RISE OF
THE LONE STAR

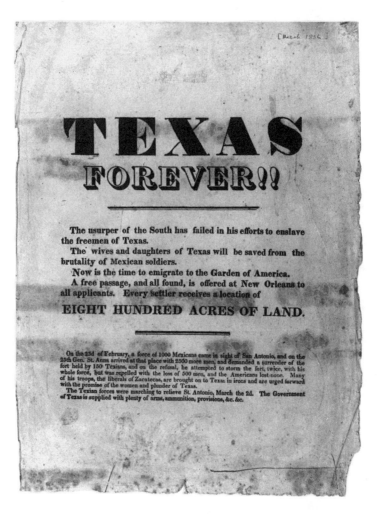

TEXAS
FOREVER!!

The usurper of the South has failed in his efforts to enslave the freemen of Texas.

The wives and daughters of Texas will be saved from the brutality of Mexican soldiers.

Now is the time to emigrate to the Garden of America.

A free passage, and all found, is offered at New Orleans to all applicants. Every settler receives a location of

EIGHT HUNDRED ACRES OF LAND.

On the 23d of February, a force of 1000 Mexicans came in sight of San Antonio, and on the 25th Gen. St. Anna arrived at that place with 2500 more men, and demanded a surrender of the fort held by 150 Texians, and on the refusal, he attempted to storm the fort, twice, with his whole force, but was repelled with the loss of 500 men, and the Americans lost none. Many of his troops, the liberals of Zacatecas, are brought on to Texas in irons and are urged forward with the promise of the women and plunder of Texas.

The Texian forces were marching to relieve St. Antonio, March the 2d. The Government of Texas is supplied with plenty of arms, ammunition, provisions, &c. &c.

RISE OF THE LONE STAR

The Making of Texas

BY ANDREAS V. REICHSTEIN

Translated by Jeanne R. Willson

TEXAS A&M
UNIVERSITY PRESS
College Station

Originally published in slightly different form as *Der texanische Unabhängigkeitskrieg,
1835/6: Ursachen und Wirkungen,* copyright © 1984 Dietrich Reimer Verlag

Frontispiece
This New Orleans advertisement offered free land to volunteers in March, 1836,
before news of the Alamo's fall had spread this far. *Courtesy Barker Texas History Center,
University of Texas at Austin*

The paper used in this book meets the minimum requirements of the American
National Standard for Permanence of Paper for Printed Library Materials,
Z39.48-1984. Binding materials have been chosen for durability.

∞

Library of Congress Cataloging-in-Publication Data
Reichstein, Andreas V.
    [Texanische Unabhängigkeitskrieg 1835/36.
English]
    Rise of the Lone Star : the making of Texas /
by Andreas V. Reichstein ; translated from the
German by Jeanne R. Willson.
        p.   cm.
    Translation of: Der texanische Unabhängig-
keitskrieg 1835/36.
    Bibliography: p.
    Includes index.
    ISBN 0-89096-318-5
    1. Texas—History—Revolution, 1835–1836.
2. Texas—History—To 1846. I. Title.
F390.R3813 1989
976.4'30—dc19   89-30386
                                              CIP

For L. Tuffly Ellis

The history of Texas seems to be largely the history of the land of Texas.

THOMAS L. MILLER

The obligation of the historian is to tell the truth about the particular phase of the past that he is discussing, and as much of the truth as he can.

EUGENE C. BARKER

Contents

Illustrations

MAP

Acknowledgments

In the course of writing the German edition of my study and revising it for the English one, so many people helped me and took interest in my work that it would actually take a little book on its own to mention all their contributions and suggestions and to thank each one of them. The following lines therefore can only give a vague idea of my gratitude toward the many people who shared my search for a better understanding of the events so far labeled the "Texas Revolution."

The initial idea of writing this study derived from my correspondence with the former director of the Texas State Historical Association, Dr. L. Tuffly Ellis, in 1979. When I was seeking a topic for my Ph.D. thesis, he set my eyes on the events in Texas in 1835–36. During my research visits to Texas in 1980–81 and 1982 he gave me a lot of invaluable hints and advice. He helped me to clarify and sharpen my premises. Most of all he nurtured the tiny flame that was my interest in Texas history, until it became what it is now: a burning fire, a deep love for Texas, its past and its present. For this I will always owe him my deepest gratitude. It is my sincerest hope that this book proves a fitting reward to his efforts.

In Europe, Professor Ernst Schulin of the University of Freiburg, West Germany, assisted in the writing of my German manuscript, which was to become my Ph.D. thesis, with valuable advice and care. Like Professor Günter Moltmann of the University of Hamburg, who helped me to revise my dissertation for the printed German edition, he showed great interest in my work. Both men provided sympathetic encouragement and were always ready to help and answer my numerous questions. Special thanks go to the German editor, Dr. Friedrich Kaufmann (who also owns the Dietrich Reimer Verlag in Berlin where my book was published in 1984), who was very enthusiastic about my study and who did a wonderful job in printing and promoting the book. I owe him many thanks for his permission to publish an English version of it without any obligations.

In Texas, the director of the Eugene C. Barker Texas History Center at Austin, Dr. Don E. Carleton; the former director of the Texas State Archives, Professor David B. Gracy II; the former state archivist, Dr. Michael J. Dabrishus; and the translator of the Bexar Archives, John Wheat, helped and encouraged me in ways that went far beyond their official duties. In long conversations and later by means of correspondence, David Gracy especially helped me enormously to clarify certain important aspects on Moses and Stephen F. Austin. Professor Walter Struve of City College, New York, gave me valuable hints on the slavery issue. Professor Malcolm D. McLean of the University of Texas at Arlington expressed great zeal for my work and helped me enormously by sending me the last volumes of his *Robertson's Colony Papers,* which were unavailable for me in Germany. I want to thank all of them for their enthusiasm and encouraging help.

From the beginning, Noel R. Parsons, editor of the Texas A&M University Press, was the guiding spirit for this edition of my study. His interest in my work, his cooperation, and his zealous efforts to see this book being published helped me to pursue my work even in difficult times. And they were difficult times indeed, especially when we could not find a source of funds to translate the German version. In Germany, Professor Werner Giesebrecht of the University of Würzburg and his wife Hertha, Professor Reinhard R. Doerries of the University of Erlangen/Nürnberg and Rolf Nüthen of the Börsenverein des Deutschen Buchhandels at Frankfurt/Main tried everything in their power to help me in that matter. Yet, when all efforts failed, Jeanne Willson, archivist at the Eugene C. Barker Texas History Center at Austin, agreed to translate my work for free. Without her, this book could never have been published. Words cannot describe how moved I was when I heard of her decision to give up her spare time for this monumental task, without asking for any compensation. It is she above all I owe my greatest thanks to. This book truly is hers as well as mine.

As it would take pages to mention all the members of the various archives and libraries who helped me in finding the sources, manuscripts and books I needed, let me simply give my whole-hearted thanks to all of them in Freiburg; Munich; Göttingen; Hamburg; Berlin; London; Washington, D.C.; New York; Cambridge, Mass.; Norman, Okla.; Lexington, Ky.; Salt Lake City, Utah; Austin, Tex.; Commerce, Tex.; Galveston, Tex.; Houston, Tex.; Huntsville, Tex.; and San Marcos, Tex.

Special thanks go to Bill O'Neal of Panola Junior College at Carthage who was so kind to grant permission to use and quote from his unpublished M.A. thesis on "Texas and Manifest Destiny."

This study was made possible to a great extent by stipends from the University of Texas at Austin, which paid largely for my research year there in 1980–81, and the German Academic Exchange Service (DAAD) which financed my research visits to Washington, D.C., and Austin in 1982.

More than anyone else, friends and members of the family always have their share when one is working on a study like this. My mother, Dr. Barbara Reichstein, in Stuttgart; my parents-in-law, Rüdiger and Gisela Böker in Hamburg; my friends Professor Thomas M. Safley of the University of Pennsylvania at Philadelphia and his wife Michele; Rolf Metten in Freiburg; and Dr. Elisabeth Arend-Schwarz of the University of Aachen helped me in numerous ways to complete this study. And especially, my wife Renate, who was always an excellent listener. She deserves special commendation for her patience with me during the past years when my mind was fixed on Texas. Without her loving care I would never have been able to write this book.

Hamburg, 1988   ANDREAS V. REICHSTEIN

Abbreviations

AHR	*American Historical Review,* Washington, D.C.
AP	Eugene Barker, ed., *The Austin Papers,* 3 vols.; vols. 1 and 2, Washington, D.C., 1924–28; vol. 3, Austin, 1927.
ARAHA	*Annual Report of the American Historical Association,* Washington, D.C.
DCRT	George Pierce Garrison, ed., *Diplomatic Correspondence of the Republic of Texas,* 3 vols., Washington, D.C., 1908–1911
BTHC	Eugene C. Barker Texas History Center, University of Texas at Austin
HOT	Walter P. Webb, ed., *The Handbook of Texas,* 2 vols., Austin, 1952, and supplement vol., Eldon S. Branda, ed., Austin, 1976
LOT	Hans Peter Nielson Gammel, ed., *The Laws of Texas, 1822–1897,* 10 vols., Austin, 1898
LP	Charles Adams Gulick, ed., *The Papers of Mirabeau Buonaparte Lamar,* 6 vols. Reprint, Austin and New York: Pemberton Press, 1968
MVHR	*Mississippi Valley Historical Review,* Cedar Rapids, Iowa
OCTR	William C. Binkley, ed., *Official Correspondence of the Texas Revolution,* 2 vols., New York, 1936
PTR	John H. Jenkins, ed., *The Papers of the Texas Revolution, 1835–1836,* 10 vols., Austin, 1973
SHQ	*The Quarterly of the Texas State Historical Association* and *Southwestern Historical Quarterly,* Austin
SSSQ	*Southwestern Social Science Quarterly,* Austin

WSH	Amelia Williams and Eugene C. Barker, eds., *The Writings of Sam Houston, 1813–1863,* 8 vols., Austin, 1938–1943
WTJ	Leicester P. Ford, ed., *The Works of Thomas Jefferson,* 12 vols., New York and London, 1905

RISE OF
THE LONE STAR

Introduction

During the 1840s the United States acquired approximately one-third of its present continental territory, with the exception of Alaska. Excluding Oregon, this increase took place at the expense of Mexico, which had inherited these lands from Spain. It was not only a territorial inheritance but also one of political preconceptions, ideologies, and way of life. For a short time after Mexican independence from Spain in 1821, it appeared as if the liberal, federal spirit of its neighbor to the north would vitalize the new republic, but centuries of central control could not simply be replaced in a day by a completely different system of government; there was a lack of resources, practicability, and also often nothing but conviction and determination on a local level.[1] When it became clear that two cultures with divergent political systems stood facing one another, suspicion, distrust, and rejection increased again on both sides.

In the course of time, as is continually reported in the literature on the subject, this difference grew to an antagonism that would necessarily lead to discord. It is emphasized that this was the antagonism of two worldviews facing each other on the two American continents: the messianic convictions of the United States—its confidence that it was creating an empire of freedom, reason, and personal happiness—and the colonial spoils system of Spain, which also kept the missionary charge of the church under its wing.[2] Protestant individualism and Catholic authoritarianism are seen here as forms of state and society in confrontation. But whether culture and political differences, which doubtless existed, can be considered a sufficient explanation for the tension that lasted for decades between the United States and Mexico must be questioned.

3

After the acquisition of Louisiana by the United States in 1803, Texas had become the boundary between these two cultures. Even the determination of an exact line between the two powers posed a problem that could scarcely be resolved. The two were united only in their contempt for the original culture: that of the Indians.

Because Mexico found the settlement and defense of the immense territory inherited from Spain to be very difficult, it attempted to adopt the U.S. system and declared itself ready for immigration, standing open to colonists from all nations. In the main it was settlers from the United States who answered this invitation, so that in this way support was given to the development of the westward movement that had acquired its own historical dimensions in the United States: "Up to our own day American history has been in a large degree the history of the colonization of the Great West. The existence of an area of free land, its continuous recession, and the advance of American settlement westward explain American development."[3]

The development of Texas was thus seen by many historians as "a chapter in the Westward Movement of the Anglo-American people."[4] More and more Americans moved into Mexican Texas. According to Walter Prescott Webb, "Potentially, Texas was a center of three conflicting civilizations—that of the Mexicans, that of the Texans, and that of the Plains Indians. The potential conflict soon became a real one."[5] This conflict of 1835–1836 went down in history as the Texas Revolution. Then, after ten years of independence, Texas was admitted as a state of the United States. These events have already received various scholarly explanations. One of the first interpretations was the endeavor to represent the Texas Revolution as a conspiracy on the part of the slave states to increase their numbers and thus their influence in Congress. Eugene C. Barker viewed the cultural differences as the origin of the disturbances.[6] The westward movement, a conspiracy between President Andrew Jackson and commander-in-chief of the Texas army Sam Houston, political conflicts, manifest destiny, and political expansionism are other catchwords with which the Texas Revolution is closely identified.

Two things are common to most studies. First, events and persons are represented as physical forces that appear out of nowhere, respond to each other upon contact, and produce reactions. Secondly, none has carefully examined this revolution alone in a single volume. The most comprehensive works, for which Texas is only one subject among many, accept it simply as having happened and begin to attempt an interpretation only upon the annexation of Texas by the United States in 1845–1846. Those who are especially concerned with Texas rely on authorities. Among them, William O. Binkley, with his book *The Texas Revolution*, published in 1952, is considered to rank first. Still, this text is only one small volume made up of four lectures. Concerning the theme he is dealing with, the author had written fourteen years previously: "The history of the struggle in which Texas accomplished the transition from a Mexican province to an independent republic has never been written."[7] To this he is constrained to add: "Although a few brief articles have thrown new light on some of the incidents or individuals involved, the comprehensive story of the movement as a whole is still waiting to be told."[8] Today nothing has changed in regard to this fact; the Texas Revolution, with all its components, has still not been examined in detail. Many questions remain unanswered.

What were the motives of the leading men in Texas, and what had brought them there? What role did Freemasonry have in the independence movement in Texas? What was the effect of land speculation? What attitude did the settlers of Anglo-American and those of Mexican origin have toward one another and toward Mexico? Are the revolution and annexation isolated from one another, or have they a connection? Is the concept "revolution" altogether justified? Does the catchword "manifest destiny" suffice as an interpretation of the event?

The present study attempts to clarify these points and, by considering all the factors, finally tries to work out what historical relationship the events in Texas have and what place they occupy in American history.

REMARKS ON THE POSITION TAKEN IN THE RESEARCH

If one considers only the extraordinary number of publications on the range of problems addressed here, any further study seems scarcely justified. As Binkley has already emphasized, however, there is still no adequate work about the Texas Revolution itself. Various individual aspects, such as battles, personalities, or diverse political and cultural activities, have indeed been treated, but without ever having been assembled into a complete picture. The main source of detailed information, which is exceedingly important and essential to this work, is the *Southwestern Historical Quarterly*, a journal published by the Texas State Historical Association.[9]

The historian still considered to have been the leader in the field of Texas history and who published much of his research in this very quarterly is Eugene Campbell Barker. He was greatly influenced by Frederick Jackson Turner and his thesis on the meaning of the frontier in American history and was thus a pioneer and model for many Texas historians.[10] Along with his 1925 biography of Stephen F. Austin, he edited the Austin Papers, a collection of original materials of the greatest importance for the years 1819 to 1836. Despite the highest esteem that is due Barker's pioneer work in this area and the observation that the present study would not have been possible without his preliminary work, two critical comments must be made.

First, Barker bases his opinions concerning historical issues almost exclusively on the statements of Stephen F. Austin, which gives his work a certain one-sidedness; next, since the appearance of his book, countless sources and collections of original material have been discovered and made accessible to the historian in various archives collections, changing the picture that was once projected by Barker. However, because of his standing as an authority, no new works have appeared about Stephen F. Austin.

Respect for his research extends also to the complex of questions having to do with land speculation and its significance for the events of 1835–1836. The overwhelming majority of historians have until now accepted Barker's scanty assessment of its importance. Only supporters of the extreme opposite thesis consider land speculation to be decisive. They maintain that speculation controlled the events of those years by means of a conspiracy—a hypothesis for which no conclusive evidence could be produced. Meanwhile, sources discovered in the National Archives in Washington, D.C., and in the Eugene C. Barker Texas History Center in Austin allow a more accurate judgment on this question than was possible for Barker.

On the whole, confidence in the authorities and uncritical copying from these authorities unfortunately characterize the largest part of the literature on Texas. One of the oldest histories has furnished, and still does furnish for many, the basis for their work: Henderson Yoakum's *History of Texas from Its First Settlement in 1685 to Its Annexation to the United States in 1846* in two volumes, published in 1855. The fundamental value of this work, which is replete with detail, will not be disputed here. It seems significant only to mention that some of Yoakum's contemporaries criticized his work severely. Besides mistakes, they charged him with considerable bias because he had been supplied with material by Sam Houston, a close friend of his, and was probably also decisively influenced by him.[11] Although this criticism is unfortunately not verifiable today, because none of the "reviewers" wrote a refutation, it is, nevertheless, questionable how indiscriminately subsequent generations of historians have used Yoakum's work. Other histories, too, often one-sided and antiquated when considered in the light of today's research, are readily quoted,[12] something that is occasionally defensible as long as their respective failings are kept in mind.

In addition to this succession of older treatises, a vast number of school books and books for children and young persons have been produced that blend anecdote, imagination, and material copied down from anywhere at all into a colorful mixture.[13] The basis for these works is often an accumulation of certain types of publications, originating in the last century and generally in narrative style, dealing with the history of Texas or of the revolution completely from the viewpoint of the author of that time and treating them as a reminiscence or a travel book for immigrants, as the story of a trip or a political paper.[14] Even though they frequently represent only the atmosphere and political tendencies of that time, for this very reason they can often still be considered as source material.

Along with these, some original sources have been printed and significantly facilitate the work of historians but, strangely enough, have found their way into the current literature only to a very limited extent.[15] Only a handful of monographs can withstand closer inspection in accordance with the current standards for historical research.[16] The nationalistic character of certain American studies from the 1920s to the 1940s is less surprising than the romantically glorified representations of the first half of the nineteenth century in the writings of modern authors.[17]

As scattered as good works on the period of 1800 to 1846 are, it becomes apparent how slight their echo is in the expansive productions that prefer to depict the revolution as a natural phenomenon and then devote themselves more in detail only to annexation.[18] Especially striking and evident today is the unlimited recommendation and recognition of publications that have a strong nationalistic and thus biased character.[19]

A more or less obvious chauvinism marks all writing of history and has a disturbing effect particularly in regard to descriptions of the Indians, the Mexicans, and Mexico in general. For the most part prejudices are simply reproduced uncritically as research results.[20]

Unfortunately, involvement with Texas history is limited to the United States, for other nations, including Mexico, and their historians apparently classify this field as "only" local history and have not yet recognized possible emanations from the events and their importance. In this sense, too, the present work, a study by an outsider, is meant to contribute to a better understanding of a historical development that is not yet complete.

PART I

Texas as a Spanish-Mexican Province

1. Incentives to Immigration

At the beginning of the nineteenth century a series of problems developed for Spain in its American provinces. The spirit of independence that had asserted itself in the successful revolt of the thirteen colonies against England spread to the Spanish empire. Not only the dreaded Americans but also an ever-larger group of Mexicans threatened the internal peace of Spanish sovereign territory.

After the United States had bought the Louisiana Territory in 1803, Texas had become the most northern province of Mexico and thus the focal point of Spanish-American politics. This befell Texas at a time when it was still only a shadowy entity. This can be determined on the one hand from population statistics and on the other from various reports that were produced time after time on the instructions of the viceroy in Mexico or the king in Spain. At the end of the eighteenth and the beginning of the nineteenth century, there were in the province of Texas (whose borders differed greatly from those of the present-day state) only three settlements of any size: Nacogdoches, which, however, was almost completely abandoned around 1820 because of disturbances bordering on civil war and the continual raids of bandits; La Bahía, which lives on under the name of Goliad, its missions and garrisons today only museums and memorials to an exciting past; and San Antonio.

When the Spaniards had established themselves after a fashion in Central America, a census was taken, usually annually, in Texas—as was done in every other province. The governor, however, limited this census to the larger settlements; consequently a claim to absolute accuracy in those statistics cannot be made.[1] For 1783 the governor, Domingo Cabello, arrived at the figure of 2,819 inhabitants in Texas, including slaves.[2] That was actually twenty-one less than in the previous year, but in 1784 there were 2,828 persons counted and 2,919 in 1785. Seymour V. Connor arrived at an estimate for 1800 of about forty-two hundred persons; in doing so he emphatically indicated his numbers were estimates and gave no sources.[3] In 1809 Manuel María de Salcedo y Quiroga, appointed governor of Texas in 1807, prepared a report for the viceroy in Mexico, Pedro de Garibay. In this document he gave the figure of 3,122 inhabitants.[4] Finally, for 1820 Gerald Ashford mentioned the number of 2,516 persons, and at that point, Nacogdoches, with its approximately one thousand inhabitants, had already been abandoned.[5] For the period addressed, a number of about three to four thousand inhabitants can consequently be assumed for Texas.[6]

To consider the numbers alone would be questionable, for it is not clear if they were arrived at through comparable statistical methods or by other means. They must, therefore, be viewed in proximity to the reports generally accompanying them which interpret these numbers and give a more or less uniform picture of the situation. They all describe the geographical riches of the province and, for the most part, speak only about the south and the east – the abundance of lakes, rivers, good land, luxuriant vegetation, and the presence of plentiful fish and game. But this superfluity, combined with the false hopes that had been aroused among colonists – hopes of an already flourishing urban civilization – had in many cases led to indolence and neglect. Continual Indian unrest and raids had decimated and laid to waste large parts of the settlements, the missions, and the fortifications, and driven many Spaniards away.

Establishing missions for the Indians, one of the three main pillars of the American policy of Spain along with military pacification and paltry attempts at colonization, had been doomed to failure by its basic concept. Whereas the French saw the Indians as trade partners, the Catholic church considered the various tribes to be a mass of heathens whose apparently miserable lives would be improved by the light of Catholic teaching and to whom it would bring salvation. In fact whole tribes were exterminated in this attempt to improve them. The basis for this lay in the missionary system of the Spaniards.

An attempt to expatiate in detail on the development, structure, and function of the Catholic church and its work in Nueva España would be unsuccessful here merely because of its enormous complexity. Since the new *Codex Juris Canonici* was promulgated by Pope Benedict XV within the Apostolic Constitution *Providentissima Mater Ecclesia* of May 17, 1917, which went into effect on May 19, 1918, there was no binding law for the whole church until then. The *Decretum Gratiani*, which had been published by Pope Gregory XIII in 1582 as the first *Corpus Juris Canonici*, had no generally valid legal effectiveness; on the contrary, special individual laws of the territorial churches held good. With the advowson bull of Innocent VI in the year 1486 the

Catholic church had laid the foundation for the influence of the Spanish crown on the management and regulation of the secular church.[7] If the two branches of the church – the monastic and the secular or parish church – were still separate in Latin America in the beginning, they became intermingled in the following period. Because of the strong missionary character of the church, an especially important function became the lot of the monastic orders, for they were to prepare the ground for the secular church.[8] The Dominicans, the Augustinians, and foremost of all the Franciscans played the decisive role in the border lands of Nueva España, especially after Charles III banned the Jesuits from all Spanish territory in 1767. In Texas it was the Franciscans in particular who were the representatives of the church, who were to prepare the way for a secular parish church.[9] They brought their monastic structure from Europe and transplanted it in the newly won lands.

Around their churches they constructed administrative areas and places to live and work for the inhabitants of the vicinity. The tribes – primarily those on the coast and along the rivers who voluntarily became Christians – had to give up their old way of life, move into the huts built for them, work hard all day in the monks' fields, and strictly follow the Catholic moral code. The women had to stay at home and busy themselves with handwork and housework.

Even though this went well for a while, a deadly apathy set in among the Indians, who were rooted in their traditions. If they secretly followed their old customs, as was continually happening, they were punished most severely when discovered. But in addition to this lack of spirit that led to a lowering of the birth rate and a higher mortality among those of middle age, the diseases introduced from Europe, such as measles and smallpox, also swiftly decimated the tribes. When life became unendurable for the Indians, they pulled themselves together and simply moved away. In this way the missions frequently failed to be self-supporting; the land was again secularized and often completely abandoned. In the regions inhabited by the Lipan Apaches and the Comanches, the Franciscans' lack of knowledge and meager readiness to learn and to adapt themselves to the situation made them victims of wars between the two tribes; they were between a rock and a hard place.[10]

Only a very few missions survived the constant ups and downs. For that reason, as the reports stressed, more soldiers were needed and, above all, more settlers who would be willing to work. But this was nothing new. The lack of initiative among the Spanish colonists was universally deplored. The stagnation of the number of inhabitants of this buffer province, small to begin with, was adequately recognized.[11] What was new was the ever-growing distrust of the neighbors to the north, which the reports unambiguously expressed.[12] If the Indians were the first reason for the stiffening of the Spanish immigration policy, the second was their ambitious neighbors, and the third was the independence movement.

Though they were not great in number, individual colonists from all parts of Europe had gone to Texas in the seventeenth and increasingly in the eighteenth centuries: Dutch, Irish, French, English, German, Swiss, and American settlers. Connor mentions a small but cosmopolitan population.[13] The heterogeneous nature of the Texas population made it easier for thoughts of independence that flowed in from the north to take hold. The French Revolution, too, had certainly been an encouragement to the men who assembled around the priest Miguel Hidalgo y Costilla in 1810 to rise up against poverty, political oppression, and the rigid caste system in the pyramid of Spanish authority.[14]

The embodiment of the might and strength of the Spanish hierarchy was the king. He was the center and stabilizing point of the whole system—at least ideally. But under Charles IV the monarchy in Spain was far from ideal. The king's first minister, Godoy, ruled over the land with dictatorial power made possible by a bloated government. After a sort of political springtime under Charles III, however, a large part of the population was no longer ready to accept this relapse. On March 17, 1808, rebellion broke out in Aranjuez. Napoleon made use of this weakness of the royal house and abruptly deposed Charles IV. King and crown prince were imprisoned in France; Spain rose in revolt, and the regime of Napoleon's brother Joseph was not recognized either in Spain or in the colonies. The rigid Spanish system began to totter. Although Hidalgo's rebellion could be put down, the center of agitation continued to smolder, sustained by the spirit of independence.[15]

On April 6, 1813, the first declaration of independence of Texas was proclaimed and on April 17 the first constitution presented.[16] But these were only short-lived. Instead of unifying the populace they only brought about severe retaliation by the government. When Ferdinand VII, the son of Charles IV, took power in 1814, he tightened the reins and disappointed all liberally inclined circles with his return to absolutism. The provinces in America were to feel clearly the strong hand of the king.[17] He dissolved the provincial assemblies and put the military at the head of the government again. In this way he departed almost totally from the liberal constitution of 1812.

The old system, now applicable again, was of strict hierarchical construction. Thus Ferdinand VII reinstituted the Council of the Indies—the Consejo y Cámara de Indias—which together with the Consejos de Castilla, Hacienda y Órdenes was consolidated on July 18, 1808, into the Consejo y Tribunal Supremo de Españas e Indias. The Council of the Indies had arisen from the Consejo Real de Castilla as a group of advisers to the king in 1517 and in 1524 received legal rank as an independent body: the Consejo Real y Supremo de las Indias. In this way it became the chief governing body and court of justice for all the affairs of the new American possessions. The Casa de Contratación, established in 1503 by Ferdinand and Isabella, which was mainly concerned with emigration and equipment, was also under its authority. The members of the Council of the Indies were appointed by the king, had to carry out his wishes, and resided in Spain without ever having seen the area of their interest. The long arm of the king in America was the *virrey,* the viceroy.

As chief executive in Nueva España the *virrey* answered only and directly to the king. Supporting him was a council, the Virreinal Audiencia, which mainly represented an appeals court in legal issues and in some cases could also be active in legislation. Subordinate to the viceroy were the provincial governors for civil and the *capitán general* for military concerns of each province. These two offices could also be joined in one person: *gobernador y capitán general.*

In 1776 a centralized administration, the Provincias Internas, was created with a *comandante general* as the supreme civil and military court standing directly beneath the crown and not answerable to the viceroy. In the course of time, however, this was often changed. In 1811 the Provincias Internas was divided into two branches: the Provincias Internas de Occidente and the Provincias Internas de Oriente, consisting of Coahuila, Texas, Nuevo Santander, Nuevo León, and the districts of Saltillo and Parras. The two *comandantes generales* were subordinate to the viceroy. The office of governor and of *capitán general* remained officially in existence, even though their authority became much less important.

From 1816 to 1821 Juan Ruiz de Apodaca was viceroy; General Joaquin de Arredondo was responsible for the inner provinces of the east, and the provincial governors were under him. Arredondo had brutally suppressed Hidalgo's uprising and was known as a declared enemy of the Anglo-Americans. Every attempt of colonists from this group to settle in Texas—if Arredondo became aware of it—was immediately thwarted. Although it was legally objectionable, he went around the viceroy and reported directly to the king. Because of his particularly strong position, the individual governors of Texas, who favored a mixed settlement of the land, had a hard time asserting themselves under Arredondo's pressure. Because his control was mainly of a military nature, civil duties were left primarily to the governors— of course depending on Arredondo's consent at the time.

At the head of the local government was the *alcalde,* with administrative and legal duties. He presided over the *cabildo* or *ayuntamiento,* a type of local council. The names *cabildo* and *ayuntamiento* were used partly for different relationships: a *cabildo* often attended to legal duties also, and the *ayunta-*

miento had more of an administrative character. Among other boards and governing bodies, only these will be mentioned here, for they were the most important for the carrying out of Spanish policies.[18]

Though the *ayuntamientos* had received more privileges in 1812, these were taken away and again entrusted to the *comandante general*. The governor at that time, Cristóbal Domínguez, characterized the mood in Texas well when he expressed the opinion that the province was hopelessly lost in its misery.[19]

The king, however, in attempting to shore up his provinces against the outside world, soon came to the conclusion that he had to alleviate the unrest that issued from within. Amnesties were granted and favorable terms promised to prospective colonists. Ferdinand VII even turned to other European nations in order to gain all the strength he possibly could for his policy of appeasement.[20] As the Spanish king set to work to bring order to the situation from within, it was obvious to observers on the spot, particularly to the last Spanish governors of Texas, that more than an appeasement policy was required to stabilize the situation in the northern provinces, above all in Texas.

Despite the filibusters, who appeared again and again and were helping to poison the political climate, the governors took up the Louisiana immigration plan once more. As was once the idea in Louisiana, the thought was to fortify Texas with colonists and thus create a buffer zone, certainly not just with Spanish citizens, but also with Catholic Americans who would have had experience with life in the wilderness and with Indians above all. Primarily intended were French and Irish colonists and those who had already lived in Louisiana under Spanish rule.[21]

In March of 1820, when disturbances again occurred in Spain because of the too harsh regency of the king, Ferdinand VII once more enforced the liberal constitution of 1812.[22] Thereupon, in November, 1820, the Cortes (Spain's parliament) issued a decree on the basis of which the donation of land by municipalities and governors was simplified, and they were granted more rights in this matter.[23] With that and with a decree concerning the guarantee of the right of asylum in Spanish territory under the auspices of Spanish law,[24] the foundation for the settlement of Texas in the following years had been established on the part of Spain.

On the American side, the Adams-Onís treaty established a foundation for the settlement of Texas. This treaty, named for John Quincy Adams and Luis de Onís, was and is one of the most important agreements that the United States has ever made and has had a lasting influence on history.

Fourteen years of intensive negotiations took place until, on February 22, 1819, in Washington, John Quincy Adams, for the United States, and Luis de Onís, for Spain, were able to sign the Treaty of Friendship, Cession of the Floridas, and Boundaries, consisting of sixteen articles, which would not be ratified by the governments until a year and a half later.[25]

Three articles in this agreement are prominent: the eleventh would become a precedent; the third would become an annoyance; and the eighth would become both. Article XI determined the assumption by the United States of claims that citizens of Florida had against Spain; Article III described the western boundaries of the United States, the boundary line between the two nations, and the express renunciation by the United States of all claims to territory west of this boundary. In return, in Article II, the United States was granted Florida. Article VIII determined that all land titles acquired before January 24, 1818, would be recognized by the United States. For decades after the conclusion of this treaty, the courts were endeavoring to establish the legality of various titles.

The problems and the literature having to do with this treaty are manifold and cannot be discussed here.[26] But the three articles listed are important for events that followed, for their role as annoyance and as precedent primarily concern Texas. Even if the United States had unequivocally renounced Texas in this agreement (it lay west of the boundaries given in the settlement), this clear declaration meant less the end of disputes than the beginning of them. This lay first in the wording of the treaty itself, because the attempt was made in Article III to describe the boundary as precisely as possible, but in Article IV it was admitted that many vague points remained. In the latter article there was mention of the convening of a commission to lay down the boundary more precisely.

Confusion arose from the history of the Spanish explorers. On their trips in the seventeenth and eighteenth centuries they had given the most diverse names to the regions, valleys, mountains, and rivers they discovered, and these were never officially coordinated. Thus for one and the same river there were often several designations.[27] Generally one of them came into general use and persisted up to the present. However, frequently other names appeared, a great advantage in cases where someone wished to extend territorial claims somewhat. But these disputes were of a paltry nature compared to the other sources of constant vexation.

Scarcely had the contents of the treaty become public when belief arose that the United States had renounced real title to the territory of Texas.[28] This view was supported by the voyages of the French explorer La Salle. Because he had once landed on the Texas coast, advocates of this Texas–United States theory wanted to suggest to a broad public that Texas belonged to the original Louisiana Territory and consequently to the possessions purchased from France by the United States. This theory carried weight because, among other reasons, President Jefferson openly supported it.[29]

In 1819 one group of adventurers, led by a Doctor James Long, even attempted to take Texas from Spain by force and join it to the United States. But this attempt failed, and the Mexicans took Long prisoner.[30] Even though this venture was a failure, it marked the beginning of attempts of various groups and individuals in the United States to revise the treaty of 1819 with respect to Article III.[31] And here the precedent-setting nature of the two other articles mentioned, VIII and XI, came especially to bear. Both expressed the intent of the United States to take into consideration the claims and legal titles of inhabitants in newly acquired territory. In connection with the dispute that arose from Article III, this could only mean for the future that, in the possible event of later occupation of Texas, land titles that were now being received from Spain would be recognized by the United States.

From a business point of view this was a very interesting idea that was immediately refuted in the newspaper in which propaganda was being made for Texas. In August 1819 the *Clarion and Tennessee State Gazette,* a Nashville newspaper, printed a letter from Texas that extolled that land in the highest terms and emphasized: "Citizens are constantly moving in with their families"[32]—at this point in time, an extravagant exaggeration.

In this style also a report was made about Dr. Long's adventure that a large number of volunteers were rushing from the United States to his standard;[33] it was also made clear that as good as all of Texas was to be found in the hands of the "patriots"—that is, of Dr. Long and his allies.[34] In addition the attempt was made to stir up enthusiasm for Texas by repeating rumors that a Swiss organization had made terms with the Spanish king and that he had sold Texas and all claim thereto to the Swiss.[35] Dr. Long could perhaps prevent this, if it was within his power. This was the equivalent of a summons to rush to Dr. Long's aid. But help did not come in the anticipated measure, and Dr. Long's enterprise was thus condemned to failure.

As wildly romantic and even patriotic as these individual events might seem at first glance, in other newspaper articles another note is joined that gives a wider-reaching meaning to the events of that year. On August 24, 1819, the following article appeared in the *Clarion and Tennessee State Gazette,* reprinted from the *St. Louis Enquirer:*

> *Province of Texas:* It seems that this beautiful province is about to be covered with adventurers. The idea of an independent state is openly advocated, and certainly we would prefer to see it anything rather than a Spanish province, or a desert according to the plan of the American ambassador at Madrid. The people of the western country are exceedingly interested in the fate of this province, because upon its fate depends in a great degree the fate of Mexico; and unless Mexico becomes free we cannot expect to come in for any share of the rich products of her gold and

silver mines. Every friend to the western country, every man who wishes to see gold and silver abundant in his country, every man who wishes to see liberty continue her march to the Pacific Ocean, must wish success to the adventurers in Texas. Success will attend them.[36]

Along with thoughts of freedom, economic considerations were being mentioned here. Spain watched over its treasures jealously and allowed no trade between its overseas provinces and the new power on the North American continent. Rumors of vast gold and silver treasure in the Spanish-American possessions had been dispersed widely from an early date.

One article alone, however, would scarcely suffice to allow any general conclusions. But on August 10, 1819, there appeared in the same Nashville newspaper a still longer article about Spanish America that is remarkable in several respects. Not only did it openly talk in 1819 about the independence of Mexico from Spain that was anticipated and considered by Americans to be necessary, but it also contained a discussion in extensive detail about how urgent it was for the economy of the United States to support and obtain an independent Mexico. The author even went so far as to recommend that the whole area simply be annexed in case Mexico proved too weak to hold its own alone. If one considers historical events up to our own time, one section of this article appears in a special light:

> In the north-west part of that island [Cuba], facing inwards towards the gulf is the port of Havanna. This port, at present an appendage of the Mexican empire . . . has been emphatically styled "the key of Mexico"! . . . We will not undertake to depict the miseries of the western country, the danger to the union itself, if this port fall into the hands of the English, or what is equally to be dreaded, into the hands of Russians. This later power has for some time been aiming at the accomplishment of this object. The question is, how is this apprehended danger and misery to be avoided?[37]

Thus along with the idea of freedom, economic interest in the area around the Gulf of Mexico was a driving force behind many who sought to free Texas from Mexico.

2. Moses and Stephen F. Austin

The Adams-Onís Treaty brought to Texas a man who was involved in financial difficulties and looking for a new field of activity: Moses Austin.

Born in Durham, Connecticut, on October 4, 1761, he was an extremely daring and farsighted businessman. He established the lead industry in the United States and was the founding father (or at least one of the founding fathers) of five American cities still in existence, traces on his road to taming the West: Austinville in Virginia, Potosi and Herculaneum in Missouri, and Little Rock and Fulton in Arkansas.[1]

As a quick-moving merchant with experience in dealing with the Spanish authorities, Austin had had plans at an early date for business connections with Mexico. It was, of course, generally known that private trade with the Provincias Internas, to which Texas belonged, was forbidden and severely punished when discovered. However, this had not stopped men like Philip Nolan, the prototype of the filibuster, from carrying on a lucrative business with stolen horses—a fact that had also become generally known. Whether Moses Austin was involved in this illegal trade at that time cannot be clearly discerned, even though among his papers there is a statement of March 24, 1801, that lists the number of horses to be taken out of Texas for trade.[2]

Nevertheless, on January 4, 1813, Austin wrote his son-in-law James Bryan that he had already communicated his views to him about trade with Mexico and such a venture appeared to be safe as well as profitable.[3] As far as can be determined, he did not pursue this plan further. One reason may have been that a friend of his, James Baird, Sr., was taken prisoner in Santa Fe with nine other merchants from Missouri toward the end of 1812 and remained in prison in Chihuahua until 1821.[4] But this failed trade expedition had as a result that Zebulon R. Pike, the leader of the group, on his return could report to the merchants of St. Louis and Missouri precise details about trading conditions with that border area of Mexico. "His expedition thus became an important factor in opening the St. Louis, Santa Fe, and Chihuahua trade and served as a spearhead for Anglo-American expansion in the Southwest."[5]

In 1812 war had broken out between the United States and England. It was the beginning of Moses Austin's financial ruin, for trade and industry disintegrated. Before his enterprises could recover from this blow, they were almost completely destroyed by the depression of 1818–1819. A mountain of debt was heaped on Moses Austin. His attempt during 1814 and 1815 to exploit his lead mine in Mine à Breton in Louisiana in a still more extensive way by using slaves, which he had had his son Stephen hire from a certain Col. Anthony Butler, failed, as did his attempt to establish a bank.[6] Moses Austin was forced to look around for something new in order to survive.

Besides his weakened physical condition, he had also a pronounced sense of family, and so it was only natural that he discuss his plans with his oldest son, Stephen F. Austin, whom he had brought up to be his partner. Born November 3, 1793, Stephen had gone to school in Colchester, Connecticut, at the Bacon Academy and afterward at Transylvania University in Lexington, Kentucky. After two and a half years of study this sixteen-year-old son was considered by Moses Austin to be mature enough to help him in his business. From 1810 to 1812 Stephen, in Mine à Breton, ran a store that belonged to his father. In the spring of 1812 Moses sent him to New York with a shipment of lead, and at the end of 1816 he entrusted his son with the management of the lead mines in Mine à Breton. But the times were not favorable enough for the young man to be able to carry on the business successfully. The mines were already no longer profitable, and Stephen could no longer hold off the downfall of his father's undertaking.

At an early age Stephen F. Austin became socially and politically committed. On June 23, 1815, he was accepted as a Freemason in Louisiana Lodge no. 109, St. Genevieve, Missouri. Two months later he began his political career; he was elected as one of two representatives for Washington County in the Territorial Legislature of Missouri and served his community in this capacity until 1820. In 1819 he barely lost election to Congress as the territorial delegate for Arkansas.[7] On July 4, 1818, as a young representative, he delivered the traditional holiday speech in the hotel at Potosi about the day and the spirit of independence in the United States. Interestingly enough, in this speech he also took up the matter of a neighbor:

The same spirit that unsheathed the sword of Washington and sacrificed servitude and slavery in the flames of the Revolution, will also flash across the Gulph of Mexico and over the western wilderness that separates in-

Stephen Fuller Austin (1793–1836), the most successful empresario in the settlement of Texas. *Stephen F. Austin Collection, Courtesy of the Special Collections Department, University of Houston Libraries*

dependent America from the enslaved colonies of Spain . . . already is the great work commenced, already are the banners of freedom unfurled in the south. Despotism totters, liberty expands her pinions, and in a few years more will rescue Spanish America from the dominion of tyranny.[8]

This last passage of the speech shows that Stephen F. Austin—even though under different premises from his father—had directed his attention to the south, to Mexico and Texas, at least by 1818. This interest took more substantial form in 1819, when the treaty between Spain and the United States became public:

> In 1819 my father proposed to me the idea of forming a colony in the province of Texas. The treaty of Dr. Onís had been brought to a conclusion; and the right of Spain to Texas appeared to be unquestionable and grants from the Spanish authorities would therefore be valid. The project was discussed by us at the Mansion house, Mine-a-Burton, for several days, and adopted.[9]

Father and son decided to use the farm in Long Prairie, which Stephen had probably already bought in 1817, as the base for their Texas venture.[10] For Stephen F. Austin, Long Prairie was the point of departure for the land speculation he was pursuing with his brother-in-law, James Perry. "Stephen F. Austin says that he has obtained property to the value of 200,000 Dollars in land and salt works."[11] This New Madrid land title specified a high rate of increase and promised high dividends, for in the area included in the land title the spot also lay that—so the rumor went—was to become the capital city of the new state of Arkansas: "the little rock." Stephen F. Austin's initial enthusiasm for land speculation was quite natural as it promised high profits to decrease the familial debts.[12]

Speculation in land was (and is) a widespread business activity that, as a form of capital investment, runs like a thread through the history of the United States.[13] The territory of the thirteen colonies was slight in comparison to the present extent of the United States. The countless political shifts in Europe and the open borders of some of the colonies, and later states, to the west allowed land speculation in the United States to run wild from the beginning. At first there was a balance between supply and demand, and as in other financial fields, one could experience great success but also great failures. In the states in the northeast, which already had firm boundaries, powerful speculation groups developed that purchased great expanses of land from Indians for trifling sums. The territory that is today West Virginia was a playground for speculation.[14] Until the end of the nineteenth century land speculation was a regular line of business in the United States. Among other things, it was of decisive importance for the development of agriculture.[15]

To the present time, land speculation is a favorite form of capital investment in broad circles, for it breathes the breath of unlimited financial growth as scarcely anything else can do: "The customs and attitudes of the frontier still flourish."[16] An appraisal of individual speculations can be produced only in tangible instances, so that the term "speculation" that will frequently be found in what follows should be understood chiefly only as a term for capital investment. The boom of speculation that appeared in southwestern Virginia at the beginning of the 1790s had also led Moses Austin to carry out various jobs such as land surveys and title registrations for investors and speculators during his time in Wythe County, Virginia, from 1791 to 1798.

So, Stephen F. Austin went to his farm at Long Prairie on Red River to get everything ready in order that settlers traveling through on their way to Texas could find a place to rest and would have a chance to provide themselves with merchandise. Just as father and son had drawn conclusions from the Adams-Onís Treaty, so they followed with intense suspense the expedition of Dr. James Long, who interpreted the treaty in his own way. Since the treaty stated, "The United States hereby cede to his Catholic Majesty, and renounce forever, all the rights, claims, and pretensions, to the territories lying west and south of the above-described line,"[17] and inasmuch as one can renounce only what one has possessed, with the signing of the treaty Spain had formally admitted that some U.S. claims to Texas did exist—which was, however, not at all the case. The United States had never had a valid claim to the territory of Texas. Thomas Jefferson welcomed this possibility of interpretation: "The treaty has had the valuable effect of strengthening our title to the Techas, because the cession of the Floridas in exchange for Techas, imports an acknowledgment of our rights to it,"[18] and Long carried these out.

In a series of letters that Moses Austin wrote to a good acquaintance, the renowned geologist Henry Schoolcraft, in the hope that the latter would find a buyer for his highly encumbered lead mines,[19] he returned again and again to the events in Texas: "Stephen F. Austin says tell Mr. Schoolcraft that two grand expeditions are now under way for the spanish country 300 families are making ready to take possession of that part of Red River with in the spanish lines which comes with in 10 miles of his plantation an other is now making up—to take possession of St. Antone under the command of a General Long."[20]

It is not possible to determine if Stephen F. Austin was more closely acquainted with Dr. Long himself or with participants in his expedition. However, at that time he lived in Long Prairie and was often in Natchitoches,[21] which is very close to Natchez, the spot from which Dr. Long and his fellow fighters had set out, and Dr. Long's venture was certainly the number one subject of conversation there: "I [Moses Austin to Henry Schoolcraft] have letters from my son Stephen, he is well and I think, doing well. Spanish matters are much spoken of."[22]

I have heard from my son Stephen, he is much pleased with his situation and states that the expedition to Texas is going on with great energy and thinks St. Antone will be in the hands of the Americans in all October next, the army and the General Long has advanced into the province of Texas and rais'd the Republican Standard and Hundreds are Daily crossing the Sabino–I understand that the first object will be to establish a provisional government and give 600 acres of land to each Soldier and Officer in the same proportion that unite themselves with the army, many men of property and reputation have already join'd both Spanish and Americans not a Royal Standard is now rais'd short of St. Antone.[23]

Although the father pushed on with the Texas project with pluck–"I shall as soon as my business is closed in this country visit St Antonia, which place I have but little doubt is now in the hands of the Americans"[24]–the son suddenly seemed to lose interest in Texas. In October of 1819 Stephen made a serious inquiry of an acquaintance, Maj. Jacob Pettit, about land and settlement possibilities in Louisiana:

When I saw you last, I believe I informed you of my determination to remove to some part of this country. I accordingly removed here last spring but am not as well satisfied as I expected. The navigation of Red River is much more difficult than expected and the country has proved to be *very sickly*. I have been sick nearly the whole summer as indeed has almost every person round me. Old Mr. G. Hearst who you know, settled near me and has lost his wife. These reasons induce me to wish for a *change* of situation, and no part of the southern country that I have seen suits me so well as the neighbourhood where you live–I therefore write you to request information on the following points–do you know of any *Small Estate* that could be purchased on a liberal credit. I am told the manner of selling property in that country is to sell, *negros* and lands, tools, &c together, on a credit. Now if I could purchase a Small Estate, of about 8 or ten working hands in that way and land in proportion it would suit me very well. I can put on four or five negros of my own the first season & as many more the 2d season.[25]

In the course of the year 1820, Stephen F. Austin distanced himself more and more from his father's project. Consequently it appears almost as a contradiction that Stephen supposedly promised his father his support at their last meeting in October, 1820, in Little Rock: "The father should proceed to the capital of Texas, and the son to New Orleans; the former to see what could be done by an application to the Spanish authorities of New Spain; the latter to make some preparatory arrangements in N. Orleans."[26]

This contradiction is resolved by closer examination. For one thing,

Stephen F. Austin wrote the report about the 1820 meeting at the end of 1829, when he had already made his father's project a success years before; for another, his laconic description gives the complete facts: Stephen was on the way to New Orleans where he no doubt was willing to give his father support. But he went there primarily "with the hope of getting employ. I offered to hire myself out as a clerk, as an overseer, or anything else."[27] The question as to why Stephen F. Austin suddenly was looking desperately for a job instead of supporting his father with his whole heart and remaining in Long Prairie or even accompanying him on his difficult journey is not so hard to answer as it appeared before. The most important thing is always to pay attention to the date of his correspondence and to put it into a frame of reference with current political and personal events.

When in October, 1819, he began to free himself from Long Prairie and to look around for other possibilities of earning money, this certainly also had something to do with his poor physical condition, as he wrote. Like his father, he had health problems throughout his life; they frequently gave him much trouble and also put him in a very depressed frame of mind. But in all probability the political situation began to discourage him also. When the Austins first conceived their Texas project, the Adams-Onís Treaty had been ratified. With the clearly defined boundary between the United States and Spain, Texas had again become unequivocally Spanish territory, and Moses Austin knew that land titles issued by the Spanish government would offer security because of this. Because once before, in 1797, he had successfully applied to the Spanish authorities for permission to settle—at that time in Spanish Louisiana—he saw no very great difficulty for himself in entering into negotiations with them again.

However, at the moment when the Austins began to put their Texas plan into effect and Stephen displayed the utmost industry at Long Prairie, James Long, that protégé of Andrew Jackson, began his invasion of Texas in June, 1819. As Moses Austin reported to Schoolcraft, Stephen followed that expedition with the greatest attention and, because of his physical proximity to the events, was always able to find out about the latest developments very quickly. So it had probably also not escaped young Austin that Long's adventure had passed its zenith in September, 1819, and danger was approaching. Long could not maintain himself alone in Texas any longer. Consequently he sought help in Galveston from the influential and powerful Jean Lafitte, who had, however, already declared that he did not want to intervene actively.

In all probability Stephen F. Austin had already heard in October of the approach of a Spanish army that had delivered a devastating defeat to the Americans on October 15, 1819. Austin, who without doubt was aware of the political situation in Mexico, certainly knew that General Joaquin de

Arredondo was the man responsible for the "inner provinces" of the east, and thus for Texas; and as was well known, Arredondo was a declared enemy of the United States. Stephen's gradual move away from his father's plans may therefore also have been determined by the fear that he would have to suffer through another disaster in one of his father's projects. His father wanted to do the proper thing and call on Texas governor Martínez. After October, 1819, however, doubt had certainly settled in as to whether Martínez—even if he would support the request of Moses Austin—could get a hearing from Arredondo. It may be assumed that after the Long affair this was extremely improbable, and Arredondo would flatly refuse the request of an American to settle in Spanish territory. That Moses Austin nevertheless started off for Texas in 1820 is understandable from his point of view. He had often taken such risks and also often been successful and made a fortune that way at an earlier time. Now he was bankrupt and had prepared the Texas project thoroughly. Of course, he had certainly also heard of Long's failure and drawn his own conclusions from it. So he had written to Washington, D.C., on January 16, 1820, and on March 9 received his old Spanish passport back.[28] His strategy was clear: he did not want to appear so much as an American but rather to document his loyalty as a one-time Spanish citizen. This was his trump card—and the last one that he had left.

For his son, the situation was different. He was young, ambitious, and was just setting out in the world. So far he had taken on two extensive financial endeavors and each time failed. The loss of Mine à Breton in the spring of 1820 had been as little his fault as the bankruptcy in connection with the New Madrid land titles in the fall of the same year, but for the ambitious young man this must have been a great shock. He had not yet been successful like his father. Now to enter again into one of his father's risky projects that, because of the political situation, could scarcely achieve success was certainly too much for sensitive Stephen. In addition, throughout his life his strong attachment to his mother was decisive for him. More important than his loyalty to his father was no doubt his wish to help his mother, who seemed to have been especially hard hit by the financial decline of the Austins.[29] Hence those letters are also understandable, in which he constantly stresses that he wants finally to stand on his own feet in order to earn money, with which he hoped to make up for the financial losses of his father. His sentence, "I know nothing as to my father's objects or prospects," was probably meant as a reassurance for his mother that he was not wasting time on fantastic schemes that would not yield anything.[30] Although Moses Austin had had unexpected success with Governor Martínez after his stay in San Antonio in December of 1820, because of an unexpected meeting with his old acquaintance, Baron de Bastrop,[31] in January of 1821, it was still not at all certain that his attempt would have any real results, even though in his typical manner he was already making the wildest plans:

> I shall settle on the Colorado within 2 miles of the sea and three days sale from the Mississippia—Where I shall lay of a town under the protection of the Spanish Government the River Colorado is situated in the province of Texas in latitude 27 N on the Spanish Main 3 days south of Mississippia 3 days sale from Havanna 5 from Jamaca 7 from St. Domingo a spot of country desirable to behold—overflowing with Wealth and Health in this situation I shall soon reinstate myself in property. I have already offers to fill up the families which will bring me about 18,000 Dollars.
>
> I have asked for leave of settlement for 300 families and 200 Thousand Acres of Land to open a Port Town at the mouth of the River. . . . If you examin Melishes Map of the United States you will find the Bay of San Bernard and the River Colorado at the mouth of which I calculate to lay the Town of Austina, which will be in afew years equal to New Orleans in Connsequence if not in wealth.[32]

At the end of March, 1821, the news reached him that his petition had been granted. The reversal of Arredondo's policy lay in a radical political change in Spain, something that the Austins could not have known about in 1820. In March, 1820, Ferdinand VII had again put the liberal Constitution of 1812 into effect in order, by generous land donations and trade allowances, to stabilize conditions in his overseas colonies and in this way put an end to the illegal infiltration of undesirable elements. The first person to benefit from this—without knowing it—was Moses Austin. Thus December 23, 1820, the day on which Moses Austin presented his proposal for a colony in San Antonio de Béxar, was the beginning of the settlement of Texas by Anglo-Americans.

When Stephen F. Austin heard of his father's success, which he had not expected, and the latter assailed him in a letter, telling him to finally put aside his doubts and join him, the son began to devote himself increasingly to his father's project. His complete turnabout in regard to the Texas plan was caused by a personal loss; on June 10, 1821, his father Moses died as the result of his exhausting journey. In his will he bequeathed to his son the mission of carrying on with the Texas project. Perhaps a bad conscience also contributed somewhat, because Stephen had refused his complete support to his father in 1820. In any case, the opportunity was presented to him here to carry on alone with an enterprise that was just beginning (and not bogged down in high hopes, as the Mine à Breton affair). It seemed suddenly to be extremely promising, and presenting him with a free hand.

Stephen F. Austin traveled around Texas from June 20 to October 1, 1821. Although in the beginning of the trip he kept his diary entries very brief, there slowly awoke in him an enthusiasm for this land, which began to make itself present in observations that became more and more extensive.[33] Although he wanted to remain in Texas in order to take care of all the affairs of his colonists,[34] who were applying to him in ever-increasing numbers for permission to settle,[35] in the spring of 1822 he found out that although Governor Martínez wanted to give him all the help he could, in the last analysis there was no legal contract between him and the new Mexican government. It suddenly seemed doubtful that in the capital city of Mexico Stephen F. Austin would be recognized as the legal heir of his father and to his father's contract, primarily because the old Spanish government was no longer in charge.

The political situation had changed from top to bottom. On February 24, 1821, Colonel Agustín de Iturbide had placed himself at the head of a revolution and declared Mexican independence, which was confirmed on August 24 of the same year by the highest ranking Spaniard in Mexico, General Juan de O'Donojú, who no longer filled the office of viceroy. Consequently, Austin saw that he must go to Mexico City in order to be able to carry out his father's plan, which he had promised to pursue.[36] On April 29, 1822, he reached Mexico City. Although he thought he would be able to take care of his business in a few days, it was not possible for him to achieve success and leave the city until April 18, 1823.

3. Political Change in Mexico

After Morelos, like his predecessor Hidalgo, had been shot in 1815, there remained only the sporadic guerrilla activity of individual, unconnected, small groups. The viceroy had eliminated all but two of these by 1819. In the spring of 1820 he gave to Colonel Agustín de Iturbide the command of an army of twenty-five hundred men, which was to destroy the last rebels under Guadalupe Victoria and Vicente Guerrero. However, instead of waging war, Iturbide agreed on a meeting, and on February 24, 1821, proclaimed the Plan de Iguala: the Mexican Declaration of Independence. This surprise move had its roots in the revolt that had broken out in Cadiz in March, 1820, among the troops that were to be sent overseas to restore peace in the province of Nueva España. Because of it, Ferdinand VII had been forced to put the liberal Constitution of 1812 into effect again. The freedom movement in Mexico, whose flames were almost extinguished, thus suddenly received new fuel.

But the Mexican independence movement differed decisively from that of the thirteen English colonies forty-five years before. True, they wished to be independent, but also not to ruin relationships with their homeland and forfeit the protection of its powerful, conservative sphere. In the Plan de Iguala Spain was praised to high heaven, the Catholic church recognized as the state church, and sovereign Mexico given a constitutional monarchy as its form of government. The conservatives were too strong, the different groups and their interests too varied for them to be able to agree on a common, liberal declaration of their autonomy like the Americans to the north. The call to freedom was the only thing they all followed – but it was also the smallest of common denominators. "Ironically, a conservative colony would thus gain independence from a temporarily liberal mother country."[1]

They wanted to be their own masters – but how was this newly won independence to be realized and the new state reorganized? Discord reigned. Nevertheless, because every group felt itself to be addressed, each one thought it could achieve what it wanted in this common arrangement: the army, the large landholders, the church, the peasants, and all those liberally inclined middle-class citizens whose free thinking convictions found expression in belonging to a secret society that had previously been officially persecuted—the lodges of the Freemasons.

At this point it is necessary to take up briefly the role of Freemasonry in Mexico. The ideas of Freemasonry had been brought there from Spain, whereas the lodges in the United States had received their character from England. This difference is important, because it is not just a matter of regional characteristics but of differences in substance and philosophy as well. English and later American Freemasonry was inspired by the thought that a liberal society can develop only in an evolutionary process through the conviction of all persons as individuals, but the fundamental idea of Spanish Freemasonry was hierarchically oriented. According to it, not movement from the bottom to the top, not the development of individual citizens, will liberalize society; rather the idea, the initiative, must come from above. So far Spanish lodges were more interested in political parties and in guiding personalities than in wide circulation. It is of decisive importance to remember that for the American Masonic lodges it was more a matter of the idea as such and its realization in daily life, and so of small steps, whereas in the countries of Central and South America the separation of big-scale politics and lodge business was often difficult.[2] As with all generalities this, too, must naturally be considered case by case.

Many of the leading men of the revolution of 1821 were Freemasons. Not only those citizens who claimed to be liberals from the beginning, but also members of the church and the army were to be found in the lodges. Colonel Iturbide, as well as many other aristocrats, belonged to the *escocese* lodge, the Scottish Rite organization.

The idea of independence that united all of them also represented the link between the young state and its neighbors to the north. The government under President Monroe was extremely well disposed toward Mexico, which seemed to be taking the same course as the United States. The Monroe Doctrine of December, 1823, prohibiting the involvement of European powers in American affairs (North American as well as South) appeared to cement a friendship that was based on the same attitude respecting essential fundamental values such as freedom, equality, and democracy. This accord was felt also by Stephen F. Austin when he came to Mexico.

In his first letter from the Mexican capital to Joseph H. Hawkins, his friend and attorney in New Orleans, Austin wrote of his expectation of returning to Texas in ten or twelve days, because, as he had been advised by the governor of Texas, the Mexican congress was informed about his plans, took his work seriously, and would handle the proposition eagerly—even though very slowly, as he had to admit. In addition, Austin mentioned concisely in this letter that a Mr. Irwin (Andrew Erwin) and a Mr. Leftwich (Robert Leftwich), as well as two Europeans, were also in the city for the purpose of applying for land grants. He noted further, briefly, that General Wilkinson had arrived in Mexico and enjoyed the confidence of the government and the friendship of a number of influential men, such as Colonel Iturbide's.[3]

Two years later Austin described his first days in Mexico City as extremely difficult. His situation had been almost hopeless—a stranger in the city, without friends or acquaintances, and unacquainted with the language. In spite of this, he said, he made connections and was able to bring his mission to a successful conclusion.[4] If one listens only to Austin's portrayal, his success would in fact be astonishing. Eugene C. Barker, until now his most recognized biographer, attributes this entirely to Austin's talent in languages, his intelligence, and ability to negotiate.[5] Though his obvious abilities cannot be disputed, small corrections in this picture must nevertheless be made.

When Austin arrived in Mexico City on April 29, 1822, he was not a solitary foreigner lost in an unfriendly city. Since April 22 Robert Leftwich and Andrew Erwin from Tennessee had been in the Mexican capital. They, too, wanted to acquire land grants in Texas. They immediately made contact with Benjamin R. Milam, who had come to Mexico City in November, 1821, with John Austin and José Félix Trespalacios (the future governor of Texas) in connection with the miscarried James Long expedition. Ben Milam belonged to the protégés of John Davis Bradburn, an American from Kentucky who had meanwhile become a citizen of Mexico and had entered the Mexican service. At that time Bradburn had much influence with the Mexican authorities and enjoyed much esteem.[6] When Austin arrived in the city a week after Leftwich and Erwin, he not only took lodgings in the same inn as they but even shared a room with them. According to the statements of Leftwich and Erwin, they quickly became friends and promised each other every possible assistance.[7] On May 5 Gen. James Wilkinson arrived in the city—the same man who had supported Philip Nolan and later also his son-in-law James Long and was a member of the Concorde Lodge no. 3 in New Orleans.[8]

At that time, along with many Europeans, there were quite a few Americans in the city who were applying for land grants, so that Austin immediately encountered a sort of American colony. The official protector of these men was the American minister to Mexico, Joel Roberts Poinsett. They helped each other out with letters of introduction, procured interpreters, because they were by no means all able to use Spanish, and now and then even had business relationships with one another. A large number of these men had been in contact with James Long or even openly supported him. It may seem strange that these Americans could quite openly apply for land grants when they had, after all, recently been noticeable for their illegal activities. The Mexico of 1822 was, however, completely different from that of 1819. It was no longer Spanish Mexico but an independent Mexico, striving after a form of government in which energetic men, loyal to the new regime, vigorous, and with business capability, were in demand – the past played no role anymore.

Thus Austin made his entrance onto a stage where there was chaotic activity, but he immediately established contact with like-minded compatriots who in addition all had common associations. Austin's attorney and friend Hawkins was also attorney for Leftwich and Erwin and, for his part, in debt to James Wilkinson.[9] If Austin did not describe all this, then it was because the others were not primarily friends but competitors whom he accompanied everywhere (though in all probability in order to be informed about their activities), but he did not help them as promised.[10] On the other hand, another common bond helped him with most of the Americans and many of the important Mexicans of the time: his membership in the Freemasons.

In his letter to Hawkins, Austin only briefly mentioned that Gen. James Wilkinson was in the city. He had arrived on May 5 and only ten days later wrote a letter of reference for Austin.[11] Aside from the mutual assistance in the American colony, it must be seriously doubted whether he would have done this for a complete stranger.

James Carter cites this recommendation as well as a letter of March 3, 1823, from Anastacio Bustamante, the *capitán general* of the Interior Provinces, to Caspar López, the *comandante general* of the Eastern Provinces, in which the former finds highly commendatory words for Austin's character as Wilkinson did later, as an argument that in this case a Freemason is coming to the aid of his fellow member. Though Freemasonry is not explicitly mentioned in the letters cited, the style and the choice of words clearly point to it.[12] This is not directly verified and in no place does Austin mention that he had identified himself or that others had identified themselves to him as Masons; on the other hand, it would be wrong to expect this, for that sort of information was handled confidentially. Still, it can be assumed as a probability bordering on certainty that Austin had identified himself as a Mason and thus made quick contact with those men who helped him in Mexico and became his friends.

On November 7, 1827, Austin was advised by a friend, the merchant William S. Parrott, whom he had met in Mexico in 1822, about political events in the capital city as well as the conditions under which Austin could get the permission of the Grand Lodge of Mexico to open a lodge in Saltillo.[13] Because Austin had not been in Mexico City again since his visit in 1822–1823, this letter, which reports in detail about the two Masonic groups in the city, can be accepted as further indication that Austin must have made known that he was a Freemason on this, his first visit, to the capital city.

Along with his connection with Parrott, he had the friendship of Father Servando de Teresa y Mier, who had introduced him to Miguel Ramos Arizpe, an influential member of congress. The latter, his brother Juan Bautista Arizpe—also a member of congress—as well as Mario Lorenzo Justiniano de Zavala, José Antonio Gutiérrez de Lara, Carlos Espinosa de los Monteros, Refugio de la Garza, and Manuel de Mier y Terán were not only Masons and had become Austin's intimate friends, they also held high office in the new nation.[14] Thus the five last-named, as members of the Congressional Committee on Colonization Questions, were decisive in the passing of a general colonization law of January 7, 1823,[15] a law that was written entirely according to Austin's conception and wishes.

When in the course of the year 1822 and also at the beginning of 1823, Austin repeatedly gave expression to his hope that he would soon be successful,[16] it was because of these men, who shared his ideas and supported his plans. With so much goodwill, even direct help, the question arises why he was not in fact able to discharge his business in Mexico City in a few days or at least weeks, as hoped.

The reason had its basis, as stated already at the beginning of this chapter, in how decisively different Mexico was politically from the United States. Even though there was a group of royalists during the American Revolution and later conflict between individual groups about the extent of power of the individual states and how strong a central executive branch should be, the royalists were nevertheless very few in number, and the later problems were questions of "how" and not of "whether." That means that federalism in the United States was basically never in question; the problems arose from the critical subject of how strong the federal bonds should be or had to be.

In Mexico, in contrast to this, there were from the beginning two camps of almost equal size: the federalists and the centralists. Both wanted to be independent, but the controversial issue was: under what constitutional arrangement? The federalists were guided by the example of the United States, but the centralists looked toward their homeland, Spain. The federalists advocated a liberal nation in the sense of a republic, but the centralists saw their future rather in a hierarchically oriented nation of a monarchic character. From the beginning this led to such great discord in Mexico that continuity and efficiency in the administration of government was not possible.

Iturbide, who had at first put a junta into force that then, on February 24, 1822, made way for a national congress, which it had itself called into being, was not satisfied with the conflict between the various circles about the national organization of the nation and on May 18 permitted himself to be proclaimed emperor: Agustín I, emperor of Mexico. On March 19, 1823, however, he had to abdicate. He had not succeeded in bridging the gap between republicans and monarchists, between federalists and centralists. Instead of this he had created two precedents that would negatively influence politics in Mexico for generations. First, when at the end of 1820 he made peace with the guerrilla leader Guerrero, he had broken his oath as a Spanish officer and committed treason to achieve his goals— however understandable this may have been. Secondly, he had dissolved the congress on October 31, 1822, after its continuous criticism of his execution of his office had become troublesome to him. Many others would follow his example in dissolving the congress as well as in committing treason. The first to emulate him in the latter was the commander of the port city of Veracruz, Antonio López de Santa Anna Pérez de Lebrón, who with his troops rose up against the monarchy and brought about Iturbide's resignation.

Stephen F. Austin experienced this confusion and agitation at first hand and sought, by advice and even suggestions for laws, to support his friends and assist the liberal, republican spirit to achieve a change for the better.[17] In this he was partially successful, for the colonization law of January 7, 1823, conformed in large part to his suggestions. His commitment to this young state secured for him the friendship and support of the republicans far beyond membership in the Masons alone.

Haden Edwards, Benjamin Rush Milam, and Gen. James Wilkinson, who were likewise applying for land grants, were also Freemasons, though less successful than Austin. His land grant was authorized on February 18, 1823; his competitors had to wait until 1825. True, membership in the Freemasons opened many doors for Austin and gave him a quick and good start, but his success rested on other factors. He was the only applicant—if there was one at all—who had a claim on an empresario contract, for he only wanted to have the old contract, made out in his father's name, transferred to himself. In addition, the arrival in Texas of the first settlers recruited by Moses and Stephen F. Austin were witness to the seriousness and responsible nature of the enterprise. Consequently, with Austin, in contrast to the others, it was a matter of reconfirmation rather than a completely new contract.

In addition, he had a good perception of the business and social structure and relationships in Mexico. Not in vain had he spent part of his childhood and youth in Louisiana under Spanish control and compared notes with his father about his experiences with the Spanish national character.[18] Thus he was well able to combine his commitment to the young Mexican nation with the tenacious pursuit of his goals. It was also not to his disadvantage to slip two doubloons (the equivalent at that time of about sixteen silver dollars) to Juan Arizpe in order to expedite his business with the authorities—a method he recommended also, for example, to his comrade-in-arms Robert Leftwich.[19]

His excellent perception of political strengths and their relationships, which is attested to by Eugene C. Barker,[20] must certainly be provided with a question mark, for in spite of all his experience Austin wrote to his brother James on May 10, 1823, that the emperor had betrayed them all and refused him and hence also all of them: "The result I hope and confidently believe will be a confederated Republic very similar to that of the United States."[21] This short passage presents an important cornerstone of Stephen F. Austin's thinking. He was convinced that things would develop in Mexico as in the United States so that the federal, republican forces would prevail, for they were stronger. Consequently, he greeted the new Mexican constitution of 1824 as a republican victory.[22]

Austin thought of himself as a Mexican citizen, as the citizen of a republic designed after a United States. But in this he was the victim of an erroneous idea with grave consequences. The Mexican constitution was a good reflection of the divided situation of Mexico. It was an amalgamation of the American constitution and the Spanish constitution of 1812—liberal, to be sure, but still hierarchical. Although on paper Mexico was now represented as a federal republic, the Spanish spirit remained alive in the content. The thirteen colonies joined together in 1776 and delegated individual rights and duties to a federal government that was weak in comparison to Mexico's, but the Mexican congress divided up the land from above into individual states, which were obligated to report to the congress.[23]

Austin did not recognize all of this at once. He realized the significance of these relationships only about ten years later, when Texas broke with Mexico and when it was already too late for correction.

4. The Americanization of Texas and Its Consequences

As previously discussed, Stephen F. Austin was not the only one who was in Mexico City applying for a land grant in Texas in 1822–1823. He mentioned two names himself: "Mr. Irwin and Leftwich are here."[1]

However, Andrew Erwin and Robert Leftwich had not come to Mexico on their own business but as agents for a company. It was the Texas Association, a group of seventy citizens of Kentucky and Tennessee.[2] When these men met for the first time and formed the plan to found a company is not known. At any rate, on February 25, 1822, a group of sixteen men from Russellville, Kentucky, gave Robert Leftwich their power of attorney to form a company in their name for the purpose of applying in Mexico for land in Texas.[3] Nine of these men were also among the seventy signers of a memorial, a petition addressed to the independent government of Mexico and witnessed by a notary, Duncan Robertson; the governor of Tennessee, William Carroll; and the secretary of state, Daniel Graham, on March 2, 1822 – four days before the news of Mexico's independence appeared in the newspapers.[4] It was delivered by Erwin and Leftwich at the end of April. According to its text, it was a petition that applied for the donation of land grants for families who intended to support themselves in Texas by farming and raising cattle.[5]

In contrast to Stephen F. Austin's applicants for settlement, who were mainly farmers and artisans,[6] the Texas Association was composed primarily of merchants, doctors, and lawyers. That they would not want to leave their flourishing businesses suddenly to wait for patronage in the wilderness or to cultivate corn is obvious, particularly since all of them, with few exceptions, were financially well off,[7] and so – in contrast to Moses Austin and his family – there was no reason for them to move elsewhere.

By 1830 only six of the seventy signers had gone with their families to

Texas; four more came in the following years.[8] Of course, this may also have resulted in part from the fact that uncertainty prevailed in regard to the legal validity of the land papers of the association.

But basically, this meager contingent raises the question of whether they really had any intention at all of transforming the settlement contract into reality or what kind of intentions the signers actually had. The purported intentions of the members are given in the petition as follows: They wanted land "for the purpose of supporting and maintaining our families by the cultivation of the soil,"[9] thus farming and cattle raising, but both activities that only a few of the signers followed. So, if occupational motivation is eliminated and legal uncertainty is, in fact, not alone sufficient to explain the imperfect realization of the plan thus expressed, the question must be raised whether this "declaration of intent" was only a pretense. But, then, what had brought these seventy men together, and what was their goal?

It is striking that a large number of them had some sort of connection, whether of relationship by blood or by marriage, of friendship, business partnership, or simply as neighbors to two men who were participants, two cousins: Felix and Sterling C. Robertson. These men – and primarily Sterling C. Robertson – were no doubt the driving force behind the whole undertaking, as later events show. So, personal connections may have brought this group together. Still, beyond this, the position of some of the participants in the public life of Nashville at that time must be considered.

Felix Robertson was one of the directors of the Farmers and Mechanics Bank of Nashville,[10] as well as a member of the board of the Nashville Female Academy,[11] a private school for the daughters of the upper class. Of the nine directors of the bank mentioned, two others besides Felix Robertson – Thomas Hill and Eli Talbot – were among the founders of the Texas Association. Two of the seven directors of the Nashville Library – Wilkins Tannehill and James Roane – were also initiators of the undertaking, as was one of the eleven directors of the Nashville Bank, George Shall.[12] In their public positions, it was easy for these men to enlist interested parties in their venture. In addition, common political views united a number of them. John H. Eaton, John Shelby, William White, and above all, Felix Robertson, John W. Overton, and Sam Houston were not only founders and shareholders of the company but also formed a circle of friends around Andrew Jackson, from which the Jackson Party or the Democratic Republican or Democratic Party, as it was later called, arose.[13]

The goal of the Texas Association was to acquire land in Texas, but not in order to settle it. On April 26, 1822, the secretary of this organization, John P. Erwin, signed a certificate of joint ownership of a share in the enterprise for the brothers Seth and Ira Ingram.[14] Through a local newspaper, the *Nashville Whig*, the members of the company were then also invited

Sterling Clack Robertson (1785–1842), one of the founders of the Texas Association, empresario, and rival of Stephen F. Austin. *Courtesy Robertson Colony Collection, University of Texas at Arlington*

to various meetings in the course of which they were called upon by the treasurer, Joel Parrish, on December 18, 1822, to pay five dollars for each share held by, or at the latest on, December 21.[15] These and later activities clearly show that their purpose was not individual settlement but traffic in land. The founding of a company as such, with offices such as president, secretary, and treasurer, as well as the issue of shares that were publicly traded in 1826,[16] shows clearly by its characteristics—which differ from those of the empresarios Austin, De Witt, Edwards, and others—that the intention was to make a business out of the settlement of Texas, and that the land they sought to gain was considered an object of trade or speculation. The Texas Association was accordingly a speculation business. As the immediate galvanization into action even before the official notice in the press of Mexico's independence shows, they had prepared themselves very carefully.

From 1823 to 1835, twenty-seven different parties concluded forty-one empresario agreements with the Mexican government[17]—"parties" because it was a matter of individual applicants and groups as well as representatives for companies. But not all of them achieved the same success.

Exactly what does "success" mean in this connection? Except for Stephen F. Austin's first agreement, which had come into effect under the old imperial law of January 4, 1823, all the settlement contracts had to satisfy two laws in order to be successful: the general Colonization Law of August 18, 1824, and the Law for the Promotion of the Colonization of Coahuila y Texas.[18] Consequently, the thirty-four empresarios were successful if they could fulfill their contracts within the legally regulated time. In accordance with their agreements they were to settle approximately 13,091 families between 1823 and 1832 in order to be successful.[19] With the average family size at that time of five persons (two adults and three children), that comes to about 65,455 individuals.[20]

In 1834, on orders from the Mexican government, Juan Nepomuceno Almonte undertook an inspection trip through Texas in order to determine whether Texas was on the verge of a revolt against Mexico, which would make a military invasion or other precautionary measures necessary. To this end Almonte was to deliver a statistical report on Texas that was to be as exact as possible. His figures came to about 24,700 inhabitants, not counting 15,000 Indians.[21] Even if the two population figures—the theoretical number of 65,455 and actual number of 24,700, which also includes individuals and slaves, making the number of families even lower—are only approximate, there is, nevertheless, a clear gap between the desired and the achieved total.

Of the 24,700 inhabitants, moreover, not all came to their land with the help of colonization agents. Even though an exact accounting is not possible, it can be assumed that at least a considerable number of settlers had come to Texas on their own initiative and found land to settle on.

On the other hand, cholera was raging in Texas in 1833 and the beginning of 1834 before Almonte's trip and claimed many a victim, but it is impossible to give an exact number. In any event, one can certainly assume that just

Land title to Peter William Crayson of July 22, 1831, issued by Stephen F. Austin (first page of three). *Courtesy Barker Texas History Center, University of Texas at Austin* about as many settlers arrived at that time as "old" ones died, so that the population was stagnant in 1833.[22] Because no other natural catastrophes took place, no appreciable number of settlers left Texas again, and even with the inclusion of those who died of cholera—with the maximum number of deaths estimated to be at 30 percent of the total population—it would roughly come to "only" 33,000 inhabitants. There remains a great difference between the theoretical and the actual number, a difference that can be explained only by the fact that not all thirty-four empresarios were as successful as they had planned to be.

Bearing in mind their respective success or failure, one can determine on closer examination that they can be divided into three groups: those who could completely fulfill their contract or contracts, those who could do so only partially, and those who were not at all successful—that is, who did not bring even one settler to Texas.

The first group is the smallest. Only two empresarios managed to fulfill their contracts totally: Stephen F. Austin and Green De Witt. In the course of the years Stephen F. Austin concluded five contracts: (1) February 18, 1823, for three hundred families; (2) February 4, 1825, at first for three hundred families, but later (April 27, 1825) raised to five hundred families; (3) November 20, 1827, for one hundred families; (4) July 9, 1828, for three hundred; and (5) February 25, 1831, for eight hundred families.[23] Green De Witt had obtained a contract for four hundred families on April 15, 1825.[24]

Fourteen empresarios or groups were partially successful. The others either made no attempt to bring families to Texas or had no success. The reasons for those failures were complex.

Benjamin D. Lovell, who together with his partner John G. Purnell, had obtained a contract for two hundred settlers on October 22, 1825, was released from his obligations when Purnell drowned on an exploratory trip to Texas, and he did not want to continue alone.

On January 2, 1833, the Mexican government declared its agreement of April 15, 1825, with Frost Thorn for the settlement of four hundred families to be null and void, because up to that time he could produce not even one hundred families on his land. This was the most frequent reason for the termination of a contract. For some of the unsuccessful empresarios the six years that each one had to settle one hundred families had actually not yet elapsed when they were given notice, but the independence of Texas put an end to their efforts. On December 22, 1836, the Congress of the Republic of Texas declared all current contracts—those not yet fulfilled—to be void.

There were, however, also men who put the blame for their totally or only partially unsuccessful effort on a rival: Stephen F. Austin. Gen. Arthur Goodall Wavell, for example, accused Austin of having betrayed him. On

July 4, 1822, he had made an agreement with Austin in Mexico City to divide between them the land that each of them should be granted. In addition, Wavell was to establish an organization in Europe that would contribute the necessary capital for this enterprise. On the same day Wavell himself submitted a petition for land. On September 10, 1822, he had already sailed for Europe and reached Liverpool on November 11. From then on he beseeched Austin in countless letters to give him news without delay about his progress in the matter of the land grant. When he finally had the documents in hand that established the claim of the two of them to land in Texas, he said, then, without further ado, he could get £20,000 for their organization.[25] But Austin held back. He appears to have written a single letter to Wavell in England, which, if it did not disappoint him, must at least have confused him.[26] Then in July, 1824, upon a further inquiry as to how things stood, Austin wrote Wavell, who was now in Mexico again: "You ask how I am getting on to which I answer not very well – and I assure you I am heartily sick of the whole business and shall gain nothing by it but losses and fatigue, and if you wish to keep out of trouble let colonization matters alone, either here or any where else."[27] At first glance the manner and matter of this letter seem odd for Austin at this time. Only once more in this period, a year and a half later, to his sister, did he speak about being tired and wanting to give up his colonization activities and leave Texas for good.[28]

Even if he often had these thoughts, he did not express them – certainly not at all to strangers, and Wavell can most assuredly not be counted among his friends. To his friends, and also to his family, Austin at this time spoke confidently of his success: the times, he said, were not always simple, but one ought not to expect too much right away, and the situation was extremely hopeful.[29]

To be sure, shortly before the letter to Wavell mentioned above, he had learned that his mother, and shortly thereafter an aunt, had died – bad news for him; he had wanted to bring them to Texas at just this time. Nevertheless, it seems improbable that he would have allowed himself to be carried away to the extent of generalizing this personal low point to a business partner and painting the whole situation in the bleakest colors.

Rather, from the foregoing it can be concluded that Austin did not want to have any more to do with his obligations toward Wavell and wanted to keep him away from his land business. The only thing that he stated he was prepared to do was to give back the money that Wavell had lent him and guarantee him a small piece of land in his territory.[30] In contrast to Austin's intentions, which at that time were primarily aimed only at the successful settlement of Texas, Wavell's letters clearly emphasize that two things were dearest to his heart: land speculation and the exploitation of mineral wealth, such as silver and lead.[31] Officially, Austin wanted nothing to do with that. How Austin came to have made an agreement with Wavell at all remains unclear. Perhaps it was in return for the money that Wavell had lent him in Mexico. Wavell later maintained that he had never gotten it back.[32] Then, on March 9, 1826, Wavell again sealed an empresario contract of his own for the settlement of four hundred families, which, however, he never fulfilled.[33]

Yet Wavell was not the only one who complained about Austin. Along with the envy that his success inevitably brought with it,[34] and enemies he acquired because he refused some of those who wanted to emigrate, for they did not comply with his idea of what was law-abiding, honest, and industrious,[35] there was another man who accused Austin of deceit that had almost ruined him: Sterling C. Robertson, one of the founders of the Texas Association.

After Erwin and Leftwich had handed in their petition and were convinced they would receive their contract from the Mexican government in a few days, Andrew Erwin left Mexico at the end of July, 1822, and traveled through Texas, where he inspected the land that the association meant to settle, and back to Nashville, Tennessee. Leftwich still remained in Mexico in order to arrange the final details and then follow immediately with the executed contract. However, it took three more years before he got the document, and it was a different contract from the one the Texas Association had anticipated.

On May 7, 1824, the congress in Mexico City had reorganized the individual states according to the new republican constitution. It had been decided in so doing that, until Texas was sufficiently populated, it would form one state with its old neighbor Coahuila.[36] In addition, in Article III the specific regulation of the national Colonization Law of August 18, 1824, was left up to the individual states. In the future, petitions for land grants had to go to the current congress of the individual states.[37] The legislature for Coahuila y Texas was assigned to Saltillo, the capital of the new joint province. For this reason, a stay in Mexico City had become unnecessary for all those who wanted an empresario contract; the place of decision was now Saltillo.

This merger of Texas and Coahuila was looked upon by many as unfortunate from the beginning and was also part of the cause of later difficulties. Originally there had been the plan to create a large inland state along with Nuevo Santander, Nuevo León, and Coahuila, for in such a large state the delegates from Texas calculated they had a good chance of later being able to split off. But by clever tactics the delegates of Nuevo Santander managed to get their own state: Tamaulipas. In the same way Nuevo León succeeded in becoming a separate state. Thus Texas and Coahuila remained unhappily wed–unhappily because Coahuila was stronger. With more inhabitants it furnished the site for the capital city and thus, according to the constitution, the seat of the executive, legislative, and judicial branches of government.[38]

This change in the political and legal situation had meant a new delay for Leftwich in his enterprise. He had made eight applications in Mexico City in reference to his petition. Because of the political turbulence, however, he had not been successful. His ninth, of August 20, 1824, he now directed to Rafael Gonzáles, the governor of Coahuila y Texas in Saltillo. Whatever the reason may have been–whether the long period of waiting in Mexico had drained him financially or he had been persuaded to do so by friends–in contrast to the previous applications, in this, his ninth, Leftwich no longer asked for permission to settle eight hundred families in Texas for the Texas Association but for himself.[39] The proposal was granted on April 15, 1825. With the contract, which was written in his own name, Leftwich journeyed to Nashville and presented the Texas Association with a bill for $10,000 for his expenses and efforts during three years in Mexico. Upon receiving the money, he would sign the contract over to the association.

The members were called upon for the payment of $205 each, which would have produced $14,350. But the amount collected was so little that Leftwich had to be satisfied with $8,000. Each one of the members was required to pay; members lost their share by refusing.[40] The small sum that was collected shows that the long years of uncertainty had allowed the interest of many in the objective of the speculation to diminish. In order to get some money in their treasury again and to increase the value of that objective, two steps were taken.

First, each share was divided into eight parts that could then be sold and treated as the actual stock certificate or share. On January 1, 1826, shares in the association were offered for sale to the public for the first time. Certainly, from this time on, confusion prevails about the number of members and, along with this, the number of securities. Although it is certain that only seventy persons had signed the petition of 1822, after 1825 there is continual mention of seventy-four signers.[41]

Secondly, the proposal was advertised far and wide in the newspapers and notice given that Dr. Felix Robertson would go to Texas with a group of men, among them his cousin Sterling C. Robertson, to survey the land and divide it among the colonists. Anyone who was interested was referred to the respective directors in Nashville, Russellville (Kentucky), and New Orleans.

However, by doing this, the association immediately violated two Mexican laws. First, according to Article 38 of the Colonization Laws of Coahuila and Texas, only the government could appoint a man who would be al-

Share No. 52 of the Texas Association issued to Robert Leftwich on October 15, 1825, the first day these shares (about 560) were issued at all. *Courtesy Barker Texas History Center, University of Texas at Austin*

lowed to survey the land and legally hand it over to settlers.[42] Secondly, according to Article 15 of the National Colonization Law, land could be owned and distributed only by empresarios if they themselves resided in Mexico.[43] It was with that article that an attempt was being made to put an end to wildly rampant speculation.

These violations of the law had no immediate consequences. They show, however, how little the association bothered about Mexico's stipulations and that they were not even familiar with them. Also there failed to be any consequences because the association had no success with its settlement.

It was clear to all concerned that Leftwich's contract was ultimately worthless for the enterprise as long as it was still in his name. On October 31, 1826, an agent was again appointed, Col. Benjamin F. Foster, who was to get the contract reassigned to the Texas Association in Saltillo, but because of political unrest in Texas, he was already back in Nashville again on March 7, 1827. Another person, Hosea H. League, was thereupon sent on the same mission with the same petition.[44]

Two things, however, began to give the Texas Association enterprise a different direction. League got scarcely any financial support from the association. Instead, on May 25, 1827, he received an official title to a piece of land in Austin's colony. He had applied for it on a visit to Texas in the spring of 1826. So now, knowing no Spanish, obviously being in financial straits, and wanting to devote himself to his newly obtained property, it was the most obvious thing for him to ask his empresario to undertake the affair in Saltillo for him.[45] Consequently, on September 8, 1827, he gave Austin power of attorney so that he could be the legal representative of the Texas Association before the authorities in Saltillo.[46] Austin took on this position on October 15, 1827, and secured the desired contract between the state of Coahuila and Texas and the Texas Association for granting land.[47]

However unimportant these details may seem at first glance, they nevertheless make it clear that—as has been mentioned frequently already—the association itself was not in a position to realize its goals as defined in 1822 and pursued them only halfheartedly, for it was, after all, primarily interested in speculation, as was well known even by the public.[48] In addition, it led to Austin's participation in the largest colonization contract ever concluded for Texas.

Important for the contract of October 5, 1827, was its expiration date: April 15, 1831. Because it was considered only as a rewriting of the Leftwich contract, the term of six years extended from the date of the agreement of April 15, 1825.[49]

But again the association undertook nothing in regard to the settlement of the territory granted it in Texas. It was rumored that the company had lost its interest in Texas, that the only one who would still show any commitment to settle Texas was Sterling C. Robertson.[50] And in the following period Robertson did attempt to settle in Texas with some families and fulfill the contract before it expired. But Robertson and his partner Alexander Thompson not only had difficulties with the Mexican authorities, they also wasted their time in the attempt to secure land and recruit colonists for other members of the Texas Association. Time ran out for them.

In a newspaper dated April 6, 1830, a letter was printed that was meant as a warning:

Be so good as to inform your friends of the Nashville Texas Association that preparations are making for extensive settlements in Leftwich's grant by persons uninterested in it, and that it is highly probable (considering the unparalleled apathy of that company on the score of settling their grant) that the Mexican government will legitimate the intrusion.[51]

The unknown writer probably is referring here to the January 30, 1830, petition of Gabriel Laisné de Villaveque, the representative of a French organization, whose application for land was received positively by many in Mexico, for a larger group of settlers from Europe approached their idea of a well-balanced, international settlement of Texas. In addition, the contract of the Texas Association was to expire, after all, on April 15, 1831. But Stephen F. Austin had already gotten busy.

On February 4, 1831, he drew up a petition to the governor of Coahuila and Texas asking to be allowed, along with his partner Samuel May Williams, to settle eight hundred families in the area that had been granted to the Texas Association. Even though his contract could be put into effect only when the other contract had expired, he asked for immediate consent to his proposal. On February 15, 1831, the land was conveyed to Austin and Williams.

Sterling C. Robertson took legal steps against this decision and on April 29, 1834, won the case.[52] The area was again granted to the Texas Association and Robertson recognized as the empresario. This affair went back and forth briefly again, but finally remained this way. Though Austin's family maintained that Robertson had won his completely unjustified suit only by means of extensive bribery,[53] Robertson reproached Austin with far more serious things. Instead of helping him, he said, Austin had aimed at enriching himself and had betrayed him.[54] In fact, Austin's action seems at least peculiar. He had been in Saltillo since January 12, 1831, because he had been elected to the congress as a delegate from Texas. There he learned of Villaveque's petition. Along with this one, there were still other applications for land grants, among them one from his secretary and partner, Sam Williams. However, this application suddenly disappeared in some way, and Austin decided to draw up a new one and act as Williams's agent.[55] He was able to present a general power of attorney for Williams,[56] on the basis of which he then received the land granted to himself and Williams. On March 5, 1831, he wrote Williams and admitted having done these things, which scarcely lived up to his image, and asked Williams, for that reason, not to allow anything about it to become public; he should at least wait until May,[57] until the contract of the Texas Association had finally expired.

In June Robertson still knew nothing about these new events, for he asked Austin for a report as to what was happening about him and the settlers; rumors were going around that land had been assigned to Williams.[58] During the proceedings on Robertson's claims that lasted for several years, William Pettus appeared as a witness on December 15, 1832. His testimony was to the effect that Austin had declared to him that he knew nothing about the title of the Texas Association, which—if this testimony is correct—was a flat lie on Austin's part.[59]

To what extent Austin's statement is true or false can be ascertained no better than the exact motive for his conduct in this affair. Whether it was as an admission of guilt or as an acknowledgment that he had done things that he had not assessed properly, he wrote to Williams on May 31, 1833: "Keep clear of speculations for the future. They are a curse to any country and will be a very sore curse to me individually. I believe they will ruin me if they have not already done it, cursed be the hour that I ever thought of applying for the upper colony."[60]

In any event, the letter contains an admission that he had been active as a speculator, at least in regard to this particular effort—something that is also confirmed by the fact that, in contrast to his four other land grants, Austin did not settle even one family there from 1831 to 1834—the time he was empresario for that area along with Williams. But whether this was actual fraud on his part or "only" taking advantage of the situation, his motives were by no means altruistic. Rather, this episode places him suspiciously near to the Texas Association, which was, of course, not the only company that wanted to make a profit by land speculation in Texas.

With all these groups and individuals the great hope was that, as in the case of the Louisiana Territory and later Florida, the United States would recognize the inhabitants' rights and demands against Mexico by taking possession of Texas. These were not idle speculations, for although the United States had in 1819 relinquished all claims to Texas, no matter in what way they were acquired, it was, as mentioned previously, talked about articulately and in public that Texas belonged to the United States and ought to be settled by Americans.[61] But even more than by all these rumors and empty talk, the hopes of the numerous speculators were supported by the fact that the government of the United States was itself attempting to "correct" the treaty of 1819 in regard to Texas.

In March, 1825, immediately after his inauguration, John Quincy Adams appointed Joel Roberts Poinsett as minister to Mexico. Poinsett spoke Spanish and had taken a long trip through Mexico in 1822 as President Monroe's political adviser. In November of 1823 Adams had made an interesting entry in his diary:

> We have no intention of seizing Texas or Cuba. But the inhabitants of either or both may exercise their primitive rights and solicit a union with

us. They will certainly do no such thing to Great Britain. By joining her, therefore, in her proposal, we give her a substantial and perhaps inconvenient pledge against ourselves, and obtain nothing in return. Without entering now into the enquiry of the expediency of our annexing Texas or Cuba to our Union, we should at least keep ourselves free to act as emergencies may arise, and not tie ourselves down to any principle, which might immediately afterwards be brought to bear against ourselves.[62]

Noteworthy is the intent of the entry at this particular time, for in both countries mentioned the American population was minimal, and there could be no reason at all for the inhabitants of Texas and Cuba to want to join the United States. In the continuation of the passage, however, Adams gives a definite indication of his motivation. He mentions concisely that Great Britain had already registered its interest in these countries. Great Britain supported Mexico solidly against the United States, for a strong United States represented a threat to England's trade in the Caribbean.[63] It is already clear here that a significant role in the power play on an international level was falling to the lot of Texas as well as Cuba.

Adams had given Poinsett clear instructions. If possible, he was to achieve the shifting of the border from the Sabine River to the Rio Grande—thus the annexation of Texas.[64] However, two things shot down Poinsett's mission. One was the so-called Fredonian Rebellion, in the course of which, on December 16, 1826, Benjamin Edwards in Nacogdoches called for a free and independent republic on Texas soil, and the other was Poinsett's own conduct.

In this connection the history of the Fredonian Rebellion is of interest only insofar as it influenced the mood in Mexico and less for the course of events in Texas itself. Along with Robert Leftwich and Stephen F. Austin, Haden Edwards had also been in Mexico City in 1822 for the purpose of obtaining an empresario contract. Like Leftwich, he was not successful—until 1825, when he received permission to bring eight hundred families to Texas. But the dilemma facing him now was that the city of Nacogdoches and other smaller settlements lay in his territory. The area was thus already settled, even though sparsely. Because of this, conflict soon arose between the new arrivals and the settled residents about the legality of land titles. The tension between the two groups grew, and in December, 1826, when Haden Edwards was away in the United States attempting to raise money for his colonists, his brother Benjamin, on his own, proclaimed the Republic of Fredonia in order to make an end to the conflict and prevail against the original settlers. To the Cherokees, whose support he tried to win, he promised half of Texas. He could, however, succeed only with the help of Austin and his colonists.

Austin, incensed, resisted the attempt to draw him into this affair. Instead, he offered Mexico his help against the insurgents.[65] He well knew that this attempt by Benjamin Edwards could have catastrophic results in Mexico, and only the immediate suppression of this uprising could show the goodwill of the other colonists and in this way save his settlement plans for Texas. The Mexicans were sending an army to Nacogdoches. At this news Edwards and his followers fled to the United States.[66] Thereupon Mexico declared the empresario contract with Haden Edwards invalid and later distributed the land in three parts to David G. Burnet, Joseph Vehlein, and Lorenzo de Zavala.

The old mistrust of the Mexicans toward their neighbors to the north was again aroused. In February, 1827, in a lead article, the important conservative newspaper *El Sol* wrote that the United States had supported the Fredonian Rebellion and should, therefore, officially relinquish all claim to Texas forever.[67] This opinion was shared by many members of the Mexican congress, as Poinsett could report to Washington, as also about his conference with President Guadalupe Victoria, in which the president communicated his regret about the article in question but at the same time gave expression to his desire that the United States might officially make known its disapproval of the rebellion.[68] Nevertheless, the United States undertook to do nothing.

The Fredonian Rebellion was, as mentioned, only a hindrance. A bad mistake undermined Joel R. Poinsett as American minister in Mexico. He was a declared republican and a Freemason. As has been explained, Freemasonry played an important role in Mexican politics at just this time. The centralists without exception met in the *escoceses,* the Scottish Rite lodges. As a countermeasure the political opposition, the liberals, began to form a York Rite lodge. Thus the Masonic lodges suddenly were playing the roles of political parties. To be sure, five York Rite lodges had already been founded in 1825, but the official charters from the Grand Lodge of New York were still lacking. Poinsett, who was a member of that lodge, was prevailed upon by General Guerrero, Miguel Ramos Arizpe, Lorenzo de Zavala, José Ignacio Esteva, and José María Alpuche to request these documents in New York.[69] Poinsett complied with this wish.[70]

The York Rite lodges soon became a strong political force in opposition to the centralists in the *escoceses* lodges. Lorenzo de Zavala, the cofounder of the York Rite lodges, a friend of Stephen F. Austin, and at a later date himself an empresario in Texas, afterward wrote that in the beginning these lodges had concerned themselves only with traditional ceremonies and Masonic activities. Only later did they turn into *juntas* that discussed political events, such as elections, laws, and cabinet resolutions. Because generals, governors, members of governing bodies, men of the church, and other influential persons were lodge brothers, the debates suddenly acquired political weight.[71] The political labels also began to change. In reference to persons, one no longer spoke of a *centralista* but of an *escocés,* and instead of *federalista, yorkino* came into use. The two groups even published newspapers. Poinsett, who had helped the *yorkinos* get started, continued to support them in their ideas, for he believed firmly in republican principles as the only true form for a government and wanted to help create a liberal state on the pattern of the United States. But by doing so he violated the basic principle of the diplomat never to mix in the politics of his host country. And it was for that exactly that he was reproached by the *escocéses* to an ever-increasing degree.

Even though Poinsett withdrew from further activity in the lodges after they had become political combat groups, he had already been branded a scapegoat and exposed to the most severe attacks. The entire anti-American sentiment in Mexico was crystallized in his person.[72] Adams, who in 1827 had given him the mission to make an offer to the Mexican government of $1 million for the territory up to the Rio Grande, had to recall him in 1829.[73] The first attempt of the United States to purchase Texas officially from Mexico had failed miserably–and not only that, the feelings of Mexicans against the United States reached a high point in the years 1827–1829.[74]

Stephen F. Austin was kept abreast of affairs in Mexico by his friends.[75] In the summer of 1830 he reported to Thomas F. Leaming in detail about the events in Mexico and gave expression to the hope that the negative feelings toward the United States and Americans were fading.[76] At the end of his report, he wrote: "As regards myself, I have made it a rule never to touch politics in this country."[77] If this sentence is to be accepted as an honest opinion, it requires a brief observation.

In November, 1827, at the latest, Austin heard about the events in Mexico around and concerning Poinsett and their political significance. That this significance had also been clear to him is shown by the letter to Leaming mentioned above. On February 11, 1828, he made application to the Grand Lodge in Mexico along with six other Freemasons to be allowed to form a York Rite lodge in San Felipe de Austin.[78] Austin, who had lived in Mexico, had numerous friends in Mexico City, and knew also about political events and relationships, apparently did not realize that the petition to establish a Masonic lodge in Texas according to the York Rite would necessarily be considered in Mexico the acknowledgment of a political predisposition. He also seemed to have forgotten that he had worked out and circulated a plan for the organization of the Mexican congress in August, 1822, and given advice in the form of reflections on the meeting to establish a constitution on January 16, 1823.[79] Even Eugene C. Barker writes about this: "This document is no doubt an example of practical politics."[80] There are even more illustrations of Austin's extremely active interest in politics.[81]

In February, 1828, General Manuel de Mier y Terán undertook a trip of inspection through Texas. The officially declared purpose was that Mier y Terán was to help prepare a border treaty between Mexico and the United States that would finally be conclusive. In the treaty of 1819 between Spain and the United States, which Mexico had entered into, the border had been only roughly described, pending a definitive agreement. It has also been one of Poinsett's concerns in 1825 to see such a document worked out. When Mier y Terán received his final instructions—significantly from Minister of War Manuel Gómez Pedraza—he was not only directed to scientifically determine the area of the U.S. border but also to inspect Mexico's military posts there and to inform the government about possible measures for further defense of the border.[82]

Mier y Terán spent a year in Texas. During this time he corresponded frequently with Austin, whom he had met during his stay in Mexico City.[83] Though Mier y Terán went primarily into scientific questions—the weather, nature, and his health—in his letters, Austin persistently wrote about trade problems and politics.[84]

It was exactly these good contacts with Austin (and information derived from them), as well as his great love for Texas—Mexican Texas!—that motivated Mier y Terán to compose a series of reports at the end of June, 1828, that decisively influenced Mexico's ideas of and about Texas.[85] In them he emphasized that Mexicans were in the minority and belonged to the lowest class. "Therefore I am warning you to take timely measures. Texas could throw the whole nation into revolution."[86]

After these observations Mier y Terán also made a list of suggestions that should improve this situation that was so gloomy for Mexico: (1) the immigration of Mexicans, Swiss, and Germans should be decisively promoted—especially by means of loans; (2) the military bases had to be improved; (3) ports for trade should be established along the Texas coast; (4) new Mexican cities must be built with government money; and (5) garrisoned cities must be set up along the Red River.

Even if Mier y Terán's statement concerning the numerical proportion of Americans and Mexicans must be viewed somewhat critically—Juan N. Almonte, in his statistics of 1834, arrived at about 24,700 inhabitants including 1,000 slaves and 4,000 Mexicans[87]—the fact remains that Texas was Anglo-Americanized.

The population count in itself was of little importance, for it primarily gave information only about the antecedents of the inhabitants of Texas. Decisive for the anxiety of the Mexicans was the behavior, the way of life, and the appearance of settlers from the United States. In his reports Mier y Terán gave numerous examples that can only be summarized here. They can be divided into four groups. The first point, which disturbed him very

José Manuel Rafael Simeón de Mier y Terán (1789–1832), head of the Mexican Boundary Commission from 1827 to 1829 and commandant general of the Eastern Interior Provinces from 1829 until his death. *Courtesy Benson Latin American Collection, General Libraries, University of Texas at Austin*

much, was the great class distinction between the two population groups. The majority of the Mexicans were poor and uneducated, for there were schools only for Americans.

Secondly, the block of Anglo-Americans consisted not only of industrious, honorable farmers but also to a great extent, shadowy elements such as fugitives, thieves, and murderers, who stayed in the border area and floated back and forth between the United States and Texas-Mexico, as the opportunity arose, and made life on the border insecure. For the sake of truth, Mier y Terán added that among them there were a few who had changed and had established an honorable existence in this, their new homeland.

But the last two points were the most alarming for him. The American colonists lived in complete ignorance of Mexican laws and regulations. Certainly here and there an *alcalde* existed and something like an *ayuntamiento*—which, however, never met; both were a farce. Officially they had become Mexican citizens and Catholics, but no regard for this could be noted among the settlers. They lived as though they were in Alabama, Tennessee, or Kentucky. They also showed absolutely no interest in the state in which they resided. This became clear, he reported, in that most families owned one or two slaves—and this was his fourth point.[88]

Even though he must be exaggerating greatly here—in 1834 among the 24,700 inhabitants only 1,000 or at most 2,000 were slaves[89]—it nevertheless angered the government in Mexico. The slavery question is in many respects symptomatic of the relationship of Texas to Mexico and vice versa. The young state, influenced by the high ideals of the French Revolution, had chosen as its motto "God and Freedom." Slaves did not fit into this picture. It was not true that Mexicans had opposed human exploitation. Countless Indians were forced to work in the silver mines and lost their lives in doing this hard work. But the term *slave* was for the Mexicans an expression too ugly and unvarnished for what they considered a necessary evil.

There was no clear law against slavery at first. On July 14, 1824, an ordinance was issued by the federal government that prohibited trade in slaves.[90] But supported by the interpretation of the alarmed Texas empresarios, this law was construed to mean that only the trade was prohibited. The slaves who accompanied Americans were not really objects of trade but "domestic servants and workers brought up with love." Austin went along willingly with this shady business, for he knew all too well that a prohibition of slavery would have frightened away many—all too many—of those who wanted to become colonists.[91] On the other hand, it was clear to him that this could be only a transitory situation. Mexico would never allow slavery for long, if only because the young country had been left to trade primarily with Great Britain, and very strong opposition to slavery was building there. Both parties, the Mexican government and the Texas empresarios, were aware that slaves would be tolerated in Texas only as an interim solution until enough settlers populated the land or until Mexico lost patience.

Although there were strong forces in Mexico that wanted to forbid slavery entirely, it had been agreed to cultivate the principle of property as well as the principle of freedom,[92] and because slaves who were already in Texas were the property of their white masters, this principle was allowed to take precedence over freedom. The ugly word "slave" was circumlocuted in that one spoke of servitude for life.[93] No matter how tightly eyes were closed in the capital city, the fact of slavery remained a thorn in Mexico's side.[94] Now General Mier y Terán's report was the last straw.

Austin, who was on friendly terms with the general and through their correspondence certainly knew about the danger threatening Americans, hastened to pour oil upon the waters and published a book in which he dealt not only with the history of his colonization efforts but also took up Mexican law in detail. The deficiencies in knowledge that Mier y Terán had discovered and pointed out with care were to be removed with dispatch.[95] In January, 1830, the little book was printed in an edition of three hundred copies. But for any corrective intervention in the relationship of Texas to Mexico, it was already too late. Perhaps these measures would not even have been taken immediately after General Mier y Terán's report if the political situation in Mexico City had not changed again.

In the election of 1828 the candidate of the conservatives, the *escocésos*, Manuel Gómez Pedraza, managed to win. The *yorkinos*, however, claimed election fraud and took the presidency by force for their candidate, Vicente Guerrero. Immediately, on September 15, 1829, he issued a law that expressly prohibited slavery in every form. Privately the president nevertheless informed the newly appointed commander of the eastern inner provinces, General Mier y Terán, that Texas was to be quietly excepted from this law.[96] Before Guerrero could take further action in domestic affairs, he first had to face the danger of an invasion.

In July, 1829, Spain, which had still in no way officially recognized Mexico's independence, landed an expeditionary corps of about three thousand men under General Isidro Barradas on the coast of the province of Tamaulipas for the purpose of reconquering Mexico. Antonio López de Santa Anna, who had meanwhile been appointed general, was able to defeat the Spanish army. This made him immensely popular. Titles such as *Salvador del País* and *Benemérito de la Patria* were offered him. Then the centralists, under Anastacio Bustamante, for their part used the precariousness of the situation and seized power in a coup d'etat. Bustamante set up a dictatorship with the support of a large segment of the army.

Finally in control, the *escocésos* took steps not only against the *yorkinos* but also against the dreaded Americans.[97] The law of April 6, 1830, was supposed to bring peace and order to Texas. In it suggestions made by Mier y Terán were adopted, such as, for example, the promotion of colonization by Mexicans and the implementation of the completion of points of defense in the north.

Two articles, however, went beyond the general's recommendations and caused a great stir. According to Article IX, all persons who wanted to cross the northern border of Mexico had to present a visa, and according to Article XI the right to settle in Mexico was withheld from the citizens of all bordering nations. All empresario contracts that had not yet been fulfilled by the date of the law were declared void. The slavery question was left untouched *expressis verbis* in Article X.[98] It was, after all, not important anymore, for Article IX and especially Article XI put an end to the immigration of Americans.

The rule, "En consecuencia se suspenderán las contratas que no hayan tenido su cumplimiento y sean opuestas a esta ley,"[99] was interpreted to mean that the two empresarios, Stephen F. Austin and Green De Witt, had already settled a hundred families and in that way fulfilled minimum requirements. Their contracts thus remained in effect, whereas the contracts of the Texas Association and the other groups reverted de jure to the state. In spite of this, Sterling C. Robertson, as has been mentioned, attempted to save his contract with Austin's help. The other companies simply continued to sell their shares in the belief the law would soon be recalled. Thus a long line of colonists started on their way and at the border were sent back again. Austin, on the other hand, was certain of the goodwill of the Mexican authorities and saw no danger for himself and his colonists.[100] But he was not alone with his settlers in Texas, and he underestimated the interplay of forces as well as the way his method of operation was really judged and interpreted by the Mexicans. He did not understand that his remarks and actions were very much political in the eyes of the Mexicians, and for this reason he could clearly be classed with one party.

PART II

The Independence Movement in Texas, 1832–1836

5. The First Resistance and Stephen F. Austin's Politics

Bustamante had seized power in 1829 and established a military dictatorship; Mexico was convulsed by fighting that resembled civil war. The folk hero Santa Anna had risen as Bustamante's opponent and fought at the head of the federalists against the centralists, who were slowly growing weaker. Though the altercations in Texas were not directly concerned, various events, in themselves insignificant, caused the discord in other parts of the country to be clearly felt.

On the basis of the law of April 6, 1830, a military garrison was established in Anahuac, a settlement on Trinity Bay, and in the harbor a customs house. Col. John Davis Bradburn became the commander of the garrison;[1] Col. George Fisher, a Serbian immigrant, became manager of the customs.

Unfortunately, both were loyal, law-abiding centralists, and Bradburn, according to his military training, a courageous, tough, demanding, and even arrogant person. He was also very correct. He interpreted the law of April 6, 1830 very strictly. When he arrested citizens for minor infractions of Mexican laws, including even Francisco Madero, the land-grant agent of the government of Coahuila y Texas when he was about to give land deeds to colonists who had lived in Texas for several years, Bradburn was probably harsh but nevertheless correct, for the land in question was within the coastal reserve forbidden to foreigners. Bradburn had a right to interfere. Madero had violated Article XI of the law. In the same way, the commander threw two lawyers in jail who had made inquiries about runaway slaves—harsh but correct.

Fisher required that all ships that sailed to or from Texas had first to pay duty to him in Anahuac, which for those ships not intending to call at this port at all was an enormous loss of time.[2]

The problem with both men, especially with Bradburn, was that the Anglo-Americans did not regard these two as actual Mexicans, since they were immigrants too. Quite a lot of American Texans thought those men would be more in line with them than with the "real" Mexican authorities. Bradburn was especially seen as one of them, as an American in Mexican clothes. But when he acted like a centralistic Mexican, he was considered a traitor, and the frenzied reactions of those Texans who found it hard to live with Mexican laws anyway showed their anger and frustration; some even took up arms in revolt against Fisher and Bradburn.

In both cases it was possible to convince the Mexican authorities that the Texans had only been driven to resistance by these two men and otherwise were loyal to Mexico, but the unrest had spread to Texas. Citizens had spontaneously gathered together.[3] They discussed Mexican politics and in letters and resolutions took sides; they were true to Mexico but only to a liberally conducted republic. Santa Anna, who was considered a champion of those values, was supported in opposition to Bustamante's tyrannical government. True to their American heritage the Texans acted in their beliefs as loyal and upright citizens.[4] But declarations of opinions were soon no longer sufficient for them. They believed they now had to act also.[5]

In order to discuss these measures, each town and each community or other kind of organized area was called upon by the *ayuntamiento* of San Felipe de Austin on August 22, 1832, to dispatch two delegates to San Felipe de Austin on October 1, 1832. The members from one district came too late, those of another stayed away; altogether fifty-five men came from sixteen districts. They met for a week, appointed ten subcommittees for the various points of discussion, and composed various resolutions. The speed with which they progressed leads to the conclusion that intensive preparations had preceded the meeting. Actually, only the "Proceedings of the Convention of Texas" are preserved. They inform us about the activities of the conference. Three petitions stand out among the ten concluding agreements or memoranda of the various committees. They were directed to the Congress of the United States of Mexico.

The first document was directed at the import duty that was much too high, particularly for essential products, according to the Texans. These were products that were absolutely necessary for living and working but could not yet be produced in Texas for the next few years, such as tools, items of apparel, books, medicine, machines, and household goods. Because the import duty for these commodities was very high, it amounted almost to a prohibition of import to the Texans. They asked, therefore, for the lifting of these particular duties.

The third request asked for a division of Coahuila and Texas, for the interests and needs of the two areas were entirely different, which was the re-

William Harris Wharton (1802–1839), son-in-law of Jared E. Groce, lawyer, and one of the leaders of the political opposition against Austin. *Courtesy Archives Division, Texas State Library*

sult not only of geography but also of the point of view of the inhabitants. Coahuila was populated almost entirely by Mexicans of Spanish ancestry; mainly Anglo-Americans were living in Texas.

But the second proposal was the longest and at the same time most important. It was aimed at Article XI of the law of April 6, 1830. It stated from all angles that (1) the law was unfair, for the Anglo-Americans were loyal citizens of Mexico, (2) it was due to these Americans alone that Texas was making progress, and (3) this law was interfering with a natural and positive development. The law was aimed directly at those who supported and could help Mexico. The conclusion was that, on the basis of all the points cited, the Congress in Mexico City could not do otherwise than to repeal this unjust law. This petition was signed by the chairman of the committee, William Harris Wharton.[6]

Born in 1802 in Virginia, William H. Wharton, along with his brother John A., was reared after the death of their parents by an uncle, Jesse Wharton, in Nashville. Jesse Wharton belonged, as did John W. Overton and Felix Robertson, to the Nashville Central Committee, which was the presidential campaign organization of Andrew Jackson and the predecessor of the Democratic Party. in 1827 William H. Wharton came to Texas as a young attorney. Probably in the spring of 1829 he met Stephen F. Austin for the first time, and from the beginning their relationship appears to have been tense if not actually very antagonistic.[7] The events themselves that led to their almost hostile association are not known, even though the strained connection between Austin and Wharton's father-in-law, Jared E. Groce, must have played a part.

Although William H. Wharton was not an empresario, he nevertheless already had such great political authority in 1832 that he was presented as a candidate for the office of president of the meeting in San Felipe de Austin in opposition to Stephen F. Austin. Austin received thirty-one votes, Wharton fifteen.[8] Both men declared themselves to be loyal to Mexico. Austin, with mild reproof, directed attention to the grievances and placed the principal fault for the unrest on the persons of Bradburn and Fisher as well as the conditions of civil war in Mexico.[9] Wharton on the other hand made accusations and emphasized the superiority of the Anglo-Americans intellectually as well as practically. It was unjust, he said, to exclude the most capable persons from colonizing, for only the Americans and not the Europeans or the Mexicans could settle Texas sensibly and make the land productive.[10]

Along with the petitions, two resolutions were passed by the participants in the meeting. First, in order to be able to deal with Indian depredations and raids by bandits, a type of citizens militia was formed, in which service was required. It consisted of one regiment divided into two battalions and twelve companies. Secondly, a standing committee was formed that could call meetings at any time and advise about the situation in Texas. This committee also immediately instructed William H. Wharton to go to Mexico to hand the petitions to the Congress.[11]

With these two resolutions Texas had created for itself, so to speak, an army and a kind of senate that could not issue any laws, to be sure, but could give recommendations. Not only was this already an anticipation of a sort of independence from Coahuila, but the meeting assumed rights for itself that belonged only to the central government in Mexico. The Mexican authorities in Texas accordingly reacted with great irritation when they heard of the meeting and its recommendations and resolutions. Even men who were close to Austin and the settlers and who recognized the necessity for reforms were offended.[12] Ramón Músquiz, who stood on friendly terms with Austin and who was the political leader of the San Antonio region, the largest and most populous in Texas, wrote Austin on October 11, 1832, very angrily and full of indignation that in the present state of affairs the action of the settlers was not only extremely foolish but above all illegal.[13]

Because of this massive opposition on the part of the Mexicans, Wharton's mission was canceled, and Austin tried to calm Músquiz.[14] It was clear that there would be no reforms if all of Texas did not demand it—that is, if the Mexican Texans did not also join in the demands of the Anglo-Americans. By their premature haste with the meeting in 1832 they had, however, annoyed that circle; this must now be repaired. So in the following months Austin visited the Mexican settlements in Texas in order to gain the approval of all the groups in Texas for the petitions to the Mexican Congress. He was successful in this and was able to convince those with whom he talked of the necessity for the reforms.[15] While the holding of a second meeting was being discussed with the settlers, he had to calm the Mexican authorities and convince them with his temperate approach. He consequently felt himself shamefully deceived when on January 3, 1833, Thomas Hastings, chairman of the Committee of Nacogdoches, called a new meeting for April 1, 1833, without having previously consulted him.[16]

The convention met in San Felipe again, on April 1, lasting for two weeks. Unfortunately, detailed minutes like those from the first meeting are not available; instead, the most important document of this meeting is the draft of a constitution for an independent Mexican state of Texas. This proposed constitution bears the signature of the president of the convention, William H. Wharton. It was to be taken as a memorandum to Mexico City by Austin.[17] Thus the roles of the two had been reversed. The constitutional recommendations made up the largest part of a packet that contained again, among other things, the request for the repeal of Article XI of the law of April 6, 1830, and for exemption from the import duty. Although Austin had complained about the method of calling the meeting, he not only welcomed the participants who arrived[18] but also collaborated on the draft of the constitution[19] and following the meeting traveled willingly to Mexico.

On July 18, 1833, Austin reached Mexico City, but, as with his first stay ten years before, no immediate settlement of his business was granted him. Two events overshadowed his stay. In the entire country, and in Texas, too, cholera had begun to rage; and the civil war between the centralists and the federalists was nearing its climax. In August, Austin composed several petitions to the Ministro de Relaciones C. Carlos García[20] and urged a speedy decision.

Meanwhile, an important change had again taken place in Mexican politics. In 1832 Santa Anna had defeated the troops of the conservative government of Bustamante, and new elections had been announced for January, 1833. The results were clear to everyone in advance. In 1833 Antonio López de Santa Anna became president of the Republic of Mexico. But for health reasons—so he said—he did not assume his office but entrusted the governing power to his vice-president, Gómez Farías, a declared liberal federalist. Today it is assumed—probably correctly—that Santa Anna wanted to wait on the sidelines, so to speak, until Farías burned his fingers by too vigorous reform so that he could appear once more as the savior of the nation, a calculation that paid off. Farías mildly curtailed the rights of the military, but those of the church, on the other hand, severely. Immediately the conservative circles called for his overthrow. Thus six weeks after the election Santa Anna returned and revoked the reforms. He was abducted for a short time by conservative groups, but he was able to escape and return to power again. This abduction, which necessarily presented a justification for, and increase in, executive power and the personal authority of Santa Anna, appears to have been staged by himself for just those reasons. From July to December, 1833, he revised Farías's reforms, then allowed him to try a liberal experiment once more, and on April, 1834, finally took over the controls— no longer as the hope and champion of the federalists, but as the advocate of a conservative centralism. Then in 1836 he also repudiated the Constitution of 1824 in favor of the Siete Leyes.[21]

Austin, who conferred personally with Santa Anna, did not achieve his main objective. Texas was not granted the right to become an independent state. But he was assured the question would be investigated and Texas would perhaps be entitled to the status of a territory. Article XI of the law of April 6, 1830, was, however, revoked, and the other problem areas, such as duty and taxes, were passed on to the appropriate ministers for decisions.[22] With these results Austin set out for Texas again on December 10, 1833. On January 3, 1834, he was arrested in Saltillo.

This happened on orders from Gómez Farías. The cause was a letter from Austin to the *ayuntamiento* of San Antonio. In this letter, dated October 2, 1833, he had advised the councilmen of Béxar to get everything ready to form a government to enable Texas to rule itself. This was also to take place if the congress refused its consent.[23] Although Austin asserted he wanted only to prevent chaos and anarchy in this way, his proposal still clearly was guilty of treason. In its answer to Austin of October, 1833, the *ayuntamiento* of Béxar with all courtesy also allowed no doubt to prevail that it refused this illegal proposal with horror.[24]

Austin remained in prison for eighteen months until he was released on June 22, 1835, because of an amnesty. From this period there have been preserved a series of letters, an appeal, and a diary that shed light on his attitude and personal motivation. His reaction to his imprisonment is marked by his failure to understand the measures taken against him.[25] In a long letter of August 25, 1834, to his brother-in-law, James F. Perry, in which he defends himself and his actions, it is striking that here and also in other places he speaks of himself in the third person. The reason for this becomes clear when one reads the end of this epistle:

Remember me very particularly to H. Austin, send him this letter, also show it to J. H. Bell, to Capt. Wiley Martin, D. G. Burnett and such other of my friends as you think proper. I wish them to know my opinion on these matters, and I wish them and all Texas to adopt and firmly adhere to the motto and rule I have stated in this letter. . . . I wish you to show this letter to T. F. McKinney and if he thinks proper, or thinks it will do any good he can inform his friends at Nacogdoches of my opinions.[26]

So the letter was meant not only as personal or private information for his brother-in-law and his sister but as a public, political statement. This was the case with several of his letters, which is especially accentuated by the fact that a series of his correspondence was printed in various newspapers.[27] Just this mixture of a private exchange of letters and a public position makes it difficult to clearly work out Austin's motives. The question is whether his private opinions and the goals that he expounded in countless documents reflected his real motives or were only politically opportune expressions.

Even his diary kept during his imprisonment must be called into question here for two reasons. First, it did not come down to us from himself, for we only have a copy made by his nephew, Moses Austin Bryan. Secondly, the style and organization seem strange for a diary.

For the first few days Austin went only briefly into the happenings around him, if he mentioned more than the date at all. But on February 20, 1834, he began less and less to describe the events around him–to whom he wrote letters and why, from whom he received mail and who visited him–but rather to give vent to his political and philosophical thoughts about conditions in Texas, the Catholic church in general and in particular, and about the future of Mexico. These commentaries, often interspersed with justifications of his own actions and attitudes, intimate that this so-called diary was also calculated to be more for publication than for personal recollection.

If the assumption is made that Austin was actually a philosophical person for whom a diary served only as a place to collect highly intellectual expositions, then the objection must be raised that his diary of 1821, made on his first trip through Texas,[28] in no way shows this profound contemplative talent and that the style and arrangement of his "prison journals" match his political statements exactly. Individual passages from his repeatedly recurring justifications are delivered as if they were to be read by others. Thus in one entry dated April 13, 1834, he explains the duties and functions of the *ayuntamiento*.[29] The brief explanatory mention of the character of the *ayuntamiento* makes it obvious that this entry was meant as reading matter for others. Most probably it was supposed to be, or actually was, published in the United States; no one in Texas would have needed such an explanation.

The question as to whether these statements written by Austin, and meant for publication, reveal his actual aims and motives would perhaps be simpler to answer if–regardless of whom they were addressed to–he had always expressed the same opinion. But this is not the case. First he praised Mexico and stressed his loyalty as a Mexican citizen.[30] Then he put this unshakable loyalty to Mexico itself in doubt in other letters.[31] In a letter to William H. Wharton he expressed himself in all clarity: "If the Govt. stands and prospers Texas must prosper under it. If the Govt. falls the bonds which bind Texas and Mexico will of course be severed by that fall, and in this event Texas can either unite herself to the North under the necessary guarentees from that Govert. or become an independent speck in the galaxy of nations."[32]

The difference between these two dissimilar groups of statements results simply from the fact, which Austin himself emphasized, that the one consisted of letters meant for everyone's eyes, and that the others were of a purely private nature and thus display his true motives.

Extensive expositions about the aims of this one man are important not only because he was a prominent and influential personality in this phase of Texas history but primarily because his statements are symptomatic of the development of Texas as a whole. But at the same time the image that prevails to the present time in historical writing about Texas and Stephen F. Austin, decisively imprinted on it by Eugene C. Barker, must be corrected. In his biography Barker drafted an evaluation of Austin that describes him as selfless, tenacious, diplomatic, devoted, modest, altruistic, and honorable.[33] On almost all these points Barker must be refuted.

It must certainly be questioned that Austin did not think about amassing wealth for himself or making big profits through land speculation. Affected by his and his father's great losses in this line of business and the unscrupulous conduct of the previously mentioned speculation companies, he certainly did express himself in some of his letters as being against land speculation in general.[34] But basically this opinion, so stoutly expounded in public, was politically determined, for he himself was accused by settlers all too often of speculation and had to defend himself against these accusations. His actions nevertheless allow doubt to arise about his statements.[35] Likewise, his attempts to secure Robertson's or the Texas Association's land grant contract for himself and his secretary Williams was probably not as completely free from speculative intentions as Austin repeatedly asserted. His outward condemnation and rejection of that type of transaction should not lead to the assumption that he had fundamentally rejected deals in land or other endeavors showing promise of profit for himself personally, or that he had withdrawn from this line of business since his New Madrid speculation.

In 1816 he had formed a company with Anthony Butler, the man from whom his father had once hired slaves, Stephen F. Austin & Company.[36] They leased stretches of the large land tract of Mine à Breton to farmers and lead smelters.[37] Not much is known about the progress and results of this venture, except that Austin had worked alone for two years with Butler's slaves, and in the last, the third year, Butler had joined in; but in that year they had not made any profit at all. Butler, who believed this to be otherwise, instituted proceedings against Austin in 1819 that did not terminate until 1833 and resulted in Austin being liable to pay about $7,000. Thus what was probably his first fairly large and independent business enterprise was not a success for him.[38] But this represented only a beginning, especially if the Long Prairie farm is considered.

His work as an empresario and the labor and vexation connected with it did not rob Austin of so much strength that after the proclamation of the Republic of Texas he went into retirement. On December 10, 1836, he was again participating in the establishment of a business organization, the Texas Railroad Navigation and Banking Company. Together with his partners, Branch T. Archer, James Collinsworth, J. Pinckney Henderson, and Thomas F. McKinney, he brought into existence the first transportation and banking enterprise of the republic.[39] Austin's share amounted to about 10 percent of the entire amount of stock issued by the company.[40] His early death spared him, of course, from having to witness the failure of the venture in the summer of 1838. Already in 1835, just after his release from prison, he had manifested interest in the plans of Samuel M. Williams to establish a bank for Texas and made all preparations to take a large number of shares.[41]

At his death Austin was the largest landowner in Texas. The records of the General Land Office show that between May 30, 1828, and February 26, 1832, he had become the owner of 87,384,516 hectares (1 hectare = 2.471 acres) of land altogether.[42] Although his brother-in-law and later administrator of his estate, James F. Perry, explained that a great part of what he owned was consumed by debts, Austin most likely was one of the wealthiest men in Texas.[43] No matter how Austin's exact financial circumstances may have appeared at his death, it must nevertheless be emphasized that his acquisition of land, as well as the generous distribution of land to his relatives,[44] was certainly determined less by a desire for property per se than by his efforts to return his family to the financial importance of the days in Virginia and Missouri before 1819. The financial failure of his father and the social decline of the Austin family associated with it were to be compensated for. He, Stephen F. Austin, would be his family's savior who would lift it out of the depression of poverty to social prestige again, to prosperity and success. If he achieved this, his position and his reputation were also established. His primary motive becomes apparent here.

Upon inspection of all his letters and political writing, it is striking how much he placed himself in the center. In connection with the colonization of Texas, he always spoke only about himself. This is especially conspicuous, for Barker so earnestly praises the noble, unselfish Austin who sought no attention, wanted to avoid notice, and did everything only for Texas, nothing for himself. But in this judgment he follows completely the image that Austin cleverly projected of himself in his own writing. He and Texas were to become synonymous.

In the picture that he sketches of himself he employs a strange mixture. On the one hand he portrays his work and his continual efforts for others; on the other he stresses that he has received nothing but ingratitude – how toilsome his work was, how much he longs for rest and retirement. This may doubtless have been one of his longings, but the question is why he never fulfilled it. Certainly life as a private individual surrounded by peace and quiet would scarcely have won for him the title Father of Texas, and he worked toward this systematically. It is only natural that he stressed to the Mexicans the unique qualities of his colony in order to acquire as much as he could for his settlers.[45] But he also definitely extolled to his fellow countrymen the role he was playing.[46]

As human and understandable as the high praise may be that Austin, with all his work and effort, rendered to himself, so little does it fit the picture of the modest, altruistic man that Barker was able to project using Austin's assertions. In addition it must seem particularly strange to anyone how obviously Austin passes over in silence the help and service of all those without whom success would never have come to him. Of course, he stresses frequently that in the beginning he was poor and without means, but he does not mention one word about the men, for instance his friend Joseph H. Hawkins, without whose help he could scarcely have survived.[47] Only once did he speak briefly about Baron de Bastrop: "The Baron de Bastrop and myself were jointly appointed the Government Commissioners to survey the lands of the settlers and issue titles to them in due form in the name of the Government."[48] With this brief, formal description, Austin is satisfied not to go further into the baron's role.

By 1805 Bastrop had already come to Texas with the retreating Spaniards as a Spanish citizen and had acquired an empresario contract to settle immigrants between Béxar and the Trinity River. In 1806 he settled in San Antonio[49] and soon rose in the esteem of the Spanish Mexican authorities because of his trustworthiness. Along with various functions that he performed for the governor of Texas, he was named as the second *alcalde* of the *ayuntamiento* of Béxar, probably on the basis of his knowledge of the English, Spanish, French, and Dutch languages.[50] It was owing only to his influence with the authorities that Moses Austin's request was heard at all in 1821. Then, while Stephen F. Austin remained in Mexico City in order to get his father's claims transferred to himself, Bastrop carried on Austin's business as his deputy. During the long period of uncertainty and the absence of Austin, Bastrop kept the colonists in line. When Austin came back again, they shared the duties of overseeing the surveying and parceling out of the land to the settlers.

Especially at this initial stage Bastrop's knowledge of the Spanish customs and language and his familiarity with the authorities were of inestimable value to Austin. The colonists accepted this, too, and expressed their confidence in him unanimously, when on September 24, 1823, they elected him representative for Texas to the legislature of the state of Coahuila y Texas. From January, 1824, until his death in 1827 he served Texas in this capacity as representative and managed to get many favorable laws passed for the Texans. There is no doubt that without Bastrop's help Austin would have progressed only with great difficulty—if at all—in his endeavor to populate Texas.[51] But Austin never mentions this anywhere. According to him, only to *his* tireless effort *alone* does Texas owe what it has become.

This trait of his was displayed very early and shocked those who could expect more gratitude. Thus a suggestion of Austin's at that time, which became known only by chance, came as a surprise to many. A copy of a letter of December 6, 1824, from Austin to Caspar Flores fell into the hands of Bastrop, who, accompanied by Robert Leftwich, Frost Thorn, and Haden Edwards, was in Saltillo in the spring of 1825. In it, on a question from Erasmo Seguin as to what plan would probably be best for settling Texas, his answer was simply, "Si acaso se puede lograr este plan propongo que se nombre por el Gov[no] á nuestro amigo Erasmo Seguin y Yo, como empresarios ó comisionados para llevar en efeto la colonización de todo el despoblado de Texas."[52] Haden Edwards reported the reaction of those men: "They were all shocked at this and could not reconcile it with his past professions. Bastrop himself affected much surprise, and was unable to account for it."[53]

As strange as such behavior seems, credit should not be completely diminished by this portrayal. There is no doubt that he was the most successful empresario, who through tireless effort decisively advanced the rise of Texas from a wilderness to a flourishing and prosperous state. This was his declared purpose—but he also wanted to enjoy the glory for it by himself. He died too soon to be able to savor the title by which he lives today in the consciousness of Texans: "The Father of Texas is no more! The first pioneer of the wilderness has departed. General Stephen F. Austin, Secretary of State, expired this day at half past 12 o'clock, at Columbia."

Thus ran the notice in the *Telegraph and Texas Register* of December 27, 1836.[54]

But verbs such as "enjoy" and "savor" seem scarcely appropriate in reference to Austin. Too strongly did his increasingly negative attitude toward life find expression in his letters as he advanced in age. Pessimism and self-pity are drawn like a thread through his correspondence. He himself certainly believed that his attitude toward life had worsened only in later years, as he wrote his cousin Mary Austin Holley on December 29, 1831.[55] But his memory betrayed him, if he thought that in the beginning in Texas he was still the completely hopeful, naive young man. On April 30, 1820, he had declared to his brother-in-law that he faced humankind with doubt, yes, even with rejection.[56] Even though his work and his fellow human beings exhausted him now and then, he nevertheless did not permit himself to be diverted from his path and his goals.[57]

Along with all his weaknesses, his vanity, his pride, and his self-pity, tenacity is the dominant trait of Austin's personality. The reason why he pushed on in spite of the annoyances that affected him so severely and in spite of much physical suffering that again and again was his lot has already been addressed. The business disasters of his father and the great indebtedness of his family in Missouri in previous years must have been perceived by him as a burden and a disgrace. His mother's family appears also to have watched this financial downfall with displeasure, for Austin continually emphasizes how important it is to him to see the family finally free of debt and to acquire for it the recognition it deserves.[58] However, because he expresses this exclusively in letters to family members, this strong motivation remained hidden from his fellow men.

But constantly and everywhere he stressed: "My object has always been, and still is, to settle and improve the country, regardless whether I made a fortune or not. . . . The credit of settling this fine country and laying the foundation for a new Nation which at some future period will arise here can not be taken from me."[59] That was what he worked for, and he achieved his goal.

With all his purposeful behavior and the array of motives indicated above, the question asked at the outset still remains unanswered: Why did he react with incomprehension upon his arrest in Mexico and what did his change of heart toward Mexico connected with his imprisonment, or so it seems, give rise to? Though before his arrest Austin had preached peace and absolute loyalty to Mexico, upon his return home he called upon the colonists for active resistance.

As has been indicated previously, Austin was of the opinion that he had kept his distance from everything political.[60] Here a misunderstanding comes to bear that probably is due to his ultimate inability to really understand Mexican or Spanish thinking. Certainly for his time an expert on the political situation in Mexico, he nevertheless applied the same standards to political events there as to those in America. Politics seemed to him to mean the same thing as membership and active participation in a party. It escaped him that his public appearance and actions and the direct position he took favoring a political alignment – that of republican federalism – by themselves represented active, political behavior in the eyes of the Mexicans. This has been addressed in the discussion of his connection with Freemasonry. His vehement intercession on behalf of the rights of the individual settlers was in Mexico an unequivocal statement against centralism, against a hierarchical authoritarian state. His statements and actions in support of the citizens of Texas were consequently not the actions of a private person but those of a publicly recognized political power.

In the face of his voluminous correspondence, his many legislative bills, and his position as empresario and later also representative in Saltillo, his frequently recurring statements that he practiced discretion and silence seem actually absurd. But again, it is understandable in light of the contrast between the two ways of thinking – the American and the Spanish.

He justified his letter of October 2, 1833, to the *ayuntamiento* of San Antonio, which was actually the reason for his imprisonment, by maintaining he wanted the best for Texas when he had urged separation from Coahuila, which was wanted by most Texans. He could not be reproached, he felt, for anything except having done all that was possible for Texas. But this was not the reason for his imprisonment. His purpose was not charged against him, but his methods. In that same letter he advised them to separate from Coahuila even if the government in Mexico should deny them this. But that was illegal, as was stressed by the *ayuntamiento* in its answer.

The welfare and development of Texas stood above everything else for Austin. For him it was above his loyalty to Mexico. His attestation of loyalty to Mexico was sincerely meant, but with the silent qualification that Texas came before Mexico; that is, his ultimate tie would be to Texas and not to Mexico. This was apparent not only in his letter of April 24, 1829, to William H. Wharton[61] but also is brought out in a February, 1832, letter from his cousin, Mary Austin Holley, to her brother-in-law in New York: "Austin added on his article on letter paper, I think, some remarks supposing the future independence of Texas, together with something against slavery. He thinks, now, it was imprudent, & as it is necessary the colony should continue for some time longer attached to the Mexican government."[62] So it was only a limited loyalty to Mexico – one for the time being; if Mexico should not prove capable to overcoming its problems, "He is resolved upon independence if driven to extremity by the blind policy of the Mexican government."[63]

Before his departure for Mexico City he wrote to Thomas F. Leaming in all clarity:

> Should it [the application for separate statehood] be refused, I think it
> will be the greatest error that the mexican govt. have ever committed –
> Texas is now able to sustain a State Govt. and cannot do any longer without
> one, & a refusal will inevitably produce a violent agitation here of some
> kind and an unprofitable & troublesome one for Mexico.[64]

That was clear! Austin had already allowed himself to be so influenced by
the War Party that he considered a violent confrontation extremely possible
if his mission failed.

Stephen F. Austin was no longer as peaceful as before and, above all, was
worn out by his efforts at mediation between the Mexican authorities and
the American hotheads. To be sure, he saw the difficulties in his relationship with Mexico and the differences from the United States, but he assessed them incorrectly. To him they were readily surmountable with goodwill, and he did not recognize their basic character. In spite of his knowledge
of Mexico, he saw the problems there with the eyes of a citizen of the United
States. To him the evolution of the United States was exemplary; if Mexico
wanted to be like it – and he really saw its political future only in this light –
then it "must pay the price by a moral resolution in which shall be overthrown all customs and the Gothic politico-religious system set up by Rome
and Spain to hold the people in subjection like beasts of burden."[65] As keen
as many of his analyses may have been, he was not objective enough to be
able to include himself in them and to grasp how he and his actions must
have affected many Mexicans.

Supported by some few very freethinking Mexican friends and driven by
an increasing, fanatical impatience, he supported and forced actions that
approached high treason according to Mexican law. The independent con-
vocation of a town meeting, the creation of a militia, and the drafting of
a state constitution with the indication that it should be put through even
against the will of the government – these things were illegal and revolutionary in the eyes of law-abiding Mexicans. Such procedures were not only
unlawful but also unnecessary to achieve reforms. One could, after all, go
through official channels, draw up petitions, and submit suggestions to the
ayuntamiento, which would then pass these on. The representative, too, could
hand in petitions. An unauthorized action on the part of the citizens was
not provided for according to Mexican law, and according to the overwhelming opinion of the Mexicans was unnecessary, even if one had to wait a long
time for reforms on occasion, and if at the time conditions resembling civil
war prevailed in the land. But that did not conform to Austin's ideas. He
was a true Mexican as long as Mexico remained true to the principles of
the United States – otherwise Texas took precedence. To that end Austin expressed the opinion that he had nothing against it if Mexico should sell Texas
to the United States, providing the conditions were favorable to Texas.[66]

One would have to assume that, for a man like Austin, with his upbringing in the United States, it was simply impossible to understand Mexico and its ideas and concepts of support for the government in their ultimate consistency and to share them absolutely like a native Mexican if there had not also been Americans who were able to do this and who regarded Austin's attitude and the actions resulting from it as critically as the Mexicans did.

John A. Williams[67] wrote Austin a long letter on December 18, 1832, in answer to Austin's request for support for the second meeting in April 1833. Williams emphasized, for one thing, how singularly it affected him that it was actually Austin who supported such illegal measures and, for another, that the majority of the citizens remained, like he, loyal to Mexico and saw no need for illegal proceedings of this kind.[68]

Consequently, Stephen F. Austin himself laid the foundation for the approaching independence movement by loyalty to Mexico that was only conditional. When on February 16, 1836, he stressed to Thomas F. Leaming, "We are at open war in Texas, with Mexico . . . ours therefore is a war of independence – our object is to form a new republic, a new nation, or to become part of the U.S.,"[69] this was not a sudden change of heart, but only the result of a development that he had foreseen at an early stage, even if he had held the hope, to which he had frequently given expression, to reach his goal by peaceful means. This hope was to be disappointed and – as it must be viewed today – had been a false hope from the beginning.

Thus Austin's loyalty to Mexico, which he himself emphasized, appears in a different light. As long as he believed he could achieve something for Texas and thus for himself with the avowal of political loyalty, he utilized it with all his might. But he let this political measure drop at that moment when he was forced to realize that even he had to subordinate himself and that his idea of a Texas patterned after the United States was not to be realized as quickly as he wished. Consequently, after his arrest, he was certain that Texas would have to separate from Mexico in the near future, even though during the imprisonment he issued messages of peace and order, so as not to aggravate the situation even more during the time of his absence.[70]

But meanwhile the situation in Texas had improved. Austin's imprisonment had created a great stir, but his authority was so great that his wishes were followed and calm prevailed. In Mexico most of the reforms proposed for Texas were passed. Article XI of the law of April 6, 1830, was repealed, and as a result a multitude of those wishing to settle left the United States for Texas. English was allowed an an official language, Texas received an additional representative in the state parliament of Coahuila y Texas, trial by jury was granted, religious tolerance was guaranteed, and, finally, Texas was divided into three administrative areas. When Col. Juan N. Almonte visited Texas in 1834 in order to see if revolutionary agitation existed there, he could

Juan Nepomuceno Almonte (1803–1869), colonel in the Mexican army and author of the famous report of 1834 on Texas. *Courtesy Benson Latin American Collection, General Libraries, University of Texas at Austin*

report only the best: Texans were friendly and peaceful and Texas was in every respect a promising, thriving community.[71] Still, new disturbances in Coahuila ruined this picture and brought anger and fear to Texas.

In March, 1833, the capital of the state of Coahuila y Texas was moved from Saltillo to Monclova. The new liberal spirit was soon overshadowed by incidences of corruption. In order to fill the empty state treasury, the representatives had decided to sell land in Texas on a grand scale. This opened

the gates to a great wave of speculation in which Austin's secretary and partner, Samuel May Williams, also participated at his own risk. All of this angered the long-established settlers. Meanwhile, Saltillo, making use of the
political confusion in Mexico City, declared that Monclova had become the
capital city illegally and chose their own governor. Santa Anna declared for
Monclova and sent his brother-in-law, Martín Perfecto de Cós, as *comandante general* of the eastern inner provinces into the agitated state to bring
order. He, however, a true centralist, scorned the liberal government in
Monclova and supported Saltillo. The governor in Monclova, Agustín Viesca,
was afraid for himself and his government, fled, and was arrested. Colonel
Domingo de Ugartechea became the new commanding officer for Texas,
and in Anahuac the customs office was occupied by Capitán Antonio Tenorio
in January, 1835.

As in 1832, disturbances, indeed, even armed uprisings, resulted over the
customs question and the renewed and increased military presence of the
Mexicans.[72] Again, as in 1832, further actions were debated. A new citizens'
meeting was called for October 15, 1835, in the town of Washington, but as
was the case in the important political events of the years before, the basic
questions of the proceedings were to be left to the man in whose assessment
of the situation most of them still had the greatest trust: to Stephen Austin.

Austin had been pardoned in the middle of July, 1835, and returned to
Texas on the first of September of that year. At a dinner in his honor in
Brazoria on September 8, he gave a speech in which he determined the course
they were to follow. This new assembly, he said, was necessary and important for unifying Texas and making it possible to effect measures for the security and defense of the country, for a war with Mexico seemed unavoidable. "War is our only resource."[73] With that, the direction was chosen for
further events.

In contrast to former times, Austin did not advise restraint and peace,
but war. As has been explained, this was no sudden change of mind caused
by the harshness and cruelty of Mexico, but an indirect admission on Austin's
part that he had made a tactical error. His goal to shape Texas according
to his wishes and to americanize it could not be achieved permanently with
Mexico but only in opposition to it.

6. The Life and Views of Texans

The position of Stephen F. Austin, as has just been developed, was considered to have tipped the scales. His voice was decisive. This implies that all the colonists in Texas did not share one opinion and therefore did not know what they should really do next. That is not to say that they did not know what they wanted – their opinions as to what was best for Texas differed.

It is not possible to produce an exact picture of the opinions of that time, for there were no general elections or polls to provide hard statistics. Nevertheless, a reliable picture can be formed by using selected statements of individuals. Along with letters, journals, and reminiscenses, political declarations and newspapers can provide an impression of the prevailing opinions and the mood of the times.

Between 1819 and 1836 nine newspapers had been established in contrast to the far greater number of announcements of newspapers. They were weekly papers that often changed their names, so that it is sometimes difficult to follow their tracks. During the critical period only the *Telegraph and Texas Register,* launched on October 10, 1835, continued publishing without extensive interruptions. The *Texas Republican,* established in July of 1834, concluded its publication when the Mexican troops marched into Texas in March, 1836. In any event, most of the newspapers before 1834 were primarily advertising journals[1] which does not lessen their research value in general but puts them in the background as a source of information in the search for patterns of opinion. The *Telegraph and Texas Register* certainly reproduced the reports and letters of various persons, but these were all official documents, not private correspondence. In order to be able to produce the most comprehensive spectrum possible of all views, it is necessary first of all to refer to private letters and memoranda.

Stephen F. Austin was the representative of a group not only in the political realm but also of a certain social level. His family had to contend with debt in Missouri, and one reason for carrying on his father's venture had been to bring the finances of the family in line. Debts and financial distress in general had been a major reason that many settlers went to Texas.[2]

At the same time, there were naturally many men who had not come to Texas because of economic necessity. One of the most notable personalities of this group was Jared Ellison Groce. Born in Virginia in 1782, he had already owned large plantations in South Carolina, Georgia, and Alabama before he settled in Texas on the Brazos River in 1822. With approximately one hundred slaves that he had brought with him, he established the first cotton plantation in Texas. One of his descendants reported that his relationship with Austin was strained—less on his part than on Austin's. "Unfortunately he aroused the jealousy of Austin who, although a great man, had his faults, and one was a desire to be chief and head of all. Colonel Groce did not go to him for advice as the other settlers did, he did not need his care and protection. This incensed Austin."[3] The reminiscenses of some other settlers were similar to the following from Mary Baylor, daughter of Joseph H. Polley: "S.F. Austin was loved and respected by every one in the colony. They mourned his death. My parents said that he had a kind word for all and did all he could for his colony. He did more for the country than anyone else and deserves all the credit as being the Head man in every thing that was done for the colonies."[4]

Only at the first glance does there seem to be a discrepancy here. The family of Joseph H. Polley had accepted Austin as their chief, as most of the other colonists did also. Groce did not need help from Austin, for he got along well with the Spanish authorities by himself. In contrast to the main body of the settlers, who had enough to do with the building of a new existence and the clearing of the land, Groce had sufficient workers at his disposal so that he could take care of his administrative problems and official procedures himself.

Inasmuch as most of the colonists came to Galveston by sea and from there up one of the numerous rivers[5] or overland with ox carts that contained all their movable possessions and with the livestock they were bringing with them,[6] the "procession" of Jared E. Groce with over fifty covered wagons and the numerous servants and their families coming from Alabama to Texas must have offered to the onlooker a strange and spectacular kind of sight.[7]

Even though Groce was the exception, he nevertheless created an opposing force to Austin. During her school days in Nashville, his daughter had met a young attorney, become engaged to him, and married him in her father's house on December 5, 1827. The young attorney who came to Texas in this way was named William H. Wharton. From his father-in-law he and

Jared Ellison Groce (1782–1836), a wealthy, independent farmer, rival of Stephen F. Austin, and head of the "Wharton Party"–the political opposition to Austin. *Courtesy Barker Texas History Center, University of Texas at Austin*

his wife received as a wedding present a piece of land: Eagle Island, with the first large frame house in Texas on it. He and his brother John A. Wharton were leaders of the opposition of Austin.[8] They also endeavored at an early time to bring Sam Houston to Texas.[9] But the opposition to Austin was not limited to them alone or directed on their initiative.

In 1827 Henry Smith came to Texas from Kentucky and busied himself as a farmer, teacher, and later also as a surveyor. In addition he stepped right from the start onto the political stage—as an absolute opponent of Mexico. He had participated with John Austin in the first disturbances in June, 1832, around Anahuac, where he was wounded. From the beginning he represented the opinion that Texas had to become independent.[10] His portrayal in history is controversial. He is pictured by some as the advocate of freedom, intelligent, generous, and affable,[11] but others describe him as a simple, stupid, and stubborn man, fawning and brutal.[12] If one takes Smith's later appearance in Texas history into consideration, the latter picture is probably more accurate than the first, flattering description; his most conspicuous characteristic was, after all, his intolerance.[13]

Four years after Henry Smith's arrival, a man came to Texas who was called by many the Father of the Texas Revolution: Branch Tanner Archer.[14] Born on December 13, 1790, in Virginia, he studied medicine in Philadelphia. In his case—in contrast to Henry Smith's—the reasons that brought him to Texas in 1831 are known. His interest in Texas made its appearance early due to his contact with Aaron Burr and his wish to accompany him on his expedition.[15] It was and is maintained that he came to Texas later only to detach it by force from Mexico and annex it to the United States as Burr intended to do.[16] The time of his move to Texas, however, arrived for Dr. Archer more or less involuntarily. In a duel he shot his cousin Dr. Crump and saw himself thus forced to find a new place of residence. At a public meeting of the citizens of the city of Brazoria on December 16, 1831, he stood up with great determination in favor of the independence of Texas. This was certainly a reason for his firm and sincere friendship with the Whartons.[17] He, too, had participated in the first disturbances around Anahuac in 1832.

One of the leading characters in Anahuac in 1832 and 1835 was William Barret Travis. Born in South Carolina on August 9, 1809, he studied law in Alabama. The marriage he had entered into on October 26, 1828, with Rosanna Cato proved to be unhappy, and so he moved to Texas in 1831, fleeing his domestic difficulties.[18] He settled in Anahuac, where he opened a law office. A historian wrote about him: "Travis was a practical, ambitious, shrewd, and adept politician with a power of dramatic written expression seldom equaled in Texas history."[19] He soon joined the opposition to Bradburn and was also promptly arrested by him. This caused him to become one of the leading men of the Wharton party or War Party, in which he appeared, together with his friend Henry Smith, as a declared opponent of all Mexicans. In 1832 he moved to San Felipe de Austin, where he entered a partnership with a man by the name of Willis Nibbs. There he found himself in keen competition with other lawyers, among them William H. Jack, Thomas Jefferson Chambers, and Robert M. Williamson, who at the same time was active as a publisher or editor of the newspapers, the *Cotton Plant* (1829–1831), the *Texas Gazette* (1830–1832), and the *Mexican Citizen* (1831). All these men also declared themselves openly to be members of the War Party. This leads us to an interesting point.

Even though it is of little significance to introduce all the opponents of Austin and his politics by name at this point, nevertheless the men who have already been mentioned show characteristics exhibited by many members of the War Party. The majority of the advocates of a harsh, if not completely hostile, course toward Mexico had come to Texas after the deterioration of the relationship between the Anglo-Americans and the Mexican authorities because of the law of April 6, 1830. Although this aspect may have more of a coincidental character, it is still informative to look at the social niveau of these men.

The predominant number of these "hawks" were doctors, lawyers, and merchants. Farmers, such as Jared E. Groce, who belonged to this group politically, were among the most prosperous in the country. Consequently, this party represented an upper class that, because of its education and economic position alone, represented a minority of the Texas settlers. Although the boundaries are fluid of course, this attempt at a demarcation nevertheless is very important.

Although the majority of the settlers were farmers and ranchers,[20] this should not lead to the conclusion that the others, as for example the men mentioned above, could live from their professional or mercantile activities alone. Only too often they were forced to plant their own corn and grain and keep cattle in order to survive. On the other hand, many farmers were also active incidentally in other occupations.[21] The fact remains, in any event, that the men leading the opposition to Austin belonged to a small group of an upper class.[22] This may actually find a partial explanation in the diverse peculiarities of their respective work, for doctors, lawyers, and merchants had far more contact with other persons, as well as with the Mexican authorities, than the average small farmer and therefore to a higher degree experienced difficulties and had to proceed in the face of them.

In a number of public appeals, Henry Smith, for example, warned and exhorted his fellow citizens not to put up with it all any longer—Texas must be organized immediately and in that way be saved from the ruin that threatened.[23] In summary he sketched the following picture:

> Texas has never been properly organized; never conveniently or well governed; always in a half way state of anarchy; and Coahuila by her great propensity for lawless innovation, has now capped the climax; and Texas is left like a bark tossed on the boundless ocean, without pilot, compass or chart, with a mutinous crew, violently dissenting among themselves.[24]

At the beginning of 1835 William B. Travis wrote to David G. Burnet that Texas and Mexico could not possibly remain together for long, for the Anglo-Americans and the Mexicans represented an absolute antithesis.[25] The *ayuntamiento* of the city of San Felipe de Austin declared in a letter to the *ayuntamiento* of the city of Béxar in January, 1833, that the Texans had suffered long enough and must now organize in order to be able to decide upon measures to save Texas from impending anarchy.[26] In February, 1833, Sam Houston described his impressions of Texas to the American president Andrew Jackson. Because Houston had not traveled over all of Texas, he was somewhat dependent on reports of his friends who had settled there, such as the Wharton brothers. For that reason it is understandable when he stresses that the overwhelming majority of Texans wanted to separate from Mexico, for they had obtained neither justice nor protection from the government.[27]

There were, nevertheless, men from that upper class who judged the general situation quite differently. One of them was Ira Ingram. Born on August 18, 1788, in Vermont, he appeared in March, 1822, as a signer of the memorandum of the Texas Association. In 1818 his name surfaced for the first time in a Nashville newspaper as the agent for *Nicholson's Encyclopedia*.[28] In 1821, along with a Mr. Lloyd, he had managed the Tennessee Book Store.[29] He later wrote his Uncle Roswell Ingram that he had studied mathematics in Tennessee for two years and in 1823 married Emily B. Hait in New Orleans. When she died of yellow fever in October, 1824, out of desperation and in order to overcome the shock, he left New Orleans and moved to Texas, where his brother Seth Ingram had already been a successful surveyor for Stephen F. Austin since 1822.[30] In January, 1826, Ira Ingram finally settled in San Felipe and there managed a mercantile establishment with his brother. He represented San Felipe de Austin at the convention of 1833 and afterward reported to his uncle that Texas must become a state by itself, and if the government in Mexico did not consent to it, it would nevertheless have to take care of this on its own.[31] But his further letters from the years following sound quite different: "As to our political relations, they are daily improving, and our prospects on this side of the picture appear to be brightening."[32]

The question of a State Government is yet undecided, and may be suspended for some time to come, but many improvements have recently been made in the local affairs of Texas, occasioned [?] no doubt by the spirit indicated by the convention of 1832 & 33, reconciling the people, for the time being, to a temporary suspension of the act of separation. An entirely new and greatly improved organization of the judiciary system of Texas is one of the effects already realized, of the general and decisive movements here one and two years ago. With this, and such other improvements as we much need, and hope to obtain, we can move quietly, and prosperously along for some time to come, attached as we still are, to the government of Coahuila. And indeed, under even partial reform, making our situation at all tolerable, I would greatly prefer temporary delay to the untried expedient of organizing immediately, with present materials, a separate State Government.[33]

There is no talk in this letter of May, 1834, of anarchy, unbearable conditions, or grievances in the administration.

Because of the reforms that had been conceded to Texas in 1833 and 1834, the situation had improved; descriptions and assessments of the political circumstances in Texas are in hand not just from persons for whom things were better—ordinary farmers also wrote letters and journals.

In April, 1835, at a time when William B. Travis had turned once again to David G. Burnet to inquire about his opinion in regard to the revolution that Travis so ardently wished for,[34] Isaac Holman, who had moved with his family and fourteen slaves from Tennessee to San Augustine near Nacogdoches, wrote a letter to Col. William Moore with the following substance:

In relation to matters of Government we are perfectly at peace—we have a order & law enacted by men of our own choosing and which is sanctioned by the Spanish Government, by which justice is generally administered in a short way to the satisfaction of the parties, without much trouble or expense—Society is much better here then perhaps you might imagine.[35]

With fourteen slaves Mr. Holman was, of course, also in a better economic situation than the average among the inhabitants. From those average farmers, however, there are also documents in which mostly only family news is to be found. But just the absence of any description of the political state of affairs and relationships can give as much information about the situation in general as a political pamphlet, if not even more. For if life under Mexican rule had been perceived as especially hard, the laws as inhuman, and the government as unjust, this would have found its expression in the correspondence of the time. The lack of any mention of unpleasantness or annoyance with the authorities is consequently an indication that the Mexican government and its regulations did not strike the ordinary inhabitants as being unusual. In their letters the settlers spoke of their daily concerns and occupations and were, beyond that, never tired of emphasizing the excellence of their new homeland.[36] Even during the war a volunteer, after a two-page description of the battles, could still describe the good qualities and uniqueness of the country for another page: "Texas is certainly one of the finest countries in the world."[37]

From letters and, above all, from memoirs we can get a good picture today of the very difficult life of the Texas colonists—a life that was dominated all too much by the fight for survival. They hardly had time to devote themselves to politics in general or to long, written political discourses in particular.

At the beginning of the Anglo-American settlement the colonists found life particularly difficult. Though in the diary of his first trip through Texas, lasting about five months, Austin described the beauty and the natural riches of the land, he nevertheless later emphasized decisively that with all the fertility of the region it was still a wilderness.[38]

Even such a well-to-do man as Jared E. Groce had a number of problems in his first year. Because of a long dry spell in 1822, he could not grow any corn, so that until the harvest of the next year his family had no bread. Sugar, coffee, and tea were likewise not to be had. There was certainly a lot of game, but it was thin and not particularly tasty. Consequently they made use of horse meat, for there were wild horses in abundance: "Thus Colonel Groce and the other colonists, during the years 1822 and 1823, subsisted mainly on the flesh of mustangs, without bread or salt."[39] Other families, too, were dependent for their nourishment on the hunt. Along with the mustang, the turkey was a chief article of food.[40]

Although life improved in later times, for the first twenty years it was difficult for settlers to provide themselves regularly with all the things they were familiar with and accustomed to in the United States. In Texas the primary and most abundant agricultural products were corn and cotton.[41] Except for cattle, cotton was the most important product in Texas until it was crowded out by the drilling of oil wells at the beginning of the twentieth century. Consequently, the Texas economy was based primarily on agriculture and cattle.[42] Luxury items such as tobacco, coffee, cigars, brandy, wheat flour, loaf sugar, and wines first were unobtainable and later available only infrequently, because supply was irregular and demand from the cash-poor settlers was variable.[43]

Just as the colonists were dependent for sustenance on what they could produce or catch, other areas of everyday life were governed by the same rule. After old clothes brought to Texas were worn out and could be mended no more, new ones were made at first out of animal skins. Later, when fiber could be had and spinning wheels (often left behind in the move to Texas because they were too bulky) were again available, new clothes could be fashioned from hand-made cloth. Clothing could very, very seldom be bought.[44]

Still, the life of the first pioneers was easier for the men to bear than for the women, for the latter missed the variety and amenities of their old homes: "Texas was a heaven for men and dogs, but a hell for women and oxen."[45] Cash for buying the amenities of a pleasant home was rarely available; necessary payments were made mostly with cows, calves, pigs, chickens, or with the only thing that was available almost in excess: land.[46]

Most houses that were built by the settlers at that time on their own property were log cabins of the simplest construction, with one or two rooms, often without windows or floors. In this way the settlers were at least to some extent protected from the rain and full heat of the sun.[47] The first settlers often lived a journey of days from each other and consequently at the very beginning had scarcely any contact with one another. There were only very few roads, and these were in very bad condition besides. A functioning postal system was not yet known even in the years of the republic.[48]

After the war was over in 1836 and the country was growing, social contacts were very much cultivated whenever possible. There was no theater in Houston until after 1838, but even before that persons knew well, and not only in the cities, how to brighten up their hard lives a bit with celebrations. Balls, weddings, or a barbecue at a neighbor's were welcome opportunities to relax from the laborious workday and at the same time become informed about all the news—social and political.[49]

But it was not just that life became easier and more pleasant for the settlers in the course of the years. It must be kept in mind that in spite of all the generalities there were considerable local differences within Texas. The farther west one went, the wilder and less populated the land was. In the cities, on the great farms in the river valleys, and on the coast persons lived better than in the interior, left to themselves.[50] Regional variations were, nevertheless, not only limited to the standard of living; the Texas of the 1830s can also be divided politically into various zones.

It must be made clear at this point that, in this early period of time, "Texas" usually means the eastern part of what is known today as Texas—that is, about a half or perhaps only one-third of the present area of the state. The rest of the land, where it was not desert, was slowly settled only after the middle of the nineteenth century.

East Texas was divided roughly into four districts: the northeast with Nacogdoches at the center, the middle section with San Felipe de Austin, and the southeast with San Antonio de Béxar as the middle point. The fourth region was the coast, with the cities of Anahuac, Galveston, and Velasco as the centers. The northeast formed a point of unity for the settlers who came to Texas overland. The border cities—even Nacogdoches—often had the reputation of being run by lawless men—by thieves and murderers, who, fleeing the laws of the United States, established themselves on the edges of Texas in the Spanish territory that was a safe place for them, and they then often lived their lives moving back and forth. For that reason the north was considered by many as a source of unrest against Mexico. It was claimed that the region's shadowy characters contaminated the political climate and the relationship between Americans and Mexicans.[51]

On the one hand, it is certainly true that many lawless men did settle in this region: they were, first, fleeing from the authorities in the United States and, secondly, were rejected by Austin and most of the empresarios who followed his example of setting up very strict standards for prospective colonists.[52] But on the other hand, these men kept quiet when it came to politics.[53] The agitators and those who fought for a free Texas or one belonging to the United States were almost without exception located in the middle regions and on the coast. The attempts of the filibusters and finally of the participants in the Fredonian Rebellion, who had all operated in and from the north, belonged long since to the past. The politically active elements lived and worked primarily in Liberty, Galveston, Velasco, Brazoria, Gonzales, Mina (now Bastrop), and San Felipe de Austin. Thus they also formed the border along the southern part of the country that was overwhelmingly Mexican, the Department of Béxar.

One of the reforms of March, 1833, had been to divide Texas into three governmental districts instead of only one: the Department of Béxar, the Department of Nacogdoches, and the Department of the Brazos. The last was the politically active middle section of Texas. Although according to Almonte there were about four thousand persons living in Nacogdoches and surroundings, only five hundred of them were Mexicans. The Department of Béxar, however, was almost exclusively settled by Mexicans. That meant that around thirty-four hundred Mexicans in the district of Béxar faced 20,800 Anglo-Americans, including slaves, in the two other districts. In the administrative area of Béxar about six hundred Americans were living.[54] Even if these figures are not 100 percent accurate, they nevertheless correctly reflect the ratio of Mexicans to Anglo-Americans in Texas, in connection with which the word "faced" used above perhaps gives rise to a false impression. Although the contacts between these two groups may have been slight, there were still a number of business partnerships and marriages between them.[55] The intimacy, however, was limited to one class of Mexicans, just as the prejudices of the Anglo-Americans that frequently arose were based on contact with another group.[56]

The one—the other: by this is meant the two layers of society that prevailed among the Mexicans in Texas. There were the few *ricos,* the officials and the rich land- and cattle owners, often themselves at one time officials who had settled in Texas after their active service was over, and there were the *pobres,* poor peasants or day laborers in the cities.[57] This social variation was rooted in ethnic problems. The *pobres* were for the most part mestizos; the *ricos* in most cases were the descendants of aristocratic, old Spanish families. The *ricos* felt more of a relationship with the white Americans than with the *pobres,* who were socially on a level with American blacks. The interests of the *pobres* were thus of no concern to the *ricos.*

It is, therefore, not strange that first Mier y Terán and then Almonte could report in their commentaries a deplorable lack of schools among the main body of the Mexican population.[58] The *ricos* mostly retained private teachers and saw no value at all in the education or training of the *pobres*. If inquiry is made about the political opinions of the Mexican Texans, it is the *ricos* who must be considered, for the *pobres* either responded with the view of their employers or did not respond politically at all. They were too poor to be able to afford an opinion. History passed by these Mexicans in Texas; for them nothing changed: "The natives were, in fact, strangers in their own land."[59]

The others—the rich families—took sides. One part joined the Anglo-Americans, the others went to Mexico after the declaration of the independence of Texas. Just as was all of Mexico, Texas too—Mexican Texas—was divided into a federal-republican camp and a centralist camp. Families such as the Seguins, Sambranos (Zambranos), Menchacas, and Veramendis could to some extent look back on more than a hundred years of personal history in Texas. Quite early a national feeling had developed among these families, pride in "their" province of Texas.[60]

Don Ambrosio Rodriguez, Don José Antonio Menchaca, Don José Antonio Navarro, Don Erasmo Seguin, and Don Juan Martín de Veramendi were the heads of rich and influential families who declared themselves for Texas as long as they lived, got along well with the Anglo-Americans, and also opposed, as the Americans did, the centralist contentions of Mexico.[61] As long as they could (Veramendi died in 1833 of cholera), they supported the Texans' struggle against Mexico.

But not only the old resident Mexicans supported the Anglos; there were also newcomers such as José Antonio Mexía[62] and Lorenzo de Zavala.[63] Mexía arrived for the first time on July 16, 1832, on the sea route to Texas as the commanding officer of a troop of three hundred soldiers advancing against the rebellious settlers in Velasco and Anahuac, and in this way engaged in saving Texas for Mexico. A Freemason like Stephen F. Austin, and actually a member of the liberal *yorkinos*, Mexía was persuaded by Austin that Texas was only demonstrating for the idea of freedom and liberality and against the centralist tendencies of Mexico.[64] Mexía never established himself in Texas, but his friend Zavala remained until his early death on November 15, 1836, in the country for which he had gotten an empresario contract to settle five hundred families on March 12, 1829, and which he did not see in person until July, 1835. Mexía and Zavala are mentioned only briefly here, in spite of their importance in Texas history, because their particular roles will be investigated in a later discussion of the land business as it relates to Texas.

Although these men fought with the Anglo-Americans against their own homeland, they were not acknowledged by the War Party, because they were Mexicans. They fought against their own countrymen because they were struggling against the dictatorial designs of Santa Anna's regime, but they did not fight, like Henry Smith and Branch T. Archer, *against* Mexico but *for* a liberal, free Mexico.[65] They acted just like their comrades in arms in other provinces, such as Yucatán, Zacatecas, and California, who rose up against a dictatorship. But without knowing it, they were supporting in this way men who were as indifferent to a liberal Mexico as to a centralist Mexico and who recognized as their real goal only the annexation of Texas to the United States. When after the war Mexicans were looked at askance in the Republic of Texas and later branded as traitors by Mexico, there remained for the committed Mexican part of the Texas population in most cases only a life of isolation and embitterment, if they were not expelled from their homes and Texas altogether.[66]

Although it was emphasized above that the simple farmer had not generally complained about irritation with the Mexican authorities, this should not obscure the fact that there were certainly problems, even though a large number of them were removed in 1833–1834 with the repeal of Article XI of the law of April 6, 1830. This had in fact amounted to an immigration prohibition for Americans and had caused a lot of bad blood, for it too often only prevented the uniting of family and friends and had not accomplished its real purpose: the rejection of undesirable elements, such as illegal aliens, fugitives, and criminals from the United States.

Stephen F. Austin once broached two subjects to Erasmo Seguin that he assumed presented problems: religion and slavery.[67] But the question of religion was actually no critical matter for the majority of the settlers. For one thing, most of them—as was mentioned above concerning private correspondence—had more important things to do than bother about questions of theology; and for another, more significantly, many of them were not at all clear about their legal situation. William P. Zuber wrote in his memoirs that the Mexican authorities had for a time allowed the Texans freedom of religion, and so a Mr. Stephenson came to them.[68]

Mr. Henry Stephenson was a Protestant minister in Louisiana who also regularly visited congregations in eastern Texas and preached there. Zuber's assertion is naturally wrong. The colonists had not been exempt from membership in the state religion but only from the requirement of paying the church tax. The activities of the Reverend Stephenson were, therefore, illegal. Because church and state received no revenue from Texas, the province was neglected in regard to religion. Thus it was possible for these false notions to take shape and be maintained.

The question of religion, however, was considered especially critical by those who wanted to become colonists and by travelers from the United States.[69] In practice it appeared that life under Catholic laws was perfectly possible for Protestants—primarily because the laws were not enforced. "As to the American settlements in Texas, they have never been required to conform to the rites and ceremonies of the Catholic religion, or to those of any other; nor have they been prevented worshiping in any way they please," wrote Ira Ingram in 1830 to his uncle.[70] With Article X of the law of March 26, 1834, the government in Mexico City even went so far as to grant religious freedom legally as long as public order was not disturbed.

The second point that Austin addressed at the outset was more critical for the colonists: the slavery question. As has already been detailed above, Texas was not a slave state in the manner of Georgia, for instance. Slaves did not yet play the great role in the general economy that they did in the deep South. From about 12 percent of the immigrating population in 1835, the proportion of slaves in the total population rose to 27 percent by 1847.[71] If this is compared with South Carolina, where blacks in 1850 made up 52.7 percent of the population, and states such as Virginia, Georgia, Mississippi, and Louisiana, whose slave population amounted to more than two-fifths of the number of inhabitants,[72] it can be seen that, much as in the case of the question of religion, slavery did not play as great a role economically in Texas as a whole as one might have surmised on the basis of frequent written inquiries to Austin from the United States, at least before the revolution.

Nevertheless, in regard to this generalization, one should not fail to consider that slavery in the Brazos district, the area settled by politically active Anglo-Americans, was already an important economic factor before the revolution,[73] and accordingly was designated by political activists as important for all of Texas. Actually, its importance for Texas as a whole before 1835 lay mainly in the realm of principle. A person should be allowed to own slaves if that was so desired; for a large part of the farmers were convinced that only with the help of slaves—even if they themselves could not afford any— would they be able to acquire a sizable plantation and thereby fortune and respect. Having slaves was highly regarded as a status symbol. Mexico, even though disapproving, looked the other way on this question, so no great difficulties arose from it for the settlers, even though the tension remained.

The Indians presented one real problem for many settlers. The reports of raids and depredations were manifold; fear was great. To be sure, Austin himself now and then characterized the Indians as savages, but he tried hard to keep things as peaceful as possible.[74] Without doubt the various Indian tribes did attack the settlers repeatedly. The question of the reasons for this and the history of the Indians in their relationship to whites is much too complex to be dealt with here. It is certainly interesting that the Spaniards and the Americans were in agreement that the Indians were the real mischiefmakers, even though they themselves had invaded Indian territory and were continually diminishing Indian living space. There were settlers, however—

though they were in the minority—who differed entirely and saw that there were Indian tribes with a very high level of culture and civilization,[75] and that it was not the Indians but the whites themselves who were the real delinquents and originators of trouble with the various tribes.[76]

Disputes again arose with the Mexicans about tariffs, which had begun to increase in 1830. It was the import tariffs that affected the Texans severely, because they were levied on essential household and farm goods. At the same time, the colonists became angry because, after years of exemption, they were also required—lawfully—to pay a public tax. But when one merchant in Anahuac, Andrew Briscoe, attempted to incite the citizens to open rebellion, he discovered that, with all their anger, they were not prepared to break the laws of Mexico.[77] The *ayuntamiento* of Liberty even went so far as to censure him publicly and remind him of his duties as a Mexican citizen, telling him that if he got into trouble with these laws, that was his problem alone.[78]

William B. Travis, who with twenty-five men and a cannon, forced Antonio Tenorio, the commander of the military garrison at Anahuac, to surrender and hand it over, was also forced to learn that the other citizens did not in any way sanction his impatient militant actions.[79] For one thing, the conduct of this group of aggressive Texans was considered ungrateful;[80] for another the attempt was made to prove that they formed an extremely small minority. A declaration on this subject was drawn up and sent to Colonel Ugartechea, who was to pass it on to General Cós. The Mexicans, however, for their part, now forfeited the goodwill of the population, partly because they demanded as evidence of their loyalty that the Texans surrender the ringleaders and agitators, which was for them out of the question.

For the Texans this demand was an expression of military despotism and consequently the first sign of the dictatorial, centralistic regime that was attempting from Mexico City to nip in the bud any political opposition. Mixed with this irritation about the centralistic tendencies of Santa Anna's government, which were becoming increasingly visible, was the anger of many settlers toward some of their fellow citizens, who appeared to be speculating in land on a grand scale by exploiting their positions as members of congress in Monclova. One of the representatives, who later was reputed to have been the worst of the speculators, was Samuel May Williams, the secretary and partner of Stephen F. Austin.

Born on October 4, 1795, in Rhode Island, Williams came to Texas in May, 1822, from New Orleans, where he had lived since 1819. In the fall of 1823 he was recommended to Stephen Austin, who desperately needed a multilingual secretary. Williams spoke fluent Spanish and French because of a rather lengthy business engagement in Argentina and had already helped Jared E. Groce and Robert Kuykendall with this ability. In this function he soon made himself indispensable to the colonists and became the most important government official in Anglo-American Texas.[81] Elected in 1835 as the representative for the Brazos district, he was mainly involved with two colleagues, John Durst and James Grant, in the legal action of April, 1835, that disposed of up to four hundred leagues of land to anyone who had enough ready cash. Of greater significance than the actual events were the motivations of those involved and the reaction of the public.

Williams alleged as his defense that the land sale had served only to fill the Monclova treasury so as to have resources at hand to use against Santa Anna and to recruit soldiers for the federalists. At least the later contracts included the condition that one thousand troops had to be raised and maintained for a year in return for the four hundred leagues of land.[82] This legal provision was aimed at Santa Anna and his government, and was also so understood in Mexico City. As soon as news of the rich land grants for the purpose of recruiting troops reached there, the laws were declared to be revolutionary and consequently null and void.

The basis for this action was a decree that Santa Anna had issued shortly before and that severely reduced the militia of the individual states. Santa Anna cleverly used the events in Monclova to express his pro forma support of the liberal government there in order to avoid open revolt. But he sent his brother-in-law, a declared centralist, to the state to attend to keeping the peace—in his, Santa Anna's, meaning of the word. Although Samuel Williams and the others understood this and sought to defend their land deals by warning of impending danger, the citizens of Texas saw these deals only as abuses by a corrupt government and its enrichment at their expense.[83] The warnings fell on deaf ears.

Most of the Texas population clung to Mexico. It was assumed that the liberals would be victorious in Mexico and that times would consequently continue to improve. The most important thing was to be able to live in peace without having to sacrifice one's principles. No matter if a group of Texans had the desire to separate from Mexico, either to become independent or to join the United States, the opinion still prevailed that the right time for either of these steps had not come. As for the first, they were too weak and so, for better or for worse, dependent too much on other nations, and the second was not worth pursuing because of the land policies of the United States. They had come to Texas, after all, just because of the liberal land-grant policy of Mexico and wanted to profit further from it. Both steps were consequently rejected as absurd by most Texans.[84]

The protestations of loyalty to Mexico seem thus to have originated less in idealistic contemplation than in practical consideration. There is an astonishing similarity here to Stephen F. Austin's behavior and attitude. This is made particularly clear by the fact that the settlers wanted to wait for his return from imprisonment in order to hear his opinion before they decided on their further course. Austin had achieved the most for the settlers up to that time with his peaceful policies. His intercession and his influence for peace in previous crises had obtained only benefits for the Texans. His policy of agreement with the Mexican authorities had brought great improvement to Texas. If he should plead in the future for peace and quiet as always before, this would be of advantage to Texas—also as always before.[85] But if he decided on war, then from a man who had otherwise always preached peace, that would mean nothing more was to be achieved by peaceful measures and taking up arms was actually the only remaining means.

No matter how strong the advocates of war may have been in the summer of 1835, Austin held the key position for determining the course of events. His person was looked upon with respect and admiration by a large number of the colonists.[86] It can be said that the opinion of the majority of Texans depended on him.

7. U.S. Economic Interest in Texas

The views of the citizens of the United States were determined to a great extent by sporadic reports from friends and relatives and by newspaper articles. In this way a completely different picture developed from one that would have reflected the reality in Texas and the opinions that prevailed there. The newspapers, which mainly operated to form public opinion, did not trouble themselves much about the actual facts, something that provoked Austin very much and frequently caused him to express his point of view.[1] But Austin's protests were just like drops of water on a hot stove. Outfits such as the Galveston Bay and Texas Land Company were making a living with land certificates that were worthless. The basis for these speculative businesses lay in the fact that the United States was trying to buy Texas from Mexico, and persons hoped to be able to make further profits there with land titles, as they had done in Florida. These thoughts prevailed everywhere: "There seems (as far I have been able to learn) a considerable disposition to speculate in the Texas lands, which can only be accounted for on the supposition that they will soon belong to the U. States."[2] And: "We are all anxious to purchase Texas from Mexico, and the subject is beginning to excite a great deal of warm discussion in the public prints."[3]

The newspapers and thus also their readers all speculated about the purchase of Texas by the United States. As has already been described, the first U.S. minister to Mexico, Joel R. Poinsett, was not very fortunate in his choice of methods, achieved the opposite of his assignment, and consequently had to be recalled from Mexico. This certainly did not diminish the intentions of U.S. president Andrew Jackson to try again. In 1830 he appointed Anthony Butler as chargé d'affaires in Mexico and immediately gave him specific instructions in his first letter.[4]

According to this letter—and subsequent ones—it was Butler's sole mis-

sion in Mexico to gain Texas for the United States. From the great array
of diplomatic responsibilities that make a legation important and necessary
in its host country–as, for instance, the furtherance of economic, social,
cultural, and political contacts–only this one small item had any importance for Jackson's administration in relation to Mexico. This clearly reveals
how weak he considered Mexico to be, a weakness that should be adeptly
exploited. At the same time the obvious fear that the Mexicans harbored
toward the United States was to be cleverly exploited as a tactical measure,
like the fear of U.S. troops and of a revolution in Texas. These remarks are
puzzling considering the fact that this letter was written in October, 1829.
In that year there could scarcely be talk of a revolutionary mood or even
intrigues in Texas. But if these were only rumors from Mexico itself as a
part of the anti-American propaganda, then Jackson devoted considerable
space to them. Above all, however, according to him, there was not a Spaniard who could not be bribed, and so Butler was given a discreet hint to
influence the members of the government with encouraging offers of money
and land. Of course, this had to be done in a decent and honorable manner,
for along with all the pressure that Jackson meant to use in this transaction,
one premise of his whole administration could not be overlooked: on no
account bring the United States into discredit and put no argument against
the United States into Mexico's hands that could be used as an excuse for war.

Jackson was consequently horrified when Butler communicated to him
by regular mail that with payments of between $300,000 and $400,000 to
certain influential persons the deal was already as good as in his pocket.[5]
Jackson wrote back that it was Butler's sole mission to conclude a trade and
boundary treaty for the use and the peace of both countries. The money
was only for the purchase of the land and keeping the peace if also to serve
in the case of vague pretensions to the land on the part of the Mexicans.
"But we are deeply interested that this treaty of session [*sic*] should be obtained without any just imputation of corruption on our part."[6]

Jackson may even have been convinced himself by the content of his letter and have written it with no ulterior motive, which, however, cannot
remove all the doubts of historians. Because of his allusion to how cor-
ruptible he considered the Mexicans to be, his instructions can be interpreted completely in Butler's sense. They were by no means as unequivocal
as he wanted to have them understood in his last letter. But basically, Jackson's
position cannot be clearly determined, for during his lifetime he himself
decided which papers should be destroyed and which preserved for the biography that he also personally commissioned. These letters–in contrast to
the one cited at first–were marked: "To be kept for the historians."[7]

In further letters also, Jackson urged Colonel Butler to finally conclude
an agreement about Texas but without being too concrete about the choice

of methods. He repeatedly hinted at imminent armed conflict and a revolution in Texas, which—he had been confidentially assured, so he said—were also being urged by speculation companies in Boston and New York.[8] Aside from the fact that often enough the U.S. government received completely erroneous information—whether intentionally or not must remain moot here—about events in Texas and Mexico,[9] the letters concerned here only confirm what was quite certainly emphasized: Texas must become part of the United States at (almost) any price; but the United States, as well as Andrew Jackson and his administration, was not to be discredited by any action or effort.

It might be asked why Andrew Jackson had chosen Colonel Butler for this delicate mission at all. He had probably known Butler since he was a child and was particularly impressed by his bravery as a colonel in the battle of New Orleans.[10] In addition, Butler had recommended himself to Jackson when in 1827 he wrote to him: "I have been into Texas. . . . It must belong to the United States and I hope that it may be one of the Acts of your administration to obtain it."[11] Still, not only Butler's lack of discretion, but also his lack of success, which he continually sought to conceal by fanciful promises to rekindle hope, led to his recall by the exasperated president in 1835. Actually, he returned to Mexico briefly once more, but again accomplished nothing for Jackson, and probably settled in Texas in 1835 or 1836.

His failure certainly was based not only on some sort of ineptitude but on the fact that Butler wanted to serve several masters at the same time. In 1833 John Charles Beales wrote him from New York asking if he would like to use his influence with the Mexican government for the Arkansas and Texas Land Company for a half-million acre "contribution" in Texas land certificates.[12] On July 27, 1835, James Prentiss, also from New York,[13] sent four letters to him at the same time; the first explained Prentiss's power of attorney, so to speak; the second—formally delivered—was an offer of a contract; the third—of a private nature—explained the conditions of the contract more specifically; and the fourth—marked secret and confidential—defined the tricky questions behind the contemplated business.[14] In summary, the following picture appeared: Butler was to attempt to purchase Texas for $10 million for the Trinity Land Company represented by James Prentiss—that is, Texas was to be granted politically to the United States and all the land was to be conveyed to Prentiss and his company. The latter was counting on about a hundred million acres from this. For it, Butler would receive a half-million acres and $5,000. For less land there would naturally be a proportionately smaller commission.

According to his letters, Prentiss derived his pretensions to this huge land transfer, for one thing, from the inability of most empresarios to settle the land that was awarded them and, for another, from the fact that he and his company had meanwhile bought up the largest part of the land scrip that was on the market. With the exception of the Austin, De Witt, and the old Leftwich—now Robertson—contracts, he and his partners owned the most rights to the land of Texas. In this region several thousand families from Europe were to be settled. This meant that Prentiss and his partners could colonize the biggest part of Texas if the legality of their title should be confirmed by Mexico. Prentiss asked Butler, in addition, to persuade the Mexican government not only to recognize the land titles but also to furnish them with rights that would make it equivalent to a sale of the land.

This commission put Butler in the uncomfortable position of sitting on the fence. On the one hand he had an official government assignment and on the other an immensely lucrative private business—two enterprises that were mutually exclusive. For the U.S. government Butler was to acquire Texas for $5 million but without recognizing the land titles and empresario contracts that were not yet fulfilled and were doubtful, in order to avoid an irritating situation like the one that had arisen in Florida. But Butler himself possessed one of these doubtful claims because of his agreements with Beales and Prentiss, who promised him land titles in the amount of a million acres, if he could extricate Texas from Mexico. His compensation from Prentiss would have been the higher, moreover. This impossibility of making things right for everyone caused Butler to fail in Mexico.

In any event, Anthony Butler was not the only one who was making an effort in Mexico to get land in Texas. Since the summer of 1833 Gen. John Thomson Mason had also been lingering in Mexico. He had approached Butler with the request that he support him in helping the company that he represented to get its rights. This company was probably the most well-known consortium that had an interest in land in Texas: the Galveston Bay and Texas Land Company.

David Gouverneur Burnet, born in New Jersey on April 14, 1788, became interested at an early date in South American politics. In 1806 he joined Francisco de Miranda's army of revolution attempting to liberate Venezuela from Spanish control. After the failure of this venture, he ran a commercial enterprise for a short while in Natchitoches, Louisiana, and then studied law. Perhaps his connections in 1818 with Benjamin Rush Milam,[15] who carried on trade with the Indians, was one of the reasons for his interest in Texas. On December 22, 1826, he received an empresario contract for three hundred families. On the same day Joseph Vehlein, a native German who had meanwhile become a naturalized Mexican merchant, also received a contract through his lawyer, Dr. John Lucius Woodbury, likewise for three hundred families. On November 17, 1828, Vehlein concluded another contract for one hundred prospective colonists. The three areas that were awarded

David Gouverneur Burnet (1788–1870), land speculator, founding member of the Galveston Bay and Texas Land Company, and president of the ad interim government of Texas in 1836. *Courtesy Rosenberg Library, Galveston, Texas*

to these two men for settlement formed a geographic unit; they were made up of two-thirds of the piece of land that had been given to Haden Edwards on April 15, 1825, for his eight hundred families and taken back again because

Manuel Lorenzo Justiniano de Zavala y Saenz (1788–1836), land speculator, founding member of the Galveston Bay and Texas Land Company, and Mexican revolutionary. He later joined the forces against Santa Anna. *Courtesy, Archives Division, Texas State Library*

of his role as ringleader in the Fredonian Rebellion. On March 12, 1829, the remainder of this old Edwards territory went to Lorenzo de Zavala, who was to be permitted to settle five hundred families.[16]

Lorenzo de Zavala was born on October 3, 1789, in the province of Yucatán in Mexico. He came from a prominent family and received a good education. At an early age he became involved in the politics of his country and was an advocate of liberal reform. In 1821, as the representative for Yucatán in the Spanish Cortes (parliament) in Madrid, he learned about the Mexican Declaration of Independence and returned immediately to his homeland, where he was elected to the Mexican congress—again from his home province of Yucatán. There he participated decisively in various constitutional and legal matters as well as in the establishment of the Masonic lodges according to the York Rite. Thus on the one hand he came into close contact with Joel R. Poinsett and on the other—because of his membership in the Committee for Colonization Questions—with Stephen F. Austin.[17] In 1827 he was appointed governor of the federal state of Mexico. Under President Guerrero he even advanced to minister of the treasury but was forced by the centralists to resign and decided in 1830 to travel to the United States because of the turbulent times in Mexico.[18]

On October 16, 1830, he participated in the establishment of the Galveston Bay and Texas Land Company together with Burnet and Vehlein. Nothing is known about its origin or the meetings and plans of the participants. The motives of the individual parties concerned can, however, be ascertained fairly easily. For Burnet, as for other empresarios as well, the greatest obstacle to the fulfillment of their contracts with Mexico consisted of the lack of sufficient financial means required for recruiting settlers, surveying, and also often for advances to the settlers for their expenditures.[19]

The three empresarios brought their contracts and their legal position into the enterprise. In return they received altogether $47,500. At the head of the organization were three lawyers and administrators, Anthony Dey and George Curtis from New York, as well as William H. Sumner from Boston. Assisting them was a seven-member board of directors. Lynde Catlin, George Griswold, John Haggerty, Stephen Whitney, William G. Buckner, Barney Corse, and Dudley Selden belonged to it until 1835. Catlin, Buckner, Corse, and Selden dropped out and were replaced in 1835 by Elisha Tibbits, Charles A. Clinton, Nathaniel Richards, and Nathaniel Lord. In addition to the three administrators, the three empresarios, and the seven directors, the company also had a lot of members or rather stockholders whose number at the beginning amounted to fifty-six and in 1849 was ninety-five.[20]

As with every other corporation the amount of profit of each individual shareholder was regulated by the number of shares or stocks owned. Outwardly the consortium appeared as the representative for Burnet, Zavala, and Vehlein, the only purpose of which was to bring settlers to Texas for the three empresarios.[21] Internally, however, it was acknowledged that the real aim and purpose of the company was to make a profit.[22] With this goal in mind the Galveston Bay and Texas Land Company advertised extensively.

With brochures, handbills, and newspaper announcements the attempt was made to acquire as many buyers as possible for the land certificates produced by the enterprise.[23] But because of the prohibition on the immigration of Americans effected by the law of April 6, 1830, these were worthless. In addition, the actions of the company were not legally irreproachable even above and beyond these statutory regulations. It was falsely promised to those who wanted to emigrate that the company could sell land de jure, when in fact the land titles that were acquired, each either for a *sitio* or a *labor*, could in the most favorable circumstances represent only a recommendation. Only the empresarios, insofar as they actually lived in Texas, along with the land-grant commissioners in Mexico, could confer on a family a legal title to the land that was being settled.[24]

Later the company behaved outwardly as if all this had not been known by them and as if they had acted most conscientiously. But not only do veiled allusions to the legal uncertainty of the situation in their land papers themselves and copies of the appropriate paragraphs from the Mexican laws in their brochures make this assertion appear very questionable; remarks of their agent, General Mason, also show clearly that they knew very well they were selling de facto worthless paper but hoped that this fraudulent act would be cleared up subsequently. They believed the settlers–once they were in Texas–would get their land, and the company itself would subsequently be recognized and installed with all the rights of the empresarios as their successor,[25] something that actually did happen in March of 1834 as a result of the repeal of the law of April 6, 1830.

In contrast to the Texas Association this consortium actually attempted to accomplish something about the settlement of Texas. One thousand families were outfitted and brought to their land in Texas. Two ships, as well as several agents, surveyors, and various advisers, were in their pay. Altogether the company estimated expenditures at $141,296.30.[26] It had sold titles to land for altogether 10,216,635 acres.[27] Offering a price of five to ten cents an acre,[28] they had thus taken in between $510,831.75 and $1,021,663.50, which amounted to a profit of between $369,535.45 and $880,367.20 after the deduction of their expenditures as they themselves calculated them. According to their expense account in 1849, they received an extra compensation of $50,000 on the occasion of the end of the Mexican war.[29]

The company, which had found many buyers for its land papers, because of the relatively high price of land in the United States–an acre cost $1.25–did not actually cheat all those who wanted to settle, for it was after all able to place one thousand families on the land. But many of those learned after their arrival that they had been deceived.[30] Even though the Galveston Bay and Texas Land Company had pointed out possible legal deficiencies in the fine print in their land papers, the favorable offer dazzled most of those who wanted to emigrate. Nevertheless, the company had fulfilled the real purpose of its existence: to yield a profit.

Its lawyers, agents, members, and directors were in addition mostly engaged profitably in another quarter. The majority of the directors, who were at the same time members, earned their living as businessmen in the broadest sense of the word. They were brokers, stock market speculators, and lawyers. They came for the most part from the region between Philadelphia, New York, and Boston. Their earnings and success were variable. To acquire exact information about their financial transactions would be very difficult and in the scope of this work, not necessary.[31]

Their pecuniary interest in Texas was not limited to the Galveston Bay and Texas Land Company. Texas, which throughout its war of independence and later as a republic remained in great need of money, issued various kinds of bonds and promissory notes. Exactly what amount Texas owed cannot be settled with absolute certainty, for not all obligations were ever claimed. In 1856 the state of Texas itself estimated the amount as $10,078,703.21. In the compromise of 1850, where things went as in the previous attempts at compromise for the preservation of the union, Texas, by an act of Congress, had gotten the promise of $10 million for the settlement of its debts,[32] a sum that in 1856 was subsequently raised to $12,750,000. Some small and middle-sized enterprises, but also many larger operations and banks, had speculated on this development.[33]

Thomas E. Davis, for example, stockholder in the Galveston Bay and Texas Land Company, had a bill of exchange for $642.77 and in 1856 received $1,037.89 for it.[34]

George Curtis, who in 1849 had placed his brother and partner Edward under guardianship and thus could also take charge of his share, was a lawyer, manager, and member of the Galveston Bay and Texas Land Company. He had a bond himself for $1,285.55. He received $5,773,63 for his and his brother's notes in 1856.[35] In 1849 he had already gotten $3,374.54 for himself and his brother.[36]

Charles H. Coffin, ordinary member of the Galveston Bay and Texas Land Company, who also possessed Texas bonds, had at his disposal only three shares. He therefore received only $186.79 in 1856 for his draft for $119. But he was the front man for the New York banking house of J. & R. Milbank & Co.[37] In 1856 this company was able to pocket the fourth largest sum that was paid out in one piece to one person or company: $408,631.67. The largest sum paid was to William W. Corcoran, George Washington Riggs, Jr., and their bank: $586,811.82 altogether.[38]

These two banking firms stand as examples of two fundamental factors in the financial and economic history of Texas: for one thing the connection of Charles H. Coffin to Milbank & Co. shows the business involvement of various large enterprises through middlemen and thus their participation, if often concealed, in speculation groups such as the Galveston Bay and Texas Land Company. Also, the political influence peddling of these financially strong circles is shown in the banking firm of Corcoran and Riggs. The election of James Buchanan as the fifteenth U.S. president and the postponement of the Civil War appears to have been decisively influenced by the lobby of the Texas stockholders.[39] This is only briefly mentioned here, for these political events represent only a later result of the relationships investigated in this work. They are, however, mentioned in order to show that the profitable transactions of individual organizations in relation to Texas cannot and should not be viewed in isolation.

General Mason was officially given a contract by the Galveston Bay and Texas Land Company on April 6, 1831, as attorney and legal representative for the three empresarios Burnet, Vehlein, and Zavala.[40] John T. Mason, born January 8, 1787, in Virginia, received an education as an attorney, was named marshal of the District of Kentucky in 1817 by President Monroe, and secretary of the Michigan Territory in 1830 by President Jackson, who was a friend of his.[41] Mason was to journey to Mexico in the name of the company and there as its long arm, so to speak, do whatever was necessary to help it achieve success. He had the right, when necessary, to engage more agents and assistants. His contact person in Mexico City was General José Antonio Mexía, whom the company had already engaged on December 27, 1830, on the advice of his friend Zavala.[42]

Mexía's primary mission was to work for repeal of the law of April 6, 1830, in Mexico City—above all its Article XI. Mexía appeared also to have speedy success. Already in the summer of 1831 there appeared in the *New York Evening Post* an article about Texas that was the result of a letter from Mexía. In this it was explained that a high-placed personage had spoken with the Ministro de Relaciones Lúcas Alamán and learned that the law of April 6, 1830, only referred to empresario contracts that had been concluded *after* the proclamation of that law. According to this there was thus no obstacle anymore to settling in Texas.[43] The high-placed personage was Anthony Butler, who had often conversed with Alamán and wished not to be named, as Mexía wrote. Interestingly enough, this letter, which was in many respects significant, did not go to the attorneys or directors of the Galveston Bay and Texas Land Company, but to James Prentiss.[44]

It is scarcely possible to define exactly the role of James Prentiss in relation to Texas, given the current state of research. Like the tip of one or several icebergs his individual acts come to light, and on the basis of these, as well as with the help of the statements of his contemporaries, the shape of his business transactions can be roughly traced. He had probably met Mexía in 1830 during the latter's stay in New York as secretary of the Mexi-

Lúcas Alamán (1792–1853), said to be responsible for Mexico's passage of the law of April 6, 1830, was at that time secretary of foreign relations. *Courtesy Benson Latin American Collection, General Libraries, University of Texas at Austin*

can legation.[45] The exact circumstances are not exactly known. Mexía himself was also interested in land in Texas. Through friends and acquaintances he acquired altogether 243,540 acres[46] and in this way avoided the legal regulations, according to which a Mexican citizen could buy only 48,708 acres. Besides this, Mexía owned in the beginning forty shares of the Galveston Bay and Texas Land Company, which he or his widow must have mostly sold, for in 1849 only three shares were still recorded in the name of José Antonio Mexía.[47]

On October 10, 1830, thus six days before the official formation of the company, a cousin of Austin wrote him that he had spoken with Prentiss the day before,[48] thus on October 9, and that Prentiss had told him that Zavala, Mexía, and others wanted to promote the colonization of their land grants with large sums of money, and that he, Prentiss, had bought shares in John L. Woodbury's empresario contract.[49] Austin's brother-in-law James F. Perry, who was at that time also in New York, likewise wrote to Austin in Texas that Woodbury might get into trouble, for it appeared that Prentiss and Mexía had bought up all his claims, and Woodbury was functioning only as their agent.[50] No matter exactly how Prentiss's claim against Woodbury appeared, it is clear that he was interested in land in Texas from the beginning.

In December, 1830, Prentiss founded the Union Land Company, which consisted of his brother Henry B. Prentiss, his son James Henry Prentiss, and himself. This company was entirely a family enterprise; no one else had any part in it. Not until 1842 did James Prentiss admit Gilbert L. Thompson into the Union Land Company. That was only a legal maneuver, for Thompson had already worked for the Union Land Company before.[51] Inasmuch as his brother and his son had meanwhile died, James Prentiss was, when the motion for compensation was entered in 1851, the sole legitimate owner: "The entire interest in the company therefore both legal and equitable became vested exclusively in James Prentiss."[52] He had bought up land papers from the Galveston Bay and Texas Land Company for twenty-eight leagues, which amounts to 123,995.2 acres.[53] In the argumentation of his lawyer, Richard S. Coxe, before the Claims Commission, he rounded the figure to 125,000 acres of land.[54] The damages arising for the Union Land Company – among them was included a chartered ship – he figured at $428,383.81.[55] This is somewhat more than three times the expenses – or losses – that the Galveston Bay and Texas Land Company claimed. Thus Prentiss was awarded more by the Claims Commission: $58,879.10.[56] But this was not all that he received. For another company, the Trinity Land Company he received $63,559.24.[57]

Prentiss had founded this company in January, 1834, again with his son James Henry, his brother Henry B., and with Gilbert L. Thompson and Stephen Cleveland.[58] Prentiss stated that the company had bought 140 leagues of land (619,976 acres) – likewise from the Galveston Bay and Texas Land Company – settled seventy-five persons on them, and altogether had expenditures of $1,506,722.08.[59] As with his other company, the Union Land Company, he claimed to have fitted out a ship for the Trinity Land Company and brought colonists to Texas with it. His brother Henry B. Prentiss, who became the official agent and legal representative of the Trinity Land Company, traveled with this ship.[60] He died in Anahuac on October 5, 1836, twelve years before his nephew James Henry Prentiss, who succumbed to an attack of yellow fever on September 22, 1848, after peace had been concluded with Mexico.[61] Henry B. Prentiss was the agent for both companies in Texas—a not at all unusual practice. Certainly doubts arise when one looks through and compares the various papers of all the enterprises.

Prentiss designated as one of the big expenses entered on the account the ship *Climax,* which was to sail from New York to Galveston for the Trinity Land Company in 1834.[62] However, this ship was also listed by the Galveston Bay and Texas Land Company in their accounts.[63] There is no mention anywhere of shared expenses. In addition, it seems strange that Prentiss, on the one hand, officially declares for his two firms only about 7 percent of the land area of the Galveston Bay and Texas Land Company territory and instead of their twelve hundred families brought only 125 colonists to Texas, but, on the other hand, claims to have had more than thirteen times the expenses of the Galveston Bay and Texas Land Company. The small expense account of his brother Henry B. Prentiss for the Union Land Company for the years 1831 to 1833[64] corresponds just as poorly with the expenditures listed as the fact that the settlers were completely destitute upon their arrival in Texas and were faced with the discovery that nothing had been made ready for them.[65]

Although nothing can be established with absolute certainty, the suspicion is strong that the two enterprises presented here by James Prentiss were only fictitious companies with the help of which Prentiss aimed to make himself a rich man. This is further strengthened by the fact that he, in contrast to the Galveston Bay and Texas Land Company and his own remarks to Butler in the letters cited above, had absolutely no legal claim to a title and thus to land in Texas.[66] In spite of having established this, the Claims Commission granted him more than twice as much as the Galveston Bay and Texas Land Company. This event, too, is at least surprising.

But it is not only difficult for the historian to analyze James Prentiss's activities accurately today. Even in his own time he knew how to cover his traces. In March, 1834, John T. Mason, the agent of the Galveston Bay and Texas Land Company, wrote in irritation from Monclova, the capital city of Coahuila y Texas, to his attorneys Dey, Sumner, and Curtis:

> The New York Company, as it is called, has been made the theme of constant abuse as a gang of speculators, wishing to overrun all Texas; and when I have denied, and called for proof, they have uniformly cited James Prentiss and his agents, who have always represented themselves, as I am told, agents of the company—Henry B. Prentiss came on in these speculations and made a nefarious contract with the commissioner Madero who died with colera; and the whole plan has been followed up by his deputy. The speculations thus engendered has alarmed all Texas and particularly the settlers in your grants, and you are blamed as identified with them.[67]

No wonder historians still repeatedly put Prentiss in a direct relationship with and dependency on the Galveston Bay and Texas Land Company.[68] But it is more probable that Prentiss only cleverly made use of the organization and preliminary work of that company in order to make money in land speculation without having to invest all too much himself. His greatest attempt, as was mentioned in the beginning, certainly went through Anthony Butler. However, it is at the same time confusing that Prentiss, when listing the members of the Trinity Land Company, instead of Stephen Cleveland, his brother Henry G., and his son James Henry, mentioned two other persons to Butler: Thomas E. Davis and Joseph L. Joseph.[69]

It is very likely that Joseph L. Joseph was one of the owners of one of the biggest dealers in domestic exchanges: J. and L. Joseph of New York. Whether he was a friend of Prentiss, and tried to get a piece of the enormous pie Prentiss set on the table or his name was simply used by the latter to impress Butler, cannot be verified.[70] Thomas E. Davis was, as previously mentioned, a shareholder in the Galveston Bay and Texas Land Company. Besides that, however, he also had an interest in the New Washington Association, which had been established in New York on October 23, 1835. Together with eleven other men—Samuel Swartwout, John S. Bartlett, James W. Webb, John P. Austin, Stephen Sicard, Walter Mead, James Treat, Lorenzo de Zavala, Joseph Avenzana, William Dall, and James Morgan—he had launched the organization, whose goal it was to erect the city of New Washington on sixteen hundred acres, to develop it commercially and agriculturally, and perhaps even to be able to develop it into the capital of Texas.[71] James Treat, Samuel Swartwout, and, of course, Lorenzo de Zavala had a share in the Galveston Bay and Texas Land Company, along with Thomas E. Davis. John P. Austin, a brother of Henry Austin and Mary Austin Holley, carried on a regular correspondence with his cousin Stephen F. Austin. Thus the latter was also informed about the activities of this company.[72] In contrast to his brother Henry and his sister Mary, John P. Austin never came to Texas but devoted himself entirely to his business in New York.

James Morgan, born in 1786 in Philadelphia, in 1830 came to Texas, where he opened a commercial business in Anahuac with his partner James Reed in 1831. About the same time Henry B. Prentiss set up a store for the Union Land Company in Anahuac, the direction of which he transferred to Dr. George Moffit Patrick. Morgan and Patrick got along with one another very well, and on November 23, 1831, Patrick married Morgan's niece Sarah.[73] Both men were also active Freemasons.[74] It is probable that Morgan came into contact with Prentiss through Patrick and through him into a relationship with Samuel Swartwout, who was a close friend of James Prentiss.[75]

At a very early stage, Samuel Swartwout had already been in touch with activities having to do with Texas. Born in New York in 1783, he was very much under the influence of his oldest brother, John. The latter was closely associated with Aaron Burr. Not only had he arranged the duel in which Burr killed Alexander Hamilton, but he had also actively participated in his Texas plan.[76] When Burr's plans had matured, he required more assistants. Samuel Swartwout became one of his lieutenants. He was to inform Burr's partner, James Wilkinson, about the state of affairs. But Burr needed more influential, well-to-do men to support him. He therefore turned to an old acquaintance: Andrew Jackson. He knew that Jackson was also toying with the thought of annexing all of Spanish America to the United States.[77] A courier was to win Jackson for Burr's undertaking but without initiating him into the affair all too exactly. Inadvertently he revealed Burr's plans, which he had learned from Samuel Swartwout: "In addition to the seizure of New Orleans, the bank would be captured, the port closed, Mexico conquered, and the western part of the United States joined to the conquered territory to form a great south-western empire."[78]

In this way Swartwout's name was connected to Burr's imperial project. Jackson judged Burr's intentions harshly because of the treachery toward the United States contained in them.[79] Nevertheless, in the course of political change Swartwout won the sympathy of Andrew Jackson and was thus appointed head of the Port of New York Authority, the most lucrative post at that time in the U.S. government, which yielded him as much as $15,000 a year.[80] He had had his first experiences with the land business in 1812 when, with his two brothers, he had established the New Jersey Salt Marsh Company, which, however, turned out to be a failure. Whether Swartwout came in contact with the Galveston Bay and Texas Land Company through Burnet is not clear. A connection might have resulted from the fact that Burnet and John Swartwout had both participated in the Miranda Expedition to Venezuela.

A typical example of the New York commercial world in its approach to Texas as a business objective was John Haggerty. He was not a man who plunged headlong into a new enterprise but waited to see how any newly founded company would develop. On September 29, 1834, he became the director of the Galveston Bay and Texas Land Company and in February, 1841, director of the New Washington Association.[81] Of the 650 shares of the latter company, he held 85; of 1,000 of the former, only 8. These figures alone actually do not have too much validity as evidence, for he certainly also owned shares through front men. Although originally James Treat was still recorded as manager of the New Washington Association,[82] in 1846 only John Haggerty, Thomas E. Davis, and Alexander H. Dana were manager and executive agents of the enterprise. In contrast to Morgan and Swartwout, who had a personal interest in New Washington itself, for Haggerty it was only a matter of profit. His name is to be found on all the documents by means of which debts and other claims were to be collected.[83] On May 21, 1836, he thus received from the state of Texas $14,417.81 for notes amounting to $9,000 for the New Washington Association.[84] But when James Morgan, who remained in Texas as general representative of the company, desperately needed money for carrying on the projects or paying the debts of the enterprise, Haggerty refused to pay.[85]

The relationship of the two men therefore was not exactly cordial, although Swartwout always tried to mediate. Haggerty, Swartwout said, had retired in 1845, had moved to the country, and did not want to have anything more to do with business activities.[86] In the face of Haggerty's brisk activity as manager and money collector for the New Washington Association, Swartwout's explanation sounds very thin. Possibly Haggerty still had shares in other land companies that traded in Texas land. At least it is known that Samuel Swartwout owned shares in the Arkansas and Texas Land Company and the Colorado and Red River Land Company.[87]

There are very few records that give information about the three companies: the Rio Grande and Texas Land Company, the Colorado and Red River Land Company, and the Arkansas and Texas Land Company. However, similar to Prentiss's enterprises, they must have had to do with only one group of businessmen, who were concealing their identity behind three different company names. All three enterprises were based on one and the same empresario contract belonging to Dr. John Charles Beales, and all three seem also to have engaged the same employees: William H. Egerton as agent,[88] Samuel Sawyer as attorney,[89] Charles Edwards as secretary and attorney,[90] and Beales certainly as empresario. Nothing is known about the directors and shareholders of this consortium. The Colorado and Red River Land Company, which claimed to have put 20,000 shares on the market, according to Beales's declaration, had expenses in the amount of 102,129.80.[91] The Claims Commission, however, decided his case in the negative, and Beales received no money.

Along with these there were many other companies in the United States as well as in Europe that aimed to make a profit from Texas. Thus John Austin from Brazoria lent his services to the Alabama Company, which intended to buy up land in Texas in large amounts for little money.[92] John Cameron, John Exter, Benjamin R. Milam, and Arthur Wavell had business connections with the English Mining Company,[93] Reid, Fairlie & Co., and Exter, Geaves & Co., for the purpose of exploiting the mineral wealth of Texas.[94]

On January 8, 1836, the Mississippi Texas Land Company was established; its eleven founders and members had joined together "for the purpose of trading and speculating in lands in the provinces of Texas & Coahuila and the contiguous border of the United States."[95] Whether this company had any business success is not known, any more than any specific information about the multitude of other organizations such as the Georgia Mississippi Land Company,[96] the Georgia Land Company,[97] the San Luis Company,[98] and the Pilgrim Company of New York.[99] They all reflect the great financial interest in Texas that prevailed in all ranks and classes in the United States. If the numerous rumors about the annexation of Texas to the United States turned out to be true and the value of the land were to rise still further, then they wanted to have a share in the anticipated profits. The above list of American companies should not give rise to the impression that they were the only ones interested; Mexican and European ventures also tried to get their share of the colonist and land business.[100]

Most American consortiums were waiting to see how events progressed, but the Galveston Bay and Texas Land Company attempted to have a direct influence on events in Mexico. As was previously mentioned, José Antonio Mexía carried on numerous conversations with leading personalities, such as the minister of war and the vice-president of Mexico. In his letter to Prentiss and also to Austin he emphasized over and over that he was just about to achieve the repeal of Article XI of the law of April 6, 1830.[101] But the most important man for the company was John T. Mason, who was in Mexico City from about June, 1833, to March, 1834.

In the beginning the Galveston Bay and Texas Land Company had attempted to win over Austin for their project.[102] But he distrusted the company and was afraid it wanted only to use him.[103] Austin and Mason met for the first time at the convention of April 1, 1833. There Mason learned about the ventures of Austin and Williams with regard to the territory of the Texas Association and of their efforts to keep others away from that project.[104] Mason also heard at the same time the discussion and decision of the delegates on the question of independent Mexican statehood for Texas. What alarmed him there was not the attempt to separate Texas from Coahuila in order to become an individual state but the resolution attached to it—which was, of course, kept quiet—to declare the empresario contracts that were still valid null and void as soon as independent statehood was achieved.[105] This was a blow that was aimed directly at the land and speculation business.

Mason would have to hurry if he still wanted to achieve something for the Galveston Bay and Texas Land Company. Austin, who had perceived Mason's fear, attempted to reassure him in a letter and to convince him that only an independent state of Texas would be a guarantee for the welfare of all.[106] But it was clear to Mason that his one chance now lay in influencing the leading personages in Mexico City and that in any event he had to steal the march on Austin.[107] He therefore left Texas with great haste and arrived in the Mexican capital a month before Austin. His plan was to bring Austin to a halt and to get the best of him by staking all his influence and, if necessary, financial resources on having Texas declared a territory. This would have had as a consequence that executive power would be exercised over Texas from Mexico City and would thus be more easily influenced.

The aims and purposes of Mason were (1) to have the empresario contracts of Burnet, Vehlein, and Zavala renewed and their rights and obligations transferred to the Galveston Bay and Texas Land Company; (2) to settle agents of the company in each of the three empresario territories, in order to satisfy the stipulation of the law, that an empresario had to live permanently in the territory conveyed to him; and (3) to attempt to buy the territory as a whole. Even if he were successful with the first two items, the last one was independent from them and a long-range objective, so to speak, whose realization required that Texas first become a territory.[108] In order to achieve this, it was clear to Mason that he had to eliminate Austin.

As little is known of any real actions against Austin as of any direct influence exerted by Mason resulting in Austin's arrest and long-lasting imprisonment, but he spoke as ill of him as he could and described him everywhere as an evil contemporary.[109] In this he was also zealously supported by one other agent of the Galveston Bay and Texas Land Company: Anthony Butler.[110] Not only did Austin know that he was making enemies such as Butler or even Zavala with his advocacy of a state of Texas, he had himself heard rumors according to which Mason, Butler, Mexía, and Zavala, with the support of Americans in Texas—probably the brothers John and William Wharton—shared the responsibility for his arrest and the length of his imprisonment,[111] and meant to get him out of the way and thus obtain a more favorable position for action. This plot against Austin and even a direct threat on his life seems to have been real, as can be seen in various letters.[112]

At the same time Butler also attempted, by means of anonymous letters that were written in a very awkward and ordinary style, to incite the colonists in Texas to an uprising against Mexico that would either have ended with Texas belonging to the United States or under Mexican military control, both results that would have been useful for him. The primitive workmanship of the letters, however, rather quickly revealed Butler as their author, which led to a further loss of the Mexican authorities' confidence in Butler himself and in the role of the United States.[113]

Though Mason was successful in his efforts to bring about the defeat of Austin's petition for an independent state,[114] Austin could in return successfully torpedo Mason's plan to have Texas declared a territory.[115] This matter remained politically unresolved, for Santa Anna was holding in reserve a final solution.[116]

The intrigues and the massive efforts of the land companies to acquire

Texas for themselves through their agents were without doubt an additional reason for Austin, back in Texas after his release from prison, to declare himself for war and Texas independence. If Mason and Butler had been successful, the biggest part of Texas would have fallen to Prentiss and the Galveston Bay and Texas Land Company, which would have destroyed Austin's plans for himself and Texas. Santa Anna was still holding back, and his hesitation probably let Austin hope the worst could be avoided.[117] But if Santa Anna rose up as the advocate of centralism and a dictatorship—as did later happen—the chances were increased for the land and speculation companies to acquire power and influence in and over Texas. Without doubt Austin saw this sword of Damocles hanging over Texas. But during his imprisonment he could openly attack only *one* enemy, who in his awkward way had cut himself off. This was Anthony Butler.[118]

Butler was, however, not successful in his intrigues. The uprising of the Texans and its results prevented a friendly agreement between him and Mexico, even though in the spring Andrew Jackson expressed his opinion otherwise to the emissary from the interim government of Texas.[119] This reference to a possible separation of Texas, even at the last minute, can be considered either as an indication of Jackson's confidence in Butler or as evidence of unrealistic belief in miracles or wishful thinking on the part of Jackson, which appears improbable in consideration of the president's personality and style of governing. But confidence in Butler on Jackson's side would seem strange, since the latter wrote as a comment in the margin: "A. Butler what a scamp."[120] Contradictions such as those in his correspondence with Butler caused historians such as Richard R. Stenberg to come to the conclusion that Jackson would have considered *any* means acceptable in order to acquire Texas for the Union.[121]

Much has been written about Andrew Jackson, his aims, motives, and his choice of methods. To reproduce everything here would not suit the direction of this work, for nothing new can be added. It was Jackson's declared intention to win Texas for the United States without risking a war with Mexico or dividing the Union over this question. But whether he actually had recourse to the medium of intrigue will always remain a matter of speculation. His statements themselves, in all their contradictory nature, allow for no unequivocal conclusion. In a letter of 1836 to Joel R. Poinsett, Anthony Butler once threatened to publish letters from Jackson that would plainly compromise him,[122] but he never carried out his intention. Until now the letters have been undisclosed.

So, along with the manifold speculations and expositions in the literature,[123] one thing remains to be done: to follow the path of the man about whom it was and still is said by many that he was another "tool" of Jackson —and moreover a successful one: Sam Houston.

8. Enter Sam Houston

The paths of Sam Houston and Andrew Jackson crossed for the first time when Houston joined the army on March 24, 1813, during the war between England and the United States. He came as a private to the Thirty-ninth Infantry Regiment, and on March 27, 1814, he participated with the rank of a third lieutenant in the Battle of Horseshoe Bend (To-ho-pe-ka) under Gen. Andrew Jackson against the Creek Indians, who were allied with the English. He distinguished himself by exceptional bravery and was severely wounded.[1] In this way he won the attention and later the friendship of Andrew Jackson. Halfway recovered, on May 1, 1817, as a first lieutenant, he was employed in the service of General Jackson's adjutant. During this time, on April 19, June 20, and July 22, he was initiated as a Freemason into Cumberland Lodge no. 8, in Nashville. Soon afterward, on October 28, 1817, he received his first official special mission in Indian affairs.

As he was particularly knowledgeable about the Cherokees—having lived among them for a few years—he first was to reassure them in regard to an 1816 agreement that had promised them land west of the Mississippi and material support in exchange for land in Tennessee but up to this time had not yet been fulfilled by the U.S. authorities. Then he was to accompany a Cherokee delegation that wanted to go to Washington to petition the president for recognition of their independence. While the Cherokee were treated with all civility in Washington but then put off again with sham and empty promises, Houston got into trouble. The secretary of state, John C. Calhoun, had no word of praise for Houston's successful effort on this difficult mission but only objected to his attire. Instead of bowing to strict Washington etiquette, Houston had appeared in the dress of the Cherokees. In addition, he was accused of having supported slave smugglers. It quickly became clear that members of Congress, who themselves had friendly con-

Samuel Houston (1793–1863), military leader for Texas independence, president of the Republic, and later governor of the state of Texas, here in 1826 as a young congressman in Washington, D.C. *Courtesy Archives Division, Texas State Library*

nections with slave dealers, had falsely accused Houston, but this produced no results. Nothing was done about the congressmen; no one apologized to Houston. His reaction was abrupt and conclusive: he resigned his commission.[2]

This was or became typical for Sam Houston. Twice more he was to relinquish his official positions. Each time it was for him a point on which he was not willing to listen to the government or public opinion in order to further his career, if in doing so he had to violate his principles. Consistency was an essential character trait of Sam Houston.

Upon emerging from the army he was without means. Consequently, he studied law for six months in Nashville, took his examination, and opened a law office in Lebanon, thirty miles away. There he gained such popularity that with Andrew Jackson's support he was appointed attorney for the Nashville district in October, 1819. But not much money could be made in this position. Therefore he gave up the office in December, 1821, in order to improve his situation in private practice, which he succeeded in doing in a very short time. His relationship with Jackson and his continually mounting popularity also brought him rank and honor with the State Guard of Tennessee, so that in 1821 he could call himself Major General Houston. His own description of the following years is laconic:

> In 1821 he was elected Major General of Tennessee. In 1823 he offered himself as a candidate for congress and was elected without opposition. In 1825 he was returned a second time to Congress almost by acclamation, so well satisfied were his constituents with his course in the House of Representatives. His popularity rose to such a height that in 1827 he was elected Governor of Tennessee.[3]

The brevity of this passage is deceptive in that it gives only a summary, so to speak, of Houston's political development during that time without going into any other enterprises, a phenomenon that is also to be found in almost all of his autobiographical writing. Llerena Friend, to date his best biographer, also noted for this period, along with the usual description of his political career, a few cultural activities, such as, for example, his short guest performance with the Dramatic Club of Nashville. As the director of the club Noah M. Ludlow mentioned in his book, Houston must have been a passable actor.[4] He belonged to a historical society—the first one in Tennessee—and gave a Masonic ball as one of eight managers. Four of the other seven managers had at least one further connection with Houston that was just as important for him as his political career, although it is not mentioned by most historians: all five—Wilkins Tannehill, Joel Parrish, John Waters, Abraham S. Hoggart, and Sam Houston—were not only Masons but also founding members of the Texas Association, a company whose goal it was to make a profit with land speculation in Texas.[5]

How far beyond this Houston was engaged in a friendly relationship with these men can hardly be determined. But various interests connected him with two of his fellow members: Wilkins Tannehill, treasurer of the Nashville Bank, was treasurer of Ludlow's drama club and also corresponding secretary from 1819 to 1821 of the Tennessee Antiquarian Society, the organization that Houston had joined in 1820.[6] On January 21, 1822, Joel Parrish was appointed by the newly designated Major General Houston to his staff as assistant adjutant general with the rank of colonel.[7] John Waters in turn was a classmate, close friend, and brother-in-law of Dr. Felix Robertson, cousin of Sterling C. Robertson, who later quarreled with Austin about land. After consulting the biographies of the other signers, one can assume that the Texas Association was a group of friends and acquaintances who wanted to try their luck in land speculation.

Next to politics, land speculation was Houston's most important field of interest, which, together with his law business, made his life as a politician possible. In those years in which politics occupied most of his time, his speculation activities remained a little more in the background and became of greater importance again when he was not actively participating in political life.

As a young congressman in 1824 he actively supported and followed Andrew Jackson in the campaign for president; John Quincy Adams won that election, however. During his second term as a congressman he worked increasingly for Jackson, who in 1828 was then able to win election.[8] In 1827 Houston won the governor's race in the state of Tennessee by a large majority. On January 22, 1829, he married Eliza Allen. On January 30 the newspapers announced he would run again. What then happened on April 8 or 9 is not known to this day. He sent his young wife back to her parents with a letter.[9] On April 16 he resigned as governor. He wrote Andrew Jackson on May 11 that his motives for these astonishing acts were of a purely personal nature.[10] They never became public knowledge and have created a rumor factory that still exists. Moreover he was not satisfied with his resignation alone; he went into voluntary exile with the Cherokees, where he remained until 1832.[11]

Some persons supposed he had resigned his governor's office only to go to the Cherokees in order to be able to make a profit out of Jackson's resettlement plan for them.[12] On the other hand, on May 21, 1829, Jackson received a letter from Gen. Duff Green that had been written to him by Dr. Marable, a congressman, and in which Houston was accused of having declared he wanted to conquer Texas or Mexico.[13]

This was also maintained with vehemence by Robert Mayo. He published a book in 1839 in which he charged Andrew Jackson with conspiracy with Sam Houston to follow Aaron Burr's old plan and separate Texas from Mexico by force. As evidence he gave first a conversation with Houston toward the end of February, 1830, in Washington, D.C., in the course of which Houston supposedly proposed to detach Texas from Mexico with the help of Indians and volunteers from the United States. He was, he said, supported in this by "a most intimate friend of his, Gen'l Van Forsen, lately of New York."[14] He had advised President Jackson of this at his own request in a letter dated December 2, 1830. Jackson's reaction served Mayo as more proof of his complicity with Houston.

On December 10, 1830, Jackson had written a letter to William S. Fulton, secretary of the Arkansas Territory, in which he informed him of Mayo's note and asked him to be on the alert.[15] Jackson said he certainly did not believe such an act was planned and considered the rumor false. The deciding factor for Mayo was not the content of this letter but its formal aspects. When looking through all his papers, Andrew Jackson in 1836 had sent back his letters to Mayo, among them the one of December 2, 1830, to which is attached the letter to Fulton marked "copy." The address reads: "Confidential Wm. Fulton Sec. of the T. of Florida—private and confidential." On Mayo's letter Jackson had noted: "Dr. Mayo—on the contemplated invasion of Texas private and confidential—a letter to be written, confidential, to the Secretary of the T. of Arkansas with copy of confidential letter to Wm Fulton Esq. Sec. to the T. of Florida."[16] However, Jackson had himself appointed Fulton secretary of the Territory of Arkansas the year before, and in the spring of 1830 named James D. Westcott, Jr., secretary of Florida Territory. This incorrect address was plain evidence to Mayo that Jackson's letter to Fulton was a sham in order later to be able to clear himself of any blame. In Mayo's opinion Jackson had failed here, and he accused him of complicity with Houston.[17]

John Quincy Adams, who had meanwhile turned into an opponent of annexation under the influence of the abolitionists, took up this issue and declared in his famous Texas speech of June 11, 1838, that Jackson had known of Houston's plans, supported them, and to conceal this had sent Mayo the original of the letter, not a copy. The letter, according to him, had consequently never been sent.[18] This caused a good deal of anger, and Jackson urged Fulton to vindicate him. Not until February did Fulton find the desired and controversial letter that, however, was addressed correctly to "William Fulton Esqr. Secretary of the Territorium of Arkansas."[19]

This confusion of dates and addresses, as well as remarks by Fulton, who would not and could not remember anything pertinent, led many authors, foremost of all Richard R. Stenberg, to take the position that a conspiracy existed between Houston and Jackson.[20] Jackson, they thought, had not acted on Mayo's hint but had written a letter to Fulton two years later and then completed a back-dated copy that he afterward addressed incorrectly.

Stenberg also sees himself proved correct in his thesis by a remark Jackson made in a letter of 1838 in which he took up the matter of that report: "Mr. Fulton's report to me which went to shew the rumors were all groundless, and that Genl. Houston had settled in Texas and was practising law there for a livelyhood."[21] The catch in this remark is that Houston did not practice law in Texas until 1833, which would indicate a later inquiry by Jackson, thus not until 1832–1833. In spite of all this, such a conspiracy cannot be unequivocally established.

It seems most probable that Jackson had the same attitude or displayed the same conduct toward Houston as toward Anthony Butler. Of course, this statement must be limited to Texas, for, in contrast to Butler, Jackson was really Houston's friend. But the president applied the same standards to Houston as to Butler. He certainly spoke with Houston about Texas and expressed his aspirations of joining Texas to the United States; of course, this could not lead to compromising the United States or the policies and person of Andrew Jackson. He explained this in his answer to Houston's letter of May 11, 1829, cited above.[22] Jackson's reasoning is interesting again — as toward Butler — in that he lay stress on his country and his honor, not the deed itself. As long as the honor of Jackson and the United States was not implicated, anything was allowed. Andrew Jackson never spoke of any sort of injustice to the sovereign state of Mexico. Only the policies and thereby the reputation of the United States must remain publicly untainted.

Because Houston had sworn on his honor not to undertake anything that could damage his country, he now had to operate carefully. A letter of July 25, 1829, from his friend John A. Wharton in Nashville, shows that not only Mayo, Jackson, Marable, and Green had heard something about his plans: "I have heard you intended an expedition against Texas. I suppose, if it is true, you will let some of your Nashville friends know of it."[23] Houston apparently did not follow up on this letter and thus took Jackson's advice of July 21, for in October John A. Wharton wrote him again: "I therefore request you once more to visit Texas. It is a fine field for enterprise. You can get a grant of land, and yet be surrounded by your friends; and what may not the 'coming of time' bring about?"[24] But Houston did not immediately follow this recommendation. First he had to settle his financial situation, for, like Butler, he had other interests too, not merely political ambition.

The business activities that have previously been mentioned occupied some room in his life. In his report to the president, Robert Mayo had spoken of Houston's financier "Gen'l Van Forsen." This was Gen. John Van Fossen, a New York financier who was involved with Houston in a bidding scandal. He had negotiated on the part of the government for a provisions contract for the Indians in connection with which Houston had bid through Van Fossen and had requested his competitors with bids lower than his to withdraw their offers. When this did not succeed, the secretary of war, John Eaton, who seems to have been involved in Houston's business, withdrew the invitation to bid on account of alleged legal defects. When these incidents became known, it led to a congressional investigation.[25]

Houston himself explained that he had done all this only for the benefit of the Indians, because he, after all, best knew their requirements.[26] In his other business dealings he did not invent such altruistic motives.[27]

Houston and two others, David Thompson and John Drennan, had bought the region of Grand Saline from Col. Pierre Auguste Chouteau for $3,000.[28] Houston had met Chouteau in 1829 when the latter had already been living with the Osages for twenty years and was one of the most outstanding personalities of the Midwest.[29] He immediately recommended Chouteau to Secretary of War John H. Eaton as agent for Indian questions.[30] At the time Chouteau was selling salt mines that belonged neither to him nor to the Osages but lay on the land that the Osages had transferred to the Cherokees in 1828. Supposedly this in turn motivated Houston in 1830 to accompany a Cherokee delegation to Washington, D.C., where he got the treaty of 1828 recognized, the Osages dispersed, and Houston's brother-in-law, Capt. John Rogers, named manager of the salt mines.[31]

In 1830 Houston acquired land in eastern Tennessee on which gold had recently been found. This was not unusual, for gold had also been discovered and mined profitably in Georgia, North Carolina, and Alabama. Houston belonged to the speculators who had bought up the land directly after the first gold strike. But before the gold in Tennessee could be profitably promoted, the gold rush of 1849 began in California and left the mines in the East and the South deserted.

In 1832 Houston described in detail the territory he had acquired and praised its advantages, so that the letter reads like an answer or an offer following an inquiry. The person addressed in this letter was James Prentiss.[32] It is probable that Houston had met Prentiss through their common friend Samuel Swartwout. Houston presumably had gotten to know Swartwout through Andrew Jackson, whose protégés they both were and also held in high regard. Already by 1826, Swartwout, Prentiss, and Houston were pursuing similar interests.[33]

The correspondence between Houston and Prentiss gives some information about Houston's goals and motives. Prentiss, too, had heard of Houston's plans and wanted to get further information from him.[34] Then in a letter to Prentiss of April 8, 1832,[35] Houston offered his services to the Galveston Bay and Texas Land Company. But in 1834 he withdrew this and emphasized that he had never had anything to do with a speculation company, a person having an interest in one, or anything at all to do with land in Texas. He was, he said, in no way eager to become active as an adviser or agent for that kind of association.[36]

This sounds like justification made in answer to accusations that, however, are unfortunately missing. There was friction in any event between him and the Galveston Bay and Texas Land Company, not only because they did not want to pay Houston for his services, as he said, but also because of considerable rivalry between him and two of their confidants: Gen. John T. Mason and Anthony Butler. He distrusted both men greatly.[37] Nevertheless, not much weight can be attributed to his disavowal, for, as has been proved, he was interested in land in Texas and was employed by Prentiss in this connection.

On June 1, 1832, Houston made an agreement with James Prentiss personally – thus not with him as representative of the Galveston Bay and Texas Land Company, as is often erroneously claimed – in which Houston declared himself to be ready to buy up as many shares as possible of the old Leftwich contract – either from Austin, who with Williams had, indeed, meanwhile gotten the land transferred to them, or from the government of the state of Coahuila y Texas. In return Houston received land conveyed from the old Domínguez contract, which, however, was to be used for the purchase of the land mentioned above. Houston and Prentiss were, then, to share the newly acquired land.[38] In all, Houston received land in Texas valued at $8,502.90 transferred to him. Of course, he could not depart for Texas immediately, as he had intended, for in May, 1832, he had to defend himself before Congress in Washington, D.C., against charges that he had beaten a member of Congress with a cane. Houston defended himself eloquently but was sentenced to pay a fine, which, however, he never had to do.[39]

Besides his financial transactions with Prentiss, into which his correspondence furnishes good insight, he was very reserved when it came to describing exactly what his primary plans in Texas were.[40] On July 10, 1832, he wrote Prentiss that he was going to leave for Nashville on the next day or the day after, to take care of the Leftwich Grant and then intended to travel to Texas.[41] This business part of his trip, however, failed in Nashville. He did not get the money that was to be placed at his disposal by the Galveston Bay and Texas Land Company for his transactions through Prentiss – the company showed no interest in Houston's services. Houston waited two months in Nashville before he left.[42] This vexing situation was brought up again in the letter to Prentiss of March 28, 1834, mentioned above, as well as in Prentiss's excuses to Houston that followed.[43]

Whether it was merely that the land business did not go the way he had imagined, or that those other plans, only mentioned by suggestion, did not make the progress that he had hoped, cannot be deduced from his words. He said that the affair concerning Texas had not functioned as he had believed it would, to his great irritation, but that all was not lost. On the next day, September 16, 1832, he was planning to leave for Texas.[44] Whatever his plans may have been, he himself considered it expedient in 1855 and 1856 to spread a cloak of forgetfulness and romance over his objectives in going to Texas and to say it was his intention to devote himself entirely to the life of a herdsman in the solitude of the prairie. But it was not granted him to carry out his plan.[45]

During the period under discussion he had nevertheless written something different to his cousin John Houston. He was about to set foot on Texas soil, he began. He had been informed that his friends had nominated him as a candidate for governor of Tennessee. If he should actually run for the office, his success was certain. The affairs in Texas were of financial interest to him and therefore had to be pursued first.[46] Houston dropped nothing more than vague hints of this kind. On July 31, 1833, he wrote to his cousin, in answer to his question about what he was doing in Texas, that he wanted to establish himself as an attorney and that he had acquired valuable land in Texas. In addition, there were a number of lesser things that he had to pay attention to.[47] However, this letter was written after Houston had already become politically active in Texas.

On December 10, 1832, he had crossed the Texas-Mexico border at Fort Towson.[48] From there the road led at that time through Nacogdoches to San Felipe de Austin. Houston stopped briefly in Nacogdoches. He called on the *alcalde*, Don Adolfo Sterne, whom he already knew from Nashville, though by the name of Adolphus Sterne, and who was a Freemason as he was.[49] Then he went on to San Felipe and on December 24 made an application there for land in which he declared he was married and had only come to Texas to make his home there and for this purpose to acquire land on the coast for the cultivation of cotton.[50]

Of course, Houston was still legally married—a divorce ensued only on November 30, 1833[51]—and also wanted land, but was it to be for the purpose of cultivating cotton and—as would have been assumed just from his words— to establish himself as the happy head of a family and a farmer? Without doubt Houston made this declaration in order to acquire the league of land that was due him only as the head of a family and not as a single person. Houston's application was immediately accepted and the land was transferred to him after the survey had been completed by Seth Ingram on January 9, 1833.[52] Still, on June 14, 1849, Houston declared in court: "that he never was a resident in said Austin's colony, nor did he intend to become one, and that he understood at the time of his receiving said grant from the said Stephen F. Austin, that he was obtaining it as a purchase."[53] On the basis of his declaration of December 24, 1832, however, his veracity must be doubted. It is certain that Houston gave his statement in 1849 only to avoid conviction in a lawsuit.

On his first visit to San Felipe he did not meet with Austin. Instead, he got together with Samuel M. Williams, who helped him with information about the Indians in Texas.[54] After Christmas he traveled on with Col. James Bowie to San Antonio. Bowie was married to Ursula Veramendi, daughter of the governor of Texas, Don Juan Martín de Veramendi, one of the most influential Mexicans in Texas.[55] In San Antonio Houston met with Comanche chiefs: before his departure from Washington, along with all his other enterprises, he had received the official government mission from Andrew Jackson to observe Indians in the southern borderlands of the United States and to learn about their movements and plans. Thus on December 1, 1832, he had immediately written a rather long letter from Fort Towson to the Indian agent in Fort Gibson, Henry L. Ellsworth, and described the situation to him.[56]

After he had taken care of his business in San Antonio, he went back again to San Felipe, where this time he met with Austin. This meeting and his impression of Austin he described many years later in a letter to Austin's nephew, Guy M. Bryan, as being harmonious and positive.[57] This letter must be read from the point of view, first, that it was written to one of Austin's close relatives and, next, was an answer to Bryan's very critical questions and accusations.

Even when eighteen years later Houston rejected all claims that he had conspired with the Wharton brothers against Austin and attempted to have him kept in Mexican prisons and instead emphasized that he had always remained constant and faithful to Austin,[58] his correspondence of that time reads otherwise: "a viper without its fangs"; "political inconsistencies"; "his want of understanding"; first "imprudent" then "pusillanimous"[59]—all these attributes scarcely fit the picture of an admirer that he later draws. Just as in his biographical writing, where his motives for going to Texas were also suppressed and a way made for romantic clichés, Houston subsequently corrected his relationship to Austin, who had meanwhile died, by assuming a different attitude.

After Houston had met with Austin in San Felipe in January, 1833, he went back to Nacogdoches, where his friends asked him to remain. In addition, they thought he ought to make himself available for the assembly of 1833, fixed for April.[60] Houston heeded this request and was elected representative from Nacogdoches to the assembly that met from April 1 to 13, 1833.

In February he had sent his first report to President Jackson about conditions in Texas: "The people of Texas are determined to form a State Government, and separate from Coahuila, and unless Mexico is soon restored to order . . . the Province of Texas will remain separate from the confederacy of Mexico."[61] Already at that time Houston began to use England's interest in Texas as a political argument and a threat. He did not go into it further but maneuvered around Colonel Butler and his conduct in Mexico. Butler, he said, had strong personal interests in Texas and was in no way making an effort to join Texas to the United States, which was really his official diplomatic mission. Instead of this, Butler, according to Houston, desired only the complete dependence of Texas on Mexico, by which was meant Texas as a territory and not as a state in itself.

All these observations he cannot have made himself, in spite of his emphasis on having traveled five hundred miles around Texas. Above all, his remark that nineteen-twentieths of the population of Texas aspired to annexation to the United States arose more from the wishful thinking of the circle around the Wharton brothers than from reality.

After the fact Houston also declared to Guy M. Bryan that he had known William H. Wharton in Tennessee and supported him for that reason, even though in 1836, during the first presidential election, he had purposely kept his distance from the two parties—the Austin Party and the Wharton Party (as he himself called them).[62] At any rate, in the convention of 1833 he helped William H. Wharton by giving him his vote in the election for president of the convention, which Wharton won. Along with Houston, Adolphus Sterne also represented the district of Nacogdoches. At this meeting Houston was chosen chairman of the committee that was to write a constitution for the would-be state of Texas. After that meeting he devoted his attention to Indian affairs again and rode to San Antonio. From there his travels took him on May 28, 1833, to Fort Gibson (now in Oklahoma) to make a report to the Indian agent. Because of his frequent and long rides Houston's war wound gave him trouble again, and he had to go for treatment to Hot Springs, Arkansas. Afterward he returned to Nacogdoches and made his living as an attorney. He celebrated Christmas of 1833 in San Felipe de Austin and departed in the spring for Washington, D.C., where he remained in March and April, 1834, with flying visits to New York.

Very little is known about his affairs in the years 1834 and 1835. He carried on a business relationship with Augustus Chapman Allen who, with his brother John Kirby Allen, was investigating various land speculation deals in Texas. Houston shared an interest in a project of the Allen brothers to build a city on the Red River. Allen kept him up to date by mail about this venture as well as about political events in Texas, while Houston remained in Washington.[63] Repeatedly there were persons who later thought they had come across Houston here and there—once in Indian garb as the leader of a five-hundred-man war party,[64] and again mysteriously by the dark of night in a small hut conspiring with others about the release of Texas from Mexico by force.[65]

In March, 1835, he was again in Nacogdoches and wrote John A. Wharton about his meeting with the latter's brother William: "I accompanied, and remained with them, until this morning; when we parted, for various routs and pursuits—I to my law business and they to the more animating pursuits of speculation."[66]

This letter, however, should not give rise to the impression that Houston himself had no more interest in land speculation. On the contrary, his activity as a lawyer was useful in the other enterprise.[67] In the Monclova speculation of 1834 and 1835, which has already been mentioned, along with Durst and Williams, José María Carbájal—the representative of San Antonio de Béxar—John T. Mason, and the former empresario Frost Thorn had acquired large areas of land.[68] Asabel Longworthy, who had bought 100,000 acres from the Galveston Bay and Texas Land Company for purposes of speculation,[69] and Samuel Swartwout had bought eleven leagues from Carbájal.[70] However, there was some difficulty with the legal transfer of this land in which Houston was also interested, and Swartwout applied to Houston also, along with his attorneys William Fortune and Frost Thorn, for a clarification of the affair.[71] Because Houston had for a long time been involved in land business and speculation, at least through Swartwout and Prentiss,[72] it is not strange that he became engaged in business with his old adversary, John T. Mason, in 1836, as Mason reported to Swartwout.[73] In addition, Mason prophesied that Houston's power and influence in Texas would become enormous, which was no great feat after the victorious Battle of San Jacinto on April 21, 1836.

More interesting here are Houston's prophecies of 1834. He believed—he wrote to Prentiss—that in one year Texas would be a sovereign state and Santa Anna would try for absolute power.[74] Four days later he underlined this statement in another letter in which he emphasized that Texas would change politically in any case, and Prentiss should not hope to acquire this land through the United States during Jackson's term as president; the Senate now in office would never agree to such a purchase. Texas would have to take care of its affairs itself and exist independently.[75] Except for a few discrepancies, Houston's predictions were correct. Santa Anna's aim of complete dictatorial power accelerated the independence movement in Texas, which did achieve independence and could not be annexed by the United States immediately for political reasons, both internal and external. But his observations about Santa Anna again make clear the intensive contact that he must have had with experts on the political situation in Mexico, for he was never there himself.

The whole design of his plans cannot yet be uncovered in its minutest detail even now, though his motives are clear as day. For one thing, he had a weakness for political glamour and grand entrances, which for him—at least verbally—could achieve high emotional pitch. He loved to step forth out of the crowd, to attract attention. In contrast to Austin, who flirted with homey reserve and modesty, Houston sought to set himself off with something exceptional. A very typical example of this is a miniature made for him in Washington, D.C., in 1830 that shows him in artistic Cherokee costume, and another is a portrait that he had made in Nashville in 1831 in which he deliberately had himself represented allegorically as Marius in the middle of temple ruins.[76] Just as Marius, he would at some future day return to important political activity—this was the message he was giving by commissioning the work.

The basis of his livelihood was at all times his legal activity and land speculation. His attention was drawn to Texas by his business at an early date, probably around 1819 or 1820, and during his first political downfall in 1829–1830 he developed plans respecting Texas that had also certainly been inspired by the adventurous enterprises of Aaron Burr and James Long. Andrew Jackson, who without doubt knew about the audacious plans of his friend and protégé, used him just like Anthony Butler to attempt to annex Texas to the United States without causing a stir, in connection with which Houston officially had to pay heed not only to the individual activities of various Indian tribes,[77] but also to report the movements of Mexican troops and their strength on the border of the United States.[78]

Both men violated the basic principle of Jackson's foreign policy; Houston was admonished and learned his lesson, but Butler did not and fell out of favor. In Texas Houston corrected and modified his ideas and plans in the face of political realities. Whoever had persuaded him that Texas was ripe for revolution—an assertion he had passed on to Jackson in the spring of 1833—had drawn a premature picture. In 1834 Houston took this into account and drew up an exact forecast for the future, evidence that politics and his plans in connection with it continued to be one of Sam Houston's strong points.[79]

Llerena Friend has given her biography of Sam Houston the subtitle *The Great Designer.* This is most certainly correct. Houston drafted a long list of grandiose plans in his lifetime; a part of them is known, and only conjectures can be made about the others. His greatest aptitude probably consisted of being able to accommodate his far-reaching plans to the immediate situation and to change them to correspond so that he repeatedly ended on top. To charge him with opportunism because of this, as his enemies did, means, however, to judge him falsely, for there were limits to his flexibility. His resignation from the army in 1818 was only one, and also the first, example—but the best was to be his loyalty to the United States, which in 1861 cost him the office of governor of Texas and won for him the admiration of John F. Kennedy, who put him in his book *Profiles in Courage* because of his firm stand: "But Sam Houston's contradictions actually confirm his one basic, consistent quality; indomitable individualism, sometimes spectacular, sometimes crude, sometimes mysterious, but always courageous."[80]

This realistic evaluation of the situation at critical moments and his loyalty to principle remove him from the crowd of other schemers of his time. Stephen F. Austin's idea of a strong and peaceful nucleus of Anglo-Americans in the midst of a newly created state of Spanish heritage struggling to survive was just as unrealistic as Mirabeau B. Lamar's later plans for an imperial Texas that reached to the Pacific. With all his weaknesses Houston showed a sense for what was possible, and his steadfastness was so compelling that in the end it allowed him alone to surpass every other Texan in honors and position.

9. Mexico's Attitude toward Texas

Houston's prophecy concerning Santa Anna was correct. After he had first allowed his vice-president, Gómez Farías, to govern and carry out reforms, which had given rise to alarm and anger among the powerful classes of society, he seized power in 1835 and reshaped the executive branch of government according to his notions.[1] This brought about intensified opposition in some of the Mexican states such as Yucatán and Coahuila y Texas. The latter, however, occupied a particular spot in the national structure of Mexico.

Had the one-time province of Texas, an outpost because of its geographical situation, never been officially treated with any particular regard, this was changed because of the great American interest in it and because of the reports by Mier y Terán and Almonte. In 1833 Tadeo Ortíz de Ayala had likewise written a report and attached his own plan to it. Ortíz had been appointed director of the Office of Colonization for Texas on August 13, 1833.[2] He wrote that the loss of Texas to the United States could have catastrophic results for Mexico, for that region was in the long run in a position to furnish all of Mexico with grain, meat, and other foodstuffs. In order to counteract the predominance of the Anglo-American settlers he suggested that two hundred German, Swiss, Dutch, and Irish families stranded in New York without money be settled in Texas. His plan, of course, never reached fruition: Ortíz died of cholera on October 18, 1833. Austin, who had heard of this mission and plan, looked upon the venture most critically—understandably, for its implementation would, after all, have frustrated his ideas of an Anglo-American Texas, "his Texas."[3]

Yet all of these reports and plans came too late for the nation that was still struggling for its own inner order. They had the effect of increasing the panic in Mexico. For to the unending harassment by the United States that for the most part was felt as a direct threat, there was added the sudden

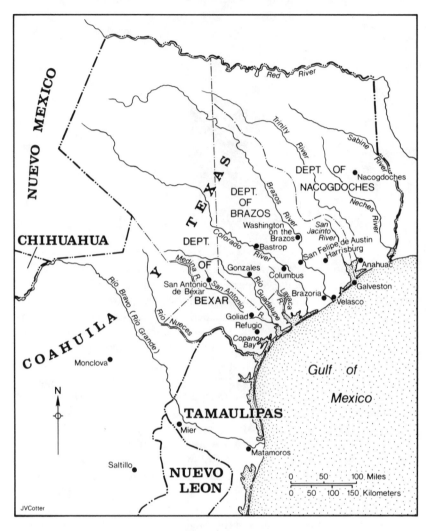

Texas in 1835

realization that the apple of discord was not old, shrunken, and worthless but rather–to retain the metaphor–an apple of pure gold.

The various newspapers of the day took dead aim at the United States as the opponent, although the pro-American *El Fénix de la Libertad* continued to write in January, 1834, that it did not believe in an American conspiracy but that Mexico of course would defend its territorial unity with force if necessary. *El Mosquito Mexicano* and *El Anteojo* emphasized that the United States was the enemy of Mexico and, in order to enrich itself with land and mineral wealth, was bringing discord to Mexico and inciting revolutionary plots in Texas.[4]

In 1836 a great number of Mexicans were convinced that the United States had caused the turbulence in Texas and that American speculators were threatening Mexico's very existence.[5] In 1837, without doubt influenced by the defeat at San Jacinto but nonetheless representative of this group and its thoughts even before the war, General José María Tornel y Mendívil wrote that the American newspapers, financed by land speculators, had promoted the uprising in Texas. While they were slandering the Mexicans, they officially glorified the crimes of the Texans, he wrote.[6]

Tornel y Mendívil, minister in the embassy in Washington, D.C., from 1821 to 1831 and minister of war during the campaign against Texas, as Santa Anna's faithful supporter and a declared conservative, presented an obvious standpoint that nevertheless was not at all that far from the truth as to what the attitude of most Americans toward Mexico was. To him, Austin was a traitor who was not only the most prominent empresario but also the ringleader of the rebellion. According to Tornel y Mendívil, Austin, with his characteristic hypocrisy, had acted in Mexico as if he were law-abiding but, shameless and deceitful as he was, he had already been carrying out his schemes. The imprisonment of a man whom the nation had always favored had been the inevitable result of his own criminal conduct.[7] Such hard words expressed a feeling that was widespread in Mexico through 1835 and after 1836 prevailed generally: they themselves had given him payment in advance with their goodwill and then were betrayed.

The fear of losing Texas caused a panic in the government—and panic usually leads to overreaction. It had certainly come to armed altercations in the fall of 1835 between Texans and Mexicans, but already in January, 1836, there existed in the provisional army as well as in the leadership of the Texans such hopeless confusion that there could scarcely have been talk of serious danger to the domestic security of Mexico.

Santa Anna, a lover of dramatic entrances and emotional gestures, nevertheless began his march against Texas in the winter of 1835 with a force of about six thousand men. Even loyal subordinates of Santa Anna, such as Lieutenant Colonel José Enrique de la Peña, criticized the hurried departure of their commander-in-chief; the events in Texas during the last months of 1835, according to him, had been investigated, and it was clearly established that the hostile actions of the colonists had been unjustified. They were the aggressors, he said, the Mexicans the assailed. The offer of Mexican friendship and help that had been repeatedly made to the settlers had been trodden under foot. From all that had been said it could be conclu-

Antonio López de Santa Anna Pérez de Lebrón (1794–1876), the general who was three times elected to the presidency of Mexico, which he turned into a dictatorship, hoped to crush the independence movement in Texas in 1835. *Courtesy San Jacinto Museum of History Association*

sively determined that war was unavoidable. It was certainly clear that it had to end as a choice between war and dishonor. However, it was necessary to prepare most thoroughly and go to work carefully, because, after all, the honor of the nation was at stake. It would have been less painful to postpone the war than to make the nation ridiculous by not observing the most elementary rules of the game.[8]

In this de la Peña reflected the thoughts of many Mexicans; war seemed to have become unavoidable, but in any case one should have proceeded and planned very calmly and not allowed oneself to venture precipitately into action, the result of which was necessarily doubtful. But Santa Anna, he said, had been as if possessed and inaccessible to every sensible argument. He had simply trusted his luck, which, however, is known not to be the most important thing in war.[9]

It should not be forgotten, in regard to all of de la Peña's remarks, that they were composed after the fact. The writer was entirely under the influence of the humiliating defeat at the hands of the Texans. The reactions in 1837 and in the following years not only reflected the views of 1833 to 1836 but also were criticism of the events of the war; for in October, 1835, there were still very different opinions in Mexico.

As was emphasized in preceding chapters, Mexico was divided, roughly speaking, into two camps: liberals and reactionaries. The liberals, under the leadership of the former Vice-President Valentín Gómez Farías, were in favor of a weakening of the military and the Catholic church, and were for a federal system of government. Santa Anna, who had at first let Farías do as he wanted, threw him out and put himself at the head of the conservative, clerical, and militaristic majority, which desired a strict, centralized government. The opposition to Santa Anna had formed around Farías and Santa Anna's onetime friends Zavala and Mexía.[10] The vice-governor of Tamaulipas, Don Vital Fernández, not only supported this opposition movement against the centralists but even advocated the idea that the northern states of Mexico should separate to form their own liberal state.[11]

This suggestion makes clear the geographic division of the opposition. The states of Chihuahua, Coahuila y Texas, Nuevo México, Nuevo León, Zacatecas, Tamaulipas, the two Californias, and Yucatán, thus the border area of Mexico, were united in their opposition to the centralists. Santa Anna reacted as quickly as he did harshly against his political opponents. Though with the help of the church he could force the liberals in California to submit to his will fairly easily,[12] he had to put down liberalism in Zacatecas with force. He himself led the army that defeated the militia of Zacatecas on May 10 and 11, 1835.

The eyes and the hopes of the liberal Mexicans were now trained on Texas. Their war cry was: "Federacion ó Muerte," and when they saw how weak they were themselves, they welcomed volunteers from the United States.[13] Mexía and Farías, who were in exile in New Orleans, attempted to gain financial support and soldiers for their cause that would provide help from Texas to save liberalism in Mexico. But for men such as Henry Smith, Branch T. Archer, William B. Travis, and the Wharton brothers, it was not a matter of preserving any sort of principles in Mexico, but only separation from that country and annexation to the United States. Mexicans like Mexía were not blind to these forces and warned about any declaration of independence for Texas, for this would unite all of Mexico against Texas. When on March 2, 1836, the Texans actually did declare themselves independent, Mexía was deeply disappointed.[14] Along with him many Mexicans felt they were betrayed; they had understood a war for the liberal principles of the Constitution of 1824 but considered themselves deceived by the Texans' desertion of Mexico.[15]

Even those who at first had still trusted in the evidences of loyalty of the group around Austin and saw in the rebellion of the Texans the defense of Mexico's freedom gave more credence, after March 2, 1836, to those who had spoken of agitation by the United States at the beginning of the uprisings: "The loss of Texas will inevitably result in the loss of New Mexico and the Californias. Little by little our territory will be absorbed, until only an insignificant part is left to us. Our destiny will be similar to the sad lot of Poland."[16]

Thus after March, 1836, one can proceed on the assumption that a united opinion prevailed concerning Texas and the United States, which had not been the case at the beginning of hostilities. Even in the army, in spite of the presumed general necessity of a campaign against the intractable Texans, there had not been agreement about whether the proper moment had been chosen for measures to keep the peace. But then events caused those Mexicans who had still been inclined to be very critical to forget their doubts. Santa Anna had prevailed—not for the first time and also not for the last.

10. The War

Disturbances had begun again in January, 1835, with the episode in Anahuac, mentioned before, in which William B. Travis with a group of armed citizens drove off the Mexican customs inspector Antonio Tenorio. The basis for Travis's militant action was mail intercepted by him in which the *comandante general* of the eastern, inner provinces, Martín Perfecto de Cós, had promised the inspector military support that he had requested in order to be able to resist the offenses against the law and the infringements of the Anglo-American inhabitants.[1] Nevertheless, the majority of all Texans condemned Travis's actions most severely[2] and sent declarations of loyalty to Mexico and apologies to Cós and the military commander of Texas, Domingo de Ugartechea.[3]

Travis wrote James Bowie on July 30, 1835: "The peace-party, as they style themselves, I believe are the strongest, and make much noise. Unless we could be united, had we not better be quiet, and settle down for a while?"[4] The Mexican command, too, at first showed itself to be obliging and making the effort to understand. On July 7, thus before the public pardon of the Texans, Cós had sent a letter to the Brazos District in which he emphasized that the Texans need not fear any troops that were sent; it was only a matter of the preservation of law and order.[5]

Then on August 1, in a letter to the political leader of the Brazos District, Cós accepted the apology of the Texans but at the same time demanded as a sign of good faith that they deliver over Travis, in order to bring him to justice.[6] Simultaneously he ordered the imprisonment of Samuel M. Williams, Frank Johnson, Robert M. Williamson, Mosely Baker, Lorenzo de Zavala, José María Carbájal, and other federalists who were suspected by the Mexican leadership of being speculators and thus as revolutionary agitators because of the law of April 14, 1835.[7] But inasmuch as these men had not participated in the Anahuac disturbances and only a part of them belonged to the War Party, this decision on the part of Cós was seen by a large part of the population as a blow against the political opposition and along with that as a sign of an incipient dictatorship.[8] They refused to comply with Cós's commands and in a number of town meetings came to the unanimous conclusion that they must call a convention for all of Texas in order to discuss the situation and the further concerted action of all Texans; the word "war" was in the air—even if only as a final expedient.[9]

Cós, who knew about the agitation of the Texans in regard to the troops that were expected, had a declaration disseminated through the press that to a great degree represented not only his views but also those of the leading Mexicans.[10] This treatise, which went in great detail into the goodwill of the Mexican government toward Texas and called upon all upright citizens to be peaceful and obedient, was delivered in the manner of a centralist form of government with the marks of a dictatorship, in which the state could determine what it considered right and little care was taken for the citizens. For many Anglo-Americans such a tone was not compatible with the principles for which their fathers had fought once, sixty years before. They saw everywhere "symptoms of tyranny dangerous to liberty" and remained faithful to the old principle: "To live free, or die in the defense of liberty and our rights."[11] If the advocates of war and immediate separation from Mexico were at first embittered by the peaceful attitude of their fellow citizens and their willingness to negotiate, the various spontaneous gatherings inclined them to be hopeful again that now finally the moment appeared to have come when they would be able to fight against Mexico.[12]

The general meeting for Texans had been called for October 15, 1835, in the town of Washington. In the meantime those who longed for war went zealously to work spreading propaganda and soliciting help in the United States. In American newspapers many letters were printed containing assurances that everyone ready to help would be richly rewarded with land.[13] However much men such as Smith, Archer, Travis, and the Wharton brothers agitated for war, Texans were in fact little in agreement as to how they should proceed.[14] They were waiting for Stephen F. Austin. His voice would be decisive and would unite the two camps.[15] As has been previously discussed, Austin had decided for war, a decision that carried with it the support and to an extent even the friendship of hawks such as Travis and Archer.[16]

The first shot of the war was fired at Gonzales. In September Colonel Ugartechea had demanded from the citizens of that city the return of a cannon that he had let Green De Witt and his settlers have in 1832 to fight Indians. The inhabitants refused to give it up. At that, Ugartechea dispatched one hundred dragoons to Gonzales. But the *alcalde* of that place had already turned for help to neighboring communities. And so on October 2, 1835, the dragoons were awaited two miles from Gonzales by a volunteer militia of 160 men under John H. Moore. Shots were fired, a dragoon was killed, and Lieutenant Francisco Casteñada ordered the retreat of the Mexicans. With that skirmish the war had begun. The flag of the men of Gonzales, which they had raised next to the cannon, and the motto painted on it, "Come and take it," became a part of history.[17]

On October 5, 1835, Stephen F. Austin wrote a remarkable letter to David G. Burnet: "My friend—All goes well and gloriously for Texas—the whole country is in arms. . . . I hope to see Texas forever free from Mexican domination of any kind. It is yet too soon to say this publically, but that is the point we shall end at—and it is the one I am aiming at."[18] Two questions must always be asked in regard to Austin's statements: To whom are they directed and for whom are they meant? Nevertheless, the assertion in this letter coincides with his actions and declarations before and afterward; the war against Mexico was waged from the beginning as a war of independence.[19]

The news of the battle of Gonzales, just as the report that Cós was moving on Texas with an army, spread like wildfire. Volunteers from all parts of the country hurried toward Gonzales. Cós, coming from Vera Cruz by sea, had landed at El Copano on September 20 with about five hundred men, artillery, and other equipment, and was marching by way of Goliad to San Antonio de Béxar. Cós reached Goliad on October 2 and left a small group of about forty soldiers there. George M. Collinsworth, the leader of a troop of about 125 Texans who were really supposed to go from Victoria to Gonzales, received word of Cós's maneuver and turned his troops toward Goliad. Ben R. Milam, Ira Ingram, and the subsequent commander of Goliad, Capt. Phillip Dimmitt, joined them. On October 9, at eleven o'clock at night, the Texans surprised the Mexicans and thus took the Presidio La Bahía del Espíritu Santo de Zuñiga, the garrison of Goliad.[20] This victory was of importance for the Texans insofar as it gave them possession of a considerable amount of powder, lead, and other military supplies that Cós had left there. In addition, the occupation of Goliad cut off his return route to the ships. At this point Cós entrenched himself with his men, probably about twelve hundred of them (his troops, Ugartechea's men, and reinforcements from Coahuila), in San Antonio de Béxar and waited.

On October 8 Austin informally created the Permanent Council out of the Committee of Safety of the city of San Felipe with members of other committees of safety, which represented, so to speak, the first government of an autonomous Texas.[21] On October 11 Austin was then chosen commander-in-chief of the military forces.[22] On October 15, according to the resolution of August 20, the consultation was to take place. All the representatives to it had also been elected, but at the beginning of October most of them were on the road to San Antonio, so that the meeting had to be postponed until November 1. Two more days passed before all the participants arrived. Not until November 3, 1835, had enough representatives come together to decide about the future of Texas—at least as they conceived it. Meanwhile Austin with his army, which he had organized to some extent by this time, laid siege to San Antonio and, in officially as well as unofficially conducted negotiations, called on Cós for peace, freedom, and the surrender of the city.[23]

The meeting lasted from November 3 to 14, 1835.[24] Branch T. Archer was elected president. In the course of the debates two different groups began to be distinguishable. The one, with Henry Smith and John A. Wharton at the forefront, was in favor of an immediate declaration of independence. The second group, under Branch T. Archer and Sam Houston, argued completely in accordance with Austin's views for a federal state of Texas that would make it possible for the liberal ideas of the Constitution of 1824 in Mexico to be victorious again.

This seems at first glance to be contrary to the statement made above that the war against Mexico was from the beginning a war of independence. This contradiction, however, can be quickly resolved. As has been mentioned before, by the beginning of 1832, if not even earlier, Austin had already been of the opinion that Texas could not belong to Mexico permanently but had to become independent at some time.[25] Branch T. Archer was already a well-known advocate of the separation of Texas. If men like he nevertheless favored a declaration for the Mexican Constitution of 1824 and thus tacitly for remaining with Mexico, they must have had particular reasons. The discussion went on for two days before the vote was taken on November 6, and thirty-three delegates voted for the defense of liberalism in Mexico and fifteen for a free Texas. The reasons for this outcome of the vote can be ascertained through inductive reasoning.

Although a warlike atmosphere existed everywhere after September, 1835,[26] Texas was militarily weak. Its army, a badly organized, untrained, and undisciplined mass of barely five hundred men, was poorly equipped, and could not hold its own against a larger, attacking, professional army.[27] There was a lack not only of food, clothing, weapons, and ammunition, but also quite generally of soldiers. If a united Mexico were to turn against Texas and send all its troops into the province, the results were clear to everyone: Texas would be completely wiped out. But by declaring for a liberal Texas in the federal union of a liberal Mexico, the hope was to drive the political camps in Mexico further apart, to acquire the support of the liberals, and above all to gain what was most important: time.

If Texans behaved as if they were basically loyal to Mexico, even if not to its government, then they could negotiate with Cós and hope that Santa Anna would bide his time. In addition, it enlisted more sympathy in the

United States for a Texas that seemed to be following a purely idealistic course.[28] It was, therefore, sheer calculation that caused the convention to appear outwardly for Mexico; that it was actually fighting for independence was clear to everyone.[29] This action was also logical because, on the one hand, warnings had arrived from the United States not to involve it officially, by any means, in a conflict with Mexico or compromise it otherwise; additionally, Mexía was in New Orleans fitting out an expedition against Tampico.[30]

Because states like Yucatán and Tamaulipas were in favor of a liberal federalism, the thought of support on the part of the liberal circle in Mexico was not at all so misguided. Further unrest in the vicinity of Mexico City itself would have occupied Santa Anna enough and kept him away from Texas for some time. In addition, the spirit of the meeting can be gathered from the results of the elections for the various offices. Henry Smith was elected governor; Sam Houston was named commander-in-chief of the Texas army; and Stephen F. Austin, William H. Wharton, and Branch T. Archer were made delegates to the United States to solicit support for Texas.

While the convention was meeting in San Felipe de Austin, the siege of San Antonio reached its climax. There had been a number of sorties on the part of the Mexicans and a few skirmishes in which James Bowie and James Walker Fannin had distinguished themselves on the Texas side.

Born in Georgia on January 1, 1804, Fannin was the only leading military personality in Texas who had received some training at the United States Military Academy at West Point. In 1834 he came to Texas with his family. He was a well-known slave trader who, however, was also interested in other types of trade.[31]

Austin, who had been given a new assignment by the convention, entrusted his command on November 25 to Edward Burleson who, after a siege of almost two months, gave orders on December 4, 1835, to withdraw into winter quarters at Goliad.[32] This order completely ignored the knowledge that the Texans had won out over the Mexicans in the surrounded city. On November 27 the rumor had spread in the Texas camp that a Mexican troop was bringing pay to San Antonio for Cós's army. A fierce fight broke out around the pack train, to which Cós even sent reinforcements from the besieged city and in which the Texans under the command of James Bowie killed fifty Mexicans while they themselves suffered only two wounded. It turned out after the victory of the Texans that the pack wagon did not contain silver for the soldiers but grass for the horses. This battle, which went down in the annals as the Grass Fight, showed that the siege was successful and that Cós was out of supplies. In addition, spies brought the news that morale and discipline among the Mexicans was decaying and that their distress was great.

Ben R. Milam asked for volunteers to disobey the command to with-draw and to storm San Antonio with him. The whole army enthusiastically followed him. After a five-day battle, in which Ben R. Milam fell, Cós was forced to surrender on December 9. One condition of the terms of capitu-lation was that Cós and his officers had to swear never again to intervene in the fight of the Texans for the restoration of the Constitution of 1824 and never again to cross the Rio Grande into Texas.[33] On December 14, 1835, Cós and his army left San Antonio and on December 15 they crossed the Rio Grande.

With that Texas was again free of hostile Mexican troops. The reaction to this fact was that Texans literally went home. They thought they had won the war with the expulsion of the Mexicans and that in the future they would be left in peace by Mexico, and so they abandoned the army. First, it was a question of preparing the fields for the next year; and then Christ-mas was just around the corner.[34] On December 25 there were still about 400 men in San Antonio de Béxar, seventy in Washington, eighty in Goliad, and 200 in Velasco. But these numbers are inexact; the "army" of Texas consisted of nothing but small groups of volunteers from Texas and the United States, and disciplinary obstacles impeded any united movement or action. On March 1, 1836, there were only two strategic points left occupied by a rather large assemblage of troops: the small garrison at San Antonio called the Alamo, with about 150 men, and Goliad, with something more than 400.[35]

Governor Smith and the Council—a type of parliament of the provisional government of Texas—also contributed decisively to the great lack of dis-cipline. In its haste the convention had forgotten to define specifically the rights and duties of these two branches of the government. The consequences were that the governor and the Council were in constant conflict with one another, and both gave contradictory orders that plunged Texas into politi-cal chaos.

The Matamoros expedition had become the great controversy. Who had first suggested it cannot be determined with any certainty.[36] The plan pro-vided that a Texas army should march into Mexico and take Matamoros, which represented a strategically important point for any eventual Mexican advance against Texas. However, whether this had been the only goal of the plan and whether strategic considerations alone had been decisive in this matter is doubtful.

Fertile soil for this obscure venture was without doubt the countless let-ters from the United States, with which the men in authority in Texas were deluged, urging them to take Mexico: "Are you not stopping too short, to halt on the confines of the province of Texas? Why not march up to the walls of Mexico, and treat with the usurper in his capital?—I could raise 20 men to go on such an expedition, where I could not raise five to defend the province of Texas."[37]

So it was, first, a matter of fulfilling the hopes of those in the United States; secondly, to give the Texans, who looked on the war as ended, a new mission in order to strengthen the army again; and thirdly, to make the most of the warlike spirit of the volunteers who had hastened there from the United States.[38] But the dissension and the ambition of each individual to carry off the laurel wreath of victory nipped all these wild plans of conquest in the bud. To go into the details of the squabbles over the Matamoros expedition here would be to go too far. Sam Houston, who refused to participate in this venture, was thereupon simply ignored by the Council and bypassed with aplomb. The command of the expedition was given, as if in a lottery, to the man offering the most at any given moment, among them at one time James Bowie and at another James Fannin.[39]

The altercations about authority and the course to be followed reached their high point when Governor Smith dissolved the Council on January 9, and the Council in a countermove removed Smith as governor and gave the office to the lieutenant governor, James W. Robinson. But Smith did not recognize this decision;[40] the authority of the provisional government was destroyed. Texas was thus, practically speaking, without leadership in the military as well as civil spheres until March, 1836. All hopes were now focused on March 1; for the Council, against the veto of Henry Smith, had called a new meeting for that date that was to draft a constitution and with it dispose of all the difficulties existing up to this time.[41]

In February the fifty-nine delegates had been elected for this meeting and they gathered in the newly laid-out city of Washington. Already on the first day of the conference the president, Richard Ellis, commissioned five men to draft a declaration of independence.[42] On March 2, 1836, the declaration was presented and it was signed on March 3.[43] Texas had now officially broken its ties with Mexico. This was, however, no unexpected step that had to be reached after a perhaps painful struggle. On December 20, 1835, the garrison at Goliad had already issued a declaration of independence.[44] But at that point the Council had not yet wanted to take notice of such public declarations, for it was still, after all, making an effort to gain the active help of the liberal Mexicans. Consequently, it was felt necessary to disapprove officially of the premature declaration from Goliad.[45]

The turn in the official attitude of Texas was brought about by two things. Mexía's attempt to carry the liberal revolution through Tampico into the heart of Mexico failed, just as other attempts at opposition to Santa Anna did. One faction of the liberals had even joined him. Even though the Texans continued to have the support of individual Mexicans such as Mexía, Navarro, Ruiz, and Zavala, help from Mexico itself could not be expected to any great extent anymore. Stephen F. Austin, who had clearly recognized this, now formally changed his stance: "I go for Indepencence for I have no doubt we shall get aid."[46] In this letter of January 7, Austin addressed, moreover, the second important point. Even though originally avoidance of diplomatic entanglements between the U.S. and Mexico had been a reason for the discretion of the Texans in the matter of independence, the three agents—Austin, Wharton, and Archer—learned what had also been revealed in letters already cited from private parties in the United States to the leading men in Texas: diplomacy notwithstanding, if Texas wanted to get material support from individuals and private organizations or volunteers for the fight against Mexico, then it had to declare its independence as quickly as possible. The three emissaries expressed this clearly: without a declaration of independence, no loans, no money, no help.[47]

Very often the Texas revolution is compared to the American Revolution of 1775–76.[48] Even though this comparison will be more thoroughly investigated at a later point, it must be stated here that when any comparison of the Second Continental Congress of the United States to the General Council of Texas is made, important differences become apparent. Whereas in the Continental Congress political and legal questions and questions of political philosophy, indeed, even questions concerning the matter of independence itself were debated,[49] the General Council, assembled to produce a constitution, after the quick declaration of the autonomy of Texas, went only hesitantly, almost reluctantly, to work to create a political framework for the new nation. The conclusion of this meeting makes a strange impression on today's observer.

George Campbell Childress is considered the author of the Texas Declaration of Independence. Born on January 8, 1804, in Tennessee, he became an attorney and later, in addition, publisher of a newspaper in Nashville, the *Nashville Banner and Nashville Advertiser.* He organized several large events in support of Texas that collected money and aid for the country that found itself in a state of war. As late as November 17, 1835, he had opened a gathering of that sort with a fiery speech in the course of which several volunteers for the war in Texas stepped forward.[50] Even though in his speech there was much mention of freedom and human rights, his motives can in no way be called exclusively altruistic. In October, 1835, he had stopped in New York and was pursuing land-speculation business. For one thing he and John C. McLemore had entered into a contract with Samuel Swartwout, Jonathan Swift, and Nicholas Biddle, the president of the Second National Bank of the United States. Childress's mission was to acquire land in Texas for Swartwout, Swift, and Biddle.[51] He did not accomplish this, however; he misappropriated the money entrusted to him and in February of 1836 turned over 42,124 acres of land to Swartwout in return for it.[52] For another, on

October 12 he had concluded a contract in the name of Sterling C. Robertson with James Prentiss, whom he described as "one of the great money operators of Wall Street." Prentiss, who stated that he had an agent under contract in England and one in Germany, wanted to bring four hundred families to Texas, according to the contract. Characterizing Prentiss, Childress wrote: "He is the greatest man here in connection with Texas."[53]

On January 9, 1836, Childress arrived in Texas, where he was taken in by his uncle, Sterling C. Robertson.[54] On February 1, as one of the two candidates of the municipality of Milam, he was elected to the Constitutional Convention. On March 1, the first day of the meeting, the five-member committee was appointed at his instigation. This corresponded to the Second Continental Congress, where five men had likewise worked on a declaration of independence.[55] But just as Thomas Jefferson had ultimately drafted it alone, Childress also probably wrote it without help from the other four. However, whereas Jefferson needed seventeen days, one night was enough for Childress; he presented the declaration on the second day of the meeting. More probable than that it was written quickly is that he had gone to Washington with an already complete draft. Yet the document surely did not require much work by him one way or the other, for it was closely modeled on the American Declaration of Independence in arrangement and structure.[56] Though the representatives of the thirteen colonies required six days more of discussion in order to accept Jefferson's work on July 4, 1776, this happened in Texas in a quick procedure: Childress read the declaration from his seat and after an hour it was accepted unanimously without change or discussion.[57] This, too, is an indication that in Texas there was no more need to struggle over the question of independence itself—it was long since a decided matter. Problems arose for the delegates over the constitution; for many of them it had been copied too much from the United States Constitution and written too little for the special needs of Texas.[58]

Two points especially seemed critical to the delegates, whose deliberations dragged on exceedingly, for each one was afraid he would damage his own interests: the question of a land law and that of the government loan to finance the war. These two subjects occupied the assembly the most.[59] Not until March 16 could they come to an agreement to borrow up to $1 million. The land law, which was introduced on March 9, was fought over until the last day.[60] On March 17, 1836, the meeting was adjourned and executive power handed over to the ad interim government elected the day before.[61] At four o'clock in the morning of March 17, David G. Burnet was sworn in as president and Lorenzo de Zavala as vice-president.[62] Now the last, decisive step to separation from Mexico had to be accomplished by the army.

On March 4 the Constitutional Convention had appointed Sam Houston commander-in-chief of the army and the militias. On March 6 they received a letter from William B. Travis, the commander of the troops stationed in the Alamo garrison, in which he asked urgently for reinforcements, for he was under enemy bombardment.[63] In this letter Travis described the situation clearly and distinctly: Santa Anna and his army had surrounded him and his men; Fannin would probably not come to his aid from Goliad, and so he urgently needed support from another quarter, for Santa Anna – if he were not stopped here – would bring death and destruction to all of Texas. The convention listened to these words, but they faded away without results. It continued to debate until the garrison had fallen and then were shocked at the horror of the war. Although some of the members became impatient, the discussions simply continued.[64] A rescue mission, however, would scarcely have been possible or even meaningful anymore, for on March 6 the plight of Travis and his men had already come to an end.

On January 6, 1836, the commander at San Antonio de Béxar, Col. James C. Neill, reported to Governor Smith by letter that his 104 soldiers were in a distressing situation and urgently needed reinforcements in order to be able to defend the city properly.[65] In addition, the rumor was going around that Santa Anna was approaching from the south with a large armed force. Houston thereupon sent Col. James Bowie from Goliad to San Antonio with about thirty men to destroy the fortifications and conduct the withdrawal of all the troops.[66] Governor Smith, for his part, ordered William B. Travis to San Antonio, also with about thirty men, to direct the evacuation. Travis submitted only reluctantly to these orders. On February 11 Neill left the city because of illness in his family and gave Travis command of the regular troops. On February 8 David Crockett arrived in San Antonio with about twelve men from Tennessee.[67] From February 14 on, James Bowie and William B. Travis shared command of the troops until, on February 24, Bowie became incapable of serving because of serious illness and Travis took over supreme command.[68] At noon on February 23, Santa Anna had reached the city of San Antonio with an army of about six thousand men. Thereupon Travis, Bowie, Crockett, and their men withdrew into the Alamo. Although the siege began immediately, it was still possible on March 1 for a small group of thirty-one men from Gonzales to reinforce the approximately 155 soldiers in the Alamo. On March 3 Travis could still send out a courier with his famous appeal for help, but then the ring of the siege was drawn tight around the Alamo.

It is superfluous to describe the battle of the Alamo in detail here; a number of noteworthy studies are already available.[69] The questions that are still unsolved can also not be answered here with final certainty.[70] At four o'clock on the morning of March 6 Santa Anna ordered the assault on the Alamo. At six-thirty the battle was over. The number of the survivors and of the dead cannot be exactly reconstructed. The 187 defenders of the Alamo were all killed; only a few women, children, and Travis's slave Joe survived. The estimates on the Mexican side range from eighteen hundred to five thousand attackers and from six hundred to sixteen hundred fallen.[71] The Americans had sold their lives dearly in any event. More important than all these numbers and detailed accounts and descriptions of heroism in the battle were the attendant circumstances and consequences on both sides.

Although Houston, as commander-in-chief, had given the order to evacuate San Antonio, Bowie and Neill remained in the city. Travis only reluctantly obeyed the order to go to San Antonio, for he aspired to a command post with the cavalry on the border. Then, when he arrived, he could not come to terms with Bowie about the command authority of each of them. As Amelia Williams wrote, the advancing Mexicans were not the greatest danger for the Texans: "that danger was internal discord."[72] In the end they had divided the authority; Travis had the command of the regulars, Bowie of the volunteers. Bowie maintained he stood higher in rank than Travis, but Travis accused Bowie of drunkenness to Henry Smith.[73] Travis in his distress finally turned to James Fannin in Goliad to get help, but Fannin did not come to the aid of Travis. Fannin had about four hundred men in his command and had entered Goliad on February 12. Amelia Williams charges that Fannin did not answer Travis's cry for help out of personal ambition. Her assumption is that, in his message to Fannin of February 16, Travis asked him to hurry to the Alamo with all his men. Then Fannin could take over command and he, Travis, would be at liberty to follow his desire to go to the cavalry on the border. Fannin, for his part, was worrying about his reputation and hoped to be further endorsed by the Council in his role as commander-in-chief.[74]

The question remains why Travis, both after he knew about the superior strength of the Mexicans and that the line of the siege had not yet become impenetrable around the Alamo, did not withdraw. An eyewitness and member of Santa Anna's staff, José Enrique de la Peña, reported in his memoirs that, because of the lack of food, supplies, ammunition, and hope of any relief, Travis was said to have promised his men on the evening of March 5 that if no help came, he would surrender on the next day or attempt to escape under cover of darkness. Santa Anna, who had supposedly intercepted information about this plan, had thereupon ordered the attack; success without drawing blood would have been no victory for him.[75] Even if this story is incorrect, which is not yet settled, it nevertheless portrays a significant trait in Santa Anna's character. He wanted to strike his opponent devastatingly. This becomes even more evident in his later decision to execute the prisoners of Goliad.

On March 14 Fannin had received Sam Houston's orders to withdraw from Goliad with all his men, for the Mexicans were advancing with a large army and Goliad could not be held any better than the Alamo. Yet Fannin did not immediately carry out the orders, but continued to hesitate. Not until March 19 did he give the orders for departure. But then it was already too late; poorly fed and exhausted, Fannin's men were surrounded by General José Urrea's soldiers and, after a protracted battle, had to surrender. The Texans were convinced that they had surrendered honorably as prisoners of war, whereas Santa Anna made use of the law of December 30, 1835, according to which all foreigners who were found with weapons in the sovereign territory of Mexico were to be treated as pirates. Thus Santa Anna gave the order to shoot all the prisoners. On March 27 this was carried out, and about 340 prisoners were executed.[76] The deaths of these men at Goliad and in the Alamo, along with all the cruelty, was for both sides strategically senseless and worthless. Santa Anna neither achieved anything by these executions nor, on the other hand, was he delayed to any extent by these battles. If Travis, Bowie, and Fannin had immediately followed Sam Houston's orders, this slaughter would probably have been avoided.

And yet the death of these men was not wholly in vain.[77] Santa Anna's brutal and in no way justifiable measures brought support for Texas from many parts of the United States, and with one blow legitimated the war against Mexico, putting the Texans into such a rage that they were able in the end to carry off the victory against a Mexican army that was far superior to them in numbers. In Mexico the negative effect of these massacres, which had horrified even Santa Anna's friends, was also clear.[78] Why he gave those commands is very difficult to establish. Even though he attempted later to give his actions the appearance of legality, the suspicion still lingers that pathological ambition and the desire for revenge allowed him to go so far.[79] At the same time, he embodied the spirit of those Mexicans who held rigidly to principles without being able to see or make distinctions. For him, as also, for example, for War Minister Tornel y Mendívil, there was no doubt where right and wrong lay.[80] Mexico's security and national unity were endangered by two things: by the liberals and by the armed insurgents who had allegedly joined the liberals. Paradoxically, Santa Anna and the circle that he represented were even occasionally supported in their inflexible conduct by the United States. When in December, 1835, he had executed as pirates the twenty-eight prisoners who were captured when Mexía attempted to establish himself in Tampico, the word from the United States was that it served those U.S. citizens right.[81] Tampico was strictly a Mexican state, and the condemned men without doubt were mercenaries.

The men who fell in the Alamo and were executed at Goliad had also been recruited predominantly among newcomers from the United States. For Santa Anna there existed no difference between them and the men from

Tampico—they were all pirates according to the law. But this time the American public denied him their support. Texas was already considered a part of the United States; friends and relatives lived there, and the newspapers reported in detail, if also often incorrectly, about the war in Texas.[82] If American support was already a determining factor in the fight of the Texans against Mexico, then Santa Anna achieved with these actions the opposite of what he had perhaps imagined. The United States was not frightened away but, on the contrary, for the first time was really drawn into the battle.[83] Still, direct intervention by the United States was not necessary.

After the extermination of the troops with Fannin, there was left only Sam Houston's part of the army of about eight hundred soldiers, who, in contrast to the troops of Travis and Fannin, were mainly recruited from Texan settlers. Although originally the number had probably stood at twelve hundred to fourteen hundred soldiers,[84] the news of Santa Anna's advance, the destruction of the Alamo, and the execution of Fannin and his men caused a general panic that had the soldiers hurrying off to their families in great numbers in order to protect them or flee with them.[85] This panic, the exodus of many settlers with their families, went into Texas history books as the Runaway Scrape. Although most of the families returned again, the alarm, the damage, and the number of victims that were to be lamented was very large.[86]

Along with the fear of Santa Anna's advancing army, anxiety and hopelessness spread because of the fact that Sam Houston with his troops did not immediately join battle with Santa Anna's army but continued to withdraw. The army, which had already been decimated by the many desertions, suffered especially from its lack of equipment. Without tents, with two covered wagons, two teams of oxen, and a few run-down horses, the Texas army offered a truly desolate appearance.[87] Santa Anna, who without doubt knew through spies about the weakness of the Texans, now committed a tactical error. Instead of forcing a decision with his superior strength, he was already so sure of success that he broke up his assembled forces and at first with only a small contingent of about seven hundred to nine hundred soldiers attempted to catch in Harrisburg the interim government, which had already fled to Galveston Island, and then he hurried along behind Sam Houston in order to finish off the Texas military force.[88] By doing this he put Sam Houston's troops in a better position numerically for one thing, and for another he exhausted his own men by the forced march. Although Houston was cursed and pressed hard by President Burnet to finally attack,[89] he continued to withdraw.

On the morning of April 21 Santa Anna was reinforced by General Cós and five hundred soldiers. With the certainty of numerical superiority he allowed his troops to rest. At four in the afternoon approximately nine hundred Texans overran the bewildered thirteen hundred to fifteen hundred Mexicans and in twenty minutes fought and won the decisive Battle of San Jacinto.[90] According to Sam Houston's official report, eight Texans were killed and seventeen wounded; the Mexicans had to lament 630 dead and 730 taken prisoner, among the latter, General Santa Anna and General Cós.[91] On Santa Anna's orders the remaining troops still to be found in Texas withdrew across the Rio Grande to Mexico. With his surprising victory at San Jacinto, Houston had won for Texas its independence from Mexico.

Still, questions remain that cannot yet be answered with absolute certainty today. Why did Houston withdraw to the San Jacinto River and only there attack Santa Anna? On April 7, 1836, Houston had written to Henry Raguet: "Don't get scared at Nacogdoches – Remember Old Hickory [Andrew Jackson's nickname] claims Nachez as 'neutral territory.'"[92] This sentence could be interpreted to mean that Houston wanted to withdraw to the American border to lure Santa Anna into a trap. A U.S. army unit commanded by E. P. Gaines was stationed there, which was to keep an eye on Indians and protect U.S. citizens. Considering the controversy over the western border of Texas, it would have been easy to maintain that Santa Anna had crossed the U.S. frontier.[93] Other historians see in Houston's long delay, for one thing, a great general waiting for a favorable opportunity[94] – a point of view that can easily be defended on the basis of the outcome of the battle alone – and for another, the time that he needed to drill and discipline the untrained crowd that he commanded.[95] He never gave an explanation for his actions himself; his reasons for it were the most simple imaginable: "I consulted none – I held no councils of war. If I err, the blame is mine."[96]

Why did Mexico accept defeat, although most of its troops were still in Texas? The shock of the defeat at San Jacinto, combined with the humiliation at having the president and commander-in-chief of the land taken prisoner, undoubtedly contributed to Mexico's panicky reaction. At the same time, all the generals and officers involved began to blame each other for their failure and the retreat. General Vicente Filisola, who had had supreme command over the main force of the troops in the absence of Santa Anna, defended himself with the argument that the army had been finished in any event and he, Filisola, had wanted to save the lives of Santa Anna and the other prisoners by his actions.[97] General José Urrea thereupon accused Filisola of lying and cowardice.[98] To de la Peña they were all sycophants and servile creatures who, robbed of their dictatorial leadership, became confused.[99]

Whatever the reasons may have been – whether sorrow about their commander and his men, whether fear for their homeland, whether inability or cowardice—the army remained faithful to Santa Anna and withdrew. The war was over; now it was a matter of securing the peace: "Tell our friends all the news, and that we have beaten the enemy . . . tell them to come on and let the people plant corn."[100]

PART III

The Republic of Texas, 1836–1846

11. The Phase of Consolidation

Even though the several thousand Mexican soldiers were on a retreat to Mexico and Texas had won its war of independence, on April 22, the day after the victory at San Jacinto, and for a long time afterward, the country was faced with financial and political ruin. Stephen F. Austin, William H. Wharton, and Branch T. Archer were endeavoring to gain support for Texas in the United States, but Texas had won the victory over Mexico alone and thereby exhausted itself economically. The army had to be paid. The land was not planted and in many places it was laid waste, for many families had left everything behind them in the Runaway Scrape. Likewise, many ventures had been destroyed in their beginnings because the Texans in their flight had often used the scorched-earth policy. San Felipe de Austin, for example, did not exist anymore – the inhabitants had simply set it afire when they departed.

In the closing phases of the war the provisioning of the army had been augmented by sea. Various ships had been fitted out; they delivered urgently needed supplies, engaged in combat with Mexican warships, and attacked merchant ships that were calling at Mexican ports.[1] This Texas "navy," officially consisting of four schooners that were supplemented by several light sailing vessels, was maintained by various merchants and by donations. Established by law on November 25, 1835, it was put into service in January, 1836. Although there were some small naval engagements, and fresh supplies to the Texans definitely depended on it, nevertheless it did not deserve the decisive role in the course of the war that many historians would like to ascribe to it.[2]

One of the merchants who made themselves particularly deserving in relation to the navy and the Texas economy in the beginning phases was Thomas F. McKinney, the partner of Samuel M. Williams. The Texas government was officially indebted to McKinney for $16,942.80 for his services, whereas his actual expenditures must have amounted to many times that amount.[3] Swartwout, too, had not only invested in land but in addition had spent large sums to support the struggle of the Texans. Although in May, 1836, he complained bitterly to James Morgan that his expenditures of more than $50,000 were lost and the Texans had robbed him of all the land he had acquired in return for good money,[4] he nevertheless invested still further in Texas. Not all contributions turned out to be so high. Henry B. Prentiss wrote to Houston that for health reasons he could not serve in the army but instead he was donating $200 for equipment.[5] Jane McManus remarked to a friend that as a woman she could not bear arms, of course, but because she owned much land, she wanted at least to buy weapons for the army.[6]

That sort of support came relatively seldom in 1835. Of course, only donations of a material nature are meant, for manifestations of sympathy in the most varied forms—such as newspaper articles or convocations—occurred in the United States from the beginning. But it was difficult for the messengers and agents to convert these sympathetic expressions into hard cash, merchandise, or credit. Two things changed this picture: for one, the declaration of independence of March 2, 1836, which had been insisted on by the negotiators Austin, Archer, and Wharton, and for the other, the news of the fall of the Alamo and the Goliad massacre. But news at that time required at least four weeks to arrive in the North from Texas.[7] There were plenty of rumors; first the newspapers printed that the Texans had won the war, then that they had lost it.[8] Andrew Jackson pressed for a definite report on the situation.[9] When the news of the Alamo and of Goliad arrived, as well as their confirmation, the Mexicans had already been defeated at San Jacinto. Consequently, it was only after the victory that volunteers and contributions in large quantity came to Texas.

Support for the Texans' fight for freedom ran like a ribbon through most of the states of the United States without showing sectional divergences, as was to happen later. Even though public opinion in states such as Virginia, New York, and Mississippi was on the whole divided, the supporters of Texas were predominantly in Louisiana, Alabama, Pennsylvania, and Kentucky.[10] In addition, the factions were not yet clearly marked by party politics, as in 1844. True, at first the newspapers friendly to the Whigs spoke against Texas, and those connected with the Democrats for it, but the dreadful news from Texas united most Americans once more behind its flag.

At the same time it must be stressed here that for many of those fighting for Texas the love of freedom or others ideals was not the determining motive for their actions but rather, primarily, material interests: "War will now be carried into the enemy's country, where gold and silver are plenty, there will be fine pickings in the interior. The war will never end until Mexico is completely our own and conquered."[11] The mixture of ideals and thoughts of profit had appeared earlier, as an article in the *Clarion and Tennessee Gazette* of August, 1819, shows: "Every friend to the western country, every man who wishes to see gold and silver abundant in his country, every man who wishes to see liberty continue her march to the Pacific ocean, must wish success to the adventurers in Texas."[12]

But not all of those who hurried to Texas were absolutely eager for precious metals; rather, for their participation in the struggle, they had been promised land of their own. Each one who had come to Texas as a volunteer received title to 640 acres; those who had reported between March 2 and August 1, 1836, received as head of a family a league and a *labor* (altogether 4,605 acres), as a single man one-third of a league (1,476 acres). These were inheritable titles that were increased by 640 acres for the relatives of those killed in the Alamo, the garrison of Goliad, or the Battle of San Jacinto.[13] These parcels of land were not looked at simply as pay, like money or natural products, but as valuable investments. As has already been mentioned, there was speculation on the annexation of Texas by the United States, which in other cases—Florida and Louisiana—had led to a considerable rise in the price of land and thus profit for the owners. This was also openly discussed in the newspapers.[14]

The appeal accordingly was soon a success. While most of the settlers who had fought at San Jacinto went home to till their fields, more and more volunteers came from the United States, until in June, 1836, the Texas army was almost twenty-five hundred strong.[15] Sam Houston, who had been wounded at San Jacinto, had been taken to New Orleans for medical treatment and had given the chief command to the then secretary of war, Brig. Gen. Thomas J. Rusk.[16] But Rusk had disciplinary problems; some of the soldiers had not gotten the news that Houston had given the command to him, and another group, newly arrived from the United States, would accept only their present leader and no other commander-in-chief.[17] Making it more difficult in addition was the fact that the army was not ready to accept the actions of the government with regard to Santa Anna.

When Santa Anna had been taken prisoner on the day after the Battle of San Jacinto, he had pronounced himself ready to sign two treaties: one official and one secret. The official treaty provided that the war was formally declared at an end, Mexico would never again make war against Texas, the Mexican army was to remain once and for all south of the Rio Grande, prisoners of war were to be exchanged, and reparations were to be given to the Texans for destroyed property. The secret treaty promised Santa Anna his immediate freedom and return home to Mexico in return for his assurance that Mexico would officially recognize the independence of Texas and the Rio Grande as its southern border upon his return. These contracts were signed by Burnet and Santa Anna on May 14.[18]

General Rusk followed the retreating Mexican troops and established his headquarters in Victoria. At the beginning of June, Santa Anna, with his secretary Caro and Colonel Almonte, were to be taken to Vera Cruz on the schooner *Invincible*. But some of the army under Thomas J. Green mutinied and prevented this; they wanted to try Santa Anna as a war criminal and hang him. Likewise, they wanted Burnet and the government to be impeached for their having concluded the Treaties of Velasco, which were rejected by many as a sign of weakness deserving only contempt. At the same time the army, which had fought against military domination by Mexico and then placed its word above that of the lawful, civil government of Texas,[19] was put into a state of alarm by news from Mexico.

Scarcely had the report of Santa Anna's defeat arrived in Mexico City than Anastacio Bustamante declared himself to be acting president and, on May 20, 1836, revoked all the measures dictated by Santa Anna and the treaties concluded by him. Simultaneously he transferred the high command over Mexico's army from General Filisola to General José Urrea. As far as Mexico was concerned, the war was to continue.[20] For this purpose a new military force was gathering in Matamoros.

The man who, on account of his bravery at San Jacinto, had been called to be Rusk's replacement as secretary of war in Burnet's government, Mirabeau Buonaparte Lamar, had meanwhile also developed into a problem case. Born in Georgia on August 6, 1798, Lamar was soon drawn to poetry and journalism. After a few publishing experiences that were disappointing for him, he went into politics in 1823 as secretary of the newly elected governor of Georgia, George Troup. On January 1, 1826, when his time in office as secretary had expired, he married and moved with his family back to his family farm.[21] In January, 1828, he established a newspaper that he published until 1833. His wife had died of tuberculosis in August, 1830. He turned again to politics, but his good luck deserted him. He was not nominated as a candidate for Congress by the seven-member board of delegates of Georgia. In 1834 his father and a sister died; his brother Lucius, probably in an attack of mental derangement, took his own life on July 4, 1834.[22] Whether these personal misfortunes were the only reason or whether financial considerations already played a role in his decision to move to Texas cannot be determined with absolute certainty. It is known that he had been told about Texas by his friend James W. Fannin[23] and in 1836 was looking after the interests of a land speculation company.[24] In July, 1835, he arrived in Texas, went back to Georgia again in November, and at the end of March, 1836, returned to Texas, where he joined Sam Houston's army.

As secretary of war Lamar represented the opinion that Santa Anna should

Mirabeau Buonaparte Lamar (1798–1859), poet, ardent Indian fighter, second president of the Republic, and gifted orator. *Courtesy Archives Division, Texas State Library*

be condemned and hanged.[25] In order to remove the troublemaker from his cabinet, Burnet appointed him commander-in-chief of the army on June 25, 1836, for Rusk was no longer in possession of any authority with the troops and had asked to be relieved.[26] However, things went no better for Lamar than for Rusk.[27] In desperation he wrote to Burnet that everything was in a state of disintegration.[28] Burnet, pressed in this manner from all sides and confronted with difficulties, took to flight by advancing. After all, he and his cabinet had been appointed by the constitutional convention only as an interim government, and in addition the rapid decay of civil and military authority in Texas had led to stagnation of help received from the United States and essentially contributed to the delay of the recognition of Texas' autonomy on the part of the United States. So, on July 23, 1836, he called for general elections to take place on September 5. To be elected were a president, vice-president, and a congress. While they were voting, Texans were also to declare whether they were for or against annexation by the United States. Only by stabilizing the situation could Texas be kept from complete collapse.

The first two candidates nominated for the office of president were Henry Smith and Stephen F. Austin. Although the latter had emphasized in various letters from previous years that he longed for rest and retirement, he was immediately ready to accept election as president, if the majority of Texans called him to this office.[29] Around the middle of August Sam Houston was spontaneously nominated at various gatherings around the country. Not until August 25 did he officially accept the nomination,[30] causing Henry Smith to withdraw his own name from candidacy—a measure that did not, however, reach the public ear, and votes were nevertheless cast for him.

At that time, as today, the question was asked why Sam Houston, after his initial refusal to be put up for election, nevertheless allowed himself to be nominated and why he hesitated so long in accepting the nomination. He himself later stated that his friendly relationship with Smith and with Austin, as well as his promise to Austin in 1833 never to run for a civil office against him, had kept him from the candidacy.[31] He had then made himself available, he said, to save Texas from stalemate, for Smith as the leader of the Wharton party and Austin as the head of the Austin party represented the opposite poles of two almost equally strong groups that would never have tolerated the victory of the other side at any time.[32] This explanation by Houston can be accepted at best only in a modified form. As the events of the election showed, Austin received nearly four times as many votes as Smith did.

Although nominated and voted for, Smith was the worst candidate possible for the presidency. William Fairfax Gray had met him in February, 1836, when he was still governor and described him in his journal as an uneducated, uninformed man possessed by extreme prejudices.[33] Smith hated Austin and blamed him for his every grievance; he reviled him whenever he could and demanded that he be hanged.[34] Not only did his implacable and intolerant behavior make him a bad candidate for the presidency, but his tyrannical administration as governor also boded no good for Texas in case of his election. Perhaps Houston only waited long enough to see if another candidate who might succeed would offer himself for election and, when this did not occur, felt forced to allow himself to be placed in nomination for the office.[35] At the same time, the long delay and hesitation may have been caused by his wound and the healing process in New Orleans, as well as by the tactical consideration that in this way he could avoid an exhausting campaign and come forward as if drafted for the office without any desire for power.

The election results—as Stephen F. Austin feared[36]—were an overwhelming success for Sam Houston. He received 3,585 votes, Austin 551, Smith 144, T. J. Green 42, T. J. Rusk 1, and Branch T. Archer 4.[37] The question is now raised why Stephen F. Austin, on whom in the fall of 1835—only a year before—the decision for war or peace in Texas had depended, had received only 15.4 percent of the number of votes Sam Houston received in this important election and in doing so only 12.7 percent of the total votes.

In August of 1836 Stephen Austin himself named two points that he had heard would be used against him to harm him and prevent his election. The one was that he had participated in the Monclova land speculation of his friend and secretary Williams, and the other that he was supposed to have been responsible for the considerate treatment afforded Santa Anna.[38] The second point he rightly rejected; "That man was saved by Gen. Houston, as you know better than I do."[39] This was true, was generally known, and still did not prevent 82.8 percent of the electorate from casting their votes for Sam Houston—a circumstance that illuminates how little weight was actually given to this argument. Significantly more difficult is any consideration of the first point.

Gail Borden, Jr., in August, 1836, wrote his friend Austin that, because of what was being said, his old friends were uncertain whether Austin had been involved in that infamous land speculation. They could not support him until he had definitively declared he had had nothing to do with these affairs.[40] Austin wrote back to Borden immediately and had his long answer printed and distributed as a flyer. His words were unequivocal: "I never had been and am not, concerned or interested in those speculations directly nor indirectly."[41] However, his denial had no effect.

But Austin was not the only presidential candidate about whom bad things were being repeated. It was circulated about Houston that he had accepted honors that did not belong to him, he was a drunkard, and his retreat from Santa Anna had been a sign of cowardice.[42] Still, these accusations obviously had no great influence on the election, which leads back to Austin and the question of why he had fallen so out of favor with Texans. Now and then the argument is suggested in the literature that many newly arrived settlers did not know Austin at all, but everyone had heard of Old

San Jacinto.[43] This supposition, however, is based on an unsound foundation, for in the fall of 1835 Austin was able to unite at least 50 percent of Texans behind him. In the following year of war it is true that some families left, but they returned after San Jacinto. Under no circumstances, however, were around 80 percent of the 1836 population of Texas newcomers in that war year when Austin was in the United States, which might have explained Austin's decrease in popularity from about 50 percent to 15 percent as a result of new arrivals. Consequently the attitude of a lot of one-time Austin adherents must have changed.

It may certainly have been significant that in the decisive period of the war he had not been in Texas but in the United States, and was supposed to be living a riotous life there, as some had charged.[44] He emphasized, of course, that along with Wharton and Archer he had worked hard for Texas, but in contrast to his earlier missions in Mexico the delegation achieved no visible results for the colonists. Perhaps also some could not accept his radical change from Mexican patriot to declared enemy of Mexico. For a man who had always represented himself as moderate, cautious in his policies, and a liberal, the words that he addressed very officially to President Jackson, to both Houses of the Congress, and to the public at large sounded strange: "A war of extermination is raging in Texas—a war of barbarism and of despotic principles, waged by the mongrel Spanish-Indians and Negro race, against civilization and the Anglo-American race."[45]

This polemic corresponded much more to the style of a Henry Smith and was in all its points contrary to what Austin had publicly stated only a year before.[46] Such "overzealousness" may have harmed him just as his immediate acceptance of the nomination for president may have done. He stressed that he had agreed to be put up for office only on the insistence of his friends and only for the public good; but he hesitated much longer when he was asked by Sam Houston to take on the office of secretary of state in the new government. Austin had been ready immediately to neglect his private life and his weakened health for the office of president, but at Houston's offer these were all at once sufficient reason for a refusal. Houston, nevertheless, had Austin confirmed by the senate for that office, and so he could no longer avoid the duty.[47]

To what extent the subject of land speculation was an important reason for Austin's sinking reputation among the settlers cannot be answered with absolute certainty. Even more than the accusation itself, his exaggerated denial, which was simply too pat, certainly harmed him. His explanation that he had learned of the extent of the Monclova speculations only a few days before the charges were made in August, 1836, completely contradicts his letters to Samuel M. Williams of April 15 and 29, 1835.[48] His vehement rejection of this speculation affair appears scarcely to have been based on his true feelings but rather on political opportunism, if one keeps in mind the letter from Austin to his brother-in-law James F. Perry from Quintana in December, 1835, in which he expressed himself at length about his land speculation objectives and related business with Williams and McKinney.[49]

When in August, 1836, he condemned Williams's actions and strictly rejected having had a part in any speculation, Williams was understandably angered and reminded Austin of their old friendship.[50] Austin became more reasonable. Nevertheless, a further reconciliation of the former partners did not come about, for Austin died on December 27 and at that time Williams was in Baltimore for the purpose of selling the land certificates of Toby & Brothers, the company associated with the Quintana Project, in which, as mentioned above, Austin was decidedly interested.[51]

Austin's defeat in the election of September 5, 1836, must thus be viewed as resulting from a combination of factors that amounted to the same thing: for the majority of Texans, Stephen F. Austin had become untrustworthy.

With the bonus of being a victorious general who had in addition cleverly kept out of political party quarrels, it was easy for Sam Houston to win the presidential election. Mirabeau B. Lamar was elected vice-president, and the majority of Texans declared themselves in the attached referendum to be in favor of annexation by the United States.[52] On October 3, 1836, all the elected delegates met in Columbia and established the First Congress of the Republic of Texas. On October 22 the interim president, David G. Burnet, stepped down from his office, and Sam Houston took his oath. At the end of November Santa Anna was released from imprisonment and at his own request taken to Washington, D.C., to confer with President Jackson before sailing for Vera Cruz.[53] Provided with a government equipped to do business, Texas now had to set to work to solve its domestic and foreign problems.

12. Domestic Policies

Sam Houston's first term as president of the Republic of Texas lasted from October 22, 1836, to December 10, 1838; his second was from December 12, 1841, to December 9, 1844. In between lay the presidency of Mirabeau B. Lamar and afterward—until February 19, 1846—came that of Anson Jones. A problem with which the Spaniards had already had to contend and the management of which clearly showed the distinct dispositions and characters of the two most important and opposed presidents, Houston and Lamar, was the Indian question.

Two tribes primarily provided the agitation in Texas: the Cherokees and the Comanches. Houston attempted to achieve a peaceful coexistence by negotiation, but Lamar sought confrontation. From the beginning Houston had had contact with various Cherokee chiefs in Texas. When war broke out in Texas, many feared the Indians would join with the Mexicans and attack from the rear. In order to prevent this, after protracted negotiations, Sam Houston for Texas and Chief Tewulle (or Colonel Bowl, as he was also called) for the Cherokees concluded a treaty on February 23, 1836. It promised the Texans the neutrality of the Indians and promised the Indians land—the land where they in fact already lived but which did not belong to them legally according to Mexican and Texan law.[1] Although the agreement kept the Texans' backs free in their fight against Mexico, it still became a fiasco—especially for the Cherokees. The Texas government simply did not recognize the treaty. Sam Houston pressured the Texas senate to ratify it as quickly as possible and tried to have a reassuring effect on Chief Tewulle: the Indians, he told him, would get the land promised them in the treaty.[2] But the senate committee handling Indian affairs, which Lamar chaired, continued to delay its report and finally, after ten months of deliberation, rejected the treaty with hypercritical legal arguments.[3] On the one hand, they said, Tewulle had not actually been the authorized agent of all the tribes cited in the text, as had been alleged; on the other hand, Houston could not have legally represented Texas, for he had received his mandate from the provisional government and it no longer existed at the conclusion of the treaty because Smith, as governor, as well as the Council had mutually dismissed each other. The Texans could not turn the land over to the Indians, becaust it belonged to an empresario contract that carried priority, and in addition there had been Indian depredations in spite of the peace treaty.

These depredations had actually been committed by other tribes than those joining in the treaty, but the committee did not distinguish here between the individual classifications of Indians. Thereupon in 1838 some of the disillusioned Indians joined Vicente Cordova, who was supposedly forming auxiliary troops for General Filisola, commander of the Mexican army in Matamoros, for a renewed attack on Texas by the Mexicans. This in turn, as well as a conspiracy by Tewulle and Cordova against Texas in the year 1835, which had been revealed, was used by Lamar, who had meanwhile become president, as the reason for announcing a war against the Indians in his message to congress of December 21, 1838.[4] Lamar called up an army and drove all the Indian tribes in the east out of Texas, except for two, which still live on their small reservation near Livingston: the Alabamas and the Coushattas.

In western Texas the Comanche tribes were a dominant force. They were also attacked by the army.[5] Sam Houston once more was able, in fact, to conclude peace with the Comanches, but fights flared up again and again until all the Comanches were driven out of Texas after the Civil War. With his policy of extermination and dispersion, Lamar not only acted in the spirit of many Texans who rejoiced at being able to hang Indians,[6] but was also in this area a much more faithful supporter of Andrew Jackson than Houston had ever been. Such a statement may be misleading, for Lamar was never a follower of Jackson and this negative attitude toward Indians was widespread in the United States.[7] Still, Andrew Jackson was the president who pursued the Indians most frankly and directly: "Indian removal . . . was the most arduous part of my duty, and I watched over it with great vigilance."[8]

In 1832 Jackson also created a precedent when he made a Supreme Court decision appear ridiculous and in fact abrogated it. John Marshall, the chief justice of the highest court in the land, had proclaimed in a decision that the old rights of the Cherokees to their land in Georgia were valid and that the state had no right to disperse them. Thereupon Jackson declared: "John Marshall has made his decision, now let him enforce it."[9] With that the rout of the Indians continued—sanctioned by the president.

Already in 1825 in the battle for the land of the Indians in Georgia a young man had come into prominence because he drew up the governor's proclamation that, in case of doubt, Georgia would march against the Creeks and Cherokees with its militia. His name was Mirabeau B. Lamar.[10]

Thus Lamar already had practice when in 1839 he again marched against the Indians. As in Georgia, so too in Texas, it was not even a matter of the protection of white settlers against the "red barbarians," as his flowery rhetoric might have intimated, but simply for land. Lamar had the idea that he could reduce the Texas debts if he drove out the Indian tribes in the east, brought the land gained in this way under public ownership, and then sold it profitably.[11] But this aroused the anger not only of Sam Houston but also of many citizens who felt betrayed by Lamar's two-faced actions. Although a legal argument not to ratify the treaty with the Cherokees had been that the land in question was part of an empresario contract and already settled by white families, now it was suddenly declared that the land belonged to the state and could be sold by it.[12] This Cherokee land bill, with which Lamar attempted to turn his idea into a law, finally failed, and not least because of Sam Houston's embittered opposition.[13]

Lamar's campaign against the Indians had cost the state, already deep in debt, $2,552,319. That was, moreover, not the only expensive venture that the president had begun. One point in his electioneering against Houston had been that Houston had practiced an inflationary policy by issuing paper money in the total amount of $800,000. But for Houston this had also been the limit, and he had prevented a law that would have set the upper limit for issuing money at $1 million.[14] The value of these notes in the summer of 1838 ran at 65 cents to the American dollar. At the end of Lamar's term in office, the amount of the notes, which had been issued in a new red design, had risen to $3,552,800. Their value in November of 1841 was between 12 and 15 cents.[15] Lamar realized now that he had to do something about this precarious financial situation.

The plan that he thereupon formed and implemented against the vote of the Congress was a fiasco. The state treasury was to be filled by means of a trade agreement with Santa Fe and Cuba. Theoretically a business connection with these two centers of trade promised great profits. Practically, however, this idea, which Lamar pursued with enthusiasm,[16] had against it, for one thing, that no relationships with Spain, to whom Cuba belonged, much less any trade agreement, existed and, for another, that Santa Fe did not lie in Texas at all but was plainly in Mexico. But it was this last point that Lamar viewed entirely otherwise. He was dreaming of a Texas empire.[17] This empire would stretch from the Gulf of Mexico to the Pacific Ocean.[18] In connection with this he rejected any thought of annexation by the United States. Texas was strong enough, according to him, to assert itself and would grow even more powerful.[19] The western border that the Republic of Texas gave itself on its own authority during its ten years of existence was just as fantastic as Lamar's plans and was never recognized by either Mexico or the United States. Texas was also at no time in a position to actually claim this territory or be able to settle or defend it.[20] Nevertheless, according to the Texas definition of the border, Santa Fe belonged to Texas. In addition, Lamar firmly believed that the inhabitants of Santa Fe would be happy to live under Texas sovereignty.[21]

All these thoughts and ideas induced him to outfit an expedition with the aim of discontinuing the old trade route from Santa Fe to the Missouri River and steering it, so to speak, to the Texas coast. On June 21, 1841, an expeditionary force of over 300 men started off, consisting of 270 soldiers, a number of merchants and reporters, and a column of twenty-one covered wagons that were loaded with merchandise worth $200,000. The long journey of almost a thousand miles through mainly desertlike territory drained the men so much that in the end they surrendered without a fight to the Mexican troops who advanced before Santa Fe. The Mexicans confiscated the merchandise and marched their prisoners on foot into imprisonment in Mexico City. In 1844 those who were still alive were freed by a general amnesty.[22]

These ventures and an unsuccessful financial policy were the reason that the Texas debt rose the most during Lamar's term in office. When he took over, the public debt amounted to $1,886,425. When Sam Houston began his second term of office, the mountain of debt had grown to $7,446,740 under Lamar's leadership. When Anson Jones lowered the flag of the republic in 1846, Texas had government debts amounting to $9,949,007.[23] But in spite of Lamar's evident incompetence in financial matters, his racism, and his excessive nationalism, during his term in office he introduced two laws that were not only immensely advanced for that time but were also of importance for the further development of Texas.

On January 26, 1839, Lamar signed the Homestead Exemption Act. This was a law protecting against home seizure. In bankruptcy sales and legal executions on the property of a debtor, the house and means of livelihood could not be seized from the head of a family. Provision had to be made that enough possessions were left to guarantee the continuation of work and accordingly the survival of the family. Although Spanish law and then Mexican law had provided for some small protection for articles such as the clothes on one's back, these provisions nevertheless were scarcely put to use. The Texas homestead act was adapted to the economic circumstances during the course of the years and remained the most advanced regulation in the United States in this sphere.[24]

The second law, which Lamar signed on the same day as the Homestead

Exemption Act, was the Education Act. It provided that three leagues of land in each county be set aside to establish schools in the county. Fifty leagues of land were to be surveyed for the creation of two universities or colleges. With the proceeds from rent, leases, or sale of these pieces of land the respective places of education were to be financed and maintained.[25] Although it then took some years before this regulation was transformed into actuality everywhere and a public school system established, the foundation for an independent, self-sufficient educational system had been set in place. One of the products of that educational policy was the founding in 1881 of the University of Texas, which owns about 2,109,000 acres of land that derives its particular value from the fact that oil was discovered on it in 1923 and with this chief source of revenue makes it the wealthiest public university in the country.[26]

For Lamar, education had been a major concern of his policy.[27] Since these concerns of Lamar particularly reflect his membership in the Freemasons, it should be emphasized here that credit universally is due the Masons for having decisively promoted and shaped public education.[28] In spite of these positive initiatives, Lamar's reputation had sunk so far in the public eye, because of the disastrous outcome of the Santa Fe expedition, that he had no political future in Texas anymore.[29]

If so much has been said up to this point about Lamar's term in office in connection with the domestic policies of the Republic of Texas, it was only because he turned to dramatic and drastic measures to solve the problems. Less spectacular but more effective was the course of Sam Houston's two terms. His efforts to achieve a peaceful understanding with the Indians by treaty were certainly devastated by Lamar's brutal actions. Beside the reassurance of various domestic groups, the main effort of his work lay primarily in the area of foreign affairs. Domestically his concerns were directed toward the army and the navy, aimed at calming them and keeping them busy, and toward the final determination of the seat of government and the finances of the republic.[30]

To explain all the complexities of these finances here would be to go too far.[31] Let it only be mentioned once more that the battle against a rapidly growing mountain of debt was a primary effort in the terms of office of each president. Because taxes could scarcely be raised and there was no wish to raise them and thus nip business and industry in the bud, other ways had to be found. One means of financing pressing work was by taking out loans, which, however, were very hard to get and only enlarged the burden of debt of the republic more quickly. Thus the formula by means of which the United States had paid its debts up to 1836 and still maintained a surplus in the household budget was relied upon: the sale of public land. Although there was an excess of it, the balance at hand did not grow: expenses mounted more quickly than income and also, the republic was forced to lure settlers with cheap lands, if not actually land that was given away for nothing, and it dared not frighten them away with high land prices.

Certainly one group profited from the sale of land: the speculators. Although at first they had even been angered by the law that had declared the Monclova transactions null and void without exception,[32] the land business had been ignited again by the distribution of land certificates by the republic. One aspiration bound the speculators to the government of Sam Houston. Both needed annexation by the United States—the one in order to be able to make the expected profit from United States land prices, and the other to be able to protect the nation from bankruptcy with the assumption of the Texas debt by the United States. Consequently, the speculators were a driving force working in the United States for a speedy annexation of Texas.[33]

13. Foreign Policy and Annexation by the United States

Next to financial policy, foreign policy was the greatest problem for the president and the congress of the Republic of Texas. Strictly speaking, the two areas can scarcely be separated, for a part of the foreign policy consisted particularly of improving the finances of the republic. For the short term the attempt was made to do this by taking out loans and for the long term by trade agreements. In order to have a good position in negotiations with the United States regarding an early diplomatic confirmation, Texas eagerly endeavored to get recognition in Europe and to be able to conclude bilateral treaties. But achieving all this was not easy, for Texas relationships with the various European powers did not depend only on mutual goodwill but decidedly on the relationship of the respective countries with Mexico and the United States. Because of their diplomatic connections with those two nations, it had not remained a secret to the Europeans that Texas had become a bone of contention between them. Recognition of Texas and any kind of trade agreement could be guided and realized only with regard to their own positions toward the United States and Mexico.[1]

Special minister James Pinckney Henderson, who was sent by President Houston in 1837 first to England and then to France, knew this well. When Lord Henry John Temple Palmerston, an especially significant person in English politics, who at the time held the office of foreign minister, received the Texas envoy, Texas was no new subject for Great Britain.

In 1825 the first American minister in Mexico City, Joel R. Poinsett, was forced to learn that the British chargé d'affaires in Mexico, Henry Ward, was already successfully working against the United States. The old mistrust left over from Spanish times, which still prejudiced Mexicans against the United States, had been somewhat reduced by the quick recognition of Mexican independence on the part of the United States—but then, because of the unseemly delay of the United States in sending a minister, it was ignited again. Ward's policy consisted of discrediting the United States in the person of its ambassador.[2] Poinsett, however, brought this about all by himself by his use of imprudent tactics and his interference in Mexican domestic policies. Butler, too, saw that he was exposed to British opposition when he was attempting to promote the purchase of Texas by the United States. This was based on two things. First, the United States was a trade rival of the British. Secondly, the British were intent on limiting the territorial expansion and thereby the enlargement of the United States' area of influence.

Here the economic motives cannot be clearly separated from the political. The Spanish trade monopoly in Central and South America had long been a thorn in the side of the British, who had therefore supported the various freedom movements with vigor. Actually, in the first phase of these struggles, they had to restrain themselves, for they had entered into an alliance with Spain against Napoleon, but after 1815 they could devote themselves again to South America.[3] In 1822 England established consular relationships with Mexico and shortly afterward recognized its independence together with that of Colombia and Argentina.[4]

When one considers that, on the one hand, toward the end of the eighteenth century England regarded the West Indian islands to be more valuable than Canada and with generous credit made the new South American states dependent on itself and, on the other hand, that 58.3 percent of the exports of the United States in 1801 went to the West Indies and Central and South America,[5] it is not difficult to understand that in this large market, which was slipping further and further away from Spain, the English and the Americans faced each other as rivals.[6] Thus in Great Britain the American efforts to buy Texas from Mexico were viewed with a certain uneasiness. When the discussion here concerns England or Great Britain, what is meant are only the government and the circles immediately around it, for up until the middle of the nineteenth century there was no interest in Texas among the British people.[7]

In contrast, after the Texas declaration of independence became known, the British House of Commons immediately devoted itself on August 6, 1836, to the problems that were seen approaching because of the new situation. Three points primarily occupied the members of Parliament. How would a recognition of Texas affect British trade? How could territorial expansion be prevented? And how should the slavery question in Texas be handled? The result of the debate was a decision to wait and see if the Texas independence movement would have a successful conclusion after all.[8]

Henderson's arrival answered that question and caused Palmerston to refer again to the other questions debated in Parliament. To be sure, he formulated the three points less as questions than as considerations that stood in the way of the recognition of Texas by Great Britain. Although trade with Mexico and the dreaded territorial expansion of the United States played an important part, the slavery question presented the greatest obstacle for the foreign minister.[9]

William Wilberforce, a member of sixty-nine welfare organizations and head of the Evangelicals, had been leading a crusade against slavery in the British Parliament since 1788. In 1807 the Evangelicals had their first success with the prohibition of the slave trade in the British colonies and in 1833 with the universal abolition of slavery in Great Britain.[10] Public opinion in Great Britain was very much set against slavery; the recognition of a country such as Texas, which had slavery written into its constitution, would therefore be very questionable, Palmerston said.[11] The only thing that Great Britain finally declared itself ready for was a trade agreement with Texas. Because no formal recognition could be achieved, Henderson journeyed on to Paris, where he arrived on March 23, 1838.

France had somewhat less difficulty than England in arriving at a mutually satisfactory relationship with Texas. The only thing that stood in the way of the immediate conclusion of a treaty on the part of France was its diplomatic relationship with Mexico. However, at just that time, this became noticeably worse. Many French citizens and merchants who lived and worked in Mexico had made claims against their host country because their property had been damaged or destroyed. The Mexican government refused to satisfy these claims. Thereupon, on March 21, 1838, an ultimatum from his government was given to Mexico by Baron Deffaudis, the French minister, according to which the Mexicans had until May 15 to pay $600,000 in damages. But they refused to pay; war was declared. After the French had first bombarded Vera Cruz from the sea, the Mexicans, under the leadership of Santa Anna—who was again styled the savior of his homeland—defeated the French in a land battle. Then the Britons, to cap it all off, intervened, for the French sea blockade was damaging British trade. A treaty of peace and friendship was concluded between Mexico and France on March 9, 1839.[12]

While this conflict lasted, France continued to delay an arrangement with Texas. Henderson tried to make clear to the foreign minister, Count Louis-Mathieu Molé, the advantages of a trade agreement with his country. Texas was an agricultural, not an industrial, country, he explained. It had raw materials to export and had to import manufactured goods—above all, luxury goods. In Texas tobacco, sugar, indigo, rice, and especially cotton were to be had of the best quality and in large quantities, and the Texans wanted to bring in the popular French wines and liquors, silks, and wools.[13] France, which certainly did not want to let England and America have any potentially profitable new market to themselves, nevertheless wished first to wait for the report of a special envoy, Alphonse Dubois de Saligny.[14] Henderson, who became impatient, suggested that France could in any event sign a trade agreement with Texas, as England and the United States had done.[15] And this did occur at the beginning of November, 1838.

Further negotiations were delayed by France, since concessions that Henderson was not prepared to make were expected from Gen. James Hamilton, a Texas diplomat soon to arrive. Tired of the dickering about percents in connection with the tariffs, Henderson finally gave in – also at Hamilton's urging – and so on September 25, 1839, a friendship and trade agreement could be concluded that provided a far better situation for the export of French goods than for the import of Texas merchandise.[16] Henderson was, to be sure, not satisfied with the details, but he had, nevertheless, brought it about that France, as the first European country to do so, recognized Texas as an independent nation according to international law. The second European country to follow France's land was Holland, where Hamilton was able to conclude agreements on September 18, 1840.[17]

England, which was now afraid it would fall behind the others, on November 13 and 14, 1840, after relatively brief negotiations, put its seal on three contracts at once with the Republic of Texas: a trade convention; a mediation pact, by which Texas would be granted a credit of over a million pounds sterling for any peace treaty between Mexico and Texas that Great Britain helped bring about; and a support alliance for opposition to slavery, which certainly brought much vexation to the Lamar government's domestic policy. The Houston faction reproached Lamar for a sellout of Texas interests.

Texas was also involved with Belgium concerning recognition and the conclusion of trade agreements. Right after Henderson's appearance in the political arena in London, King Leopold I considered opening relations with this aspiring new republic in order to help the progress of the economy of his kingdom, which had also become independent, from the Netherlands, only very recently. But throughout the long negotiations the Belgian government could not reach any resolve, and so there remained only attempts and treaty drafts that were never ratified.[18] The results were similar to those of the treaty of friendship, trade, and shipping between Texas and the free Hanseatic cities of Lübeck, Bremen, and Hamburg. It was drawn up on April 17, 1844, by the Texas representative in the Netherlands, William Henry Daingerfield, and the resident minister of the three Hanseatic cities in Paris, Vincent Rumpff, but could not be ratified by the Texas government anymore.[19]

As a second concern, along with diplomatic recognition, the Texas intermediaries were involved in trying to borrow money from various European states. These negotiations, however, failed. If one disregards the diplomatic and constitutional implications, no great success was achieved for any length of time by the concluded trade and friendship treaties either. France's envoy to Texas, Dubois de Saligny, allowed himself some unautho- rized actions and improprieties, was more interested in his own well being than that of France,[20] and contributed little to a positive relationship be- tween the two countries.[21]

England, which had less interest in Texas itself than in its position in the interplay of forces between Mexico and the United States primarily endeav- ored to achieve something for Texas in Mexico–that is, to prevail upon the two countries to come to an amicable settlement–an undertaking that the Britons intensified still more when the rumors of an annexation of Texas by the United States became considerable.[22]

Texas and Mexico did try, of course, to find a peaceful solution to their problems, but ideas about the "how" were fundamentally divergent. The Texans investigated various ways to persuade Mexico to recognize their in- dependence. From diplomatic advances with the aid of British offers of media- tion to guarded threats of support by the Texas navy of the rebellion that was again heating up in Yucatán, the governments of Lamar and Houston left nothing untried to motivate Mexico to be more reasonable.[23] Mexico, on the other hand, let it be understood that it was ready to forgive and forget the horror and injustice of the war, if only Texas would recognize Mexican sovereignty. That in turn was unacceptable to the Texans.[24] How- ever, diplomatic advances on the part of both sides were not the only way to promote their claims.

Rumors that Mexican troops were marching into Texas again circulated furiously in the early years of the republic, to be sure, but beyond massive troop concentrations in the vicinity of the Rio Grande, the Texas-Mexican border, Bustamantes' plan to retake Texas did not develop. Santa Anna, who had sunk greatly in public esteem because of his defeat and capitulation, rose again in the favor of the population because of his victory against the French on December 5, 1838, and was once more elected president. But the hopes that many Texans attached to his election–that he would honor the Treaties of Velasco that he had made and recognize Texas–was not fulfilled. Instead, he took the miscarried attempt of Texans to conquer Santa Fe as cause to put an army on the march against Texas once more. General Rafael Vásquez moved into Texas and on March 5, 1842, took San Antonio with- out resistance.[25] But the Mexicans made no preparations to stay. Actually, other parts of the army had taken Goliad and Refugio; but after a two-day stay the troops left Texas again without having done any material damage. As a result, all of Texas was thrown into a frenzy of wild enthusiasm for war, in which many hoped to gain immortal fame by conquering Mexico.[26] Only with effort could Houston apply brakes to the forces that, by march- ing into Mexico, wanted to prevent a renewed Mexican invasion, which seemed to be prefaced by General Vásquez's military action.[27] But inasmuch as there was no question of such an invasion and it quickly became evident to everyone, the militia that had gathered to defend San Antonio soon dispersed.[28]

Consequently, Texas was completely surprised by the second Mexican wave of aggression under General Adrian Woll on September 11, 1842. Like his predecessor Vásquez, Woll took San Antonio without a fight but, in contrast to him, intended to stay there. Sam Houston declared a general mobilization.[29] After an engagement on Salado Creek, six miles east of San Antonio, on September 18, that caused far more casualties to the Mexicans than to the Texans, General Woll withdrew to Mexico on September 20 and from there sent out negotiators on September 26 to conclude an armistice. This was signed in 1844 but never ratified, for it stated that Texas was a part of Mexico.[30]

In contrast to Houston's success in calming the Texans in March and April of 1842 and preventing rash action, in December a group of three hundred men under Thomas Jefferson Green and William S. Fisher disobeyed the orders of their commander, Gen. Alexander Somervell, to turn back from Laredo to their winter quarters at Gonzales and instead marched into Mexico. Like the Santa Fe expedition, this venture—called the Mier expedition after the place of the Texans' defeat—was a complete fiasco.[31] The survivors were taken into Mexican captivity and not released until 1844 with their fellow Santa Fe prisoners when Santa Anna was overthrown and José Herrera came into power. Herrera's latitude of action in what followed was, however, limited not only by an opposition that was gaining strength and was a threat to him but also by the annexation negotiations that were meanwhile being conducted openly between the United States and Texas.

The question of annexation was always the center of relationships between the United States and Texas. As has been mentioned, at the election for the various offices of the Republic on October 5, 1836, the Texans were also to cast their votes for or against annexation. The majority of Texans voted for union with the United States.[32] William H. Wharton, who had been sent to Washington as a special ambassador, first to achieve recognition of independence and then annexation, was—as was all Texas—thunderstruck when Andrew Jackson, the man who had sought with all means available to him to buy Texas from Mexico, advised caution in a message to the Congress of the United States on December 21, 1836.[33] For Wharton this was especially incomprehensible, for on June 1 of that year, at an evening meal in the family circle, the president had given him to understand that he was negotiating with Mexico and that Texas would soon be ceded to the United States.[34] Not only had President Jackson apparently, and for many inexplicably, changed his mind, Sam Houston too posed a riddle for

Wharton and other contemporaries as to where he stood on the question of annexation.

At the end of May, Wharton reported for the first time that a rumor was abroad to the effect that Houston was against union with the United States.[35] James Morgan, who was certainly critical of Houston, if not absolutely hostile to him, launched letters to the public several times in which he accused Houston of working against annexation, and which then brought strong denials from Wharton.[36] Ashbel Smith, who was in England and France from 1842 to 1844 as chargé d'affaires for Texas, had close contacts with Houston and was of the opinion that Houston was basically against annexation and favored a union in the beginning only on account of the weakness of the young republic.[37]

The basis for the question as to where Houston actually stood on annexation lies not only in rumors and the opinions of other persons but in his own contradictory statements. He informed his cousin John H. Houston on November 20, 1836: "By all means get Texas annexed to the U. States,"[38] and to Robert A. Irion on March 19, 1837: "Annexation wou'd have rendered me truly happy, and secured all that we contended for."[39] But he then appeared either to have changed his opinion by May, 1844, or never to have made up his mind absolutely, when he wrote to William S. Murphy: "The Union of Oregon, and Texas, will be much more natural and convenient, than for either separately to belong to the U States."[40] But taken out of context these lines falsify Houston's intentions, which are clearly revealed in this letter and elsewhere.

To him it was clear, as it was to Andrew Jackson, that Texas and its annexation by the United States stood not as a problem isolated in space, but as an entity that was nationally as well as internationally at the mercy of various forces. The connection that Houston was establishing in his letter to Murphy, the American chargé d'affaires in Texas, between Oregon, California, Chihuahua, Sonora, and Texas was a warning and a threat to the United States should the annexation negotiations still fail. Many times in the years 1844 and 1845 Houston had to play that card and permit it to be played—namely, that Texas could maintain itself independently and choose its partners how and where it wanted. But the whole time he knew that only annexation to the United States was reasonable and desirable, though it was also necessary that favorable terms should be effected for Texas.[41] So when there were difficulties in the negotiations, Houston would immediately emphasize that they were strong enough, if need be, to be able to remain independent.[42] And not only Houston had to use such tactics; Andrew Jackson's hands were also tied.

Two big problems faced him in relation to Texas: one foreign and one domestic. As was previously mentioned, it was his declared aim to gain Texas for the Union. Anthony Butler had, however, foundered in this mission, for he had not understood that to Jackson the reputation and unity of the United States were still above any territorial gain. William H. Wharton had also not understood the motives of the president when, at the dinner mentioned above, he protested vigorously against a settlement between the United States and Mexico, which would have brought Texas into the Union through negotiations.[43] He had not recognized that Jackson could agree to an immediate annexation only if Mexico separated voluntarily from Texas or if an aggressive act of the Mexicans against the United States justified American intervention and entry into Texas.

Jackson believed that the latter possibility was the more likely, and for that reason he ordered Gen. Edmund P. Gaines to the southwest border of the United States to protect the white settlers from Indian attacks. Immediately upon his arrival Gaines also spread reports that danger threatened by the Indians was forcing him to intervene there. Encouraged by Jackson's own dubious actions in 1818 against the Indians of Florida, Gaines invented the rumors and messages, for the Indians at that time were completely peaceful in the area.[44] Spurred on by calls for assistance from Austin and entreaties from Houston, Gaines crossed the border and for a time occupied Nacogdoches.[45] This happened, however, *after* the Texans had won at San Jacinto and no reason existed anymore for intervention by American troops. Because no danger was present, Gaines had violated Jackson's precept of neutrality. Although Jackson sanctioned the action against the Indians, he condemned the breach in existing treaties between Mexico and the United States.[46] Gaines had again, just as Butler had, discredited Jackson himself and the United States in general with the Mexicans by his legally questionable conduct. The Mexican minister in Washington, D.C., Manuel de Gorostiza, protested vigorously against U.S. involvement in Texas. The State Department rejected the protests, but Jackson could therefore make no allowances in Texas. As much as he wanted to include this territory in the Union, he could now do nothing hastily, if he did not want to provoke a war with Mexico and submit the unity of the United States to a test of strength.

Slavery and, connected with it, sectionalism had become a great problem for which a generally satisfactory solution could no longer be found. It was only a matter of delaying an open break or armed conflict as much as possible by compromise. Because it was a stubborn struggle between two relatively equal forces—the North, which was becoming ever more industrialized, and the agrarian, feudalistic South—each side watched the other suspiciously in order to be able to act immediately against any unilateral increase in strength.[47]

Texas, which had written slavery into its constitution, would strengthen

173

the Southern states, a situation which many Northerners feared. During the debates in Congress about the rights of the slaveholding states and the demands of the abolitionists from the Northern states, Texas had become the snag on which lines of argument were caught.[48] Although the abolitionists in the House of Representatives, led by John Quincy Adams, who had been converted to a declared enemy of slavery by Benjamin Lundy, saw in Texas an attempt by the slaveholders to increase their influence, many Southerners reproached the Northerners for deserting their brothers and sisters and abandoning Texas to the Europeans. But attempting to see the conflict over Texas only from the aspect of the North and the South, of abolitionist and those who favored slavery would be to oversimplify it and consequently to adulterate it.

The expansionists, who often had close connections with the land speculators and thus furnished a further reason to reject Texas, also provided irritation and the further development of two camps.[49] In this connection affiliation with the opponents, as with the supporters, can scarcely be determined along regional lines alone. There is one criterion that helps to characterize the two camps in addition to the North-South preference: the division by political parties.

As has already been discussed in reference to the support for the Texas War of Independence, American political opinion at that time was divided according to the party allegiance of those concerned. The two parties, the Whig Party and the Democratic Party, were, however, not totally united internally but broke down in the South and the North to some extent into very recognizable little groups and factions, which often led to disagreement and conflict within the parties themselves.[50] In general, however, one can begin by assuming that the Whigs at first declared themselves to be against the annexation of Texas, and the Democrats were for it. This party structure was continually changing and changed considerably under various political influences in the ten years of the Republic, so that one cannot start altogether from a fixed pattern in the Texas question at that time.

When the problem of annexation appeared in 1836, it faced a broad front of rejection. The opponents of slavery and the Whigs had banded together against the Democrats.[51] Even though the abolitionists and the Whigs are all too often treated as one, this is wrong unless a distinction is made within the Whig Party. The parties were, after all, not homogeneous structures but broke down into regional components that were always fighting. In the election for the presidency in 1828, the Democrats could still be designated in general as the party of the South, while the Whigs had to be viewed as a coalition of various regional and political strengths that coincided chiefly only in their opposition to the policies of Andrew Jackson and the Democrats.[52] Although the Whigs in the North stood opposed to the acceptance of Texas into the Union because of their opposition to slavery, in the South they nevertheless expressed themselves as being against annexation exactly because of their support of slavery. If this sounds paradoxical, on closer reflection the motives are completely intelligible.

The Whigs in the Southern states belonged for the most part to the plantation aristocracy. However, it was this very group that spoke in the beginning against the annexation of Texas, for an independent Texas had more advantages for them. For one thing, they were afraid of the competition of the cheap, good, and abundantly available cotton from Texas, and for another they were hoping for help in the case of necessity.[53] Some men in the Southern states foresaw that the break with the North was unavoidable. They already surmised quite accurately at that time that Great Britain would wait it out and not help the Southern states in an armed conflict. The economically stronger North was not dependent on trade, as the South was with its agricultural products, and would win the war that must inevitably come. But England and other nations would carry on trade with an independent Texas. Texas as a free nation could assist the South and help it to victory in the war, as the former governor of South Carolina and future ambassador extraordinary from Texas, James Hamilton, wrote to Mirabeau B. Lamar in 1838.[54]

Jackson's policy consequently faced the abolitionists and a united Whig opposition. Because a presidential election was to take place again in 1836, Jackson could not act in the Texas question, as earlier in the bank crisis, and put through his views (almost) alone against all others.[55] Even though they were in the minority as opposed to the Democrats, the Whig opposition was nevertheless so strong that the outcome of the election did not appear half as certain as Jackson would like to have seen it. Daniel Webster, determined opponent of Andrew Jackson as well as of his expansionistic ideas, together with Henry Clay and John C. Calhoun, leader of the opposition, had affixed the label "King Andrew" to Jackson.[56] Because Jackson, thinking dynastically, had actually already chosen his successor and wanted him—his vice-president, Martin Van Buren—to become the next president of the United States, he did not dare to take any risk and rashly endanger Van Buren's election. After he had won, there would still be enough time.

These tactics were publicly transparent. Newspapers printed in all clarity their doubts about Jackson's "sudden" love of neutrality. He had used General Gaines as a scapegoat, they reported, to secure Texas for the Union while being able to stand there innocently himself.[57] So Jackson, who was aware of these reproaches, intentionally and out of pure political calculation restrained himself in regard to Texas without having changed his opinion concerning the territorial expansion of the United States in the slightest.

Martin Van Buren won, though only by a relatively close margin. In his election in 1828 Jackson had had 139,222 more votes than John Quincy Adams, and in 1832 actually 157,313 more than Henry Clay (and 124,205 more than all the opposing candidates together). Martin Van Buren could record for himself only 26,022 more votes than his competitors.[58] In order to make the way ready, on March 3, 1837, his last day as American president and as his last official function, Andrew Jackson recognized the Republic of Texas. Now it was incumbent on his successor to complete the work.

Still, although Martin Van Buren had gotten an operative majority as a start, he could not make use of it to annex Texas.[59] Economic problems required all his time. In addition, in 1838 John Quincy Adams once more rose to his old, rhetorical greatness and in a long speech that became famous condemned any admission of Texas and the spread of slavery that was associated with it.[60] Van Buren's rather unfortunate policies gave the Whigs so much impetus that in 1840 their candidate, William Henry Harrison, was able to defeat the incumbent Van Buren in the presidential election.[61] But, on April 4, 1841, one month after taking office, Harrison died of pneumonia. He was the first president to die in office, and with him died the program of the Whigs.

His successor, John Tyler, fell out with the party that had installed him as vice-president and was excluded from it. All the Cabinet members, with the exception of Daniel Webster, whom Harrison had named secretary of state, resigned. The rug had been pulled out from under Tyler domestically speaking, and so he turned increasingly to foreign policy, in which the president had more latitude. Webster saw it as his mission to divert Tyler from Texas and to finally conclude a treaty with Great Britain concerning the course of the Maine boundary, unsettled since 1783, which was accomplished with the signing of the appropriate document on August 9, 1842.[62] But on May 8, 1843, Webster also handed in his resignation. It had become clear to him that he could not restrain Tyler from his expansionistic plans. Men such as Thomas W. Gilmer, former governor of Virginia, and Robert J. Walker, senator from Mississippi, wrote letters that portrayed with great eloquence the advantages and urgency of the annexation of Texas and that aroused much attention through their distribution in newspapers. Gilmer, as well as Walker, who like Duff Green, Samuel Jaudon, N. Beverly Tucker, and Caleb Cushing, belonged to President Tyler's advisers, were, like the others, heavily involved in land speculation—among other places, in Texas—and were active as agents in the sale of land papers.[63]

As a successor to Webster, Tyler appointed the former secretary of the navy, Abel P. Upshur, from Virginia, who, in contrast to his predecessor, was a declared proponent of slavery. Tyler and Upshur now promoted the negotiations with Texas. On April 12, 1844, the Texas representatives Henderson and Van Zandt and John C. Calhoun, successor to Upshur, who had died, signed the annexation treaty. It provided for Texas to be admitted to the Union as a territory; all public property, including land, to be transferred to the United States; and the assumption by the United States of Texas debts up to $10 million.

On June 8, 1844, however, the Senate of the United States rejected the document by a vote of 35 to 16. On September 2, 1844, Anson Jones became president of the Republic of Texas, and in November, 1844, the Democrat James K. Polk was elected eleventh president of the United States. His campaign platform, "Re-annexation of Texas and Re-occupation of Oregon," brought him 38,181 more votes than his Whig opponent, Henry Clay. The regionally extensive distribution of agreement with Polk's expansionistic program can be seen in that he received 170 electoral votes and Clay only 105.[64] Negotiations between Texas and the United States began anew.

On February 27, 1845, the Senate of the United States voted for the annexation of Texas as a state and not as a territory.[65] On July 4 of that year, at a meeting called just for that purpose, the Texans voted likewise for annexation and at the end of August submitted a draft of a state constitution to the American Congress, which was accepted on December 29, 1845. With that, Texas had become constitutionally a state in the United States. The official conveyance ceremony took place on February 19, 1846, which Anson Jones concluded with the words: "The final act in this great drama is now performed: the Republic of Texas is no more."[66]

The dates of this "great drama" can easily be arranged in sequence, but as a mere compilation they raise questions. How was it that the Senate rejected an agreement in 1844, which Tyler as well as Upshur and Calhoun had been certain would be accepted with a two-thirds majority?[67] When the Senate had refused to accept annexation in the summer of 1844, how was it that a president was then elected in the fall of the same year who had declared himself in favor of this particular measure? Why did it still take more than a year from the time of Polk's election before Texas ran down its flag? All these questions find their answers in the shift in importance taking place at that time from domestic processes to the predominance of foreign developments.

The senators had rejected the first annexation treaty because the danger of a biased concession of advantage for the Southern states was contained in it. To accept Texas as a territory would have meant that on a later occasion three or four states could be created out of the region, which in a single leap would have led to a preponderance of Southern states in Congress. Further, some senators raised the argument that English abolitionists were working in Texas to do away with slavery there forever—an argument that was dismissed, even by many Southerners, as ridiculous.[68] Furthermore, many

Whigs feared a war with Mexico would be instigated by accepting Texas in the Union.[69] Because the elections were now imminent, no one wanted to incur the displeasure of the voters and burn their fingers on the hot iron of Texas. The Democrats decided to offer the annexation of the Oregon territory, which was claimed by both Great Britain and the United States, as a counterweight to the acceptance of Texas. As an advocate of this clearly expansionistic policy, James K. Polk, a faithful follower and student of Jackson, was elected. The Democrats stood united behind Polk and represented a clear policy, so it was not difficult to beat Henry Clay, who was not able to unite the Whigs.[70]

Although in 1844 the Senate was still cautious, because it was not known how the voters would react to such an expansionistic program with all its dangers, with the November election it had received a clear mandate for the expansion of America. To attempt to base the change on election-related events alone would, nevertheless, prove wrong, for a change in foreign policy had also begun to be distinguishable, which for many Americans had a more threatening effect than even a war with Mexico. Propaganda for the annexation of Texas had originally employed the argument that Great Britain was actively trying to help abolish slavery in Texas. Put that way, the statement seemed absurd to many slaveholders, for the attitude of the Texans was known. By virtue of a complex development that, however, slowly became clear to the public, the British onslaught suddenly appeared in a different light.

With the help of France, England had presented its case in Mexico and had suggested an agreement according to which Mexico would recognize Texan independence and it would in turn be guaranteed by England and France.[71] This was the British reaction to the rumors taking shape in Europe that the United States was about to annex Texas. These reports forced the British government to act if it wanted to prevent the union.[72] Whether this was its only aim or just an interim measure can still not be answered with certainty.

In Washington, D.C., reports arrived from Mexico that Great Britain was also trying to acquire California for itself.[73] That was no misguided idea, for since the beginning of the nineteenth century Great Britain had manifested an interest in the Pacific Coast and begun to develop a strong trade base. But the west coast of America was only a harbor and point of departure for the continually growing East Asian trade that occupied many large British firms. Since the 1830s, the British East India Company's trade with China had become ever stronger and more profitable in spite of China's restrictive policy. Wood and, above all, sea otter skins were the main objects of trade of one of the greatest financial enterprises of its time; by its merger with the North West Company in 1821, the Hudson's Bay Company had risen to be almost the exclusive master of the Oregon territory. But after the Opium War of 1839 and the official treaty of 1842 with China, British foreign trade was devoted more directly to the East Asian area. Interest in Oregon declined gradually.

Another European power also had great trade interests in the Pacific region and bases in California; after 1812 the Russians were located in Fort Ross, north of San Francisco, which controlled that important harbor area. Actually in 1824 and 1825 the Russians, after negotiations with the British and the Americans, had fixed the border of Russian Alaska at 54°40′ latitude, sold Fort Ross to John Augustus Sutter in 1841, and thus apparently withdrawn from the area,[74] but how far their interests in it actually went is difficult to ascertain. In 1838 or 1839 a plan was formed in Texas to establish diplomatic relations with Russia, for it was not burdened with prejudices either by colonies or slavery. Furthermore, the plan provided for actually realizing the claim to California with the help of British capital in order thus to enter into a firm trade alliance with Russia and Great Britain.[75] Apparently, however, nothing ever came of this scheme, which provided for the immediate dispatch of emissaries to St. Petersburg, even though Lamar was informed about the affairs of the Russians in California[76] and an engineer from the Russian Navy, a Mr. Pepin, in the company of both *Abbé* Anduze, a French agent and chaplain of the French fleet, and Mr. William A. Slacum, a special agent for the United States observing Russian activities on the Pacific Coast, surfaced in Houston in April, 1839, and, after a trip through the interior of the country, went back to the United States, again with Mr. Slacum, at the beginning of May.[77]

If these details might seem insignificant at first glance, they gain in importance through the remark of the American secretary of war, Joel R. Poinsett, who stated to the French chargé d'affaires in Texas, Dubois de Saligny, in regard to California: "There is where both the English and the Russians hope to be some day; but we know very well how to forestall them and get there ahead of them."[78] His opinion was to prove right in the end. The reports and rumors of the exercise of influence of European powers on the North American continent in a way that was likely to reduce the full scope of U.S. trade and hinder the impulses of the expansionists exerted a strong influence on the general mood of the population in the United States, something that Polk helped decisively.

The Texans, who played cleverly on this fear, were involved pro forma in negotiations with England, France, and Mexico; and so the Mexican foreign minister, Luis Cuevas, signed the first papers on the way to the recognition of Texas on May 19, 1845.[79] But the British advances were destined to fail. The British foreign minister, George Hamilton Gordon, Earl of Aberdeen, had received reports about the political atmosphere in the United

States and saw that the situation was critical for Great Britain. But in no case could a war with the United States be risked, and since the alliance with France began to drift apart, the French foreign minister, François Guizot, was forced to tell the Mexican emissary in Paris in June, 1845, that neither France nor England could ever manage to give guarantees that would force them to take up arms. Morally, however, he said, they were firmly on the side of Mexico.[80] In this way the diplomats of Europe had recognized the annexation of Texas by the United States as a fait accompli.

The evolution of Texas from a Mexican province to an independent republic was concluded. Texas had become the twenty-eighth state in the Union.

Conclusions: A Case of Manifest Destiny?

On August 23, 1843, the Mexican foreign minister José María Bocanegra had given the emissary of the United States, Waddy Thompson, to understand *expressis verbis* that the Mexican government would consider admission of Texas into the United States as a direct declaration of war.[1] Then in 1844 it was known in Mexico exactly what it might expect from a man like Polk. The Mexican minister in the United States, Juan N. Almonte, wrote on August 18, 1844, to Foreign Minister Bocanegra that an election victory for Clay would mean peace and justice for Mexico; a Polk victory would mean annexation and with it, war.[2]

In his first address to the American Congress on December 2, 1845, Polk, in confirmation of the Monroe Doctrine, had cautioned the European powers once more against any interference on the American continent. Although he was especially addressing the Europeans, he stressed the neutrality of the United States toward *all* other nations. When he declared that the people of the American continent had the right of self-determination in that no one had the right to interfere, he was referring only to the United States. His generally formulated thesis that the United States had not intervened in the internal party disputes of other countries or attempted to introduce its own political system into other lands by means of intrigue, diplomatic activity, or force was false. His words conformed to the truth no better than did those of the declaration of war on Mexico of May 11, 1846.[3] It is even possible that he knowingly made false assertions.

James K. Polk belonged to the inner circle of the faithful around Andrew Jackson. Together with Thomas Hart Benton, he had helped Jackson in 1834 to win the Bank War against Nicholas Biddle and in this way earned his spurs in Congress as a tough fighter.[4] Polk, Benton, Jackson, and Sam Houston were close friends, opponents of a division of the Union over the question of slavery, and declared expansionists.[5] As a protégé of Andrew Jackson, Polk must have known about Jackson's foreign policy and thus also about the missions and work of Joel R. Poinsett and Anthony Butler. Both men had instructions, as has already been described, to meddle in the internal affairs of Mexico in order to gain Texas for the Union.

Their mission failed, for, like most Americans, they did not understand Mexican national pride and to some extent did not want to acknowledge it. *La raza,* the intellectual-cultural and ethnic bonds that make it possible for Mexicans to hold together in the face of external threat in spite of the prevailing class differences and even to overcome party differences, remained incomprehensible to the overwhelming majority of U.S. citizens. Completely insensitive, they considered their ideas to be transferable without ado to another culture. Still, it was not only the recognition of an independent culture and tradition that they denied to Mexicans; they faced their neighboring country and its claims with just as much hostility as they showed toward the Indians.[6] For Polk, his cabinet, and a large part of America it was inexplicable why Mexico, crisis-ridden and almost bankrupt, did not finally recognize the autonomy of Texas and, in addition, would not sell California to the United States. They overlooked the fact that they themselves would not sell one square millimeter of their own land to another nation and did not recognize how little actions of this kind could be reconciled with Mexican national pride.[7]

Contrary to his peaceable address of December, 1845, and the supposedly dismayed reaction to the armed altercations in May, 1846, Polk was already firmly resolved to make war against Mexico and to acquire for himself the territories of Texas, New Mexico, and California by force.[8] Moreover, completely in the spirit of Andrew Jackson, he advocated the view that Mexico had no claim at all to Texas, for that area actually belonged to the Louisiana Territory, which Jefferson had bought from France and which Adams had unjustifiably surrendered to Spain in 1819. This completely untenable claim and contention, based on La Salle's journeys,[9] in which Jackson and his followers had immersed themselves, led to the notion that Texans had always been Americans who had just had to defend themselves for a short time against a wild and unjustified Mexican despotism.[10] Accordingly, the fixing of the southern border of the United States as it was dictated in the peace treaty with Mexico on February 2, 1848, was, in the eyes of the expansionists, less an appropriation of foreign territory than the manifestation of native entitlement.

This digression on the expansionists, who determined the policies in the United States at that time and so also exercised their influence on the fate of Texas, raises the question of what had actually caused the Texas War of Independence. For John Quincy Adams, as an opponent of the expansionists, it was clear that it had been a conspiracy of the slaveholding states that had secretly brought "their people" to Texas in order to be able to play a more important role in Congress. In support of this, Adams could refer to the man who had reported these things: the committed Quaker and abolitionist Benjamin Lundy.

Born in New Jersey on January 4, 1789, Lundy became active in the antislavery movement in 1820. He was a proponent of the theory that free blacks should be settled in thinly populated areas and thus the problem of slavery could be solved. On the strength of this idea he visited Canada, Haiti, and also Texas. In June of 1832 he came to Texas for the first time, searching out land for his plan to make it possible for free blacks to settle. Later he journeyed twice more to Texas, the land that seemed to him to be best suited for realizing his design,[11] in the summer of 1833 and the summer of 1834, when he met Colonel Juan N. Almonte, with whom he quickly became friends. He also officially received an empresario contract on March 10, 1835, for land on the Rio Grande that at this time lay in the province of Tamaulipas. But the realization of his venture never came to pass, for war broke out in Texas.

To Lundy it was immediately clear that this conflict had been contrived by slaveholders and land speculators in order to join Texas to the Southern states. This idea of a potent conspiracy had already occurred to him in San Felipe de Austin on his second visit in Texas, when he had a serious disagreement with slaveholders. His close contacts with the opponents of slavery and with Mexicans, who were very critical of the overt practice of slave ownership, supported him in his "observations": "There is many a wolf in Mexico, from our country, in the guise of sheep."[12]

One of his acquaintances assured Lundy that Austin was playing a double role and was interested only in the spread of slavery and his own personal power. This as well as other conversations and his own reflections found their way into his famous pamphlet *The War in Texas; a Review of Facts and Circumstances, Showing That This Contest is the Result of a Long Premeditated Crusade against the Government. Set on Foot by Slaveholders, Land Speculators, & c. with the View of Re-establishing, Extending, and Perpetuating the System of Slavery and the Slave Trade in the Republic of Mexico*, which appeared in Philadelphia in 1836. Lundy's ideas created the matrix and source for the abolitionists and countless articles and books.

In Great Britain, too, between 1837 and 1847 some volumes, as well as articles in newspapers and magazines, were published about Texas.[13] Most of them were works of propaganda that took a position for or against relations with Texas. William Kennedy's book, *Texas, the Rise, Progress, and Prospects of the Republic of Texas*, published in 1841 in London, was composed more on the line of essays and aimed as an appeal for trade relations with

Texas for commercial reasons.[14] David Urquhart's little book from the year 1844, *Annexation of the Texas, a Case of War between England and the United States*,[15] was entirely positioned on the side of Benjamin Lundy and William E. Channing, the Unitarian from New England who had caused a lot of talk with an open letter to Henry Clay on August 1, 1837.[16]

The conspiracy theory received nourishment only from the fact that Texas was officially a slaveholding country. In 1835–1836, however, slaves could not have made up more than 10 percent of the entire population, according to relatively accurate estimates.[17] Only after 1836 did the percentage of slaves in Texas begin to rise as the result of an increased flow of settlers. Slave work began to be economically of importance for all of Texas only in the years of the Republic.[18] The proportion of slaves in Texas rose from 10 to 12 percent in 1835 to 30 percent in 1860, putting it in ninth place among fifteen slaveholding states, after South Carolina with 57 percent, Mississippi with 55 percent, Louisiana with 47 percent, Alabama and Florida each with 45 percent, Georgia with 44 percent, North Carolina with 33 percent, and Virginia with 31 percent.[19]

To understand how these numbers came about, it is important to know the origin of the Texas immigrants. The statement, which was often made and called upon by the abolitionists as evidence for their conspiracy theory, that in the overwhelming majority of cases the Texas settlers had done their recruiting from the South and thus from slaveholding states and so in deed and word had been pure and simple propagators of slavery is in its simplicity false as an analogy.[20] It is true that the proportion of immigrants from the Northern states was in general small and in the immigration during the years 1850 to 1860 did not exceed 2 percent.[21] It is just as true that about 50 percent of the settlers in eastern Texas between 1836 and 1840 came from the states of Alabama (45 percent slaves in 1860) and Tennessee (25 percent slaves in 1860).[22] These were, nevertheless, only the states from which they had directly come, not the actual place of origin of the families.

In the eighteenth century, after the years of the American Revolution, a stream of settlers had moved to the West out of the states of Virginia and Georgia, over the Allegheny plateau into the valley of the Mississippi, and from there to the south.[23] So even those families in eastern Texas who had entered from the Southern states did not represent old, settled Southerners but constituted a part of that southwest migration because of which they were less closely bound to the traditions of the classic Southern states but had rather created their own. Texas thus was made up of a frontier society that, differing from the South and the North, had produced its own customs and principles.

On the Gulf Coast, settlers from the Northern states were represented more numerously than in the east, south, and southeast, where, next to the Mexicans, Germans represented the largest group of non-Anglo immigrants, with about 47 percent.[24] In addition, immigrants from the states with few slaves fundamentally outweighed those from slave-rich states.[25]

Along with all these numbers and statistics it must again be emphasized that many of those from the United States who wanted to settle did write to Stephen F. Austin and others for information about the Mexican laws concerning slavery and thus showed how important this question was for them, but disturbances never came about in Texas because of slavery. Mexico had excepted Texas from all regulations concerning it and looked the other way in regard to the slaveholders—even if reluctantly. Consequently, there was no reason for the Texans to complain about Mexico on this point. When even today writers speak of the important bearing that slavery is supposed to have had for the Texans and see it, or the threat of its abolition by Mexico, as a fundamental reason for the beginning of the war against Mexico, then they are being taken in by the political activists, the hawks, who had a habit of talking about Texas when they really could mean only themselves.[26] As has been described already, the hawks were in general concentrated in the Brazos district. There slavery played a large part on account of the agricultural use of that area—far greater than for the rest of Texas. The hawks thus had a justifiable reason to worry, for Mexico would not tolerate slavery forever. But they did not represent the majority in Texas, and for them the slavery question was at most a cause for bad feeling but never a motive for armed conflict. In addition, it should be mentioned finally that there is no indication at all of immigration directed by the slaveholding states or any further conspiracy of plantation owners supporting the thesis of the abolitionists that the Texas War of Independence was just a plot of those states.

Substantially more scholarly weight has been given to the theory of cultural conflict as a cause for the war of the Texans against the Mexicans. Up to the present in most historical discussions about that period the opinion is advocated that the real reason the province of Texas broke away from the Mexican nation was that the quantity of distinctive culture and customs that existed was so great that coexistence of the two ethnic groups for any length of time was made impossible in any event.[27] Here almost all work is influenced by a publication by Eugene C. Barker from the year 1928: *Mexico and Texas, 1821–1835*, a book that is based partially on Barker's previous articles. In annotated bibliographies even today the report of "excellent" is given to this publication,[28] praise that, considering that during the last sixty years an array of sources was discovered, must at least be looked at as questionable.

In the chapter on grievances in Texas, Barker refers exclusively to testimonials by Stephen F. Austin, official statements and reports of the Mexicans, and papers of the extremely active hawks in Texas. He himself admits that he had no other source material at his disposal.[29] But, as has already been developed in the preceding chapters, the documents of settlers that have meanwhile been acquired render a completely different picture. Contact between Mexicans and Anglo-Americans actually was relatively slight because of geographical realities as well as often because of language difficulties and, not least of all, because of the pride of the Americans on the one hand and of the Mexican upper class on the other.[30] But no tense or hostile atmosphere prevailed, and they lived on peacefully with one another with any number of business and commercial ties. They got along well even with the Mexican troops and their commanding officers.[31] The contemptuous disparagement of the Mexican soldiers appeared only after the events of the war.

The Fredonian Rebellion, which had resulted from quarrels about land rights; the struggles in Anahuac in 1832, which had arisen because of the strict rule of the military commander John D. Bradburn who came from Kentucky; and the fight between Martin de León and Green De Witt, which had likewise developed from land disputes and smuggling incidents, in no case represented ethnic problems. When Barker writes that the Mexicans distrusted the Anglo-Americans and then at the end states: "At the bottom the Texas revolution was the product of the racial and political inheritances of the two peoples,"[32] this is a misleading oversimplification.

It is true that in official circles and in Mexico City fear of pressure from their northern neighbors was great, and infiltration and with it a gradual separation of Texas was feared. But in Texas itself the peacefulness and industry of the settlers was attested to by Mier y Terán and also by Almonte. Mier y Terán feared only that the Anglo-Americans might push the Mexicans to the wall by force of numbers and consequently wanted to see a further *growth* of the stream of settlers prevented; satisfaction with the Anglos per se existed, and there have been and are disturbances in every community.[33] Settlers had certainly been allowed to come into the country when in government circles fear of the United States had already begun to appear, for the activity of the Anglo-Americans promised much for Texas, and it was mainly the adventurers and the official policies of the United States that were viewed with distrust and alarm.

In Mexico City the hope had existed that it was possible to harness and integrate the industrious, resolute nature of the Anglos into a uniformly distributed and structured heterogeneous society with members from various nations. The ever more distinct homogenous character of an Anglo-Saxon community, which was becoming more and more a foreign body within their union, worried the Mexicans. The attestation of loyalty on the part of Austin, whose voice possessed some political weight in Mexico, and his followers made it possible to some extent to silence for a time the warning voices in the capital city.

The majority of the settlers harbored basically no contempt for their Mexican neighbors, but relative to this, attention should certainly again be directed here to the social differences in the Mexican-Texan society and its division into *ricos* and *pobres* that influenced the attitude of some Anglo-Americans. There were, nevertheless, Texans such as Henry Smith and William B. Travis who basically hated and were contemptuous of Mexicans, made themselves noticeable by their rabble rousing, and consequently distorted the picture. But these forces were plainly in the minority. Barker's first assumption, that an underground ethnic movement had led to the breakup, must accordingly be rejected in its one-sidedness as unfounded and false. A somewhat different evaluation can, on the other hand, be applied to the second point, which immediately leads to a third complex of theories respecting the Texas War of Independence.

Barker speaks of a political heritage that caused the settlers to come to blows with the authorities in their state. In the first years the newcomers had difficulty in Texas finding their way about in the Spanish-Mexican legal system. Spanish was the official language and a problem for many in the beginning. For citizens who were accustomed to self-government in its simplest form and the jury system, it meant a great change to submit to a hierarchical government and a complicated type of appeals court that was interwoven with the administrative branch of the government.[34] At first, with special authorization by the government, Austin looked after various administrative duties and was an intermediary between the authorities and the settlers. In spite of this, there were difficulties, and these were discussed at the conventions of 1832 and 1833. In Saltillo and Mexico City a deaf ear was not turned to the Texans' complaints and suggestions for change, and with the reforms of 1834 all of their requests were fulfilled except for granting them their own state – that is, separation from Coahuila, which had to be refused on the grounds that the population was numerically still too small. These irritations and quarrels with the authorities and the government subsided gradually and would have been no reason for war even at the time they were most severe.

Frequently the theory is proposed that, because of the violently advocated centralism of Santa Anna, the war had begun as a fight for democracy and for the Constitution of 1824 and was thus a struggle of democracy against a dictator, comparable to the attempts in Yucatán and Zacatecas.[35] This theory contains useful elements, but nevertheless it is not completely satisfactory as an attempt at a general explanation for the events of the years 1835 and 1836. For the Mexican Texans who took part in the struggle it certainly is true, but for the Anglos, scarcely. In the beginning phases of the war the settlers got their bearings from the watchwords and conduct of the politically active hawks who, with Austin's vote, determined the policy of that time. From the beginning, as has already been mentioned, this leading group was, however, in favor of the separation of Texas from Mexico, but they restrained themselves for the sake of political expediency. Men such as Stephen F. Austin, Sam Houston, Henry Smith, David G. Burnet, the brothers John A. and William H. Wharton, William B. Travis, James Bowie, James W. Fannin, and Anson Jones[36] were convinced that Texas had to break loose from Mexico. Austin had certainly admitted numerous times that the initial declaration for the liberal Constitution of 1824 had been only eyewash and pure opportunism. Centralistic governments and would-be dictators had existed in Mexico before 1835 without having it result in disturbances or even armed uprisings. Up to that point Austin had also successfully mediated between the government and the settlers in the case of disputes. Why did the system break down this time?

In Mach, 1835, Dr. Pleasant W. Rose referred to lawyers and land speculators as the real cause of disturbances.[37] In contrast to his statement, a large part of today's research nevertheless presumes that land speculation played no great role in the origin of the war.[38] Moreover, to refer again to a work by Eugene C. Barker, after investigating the sources available to him, he nevertheless expressed only cautiously the thought: "One may, however, venture the opinion that neither the speculators nor the speculations had much to do directly with causing the revolution."[39] In his article Barker considered only the Monclova speculation and its influence on the settlers but did not take into account the complicated interplay of the speculators in New York, Mexico City, and Monclova. Furthermore he went from results to causes and paid no attention to the inherent dynamics of certain events that gave a new direction to actions that were originally planned differently.

In Article XXIV of the Colonization Law of the state of Coahuila y Texas of March 24, 1825, it had been specified that Mexicans alone might buy up to eleven leagues of land. The prices for one league were set at $100 for pasture, $150 for unirrigated arable land, and $250 for irrigated real estate.[40] Between 1825 and 1832 176 parcels were sold. Inasmuch as only few Mexicans could afford these prices, they were quickly sold off to interested foreigners.[41] One of those interested parties was Stephen F. Austin, who had to pay only $1,000 for three of the parcels—a further indication that he could not have been as poor by far as he always maintained.[42]

These real estate transactions were the first land speculation in Texas and nevertheless aroused no notice at all; for one thing they were done privately and not generally known about, and for another they were done between Texans themselves or friends and relatives in the United States, so that if there was any knowledge about these proceedings, there was no feeling of interference from outside. An uproar arose only when in several laws of 1834 and 1835 land speculation was promoted in a great way and a couple of names were caught in the crossfire of criticism. Then articles appeared in newspapers complaining that land was being sold in great quantities at cheap prices and thus the creation of monopolies and an influx of foreign enterprises, indifferent to Texas itself, were being favored.[43] Persons saw in the large purchases of land a disgraceful self-enrichment of their fellow citizens who had unscrupulously misused their offices as representatives.[44] Those who were thus condemned, as for example Samuel M. Williams, defended themselves among other ways with the argument that no one had gotten excited when John T. Mason acquired 300 leagues of land in the same way in 1834.[45] Although the settlers were not particularly interested in Mason's activities, because he and his transactions were not and never did become very well known in Texas, his activities in Texas in 1834 and those of the congressional representatives in 1835 attracted some attention in Mexico City, even though for completely different reasons from those existing among the Texans.

In government circles the speculation of 1834 and 1835 sent up two different alarm signals. The United States had already been making attempts for a considerable length of time in Mexico City to buy Texas. These offers went along with extremely dubious tactics on the part of American diplomats, which discredited the entire foreign policy of the United States. Although the pressure from official sources was already irritation enough, in addition the representatives of private organizations took the lead with their pitches. However, they operated more capably insofar as their offers were less humiliating to Mexico than the more demanding propositions of the government and relied on the temptation of lucrative side deals from willing state officials. Although the companies also speculated on the future annexation of Texas so as actually to be able to realize their profits, in Mexico City they attempted "only" to acquire privileges for themselves and land in Texas without directly irritating Mexico's sovereign rights. As the letters of Mexía and Mason prove, many influential men, from the attorney general and the minister of the interior to the president himself, were not at all disinclined to grant certain rights to the petitioning enterprises for appropriate sums, particularly when this went on privately and was not connected with any official land loss and thus loss of prestige. Even though no absolute evidence of a direct bribe with the resulting official action has been found, it can still be assumed with a probability bordering on certainty that the news from Monclova that public land was being sold at cheap prices *en gros* caused dismay in the Mexican capital on the part of a number of persons who had thought to dispose of the land themselves.

In addition, these land sales were linked to political motivation. Governor Viesca, who belonged to the liberal party, explained that the land was sold to be able to finance the opposition to the centralists under Santa Anna. Disturbances in Coahuila and other provinces lent weight to his statement. Whether Viesca's explanation was the truth or not, Santa Anna had double the reason to proceed against the government of Coahuila y Texas. He was, nevertheless, clever enough to declare himself officially on the side of the elected governor, but immediately sent the declared centralist Cós to Monclova to attend to peace and order. This military measure coincided with another one. The customs officials in Texas could not maintain their authority and had asked for military support against grumblers and rowdies.[46] So Cós had two missions before him.

Now in the advance of the Mexican army, one group, which in 1834 had almost completely lost its hold in Texas, saw its chances rise again: the War Party. The men who wanted to separate Texas from Mexico at any price and join it to the United States used the opportunity and spread the most hair-raising rumors: several thousand soldiers were on the march to Texas; they were going to free all the slaves and, together with the Indians, they were going to subjugate the Texans under the dictatorship of Santa Anna and the Catholic church and force them to pay immensely high taxes.[47] Furthermore, Texas was to be declared a territory, and Great Britain was going to help Mexico defeat the Texans.[48]

Even though many persons saw through this clumsy propaganda,[49] it still made some settlers feel insecure, particularly because Cós actually did turn up with a fighting force. In addition, the news of Santa Anna's brutal military action against his liberal opponents did not exactly serve to calm and soothe the anxious and angry people. Cós, it is true, did endeavor to make it intelligible to the Texans that no action at all was planned against them and that he wanted only to reestablish order in general,[50] but in Texas they could not agree on whom they should believe, the hawks or the doves. The decision was to fall to Stephen F. Austin. In a similar situation in 1832 he had saved the day and established peace. The reputation preceded him that he knew the Mexicans best. He had also spent the most time in Mexico City, even though partly as a prisoner. He knew the leading politicians, and up to that time Texas had always fared well with his decisions. Austin came and for the first time spoke in favor of armed resistance, of war. In this decision, too, land speculation again had a decisive part.

As has been mentioned previously, the settlers knew scarcely anything about Mason's activities, but the delegates in Monclova and Stephen F. Austin did. Austin had certainly met with Mason for the first time on April 1, 1833, and afterward was in bitter rivalry with him. The intrigues in Mexico City had showed Austin how dangerous these companies could be and how they were finding more and more of an ear with the Mexican government. If he wanted to save Texas for himself and the settlers, then Texas had to be separated from Mexico by force before his influence in the capital city was completely gone and the political decisions were made only by henchmen of certain enterprises. Whether these ideals of his and the decision resulting from them corresponded to the actuality can hardly be verified, even though it must firmly be concluded that after his meetings with Santa Anna, Butler, Mason, and others this picture must have been drawn clearly for him. A man like General Mier y Terán could perhaps have stepped in here once again as a mediator and restored Austin's faith in the stability of the Mexican government as well as also mediated in Texas between Cós and the settlers. But Mier y Terán had committed suicide on July 3, 1832.[51]

Consequently, in the search for the causes of the Texas War of Independence of 1835–1836, contrary to previously prevailing opinion, land speculation must receive a position of great importance. It was directly and indirectly one of the main reasons for the war between Mexico and Texas, for it influenced the decisions of the Mexicans and made the citizens of Texas overalert.[52] What tipped the scales, however, was Stephen F. Austin's decision to fight. This statement is not meant to diminish the impression that the news about Santa Anna's dictatorial ambitions had on the settlers. In like manner, Cós's action to require the surrender of the so-called agitators—and his cleanup of the few more unpopular liberals—was legal, to be sure, but politically just as inept as his military actions and the obvious attempt to disarm the settlers. But events of this kind and centralistic governments had existed before without leading to an open break. Here likewise Santa Anna's later behavior, his storming of the Alamo, the order to shoot at Goliad, and his actual installation as dictator in 1835 cannot be taken as evidence for the decision of Austin and others in 1835. Perhaps things *would* have gone badly in Texas in the long run under his leadership—but it cannot be *proved*, for his actions against the Texans in the war must also be seen as a reaction to their declaration of war, which for him was a clear case of rebellion and at the same time represented an attempt by the United States to conquer Texas by force of arms. Many of his actions in 1836 and afterward can consequently be cited as effects and not as causes, which should neither excuse them nor justify them. The judgment of Mexican historian Elesio Paredes is short and to the point: "Santa Anna was a bad Mason and a bad Mexican."[53]

Here Paredes addresses a further point that has already been introduced in this study. The question is asked: What role belongs to Freemasonry in the conflict between Mexico and Texas? Although exact dates are missing, it is assumed today that about 1 to 2 percent of Texans were Masons. In relation to this insignificant percentage, the high proportion, never less than 30 percent, of Masons exercising critical functions and connected with important political decisions is striking.[54] The interim president, David G.

Burnet, his vice-president, Lorenzo de Zavala, the secretary of the interior, and the three successive secretaries of war were likewise Masons, as were the three presidents of the Republic of Texas, all four vice-presidents, all secretaries of the interior, and numerous other high officeholders. Altogether in the interim government 50 percent of all the members of the executive branch were Masons; in the first administration, 78 percent; in the second, 88 percent; in the third, 86 percent; and in the fourth, 100 percent. In the highest courts of the Republic at least 50 percent of the judges were Masons.[55] It can, then, be assumed straightaway that Texas politics in the years 1832 to 1846 was decisively determined and shaped by Masons. The influence of Freemasonry, especially on educational policies, consequently cannot be underestimated,[56] even though on the other hand disagreement must be registered with James D. Carter, who with regard to Texas and Mexico, speaks definitively of a battle of the Freemasons against tyranny contrary to his own findings.[57] This one-sided allotment of roles overlooks the fact that there were numerous Masons in the highest offices of Mexico and that the war in Texas was not at all a battle for a liberal Mexico but from the beginning for a free Texas.

The significance of Freemasonry in the dispute with Mexico lies elsewhere. It created a bond that brought very dissimilar men together and let them act. Contrary to all the accepted representations of Texas history, it was not simply that some men came to Texas by chance and there somehow found themselves united against Mexico, but rather that they already had a common basis in their lodge membership and could unite and utilize a connective network that furnished introductions and helped newcomers to be integrated quickly. Just as Freemasonry in the American Revolution united leading persons like Samuel Adams, Benjamin Franklin, Paul Revere, and John Hancock in ideals and organization,[58] it must also be seen in Texas almost as a foundation on which the players were put into relationship with one another. Freemasonry thus was not a cause of the Texas War of Independence but a combining force of individual strengths without which the political development in Texas would have advanced at a considerably slower pace.

From the foregoing, Carter can also be refuted when he says: "The Texas Revolution was an ideological war,"[59] for in the main it was a struggle for local power. Not only is his thesis of the "ideological war" wrong, his term the "Texas Revolution" must also be questioned. Although all the texts use it, it is doubtful whether the events of the years 1835 and 1836 can be grasped by means of the concept of revolution.

When this designation was used for the first time for this armed conflict cannot be determined. The participants themselves spoke in the beginning mainly of war, battle, and liberation. A newspaper in New Orleans was using the term "revolution" on November 17, 1835;[60] Sam Houston used it on January 26, 1851, in a speech in Philadelphia;[61] and his friend Henderson Yoakum by emphatic use in his history book in 1855[62] lent it historical weight that allowed it to recur as the established form in all treatments up to the present day.

"Les révolutions sont les changements tentés ou réalisés par la force dans la constitution des sociétes."[63] With this sentence Arthur Bauer in 1908 defined revolution as social change in society by means of force. As handy as this definition sounds, it in turn raises a number of questions. What is change? What is force? What is society? In its effort to work out a comprehensive definition and exact description of all the characteristics intrinsic to revolution, modern research on revolutions has come far but still has not reached its objective.[64] The various assessments from social psychology, politics, history, and sociology, with all the constraints of their specialties, still leave so many gaps that empirical use of these theories raises more questions than it finds answers. Because it is not the mission of this work to test the individual theses as to their convincing nature, it will be sufficient to use a few general criteria common to all theories to determine whether a revolution did take place in Texas.

Using the methods of the social psychologists, Ted R. Gurr has described revolution—expressed in simple terms—as a process of individual and collective frustration directed toward aggression, in which the renunciation of satisfying needs of the individual leads to relative deprivation and allows a collective violence potential to build up.[65] Chalmers Johnson sees revolution sociologically as the answer to a particular crisis in a particular social system,[66] whereby it differs in general from rebellion by its inherent ideological direction of impact.[67] Charles Tilly attempts to interpret revolution as a pure political process, a power struggle of revolutionary groups with a government defending itself with force.[68] When Hannah Arendt stresses that only where the pathos of a new beginning prevails and is combined with the idea of freedom is a revolution present,[69] then one would be inclined at first glance to affix the term "revolution" to the events in Texas, for there was no lack of pathos in the speeches and writings of leading men such as Austin, Houston, and Lamar; and in all their statements they wanted to be sure that their struggle was understood as an expression of the aspiration for freedom of American derivation. Such an application, however, would mean a false interpretation of Hannah Arendt and the all-too-literal acceptance of the flowery speeches of the Texas leadership. The pathos about which Hannah Arendt speaks refers to a broad emotional surge in the population, in which in addition the concept of the freedom to be won must be deeply rooted.[70]

193

From what has already been said, it can be perceived that these criteria were not fulfilled in the war of Texas against Mexico. The shortcomings in the Mexican political system, which the settlers were still complaining about in 1833, had been reduced by 90 percent by 1834. No one in Texas was oppressed because of origin, language, religion, or political views. The separatists certainly tried to convince the population that there was danger in delay and that the oppressors were on the march, but it was only a matter of propaganda, as has already been described, and it was also understood as such.[71]

The other theories likewise do not prevail upon closer investigation, for neither a social crisis nor a reservoir of frustration nor an ideological alignment of the war in Johnson's sense applied. The closest application would be to advocate Tilly's power struggle, but on closer analysis this model also breaks down, for the thrust of the struggle of the Texans was not at all aimed at a change in the political system in Mexico or in Texas as a part of Mexico but at separation. No one wanted to change anything in Mexico itself. They were not turning against an oppressive system of government but rather against cohabitation with and in a foreign nation. Even though Johnson discusses how rebellions can develop into revolutions,[72] and it is kept in mind that the settlers actually were fighting against Santa Anna and for their freedom in 1836, nevertheless, the argument just addressed comes to bear again here, that it was not at all the aim of the Texans to create a liberal Mexico or to make social change but to annex themselves to the United States. If the concept of "Texas revolution" is to be kept as a term, it must nevertheless be firmly established here that in the scholarly sense there was no revolution in Texas.[73]

If the concept of revolution is rejected for the events in Texas in the years 1832 and 1836, then a comparison with the American Revolution of 1776 is not appropriate, at least terminologically. Nevertheless, parallels were drawn here very early and served many Texans, along with their expression of close relationship, as the legitimation of their own actions.[74] Only very few Texans applied this comparison to a declaration of loyalty to Mexico: those who actually behaved as revolutionaries, along with the Mexican Texans, in that they held to their loyalty for the liberal Mexico of 1824 and revolted against the centralism of Santa Anna. But the words of that clear-sighted minority have been pushed aside and forgotten:

> You are told that it is your interest to become a free and independent people; and you are told that a rise in the value of your lands is of more importance to you than your oaths and obligations. . . . An independent government would, we admit, be better suited to the genius and interest of those who might be in power: it holds out as inducements, honors, and titles, and offices, and salaries; but to those in the ordinary ranks of life, it brings poverty, and toil and war, and taxes.[75]

Such declarations naturally evoked reactions: "The crisis had come, and it was time for every patriot to speak out,—but I solemnly declare, I was actuated by motives wholly unselfish."[76]

This attitude is also readily attested to for the actors of the time by many historians. They see, or saw, in the struggle of the Texans clear parallels to the American Revolution of 1776.[77] Those similarities that are continually affirmed must, however, be characterized as false for the same reasons that the term "revolution" was rejected. The argument that in both cases disputes over duties and taxes played a main role can be disproved by statements already made here. The founding fathers of the United States labored in long debate to combine their various ideas into a general consensus in order to create an actual government based on the concepts of the Enlightenment, but in the two conventions of 1835 and 1836 much more banal matters were at stake—the formation of militias and the settlement of land distribution. Ideological problems did not exist for them—they simply adapted the appropriate American example and got into disputes only about how the documents in question should be changed so that they conformed better to the situation in Texas.

In addition, the constitutional convention held in 1836 cannot be compared with the convention of 1776 for a further reason and one that appears to be a formality at first. The delegates of 1776 came from families who had lived in the colonies for a long time. They were familiar with their country and its special problems. Therefore they were well suited for their task. In contrast to this, 83 percent of the delegates in Texas had arrived after 1830; 42 percent had moved into Texas after Austin's trip to Mexico City in 1833, and 29 percent of them had come even after the war had broken out in 1835. Whatever the accurate numbers might have been, it is extremely unlikely that between the outbreak of the war in October, 1835, and the first sessions of the convention in March, 1836, 29 percent of all Texas settlers should have moved into Texas. Although quite a few settlers turned their back on Texas in the Runaway Scrape in the months of January, February, March, and April, 1836, a large number of them came back after the victory of San Jacinto and cannot thus be counted as new settlers. Even if someone would be tempted to call this a quibble over numbers, the difference is still striking: whereas the delegates of the Continental Congress were members of old families who were very familiar with the cultural, political, social, and economic background of their country, at least one-third of the members of the convention in Texas could not have had a profound knowledge—if any at all—of their new homeland, because they had only just arrived. They might reflect the large number of volunteers coming to Texas, and thus the change that took place in Texas after the war, but they did not represent the Texas of old, the Texas that had existed prior to autumn of 1835, the Texas of Stephen F. Austin, Green De Witt, and others.[78]

Though it is not meant to advance the claim of having found a parallel that can be established exactly by scholarly means, a comparison of the Texas War of Independence with another violent conflict on the North American continent intrudes.

> Since this last condition characterized the case of the Americans in Texas under Mexican control, a serious clash was inevitable.[79]

> The two cultures still would have clashed even if all the Negroes had been free.[80]

The first quotation refers to the Texas "revolution," the second to the American Civil War. Both authors—entirely independent of one another—found it appropriate to characterize the respective conflicts as the inevitable collision of two cultures. Both were wars of secession, even if one was won and the other lost; both cases concerned the fact, among other things, that persons thought they could and should take freedom for themselves and renounce a union that they had at one time entered into voluntarily. Both of them, the Texans as well as the Confederates, were closely related in their feeling of superiority over the system of government to which they had once given the oath of solidarity.

Stephen F. Austin in his irritation at the ingratitude of "his" settlers had found appropriate words several times: "I do say that North Americans are the most obstinate and difficult people to manage that live on earth."[81] "[It is] a principle which is common to all North Americans, a feeling which is the natural offspring of the unbounded republican liberty enjoyed by all classes in the United States; that is, jealoucy of those in office, jealoucy of undue encroachments of personal rights, and a general repugnance to every thing that wore even the semblance, of a stretch of power."[82]

Austin so described the "mind of the west," the character of those pioneers who, through generations of wandering, had learned to trust only themselves. It is nevertheless impossible to define such a heterogeneous group as the settlers in universally valid terms. It is astonishing how, as a matter of course, American historians attach to their own fellow citizens for all events attributes to which they would almost like to affix an excusable character: "a race of aggressive and unruly American frontiersmen" is what they are called, not only by Frederick Merk.[83] But this assertion, which reveals more about the historians than about history, must be contradicted here.

On the strength of the foregoing study a picture is revealed that falls into two pieces. First, there was the simple settler who had seen himself driven to look for a new home, mostly for economic reasons; and then there was the adventurer whom Theodore Roosevelt described in his treatise *The Win-*

ning of the West.[84] In spite of the fractiousness of character in his fellow citizens that Stephen F. Austin attested to, with all the trouble of living with such persons and managing and governing for them, they nevertheless rejected an armed uprising and the aggressiveness of the activists, the War Party, as the sources universally show. Expansionists and adventurers such as Travis,[85] Fannin, Smith, Chambers, Archer, Wharton, and Williamson understood how to use the advantage of the moment aptly, when a crisis appeared anew in Mexico's political system, and took things into their own hands.

To this picture of two parts John Louis O'Sullivan, the publisher of the *New York Morning News* and the *Democratic Review,* in 1845 gave a name that was to join both parts into a positive whole: manifest destiny.[86] Considering the two forces, the moderates and the activists, John W. O'Neal comes to the conclusion: "Manifest Destiny, therefore, was the basic, essential cause of the Texas Revolution."[87] By that he implies either that manifest destiny is a characteristic attitude, a basic position, or a motivation that was common to all Texans or that, on the contrary, all alignments occurring in Texas can be combined under that concept. Now what is manifest destiny?

Albert K. Weinberg has chosen for his study on this topic the subtitle *A Study of Nationalist Expansionism in American History*[88] and thus immediately supplied a definition: manifest destiny is a term for national expansionism and thus for an attitude. Weinberg describes in full detail the various usages and senses that this concept has received. It became a general term for "a natural right on the part of our race, to possess the earth,"[89] for a geographical predetermination, for a crusade for freedom, for a religious-philosophical idea of fulfillment, and for the vindication of the nation.

Although the book does include all the intellectual and philosophical aspects by which the expression was shaped and used, it nevertheless ignores many real aspects and often creates a one-sided picture. The premise of the author, in which he chooses U.S. expansion as an ideal area for study because the U.S., according to him, is morally unobjectionable on the whole and has progressed without great tragedies,[90] already exposes the same nationalistic attitude that also characterizes the works of Justin H. Smith.[91] Because Weinberg anticipates the evaluation that really could and should be given only after the consideration of the facts and relationships, he has already fixed a course that reproduces the reality of the time in a distorted manner.

His discussion of one of the truly great tragedies–and here only Weinberg's terminology is used–shows clearly the dilemma that he cannot resolve. When the Cherokees were to be driven out of Georgia in the 1820s and then after a rather long legal and political tug-of-war actually were driven out, the divine mandate to subdue the earth and make it useful was given as the reason for the dispersion. The "savages" transgressed against this commandment, for they "only" hunted and wandered about, whereas the whites cultivated the land in the sense of that divine stipulation.[92] These arguments did not prove to be handy enough, however, for specially appointed government commissions had to concede and recognize that the "savages" were not at all savage but, on the contrary, led a very civilized life in cities, at universities, and on the land cultivated by them. Thereupon the word of God was interpreted in Georgia to mean that the earth should be cultivated only by the white race and not by the red. Although Weinberg sees and describes all this, he does not delay long over an attempt at an explanation; he simply accepts the contradictions and weaknesses in the chain of arguments of the time, refers to other authors, and goes on to the next point in his work.[93] Twice he briefly addresses economic factors—the great desire of many individuals to acquire valuable land cheap and the discovery of gold in Georgia—but lets these facts stand alone without balancing them against his detailed description of the intellectual background.

When Weinberg repeats the words of the governor of Georgia that only whites were considered as the fulfillers of the divine plan, he shows that, by bending the argument to fit the idea, philosophy had to take a place in the background and serve the whites' economic aspirations. This becomes obvious also in another connection when Weinberg asks why a merger of expansionism and the ideal of freedom did not set in until the 1840s.[94] He attributes this to altruism and to an egoistic need for protection of their own country—the United States—by many citizens.[95] On the basis of the relationships worked out in the study at hand this statement must be limited. Without doubt there were numerous persons whom Weinberg's characterization fits, just as, however, for a great number of persons the phrase "extension of the area of freedom" was only an added justification for personal goals. In the first category Stephen F. Austin and Anson Jones would be placed, and in the second Henry Smith and William B. Travis. As has already been discussed, the argument of self-defense against British and French interests in relation to Texas, New Mexico, and California was for many only a pretense and not actual.[96] The *real* fear of British strength restrained the United States from annexing Canada—and Canada would not voluntarily allow itself to be annexed so easily as the United States proposed in 1911.[97] On the other hand, there should be no doubt here that there were a great number of politicians, military men, merchants, and industrialists who saw in Great Britain mainly strong and threatening competition.[98]

But in every political phase the expansionists also had a considerable number of opponents to whom Weinberg devotes a few words only when they accepted matters as already accomplished facts and in part made their peace with them.[99] Moreover, he speaks as a rule too generally of "the

Americans," which in this connection is especially dangerous when one considers that Polk with a declared expansionistic program was elected by "only" 49.5 percent of the population.[100] Although certainly the majority of American citizens were in no way opposed anymore after the land was won, Daniel Webster fought to the end against the expansion of the United States for he liked to imagine the areas of Texas, California, and Oregon as independent countries or as a confederation.[101]

It might be said that such criticism was inappropriate in a work that has set as its goal the illumination of an ideology and not, for example, of a period of time. This could be said only if one did not perceive in doing so that it was just the massive criticism that the expansionists continually met with[102] that drove them to justifications that took on an ever-stronger religious character. The legitimacy of the criticism was exactly what made those who were thus attacked move their actions into the realm of divinely inspired missions in order to cause the disagreeable admonishers to be silent.[103] The expression "manifest destiny" originated in 1845, thus just as the continental expansion of the United States neared its end with the annexations of Texas, Oregon, New Mexico, and California achieved in quick succession. The phrase "manifest destiny" consequently presents itself as a subterfuge—as a reaction and not as a cause.

In spite of the brevity of this explanation, it would be wrong, too, to generalize the foregoing thesis for many persons actually believed in manifest destiny. Introduced as a slogan for propaganda purposes, this expression determined the thoughts and actions of a great number of persons. But to want to use it as a general descriptive term for the spirit of an age, as Weinberg does, ignores the abundance of ideological attitudes in America and their origins in the nineteenth century, as does the assertion that this attitude was the main cause of the development of Texas.

Men like Clay and Webster in the tradition of Jefferson joined the idea of freedom with that of democracy and so could subordinate themselves personally. However, this relationship was disturbed for many expansionists such as—to remain with the example of Texas and to name only a few—James W. Fannin, William B. Travis, John A. Wharton, Robert M. Williamson, Henry Smith, and Thomas J. Chambers; democracy was for them a structure that had to submit to their idea of freedom, which was in reality unbridled egoism. The spatial expansiveness of frontier society allowed more room for such persons than did the always more severely delineated narrowness of the North, and thus, in the border areas of Anglo-American culture, made them into rebels against the traditional order.[104]

Along with their unrest, land hunger drove many of these men to Texas, New Mexico, and California. In the speech before the Democratic Party in New York on February 22, 1848, which has been cited above, Sam Houston said: "There is not an American on earth but who loves land."[105] This sentence is for the most part correct in its universality, whereas Elgin Williams's conclusion from it—"every colonist was a land speculator"[106]—is completely overdrawn. He infers this from a statement, which he quotes incorrectly, by William R. Hogan, who quite correctly proposes a three-stage classification.[107] The settlers, for whom land was vital as the basis for their livelihood and not as an object of speculation, nevertheless often found themselves forced to compensate for failures in their harvests or cattle by selling land. The middle class, if it can be called that at all—men such as Houston or Austin, who had enjoyed an education—attempted to make money by small to medium land speculations.[108] Then in the twilight there prospered the machinations of the large companies, which were active from the very beginning in the United States and brought land speculation into general discredit[109]—one reason why Sam Houston kept his considerable activities in this area quiet and Stephen Austin vigorously denied corresponding rumors concerning himself and loudly condemned speculation as such.

When Michael P. Rogin writes, "Land was the major investment opportunity in early America,"[110] this is no new discovery; for Michel Chevalier, who traveled through the United States from 1833 to 1835 on a commission from the French government in order to see for himself various technical developments, conducted general studies concerning the American mentality, as did Alexis de Tocqueville, and determined that:

> Everybody is speculating, and every thing has become an object of speculation. The most daring enterprises find encouragement; all projects find subscribers. From Maine to the Red River, the whole country has become an immense *rue Quincampoix*. . . .
> I said that every thing has become an object of speculation; I was mistaken. The American, essentially practical in his views, will never speculate in tulips, even at New York, although the inhabitants of that city have Dutch blood in their veins. The principal objects of speculation are those subjects which chiefly occupy the calculating minds of the Americans, that is to say, cotton, land, city and town lots, banks, railroads.[111]

All these were things in which Austin was interested during his life—so according to Chevalier he was a typical American. Austin, whose goal it was to establish an American state in Mexico in the spirit of Jefferson,[112] must have realized that he would neither be useful to the pan-Americanism of Jefferson nor would he achieve his own personal desires of recognition, prosperity, and influence in Mexico, and thereupon voted for the war of secession.

It was a war that Santa Anna and his supporters wanted to wage, on the one hand, to eliminate opposition forces in Coahuila, to provide for order in Texas, and to put an end to uncontrolled land sales, for they were themselves interested in land speculation. On the other hand, the Mexican troops were what those Texans wanted who needed a war to free Texas from Mexico. Nevertheless, it was not a matter of any kind of conspiracy. Sam Houston did not need any mandate from Andrew Jackson to join Texas to the United States in his own way. He knew what his mentor thought, and he wanted and intended to be able to combine this with his own enterprises. The land speculators, the expansionists, and those who were fighting for their own glory also entertained no conspiratorial plans. As they had done before, they sought to exaggerate the almost daily quarrels and smaller disturbances, something they were successful in doing in 1835 on account of the advance of Mexican troops and the land speculation in Monclova. Austin's word, however, was crucial. Without his call to battle, the disturbances would probably have faded away again. The war of 1835–1836 was not inevitable. The individual strands in the bundle of causes that must be seen in proximity as almost equivalent in their size and stratification were, when regarded separately, not enough reason for war. Only the combined effect of land speculation, political insecurity, military action on the part of the Mexicans, and the persistent action of the expansionists led to a widespread readiness for war. The importance of Austin in tipping the scales certainly shows the relative weakness of each individual strand. Any monocausal attempt at an explanation of Texas' war of independence of 1835–1836 can therefore not be valid. The disturbances among the people and with the authorities, which had been brought about by the factors described, represented the powder keg, so to speak, that Austin's word, as the spark, caused to explode but which could also have been made harmless by him. If Austin had negotiated with Cós, as he suggested, what passed into history as the Texas revolution would with some certainty never have happened.

In spite of everything, Texas would in all probability have become a state in the United States. The expansionists and the speculators, who had made one of their own president in the person of Andrew Jackson and were the determining force in the politics of the United States from 1828 to 1845,[113] not only exercised a strong influence on politics in those years, they also had the personalities to carry their plans through. After Jefferson had, with the purchase of Louisiana, set the example of territorial expansion, Florida, Texas, Oregon, New Mexico, and California followed in logical sequence.[114] This is no modern interpretation, for many persons saw this development, as has already been described, and calculated on the strength of it great profit for corresponding speculation.[115]

The events in Texas consequently are arranged in a clearly recognizable evolution; they were not chance, just as the meeting of those persons who determined the destiny of so many persons was not mere chance. Without any conspiracy the expansionists achieved their goal, favored by events that they had partially set in motion themselves and others that occurred as a reaction to their behavior. The settlers, to whom for the most part the battle for survival was more important than politics, were pulled into the whirlpool of events.[116] The idea of manifest destiny was only one part of the evolution of Texas; on account of its religious-philosophical content, it was applied like a hastily donned veil that developed into a second skin for many expansionists and thus in turn—wrongly—to a magnified attempt at an explanation for their deeds. The historical process that ran its course in Texas consists of an unbreakable chain but at the same time exhibits its most important link. With Texas, the continental expansion of the United States in the first half of the nineteenth century had reached its zenith, for apart from Oregon, the United States could no longer pursue its way to the Pacific by peaceful means. In recognition of this, the phrase "manifest destiny" was created to cover up the fact that, already in the case of Texas, the United States had no right to interfere in the affairs of other sovereign states only to enlarge its own territory. At the same time, this segment of Texas history portrays the development of American frontier society; in addition, the problem of slavery and the Indian question cause the development of the territory of Texas from a Mexican province to the twenty-eighth state in the United States to appear as one of the most important segments of American history, one that almost possesses the character of a prototype.

Notes

INTRODUCTION

1. See Claudio Véliz, *The Centralist Tradition of Latin America,* p. 155.

2. Victor A. Belaunde wrote aptly about this: "The Portuguese advance was one of pioneers, not of settlement; and the Spanish advance had the same character, a search for El Dorado, the establishment of missions, and the dissemination of religious propaganda" ("The Frontier in Hispanic-American History," *Annual Report of the American Historical Association* 1 [1922]: 300 [hereafter cited as *ARAHA*]).

3. Frederick J. Turner, *The Frontier in American History,* p. 3.

4. Subtitle of Eugene C. Barker's book, *The Life of Stephen F. Austin, Founder of Texas, 1793–1836.*

5. Walter Prescott Webb, *The Great Plains,* p. 165.

6. "Texas once settled, the revolution was the inevitable result of the racial inheritances of the two peoples thus brought into political union with one another" (Eugene C. Barker, *Mexico and Texas, 1821–1835,* pp. iv–v).

7. William C. Binkley, *Official Correspondence of the Texas Revolution, 1835–1836,* 1:v. (hereafter cited as *OCTR*).

8. William C. Binkley, *The Texas Revolution,* p. v.

9. The journal appeared for the first time in 1898. Its original name, *Quarterly of the Texas State Historical Association,* was changed in 1912 to *Southwestern Historical Quarterly* at the suggestion of Professor Barker (hereafter cited as *SHQ*).

10. See also William C. Pool, *Eugene C. Barker, Historian,* pp. 142ff.

11. See Amelia Williams and Bernhardt Wall, *Following General Sam Houston from 1793 to 1863,* p. 243, as well as the "Report of James Hampton Kuykendall," vol. 2, book XI, pp. 2–3, James Hampton Kuykendall Papers, Barker Texas History Center, University of Texas at Austin (hereafter cited as *BTHC*).

12. Here should be mentioned especially Hubert H. Bancroft, *History of the North Mexican States and Texas;* Dudley G. Wooten, ed., *Comprehensive History of Texas;* Henry Stuart Foote, *Texas and the Texans; or, Advance of the Anglo-American to the Southwest;* John Henry Brown, *A History of Texas, 1685–1892;* David B. Edward, *History of Texas;*

Frank White Johnson, ed., *History of Texas and Texans;* and William Kennedy, *Texas: The Rise, Progress, and Prospects of the Republic of Texas.* Although Bancroft's work treated a wealth of material, it contains many errors. Wooten reproduced various works, among them Yoakum's. The biases of the articles could often not be avoided. Foote was, as Kennedy was also, an author who wrote for reasons of propaganda and therefore consciously drew a one-sided picture; Foote wanted to speed up annexation and Kennedy, to arouse England's interest in Texas. Brown suppressed every criticism of Texas and the "revolution," and Edward wrote entirely from a pro-Mexican point of view, which hurt him a great deal and forced him to move away from Texas to the North. In spite of their frequent errors, all these works are usable as long as one is aware of their failings and uses them critically, which unfortunately is not done by too many historians.

13. See, as examples, Anthony G. Adair, *Texas: Its History;* Carleton Beals, *Stephen F. Austin, Father of Texas;* Anna J. Pennybacker, *A History of Texas;* and Lewis W. Newton, *Texas, Yesterday and Today.*

14. See the anonymous pamphlet *Visit to Texas: Being the Journal of a Traveller;* Henry Bruce, *Life of General Houston;* William Bluford Dewees, *Letters from an Early Settler of Texas;* Mary Austin Holley, *Texas;* Arthur Ikin, *Texas: Its History, Topography, Agriculture, Commerce and General Statistics;* Frédéric Leclerc, *Le Texas et sa révolution;* Charles E. Lester, *The Life of Sam Houston;* John J. Linn, *Reminiscences of 50 Years in Texas;* José María Tornel y Mendívil, *Tejas y los Estados-Unidos de América, en sus Relaciones con la República Mexicana;* David Urquhart, *Annexation of the Texas: A Case of War between England and the United States;* and Charles Sealsfield, *Das Kajütenbuch, oder Nationale Charakteristiken.*

15. Among these compilations of source material are Eugene C. Barker, ed., *The Austin Papers,* 3 vols., the two-part vol. 1 was published as *ARAHA,* vol. 2, for the year 1919, and vol. 3 was published by the University of Texas Press (all three hereafter cited as *AP*); Amelia W. Williams and Eugene C. Barker, eds., *The Writings of Sam Houston, 1813–1863* (hereafter cited as *WSH*); Charles Adams Gulick, ed., *The Papers of Mirabeau Buonaparte Lamar* (hereafter cited as *LP*); the previously mentioned Binkley, ed., *Official Correspondence of the Texas Revolution (OCTR);* John H. Jenkins, ed., *The Papers of the Texas Revolution, 1835–36* (hereafter cited as *PTR*); George Pierce Garrison, ed., *Diplomatic Correspondence of the Republic of Texas* (hereafter cited as *DCRT*); Hans Peter Gammel, ed., *The Laws of Texas, 1822–1897* (hereafter cited as *LOT*); Nancy Barker, ed., *The French Legation in Texas;* Ephraim Douglass Adams, ed., "Correspondence from the British Archives concerning Texas, 1837–1846," *SHQ,* in 24 parts, vol. 15–21 (1912–17); and Anson Jones, *Memoranda and Official Correspondence Relating to the Republic of Texas: Its History and Annexation, 1836 to 1846.* The *WSH* are distinguished by a thorough editing; the *PTR* are unfortunately full of errors, which, however, diminish the value of this compilation only slightly. A very good collection of more recent source material that for the first time sheds some light on land speculation in Texas after the revolution is found in Feris A. Bass and B. R. Brunson, *Fragile Empires: The Texas Correspondence of Samuel Swartwout and James Morgan, 1836–1856.* Also on this point attention should be called to the excellent edition of the papers dealing with the Robertson colony, edited by Malcolm McLean, *Papers Concerning Robertson's Colony in Texas,* 14 vols. (to date).

16. Among these are Llerena Friend, *Sam Houston, the Great Designer;* William Ransom Hogan, *The Texas Republic: A Social and Economic History;* Donald W. Meinig, *Imperial Texas: An Interpretive Essay in Culture Geography;* Margaret Swett Henson, *Samuel May Williams: Early Texas Entrepreneur;* and David J. Weber, *The Mexican Frontier, 1821–1846.*

17. Here come to mind especially T. R. Fehrenbach, *Lone Star: A History of Texas and the Texans,* and William H. Goetzmann, *When The Eagle Screamed: The Romantic Horizon in American Diplomacy, 1800–1860.* Although Fehrenbach makes an effort to put aside his local patriotism (something that he often does not at all succeed in doing, but instead offers a convincing command of facts), the pamphlet by Goetzmann, who otherwise enjoys an excellent reputation as a scholar, has a very disturbing effect because of an extreme accumulation of errors in regard to well-known facts, which lead the author to quixotic conclusions. Apart from the author's strange labeling as "romantic" that part of American history which he himself characterizes in his introduction as violent and loaded with conflict (p. xiv), the extreme one-sidedness and frequency of error of the pamphlet make it an example of how history should not be written today.

18. See Rush Welter, *The Mind of America, 1820–1860;* Robert E. Riegel, *Young America, 1830–1840;* and David M. Potter, *The Impending Crisis, 1848–1861;* as well as Robert Selph Henry, *The Story of the Mexican War,* 2nd ed. Unfortunately even in the recent past "special" treatments of Texas have appeared that also stress the "physical" character of history and because of their exclusive use of long-familiar material are superfluous. To these also belongs, e.g., David M. Vigness, *The Revolutionary Decades, 1810–1830.*

19. The book in first place here is Justin H. Smith's two volume *The War with Mexico* (1919). Although it is based on a great quantity of material, upon closer inspection a bias in the use of sources becomes apparent that causes Mexico's behavior to be misrepresented. The only work that, in addition to emphasizing the unquestionable importance of Smith, offers legitimate criticism, is the study by Gene M. Brack, *Mexico Views Manifest Destiny, 1821–1846.*

20. A complete recital of all the works would be going too far here. Because this phenomenon appears even in such otherwise excellent discussions as David M. Pletcher, *The Diplomacy of Annexation: Texas, Oregon, and the Mexican War* – consider Pletcher's shortened and consequently adulterated version of the statement of Pedro María Anaya, the Mexican minister of war, on pp. 353–54 – it is not surprising when handbooks of Texas history like Seymour V. Connor, *Texas: A History,* which are otherwise accurate and clear, represent the Mexicans as lazy and slaves to authority and the Indians as brutal savages. For the origin and history of this racism, see the exemplary study by Richard Drinnon, *Facing West: The Metaphysics of Indian-Hating and Empire-Building.*

CHAP. I. INCENTIVES TO IMMIGRATION

1. The census reports for the years after 1783 that were obtained and collected in the Nacogdoches Archives suffer not only from their incompleteness – for many

years there only exist figures for one city or another—but also from their inaccuracy. For the year 1785 in San Antonio 1,579, in La Bahía 621, and in Nacogdoches 433 persons were counted, which altogether makes 2,633. But in the summary report a total of 2,919 is given, which leads to the question as to why the individual reports and the summary report differ by 286 inhabitants, or what different methods were used in the individual cases. See the census reports concerned in the Nacogdoches Archives, Texas State Archives, Austin, Texas.

2. See the year 1784 in "Census Reports," Nacogdoches Archives.

3. Connor, *Texas,* pp. 56–57. Complete population figures are unfortunately not available for Texas in this period. Although the cites of La Bahía and Nacogdoches experienced an increase, however slight, between 1786 and 1793, a loss of about 1,080 inhabitants occurred in the thirty years from 1785 to 1815 in San Antonio de Béxar. For a closer comparison, see the "Census Reports," Nacogdoches Archives.

4. See the good translation of the report along with an introduction by Nettie Lee Benson, "A Governor's Report on Texas in 1809," *SHQ* 71:603–15.

5. Gerald Ashford also gives no exact source. Compare his *Spanish Texas,* p. 229.

6. Completely different numbers are given by Henderson Yoakum. For 1744 he gives 1,500; for 1765 only 750; and for 1806 the splendid number of 7,000 inhabitants in Texas, without verifying these numbers, of course. Particularly for 1806 his data appear to be purely speculative, for they are not verified anywhere or supported by any other writer. See Yoakum, *Texas* 1:87, 97, and 138.

7. The church in Spain had already entered into alliance with the state at an early time. In the bull *Universalis Ecclesiae* Pope Julian II had agreed with the conditions of Ferdinand of Aragón and blessed the advowson system, a system that promised the church power and influence in the New World, too, but at the same time made it a tool of the crown in the conquered lands. With the later development of the *vicariato* policy, the Spanish king then even became the representative of the pope in America. See N. M. Farris, *Crown and Clergy in Colonial Mexico,* pp. 7ff.

8. According to the bull *Universalis Ecclesiae* of 1508, the viceroy officially presided over the church in Latin America. The parish church was answerable to him. The responsibility for the monastic churches lay with the papal court, even though the crown also sought increasingly to gain influence here, which it partially succeeded in doing. For an introduction and a more comprehensive reading list, see Michael C. Meyer and William L. Sherman, *The Course of Mexican History,* pp. 184ff; and Thomas C. Barnes et al., *Northern New Spain: A Research Guide,* pp. 57ff.

9. See also Herbert Eugene Bolton, *Texas in the Middle Eighteenth Century,* pp. 5ff.

10. See Fehrenbach, *Lone Star,* pp. 59ff.

11. See the report of the Marquis de Rubi of April 10, 1768: "Digttamen, que se orden del Exmo señor Marques de Croix, Virrey de este Reyno expone el Mariscal de Campo Marques de Rubi, en orden a la mejor Sittuazion de los Presidios, para la defensa, y exttension de su Fronttera a la Genttilidad en los Confines al Nortte de este Virreynatto." The report of the council of war of the province of Chihuahua of June 9–15, 1778; and the report of the Franciscan, José Francisco Lopez, of August 4, 1785 (Ernest Wallace and David Vigness, eds., *Documents of Texas History,* 1:22ff.).

12. For more details about the rise of Spanish distrust see John Rydjord, *Foreign Interest in the Independence of New Spain,* pp. 206ff., as well as Benson, "A Governor's Report," *SHQ* 71:603–15.

13. Connor, *Texas,* p. 57. Statistics for La Bahía in 1819 in the Nacogdoches Archives give 838 inhabitants; the groups included are as follows:

	Hombres	Mujeres
Europeos	249	240
Espanoles	145	118
Id. Cast y Mestis.	43	41
De orígen Africano	1	1

14. The Yanaguana Society report concerning the Casas and Sambrano revolution in 1811 states that an agent of Napoleon in Mexico, Octaviano d'Alvimar, promoted ideas of freedom and independence in order to cause a weakening of the Spanish empire, which would have had three advantages for France: Spain would have been weakened, French trade extended, and the countries more open to the political influence of France. See Frederick C. Chabot, ed., *Texas in 1811,* Yanaguana Society Publications, vol. 6.

15. For more details about the history of Hidalgo's rebellion, see Meyer, *Course of Mexican History,* pp. 285ff., and Charles Cumberland, *Mexico: The Struggle for Modernity,* pp. 113ff.

16. See the translation of the text in Wallace and Vigness, *Documents of Texas History,* pp. 39ff. For details of the history of the first revolution in Texas in 1811, its development, and the influence of the ideas of the American and French revolutions, see Julia K. Garrett, *Green Flag over Texas,* pp. 41ff.

17. See the report of the minister of foreign affairs to *Comandante-General* Arredondo of May 24, 1814, in Mattie Austin Hatcher, *The Opening of Texas to Foreign Settlement, 1801–1821,* pp. 346ff.

18. For details of Spanish government in America, see Joseph Clark, *A History of Texas,* pp. 80ff., as well as Roger B. Merriman, *The Rise of the Spanish Empire in the Old World and in the New,* vol. 3, *The Emperor,* pp. 618ff. For the later development under the Bourbons, see Pedro Aguado y Bleye, *Manual de historia de España,* vol. 3, *Casa de Borbón,* pp. 611ff.

19. Dominguez to Arredondo on May 22, 1814, in Hatcher, *Opening of Texas,* p. 247.

20. See Ferdinand VII's "Circular of the Spanish Government to Friendly and Allied Powers, Relative to the Bases of a Pacification between Spain and Spanish America,–Madrid, 17th June 1818," in *British and Foreign State Papers, 1817–1818,* 5:1217–20.

21. For the whole affair of the settlement of Texas in the last years of Spanish rule, especially the various plans on the part of the Spanish, the Germans, and also the Swiss, see Hatcher, *Opening of Texas,* esp. pp. 224ff., as well as "The Louisiana Background of the Colonization of Texas, 1763–1803," *SHQ* 24:169–94. For details about the Louisiana immigration plan, see Gilbert C. Din, "The Immigration Policy of Governor Esteban Miró in Spanish Louisiana," *SHQ* 73:155–75.

22. See the translation of the royal manifesto: "Manifesto of the King of Spain

to the Nation, Madrid, 10th March 1820," as well as the corresponding declaration for the colonies in America, "Address of the King of Spain to the Inhabitants of the Spanish American Colonies: Madrid, March 1820," in *British and Foreign State Papers, 1819–1820,* 7:280–84.

23. See the complete text in *Coleccion de los Decretos y Órdenes que han expedido Las cortes ordinarias,* 6:345–47.

24. See the complete text in ibid., p. 152.

25. The exact text of the treaty is quoted in William Malloy, ed., *Treaties, Conventions, International Acts, Protocols, and Agreements between the United States of America and Other Powers, 1776–1909,* Sen. Docs., vol. 48, pt. 2, pp. 1651–57.

26. See Charles E. Hill, *Leading American Treaties,* pp. 151ff., and the bibliography, pp. 174ff., as well as the extensive bibliography in Michael H. Harris, *Florida History: A Bibliography;* pp. 75ff.

27. See the article by Isaac Joslin Cox, "The Southwest Boundary of Texas," *SHQ* 6:81–102.

28. That this alleged claim was based only on speculation and rumors and was completely unsupportable is proved very well by Cox, ibid.

29. Jefferson to M. Bowdoin, July 10, 1806, in H. A. Washington, *The Writings of Thomas Jefferson,* 5:17ff. (hereafter cited as *WTJ*).

30. For the life and attempted revolution of Long, see Mirabeau B. Lamar, "Life of James Long: General Long's Attempted Settlement of Texas," *LP* 2:51–134.

31. On June 16, 1818, there appeared in the Nashville newspaper, the *Clarion and Tennessee State Gazette,* on p. 5, the following report: "Louisiana: The following remarks on Dr. Robertson's map, copied from a Natchez paper, give most important intelligence: The First object which attracts the eye of an American, in examining this map, is the astonishing difference in the claims to territory between the United States and Spain. . . . We cannot forbear expressing surprise, when we see the proposed western limits of Louisiana, by the secretary of state of the United States to Don Onís minister of Spain, near the gov'nt of the U.S. by which the president, offers to relinquish two-thirds of the territory claimed under the purchase of Louisiana. . . . We recollect that under every administration since that purchase, it has been maintained that our claim extended to the Rio del Norte–Now if that claim be founded in justice, as we have a right to believe it was, the American people will cheerfully defend it, notwithstanding the fears that some may feel from the power of confederated Europe."

32. In addition, in a letter printed under the heading "Extracts of a letter from a gentleman in the Province of Texas, under date of 21st, July, 1819," it is reported: "This is certainly the most healthy, beautiful and fertile country I have ever seen."

33. Letter of August 6, 1819, from the "Republican Army of Texas," printed in the *Clarion and Tennessee State Gazette* on September 7, 1819.

34. Ibid., an article of October 5, 1819, p. 4.

35. Ibid., September 28, 1819, under the heading "Important."

36. Ibid., August 24, 1819.

37. Ibid., August 10, 1819, p. 3.

CHAP. 2. MOSES AND STEPHEN F. AUSTIN

1. For the life of Moses Austin, see the extremely accurate and excellently re-searched biography by David B. Gracy II, *Moses Austin: His Life,* here p. 231.

2. *AP* 1:69.

3. *AP* 1:222–23.

4. See Robert G. Cleland, *This Reckless Breed of Men,* p. 122, in connection with a letter from James Baird, Sr., to Stephen F. Austin of October 10, 1821, in *AP* 1:416ff.

5. Cleland, *This Reckless Breed,* p. 122.

6. See Barker, *Life of Stephen F. Austin,* pp. 21ff; as well as Gracy, *Moses Austin,* pp. 169ff.

7. Barker, *Life of Stephen F. Austin,* pp. 21, 29; and Gracy, *Moses Austin,* pp. 164, 182.

8. Leo M. Kaiser, "Stephen F. Austin's Oration of July 4, 1818," *SHQ* 64:78–79.

9. Mary Austin Holley quotes her cousin Stephen thus in the draft of a biography, "The Life of Stephen F. Austin." Mary Austin Holley Papers, *BTHC,* pp. 17–21.

10. For Moses Austin's intention to settle three hundred families on 200,000 acres of land, the base in Long Prairie was of decisive importance, for it lay only ten miles from the Texas border. For the purchase of Long Prairie, see Gracy, *Moses Austin,* pp. 179–80.

11. Moses Austin to Henry R. Schoolcraft on July 4, 1819, Schoolcraft Papers (transcripts from the Smithsonian Institute), *BTHC.*

12. For details, see Gracy, *Moses Austin,* pp. 180, 198.

13. For the difficult complex of topics concerning speculation, see Allan and Margaret Bogue, "'Profits' and the Frontier Land Speculator," *Journal of Economic History* 17, no. 1 (1957): 1–24.

14. For the beginnings of speculation, see Frederick Merk, *History of the Westward Movement,* pp. 100ff.

15. David Brion Davis writes: "Speculators had always helped to shape the character of American agriculture. The great theme of American settlement was the continuing contest of will between absentee owners and the squatters who first developed the land and who often had some partial claim of title" (Bernard Bailyn, ed., *The Great Republic,* p. 445).

16. Thus John Delafons, *Land-use Controls in the United States,* p. 6.

17. Malloy, *Treaties,* p. 1653.

18. Jefferson to James Monroe, May 14, 1820, *WTJ,* 12:160–61.

19. Moses Austin had met Henry Rowe Schoolcraft (1793–1864) at Herculaneum on July 23, 1818, during an expedition of the latter through Missouri and Arkansas. Schoolcraft was a respected, well-known, and competent geologist and ethnologist. See his report on Moses Austin's lead mines at Mine à Breton in Henry R. Schoolcraft, *A view of the lead mines of Missouri,* pp. 6, 19ff., as well as his diary, *Scenes and Adventures in the Semi-Alpine Region of the Ozark Mountains of Missouri and Arkansas, which were first traversed by de Soto, in 1541,* p. 38. For the relationship of the older Austin and Schoolcraft, see Gracy, *Moses Austin,* p. 183.

20. Moses Austin to Schoolcraft, July 4, 1819, Schoolcraft Papers.

21. Moses Austin wrote to Stephen's brother James on August 12, 1819: "You ought to write him and direct your letter to Nachitoches—he will get them" (*AP* 1:346–47).

22. Moses Austin to Schoolcraft, July 26, 1819, Schoolcraft Papers.

23. Ibid., August 18, 1819, Schoolcraft Papers.

24. Ibid., September 17, 1819, Schoolcraft Papers.

25. Stephen F. Austin to Maj. Jacob Pettit from his farm Long Prairie on October 5, 1819, Natchez Trace Collection, *BTHC*.

26. Stephen F. Austin, *Establishing Austin's Colony*, ed. David B. Gracy II, p. 2.

27. Stephen F. Austin to his mother Maria, January 20, 1821, *AP* 1:373.

28. See J. Meigs to Moses Austin, March 9, 1820, *AP* 1:356.

29. See James A. Gardner, "The Life of Moses Austin, 1761–1821" (Ph.D. diss., Washington University, 1963), p. 28, as well as Gracy, *Moses Austin*, pp. 135–36, and Stephen F. Austin to James Bryan, April 30, 1820, *AP* 1:373–74.

30. Stephen F. Austin to his mother, January 20, 1821, *AP* 1:373–74.

31. For the meeting of Austin and Bastrop, as surprising as it was fateful, as well as Austin's experiences in San Antonio and the role of Bastrop, see the results carefully researched by David B. Gracy in *Moses Austin*, pp. 201–204. And yet, even David Gracy can only guess at their first encounter, which is still shrouded in mystery. The few "reports" about this first meeting of Bastrop and Austin are extremely vague. Stephen F. Austin wrote his brother James in 1829: "They [their father and Bastrop] had seen each other once before in the United States, having met at a tavern when travelling, many years previous" (quoted in Dudley Wooten, *A Comprehensive History of Texas, 1685–1897*, 1:442). Mary Austin Holley in her draft of a biography, "The Life of Stephen F. Austin" (Mary Austin Holley Papers), states on page 20: "In crossing the public square with this determination he accidentally encountered the Baron de Bastrop, one of the local magistrates, with whom (as the reader will recollect) he became acquainted during his visit to Missouri many years before. . . ." Her remark "as the reader will recollect" leads to the assumption that she had written about this first meeting in detail. Unfortunately, this part of her manuscript is missing. That the older Austin had met Bastrop in a tavern in New Orleans is also reported by Clarence R. Wharton in his book *Texas under many flags*, 1:128: "Bastrop and Austin had met in a restaurant in New Orleans some years before. . . ." Yet, David Gracy has his doubts about Wharton's sentence: "The word 'restaurant' was not in common use in the early 19th century when Austin and Bastrop met. They would have called the place a 'tavern' or 'inn.' This fact suggests that perhaps some one of Wharton's researchers may have gotten his data confused and introduced a fact that he *thought* he had found. On the other hand, it is equally possible that Wharton was merely trying to use terminology contemporary to his readers" (David Gracy, letter to author, January 12, 1983). In any case, the mystery of where Austin and Bastrop had met for the first time remains unsolved. Philipe Enrique Neri, Baron de Bastrop—or Philip Hendrik Nering Bögel, which was his real name—is even today a vague figure in Texas history. The little that is known about him has been compiled by Charles A. Bacarisse in "Baron de Bastrop," *SHQ* 58:319–30, and Woods Moore, "The Role of the Baron de Bastrop in the Anglo-American Settlement of the Spanish Southwest," *Louisiana Historical Quarterly* 31:606ff. Bastrop, who

had been occupied with two settlement plans for Texas and was also involved in land speculation, was supposed to have had contact with Aaron Burr and Dr. James Long. See Elgin Williams, *The Animating Pursuits of Speculation*, p. 44.

32. Moses Austin to James B. Austin, March 28, 1821, *AP* 1:384–85, and April 8, 1821, *AP* 1:385ff.

33. See Austin's travel journal, Eugene C. Barker, ed., "Journal of Stephen F. Austin on His First Trip to Texas, 1821," *SHQ* 7:286–307.

34. Austin to Major Jacob Pettit, Long Prairie, October 5, 1819, Natchez Trace Collection.

35. See *AP* 1:419–63.

36. See Austin to his mother Maria, July 13, 1821, *AP* 1:401–2.

CHAP. 3. POLITICAL CHANGE IN MEXICO

1. Meyer, *Course of History*, p. 294.

2. Ulrich von Merhart, *Weltfreimaurerei*, p. 326; H. L. Haywood, *Freemasonry and Roman Catholicism*, pp. 117–18; and for the beginnings of Freemasonry in Mexico, Lillian E. Fisher, "Early Masonry in Mexico (1806–1828)," *SHQ* 42:198–214.

3. See Austin to Joseph H. Hawkins of May 1, 1822, *AP* 1:504–505.

4. Stephen F. Austin to his fellow citizens, June 5, 1824, *AP* 1:815–17.

5. Barker, *Life of Stephen F. Austin*, p. 69.

6. See Margaret Swett Henson, *Juan Davis Bradburn: A Reappraisal of the Mexican Commander of Anahuac*, pp. 38ff.

7. See "Robert Leftwich's Mexico Diary and Letterbook, 1822–1824," in Malcolm D. McLean, ed., *Papers concerning Robertson's Colony in Texas*, Introductory vol., pp. 107, 128–29.

8. For Wilkinson's activities and his membership in the Masons, see Connor, *Texas*, pp. 58ff., and James David Carter, *Masonry in Texas*, pp. 211ff.

9. See McLean, *Papers concerning Robertson's Colony*, 1:liv–lviii.

10. Ibid., Introductory vol., pp. 67, 72, 482ff. As he did to Leftwich, he also disparaged his colonization affairs to Arthur G. Wavell in order to scare away any troublesome competition. Compare this with note 30 in chap. 4, below.

11. *AP* 1:516–17.

12. Carter, *Masonry in Texas*, p. 220.

13. *AP* 1:1707ff.

14. For the political role of those men as well as their lodge membership, see Barker, *Life of Stephen F. Austin*, pp. 51ff., and Carter, *Masonry in Texas*, pp. 219ff., along with further information in notes.

15. See Juan Mateos, *Historia Parlamentaria de los Congresos Mexicanos*, 2:57ff.

16. Thus in many letters to friends and relatives; see *AP* 1:505, 517, 530, 534, 536, 555, and 566.

17. For Austin's various activities in Mexico see Barker, *Life of Stephen F. Austin*, pp. 43ff.

18. For Austin's estimation of the Spaniards, see his letter to Mary Austin Holley of August 21, 1835, *AP* 3:101ff.

19. See McLean, *Papers concerning Robertson's Colony*, Introductory vol., pp. 482–83, 561–62.

20. Barker, *Life of Stephen F. Austin*, p. 69.

21. *AP* 1:638–39.

22. Austin to Caspar Flores, December 6, 1824, *AP* 1:984ff.

23. For the similarities and differences in the constitutions of the United States, Spain, and Mexico, see the very good essay by James Q. Dealey, "The Spanish Source of the Mexican Constitution of 1824," *SHQ* 3:161–69.

CHAP. 4. THE AMERICANIZATION OF TEXAS AND ITS CONSEQUENCES

1. Austin to Joseph H. Hawkins, May 1, 1822, *AP* 1:505.

2. The name Texas Association surfaces for the first time on April 26, 1822, on one of the land shares given out by the company. Before that the group appears first only under the simple designation Citizens of the United States of America and later until 1822 under the name Nashville Company. See McLean, *Papers concerning Robertson's Colony*, 1:364, 416.

3. See ibid., Introductory vol., pp. 46, 292ff.

4. Officially news of Mexican independence was made known by means of a communiqué from the new government on January 8, 1822. This announcement first appeared in Nashville, Tennessee, in the newspaper, the *Nashville Whig*, of March 6, 1822, p. 2.

5. McLean, *Papers concerning Robertson's Colony*, 1:364ff.

6. See the individual inquiries and applications written to Austin, his family, and their representatives, from various persons who wanted to become colonists, *AP* 1:421ff.

7. This is apparent from the biographical sketches that McLean has compiled for the signers of the memorial, *Papers concerning Robertson's Colony*, 1:xliiiff.

8. These figures are the best that could be ascertained by following the paths of the various families involved.

9. McLean, *Papers concerning Robertson's Colony*, 1:367.

10. For a complete list of the directors, see the *Clarion and Tennessee State Gazette*, January 13, 1818, p. 3.

11. See the *Nashville Republican and State Gazette*, May 8, 1821.

12. See the *Clarion and Tennessee State Gazette*, January 6 and February 3, 1818, p. 3.

13. Robert V. Remini labels this group "the Nashville cronies" (*Andrew Jackson and the Course of American Freedom, 1822–1832*, pp. 108, 409n30.

14. McLean, *Papers concerning Robertson's Colony*, 1:416.

15. See the *Nashville Whig*, December 16, 1822, p. 3. For previous meetings, see ibid., October 30 and November 6 and 20, 1822, p. 3.

16. McLean, *Papers concerning Robertson's Colony*, 2:399.

17. For the individual contracts, see Mary V. Henderson, "Minor Empresario Contracts for the Colonization of Texas, 1825–1834," pt. 1, *SHQ* 31:294ff.

18. See a translation of the law in *LOT*, 1:27–30 and 97–106. The law can almost

be called the Lex Austina, for it can be attributed entirely to Austin's proposal.

19. Henderson, "Minor Empresario Contracts," pp. 300–301.

20. Concerning these statistical averages, see Barnes F. Lathrop, "Migration into East Texas, 1835–1860," *SHQ* 52:1–31, 184–208, and 325–48. For the size of families, see his table 13 on p. 333.

21. See Juan N. Almonte, "Statistical Report on Texas, 1835," *SHQ* 28:177–221.

22. For cholera in Texas, see J. Villasana Haggard, "Epidemic Cholera in Texas, 1833–1834," *SHQ* 40:216–30.

23. For details, see Virginia H. Taylor, *Spanish Archives of the General Land Office of Texas*, pp. 36ff., as well as Barker, *Life of Stephen F. Austin*, pp. 125–26.

24. For Green DeWitt's empresario work, see Ethel Z. Rather, "DeWitt's Colony," *SHQ* 8:95–192.

25. Arthur Goodall Wavell to Austin, November 16 and 21 and December 2, 1822, *AP* 1:553–56; December 10, 1822, *AP* 1:558–59; January 23, 1823, *AP* 1:572ff.; February 17, 1823, *AP* 1:576ff.; and May 22, 1823, *AP* 1:646–47.

26. Whether Austin had rebuked Wavell or accused him of self-interested intriguing is not evident, for Wavell intentionally was not about to establish anything in writing. See Wavell to Austin, February 17, 1823, *AP* 1:577.

27. *AP* 1:869; the date cannot be exactly determined.

28. Austin to Emily M. Perry, December 12, 1825, *AP* 1:1238–39.

29. He wrote on July 31, 1824, to his friend Ramos Arispe: "Muy apreciable dueno mio, Tengo la satisfaccion de participarle á U que he completado por fin las 300 familias que el Supremo Gobierno de la nacion Mexicana me Autorizó establecer en esta provincia," *AP* 1:863; to his mother he observed on May 4, 1824: "Our prospects are now beginning to look up," *AP* 1:785; and to Mrs. Joseph Hawkins, the widow of his friend, on April 20, 1824: "The affairs of this colony are prosperous and highly flattering . . . all goes well," *AP* 1:775.

30. Austin to Wavell, *AP* 1:869.

31. Compare n. 25, above.

32. Wavell to Ashbel Smith, February 28, 1851, Ashbel Smith Papers, *BTHC*.

33. Wavell never had any intention of settling the land granted him in order to fulfill his contract with the Mexican government. He was concerned primarily with the exploitation of the mineral wealth. For Wavell's attempts to establish himself profitably in Texas, see Robert W. Amsler, "General Arthur G. Wavell: A Soldier of Fortune in Texas," *SHQ* 69:1–21 and 186–209; Henderson, "Minor Empresario Contracts," *SHQ* 32:16ff.; and the letter of John Exter to Benjamin R. Milam, March 18, 1828, Milam-McKinney Collection, *BTHC*.

34. Austin constantly had to defend himself against the reproach that he was only lining his own pockets. For example, see his letter to his settlers of June 5, 1824 (*AP* 1:820–21).

35. See also Eugene Barker's description of William Fitz Gibbon and his two stepsons, in Barker, *Life of Stephen F. Austin*, p. 87.

36. See the text of the law in *LOT*, 1:61ff. For the discussion in Mexico about the division of the provinces, see Nettie Lee Benson, "Texas as Viewed from Mexico, 1820–1834," *SHQ* 90:241–42.

37. *LOT*, pp. 97ff.

38. For the problems that arose from the union of Coahuila and Texas, see Charles A. Bacarisse, "The Union of Coahuila and Texas," *SHQ* 61:341–49.

39. See "Translations of Empresario-Contracts," p. 22, Spanish Archives, General Land Office, Austin, Texas.

40. So says a newspaper announcement, *Nashville Whig*, August 6, 1825, p. 3.

41. Compare the letter from Hosea H. League to Austin, September 10, 1827, *AP* 1:1680ff., with the signatures on the petition in McLean, *Papers concerning Robertson's Colony*, 1:369ff. For the uncertainty concerning the division of the shares and their distribution, see ibid., 2:55ff. Interesting here is the presence already at this point of two participants and directors of the association, both of whom played a role in the coming events in Texas: Ira Ingram and Sam Houston.

42. *LOT* 1:104–105.

43. Ibid., p. 98.

44. McLean, *Papers concerning Robertson's Colony*, 3:230ff.

45. League to Austin, August 28 and September 10, 1827, *AP* 1:1677–78 and 1679–80.

46. McLean, *Papers concerning Robertson's Colony*, 3:278ff.

47. For the text of the contract, see "Translations of Empresario Contracts," pp. 34–36, Spanish Archives, General Land Office. Why the company, which for the sake of clarity has been labeled Texas Association in this work, had its name changed from the Nashville Company to the Texas Association at this time is not evident. On July 23 and 30, 1825, in the *Nashville Whig* the following notice appeared on the first page: "Texas Association, Attend! Those persons who claim to be stockholders in the company of which Capt. Leftwich is agent, denominated the 'Texas Association' will attend at the room of Decker & Dyer on Saturday evening the 23d inst. July 16, 1825."

48. See a newspaper report in the *Kentucky Reporter*, August 1, 1825, quoted in Barker, *Life of Stephen F. Austin*, p. 291n23.

49. McLean, *Papers concerning Robertson's Colony*, 3:301.

50. See Amos Edwards to Austin, July 7, 1828, *AP* 2:68ff.; and William H. Wharton to Hosea H. League, September 12, 1828, Benjamin C. Franklin Papers, *BTHC*.

51. An excerpt from an unsigned letter of February 25, 1830, from Rio Brazos de Dios, Austin's Colony, Texas, printed in the *Nashville Republican and State Gazette*, April 6, 1830, p. 3.

52. See John and Henry Sayles, *Early Laws of Texas*, vol. 1, decree no. 285, art. 78, p. 125.

53. See Oliver Jones to James F. Perry, June 10, 1834, *AP* 2:1062–63, and Moses Austin Bryan to James F. Perry, June 26, 1834, *AP* 2:1063.

54. Robertson in his declaration to the governor, Archivo de la Secretaria de Gobierno, Saltillo, Coahuila, vol. 38, legajo no. 29, 1834, expediente no. 1293, pp. 132, 153ff.

55. He explained this himself in a letter to Samuel M. Williams of February 5, 1831, *AP* 2:594–95.

56. This power of attorney is controversial in the literature, for it was totally uncustomary to give a power of attorney without a statement as to the region to be settled and the number of families. Consequently, Malcolm McLean attempts

to show that Austin forged this power of attorney. See McLean, *Papers concerning Robertson's Colony,* 5:51ff., and in contrast Barker, *Life of Stephen F. Austin,* pp. 297–98 and n. 54.

57. Austin to Williams, March 5, 1831, *AP* 2:607.

58. Robertson to Austin, June 7, 1831, *AP* 2:664.

59. For more about the controversial testimony of William Pettus, see Barker, *Life of Stephen F. Austin,* pp. 300ff.

60. Austin to Samuel M. Williams, May 31, 1833, *AP* 2:983–84.

61. This is clearly stated by the congressman from Kentucky, Henry Clay, before the House of Representatives on April 3, 1820, in Daniel Mallory, *Life and Speeches of the Hon. Henry Clay,* 1:394ff. Also Thomas Jefferson to James Monroe, February 4, 1816, in H. A. Washington, ed., *Writings of Thomas Jefferson,* 6:550ff., and Jefferson to Monroe on May 14, 1820, in *WTJ* 12:160–61, as well as various speeches and pieces of propaganda in David Woodman, *Guide to Texas Emigrants,* pp. 76ff.

62. Charles Francis Adams, ed., *Memoirs of John Quincy Adams,* 6:177–78.

63. See J. Fred Rippy, "Britain's Role in the Early Relations of the United States and Mexico," *The Hispanic American Historical Review* 7 (1927): 2–24.

64. See "Extract from a letter, No. 5, from Mr. Clay to Mr. Poinsett, dated Department of State, September 24, 1825," *American State Papers, 1826–28, Foreign Relations,* 6:581–82.

65. See also the proclamations and correspondence of Austin and others, *AP* 1:1553–76.

66. For the Fredonian Rebellion, see Edmund Morris Parsons, "The Fredonian Rebellion," *Texana* 5 (1967): 11–52; Connor, *Texas,* p. 84; and Barker, *Life of Stephen F. Austin,* pp. 148ff.

67. *El Sol,* February 20, 1827.

68. Poinsett to the current secretary of state Henry Clay, February 21 (Despatch 74) and March 8 (Despatch 77), 1827, "Despatches from United States Ministers to Mexico, 1823–1906," vol. 2 (August 17, 1825–April 18, 1827), Record Group 59, National Archives, Washington, D.C.

69. See Carter, *Masonry in Texas,* pp. 196ff.

70. Reported by W. S. Parrott in his letter to Austin of November 7, 1827, *AP* 1:1708. On the other hand, Parrott does not appear to have been an exemplary contemporary. Originally a dentist, soon after his arrival in Mexico he turned to more lucrative affairs like land speculation, brokerage, money lending, and the importing of unspecified merchandise. From September, 1834, to July, 1836, he occupied the office of an American consul in Mexico City. He is supposed to have contributed considerably to the anti-American feeling in Mexico by his conduct. See also Brack, *Mexico Views Manifest Destiny,* pp. 89ff.

71. Lorenzo de Zavala, *Ensayo Histórico de las revoluciones de Mexico desde 1808 hasta 1830,* 1:263ff. and 2:11ff.

72. For the public discussion about Poinsett, see Brack, *Mexico Views Manifest Destiny,* pp. 32ff.

73. See Lucia R. Douglas, "John Quincy Adams and the Texas Question" (M.A. thesis, University of Texas, 1927), pp. 20–21.

74. Almost the entire edition of *El Sol* for August 8, 1829, consists of hate letters directed at Poinsett and the United States.

75. See William Parrott to Austin, November 7, 1827, *AP* 1:1707–1708.

76. For the special relationship between Austin and Leaming, see Andreas Reichstein, "The Austin-Leaming Correspondence, 1826–1836," *SHQ* 88:247–82.

77. Austin to Leaming, June 29, 1830, Thomas F. Leaming Papers, *BTHC*.

78. McLean, *Papers concerning Robertson's Colony,* 3:327.

79. Printed in *AP* 1:538ff. and 568ff.

80. Concerning the latter document to the *junta nacional instituyente,* see Barker, *Life of Stephen F. Austin,* p. 72.

81. In this connection Austin's attempt to become a delegate to the congress from Arkansas should be kept in mind. See Barker, *Life of Stephen F. Austin,* p. 22.

82. Pedraza to Mier y Terán, September 12, 1827, quoted in Ohland Morton, "Life of General Don Manuel De Mier y Terán," pt. 3, *SHQ* 47:39–40. For Mier y Terán's trip and its political implications, see Benson, "Texas as Viewed," 268ff.

83. See Morton, "Life of Mier y Terán," pt. 2, *SHQ* 46:243.

84. See Mier y Terán to Austin, May 17, 1828; June 24, 1828; July 8, 1828; August 5, 1828; September 29, 1828; March 12, 1829; and September 28, 1829, in *AP* 2:40, 51ff., 70, 87, 120–21, 181–82, and 260–61; and also Austin to Mier y Terán, May 29, 1828; June 30, 1828; December 29, 1829, in *AP* 2:42ff., 56ff., and 306–307.

85. Morton goes so far as to maintain: "Following his inspection of Texas from February 1828 to February, 1829, Mier y Terán wielded a greater influence in Texas than any other man in Mexico of his day. From the time of his first visit until his tragic death in 1832, he was the eyes, ears, and possibly the brains of Mexican officialdom in Texas" ("Life of Mier y Terán," pt. 4, *SHQ* 47:140).

86. Mier y Terán to President Guadalupe Victoria, June 30, 1828 (Alleine Howren, "Causes and Origin of the Decree of April 6, 1830," *SHQ* 16:395ff.).

87. See Juan N. Almonte, "Statistical Report on Texas, 1835," *SHQ* 28:177–221.

88. See Mier y Terán's report in Howren, "Causes and Origin," 395ff.

89. Almonte, "Statistical Report."

90. *AP* 1:852–53.

91. See the many applications to the Mexican government and letters from Austin and to him from settlers, *AP* 1:809ff., 827–28, 832ff., 863ff., 892, 996ff., 1020ff., 1046ff., 1060, etc., as well as *AP* 2:2ff., 27, and 285.

92. See Austin to John Durst, *AP* 2:288–89.

93. See *AP* 2:46, as well as the reaction in the United States, *AP* 2:74–75.

94. See Barker, *Life of Stephen F. Austin,* pp. 201ff. and notes.

95. See Gracy, *Establishing Austin's Colony.*

96. Barker, *Life of Stephen F. Austin,* p. 20, and n. 100.

97. For the situation in Mexico, see Meyer, *Course of Mexican History,* pp. 316ff., and bibliography, pp. 322–23.

98. See the translation of the text in Wallace and Vigness, *Documents of Texas History,* pp. 66–67.

99. As quoted in Barker, *Life of Stephen F. Austin,* p. 266, and n. 21.

100. See Austin to Leaming, June 29, 1830, Thomas F. Leaming Papers.

CHAP. 5. THE FIRST RESISTANCE
AND STEPHEN F. AUSTIN'S POLITICS

1. For Bradburn's biography, see the study by Margaret Swett Henson, *Juan Davis Bradburn: A Reappraisal of the Mexican Commander of Anahuac.*

2. For the disturbances in 1832, see Forrest E. Ward, "Pre-Revolutionary Activity in Brazoria County," *SHQ* 64:212–31.

3. See *LP* 1:97–98.

4. "Address Setting Forth Grievances to Col. J. A. Mexía," June 13, 1832, *LP* 1:142–43, and "Citizens Meeting," July 2, 1832, *LP* 1:137.

5. *LOT* 1:477.

6. Ibid., pp. 479–503.

7. For Jesse Wharton's membership in the Nashville Central Committee, see Robert V. Remini, *Andrew Jackson and the Course of American Freedom, 1822–1832,* p. 409n.30. For the poor relationship between Austin and Wharton, see the beginning of Austin's letter to Wharton of April 24, 1829, *AP* 2:207–208.

8. See the "Proceedings of the Convention of Texas," *LOT* 1:481.

9. See Austin to Col. Elosua, August 21, 1832, *AP* 2:846ff.

10. William H. Wharton in his petition to the Mexican Congress, *LOT* 1:486ff.

11. For these two resolutions and the instructions to Wharton, see *LOT* 1:495–501.

12. "Miguel Muldoon to the Public," *AP* 2:854–55.

13. *AP* 2:874–75.

14. Austin to Músquiz, November 15, 1832, *AP* 2:888–89.

15. Barker, *Life of Stephen F. Austin,* p. 353.

16. Austin to Samuel M. Williams, January 12, 1834, *AP* 2:1024–25, and Barker, *Life of Stephen F. Austin,* p. 359, and n. 23.

17. *AP* 2:946–47, and Wallace and Vigness, *Documents of Texas History,* pp. 8off.

18. *AP* 2:934ff.

19. Ibid., p. 940.

20. Ibid., pp. 992ff.

21. For Santa Anna's policies and his rise, see Oakah L. Jones, *Santa Anna,* esp. pp. 40ff.; Mena L. Flores, *El General Don Antonio López de Santa Anna;* Meyer, *Course of Mexican History,* pp. 324ff.; and Connor, *Texas,* pp. 97ff.

22. See Austin to Williams, November 26, 1833, *AP* 2:1016, and Barker, *Life of Stephen F. Austin,* pp. 374–75.

23. *AP* 2:1007–1008.

24. Ibid., pp. 1012–13.

25. See Austin to Williams, January 12, 1834, *AP* 2:1024–25, and to George Fisher, *AP* 2:1033ff.

26. *AP,* 2:1083, as well as the postscript of August 26, *AP* 2:1084.

27. See Samuel Parkman to Austin, August 1, 1828: "A desire which I have for some time entertained to have a knowledge of the distinguishing characters of the Province of Texas has been of late much increased by the perusal of some of your letters published in the papers of this country [Missouri]" (*AP* 2:85). Compare corresponding Austin letters in *AP* 2:264 and 336. Austin himself had planned the pub-

lication of a number of his letters from the beginning and had this carried out by friends in the United States: "Such parts of my letters as you cause to be published calculated to give information to the settlers, I hope the newspapers in Mississippi, Tennessee, Kentucky, and Missouri, will republish" (Austin to Joseph H. Hawkins, July 20, 1821, *AP* 1:402ff., which Hawkins arranged to have printed in the *Arkansas Gazette,* October 6, 1821, and the *Louisiana Advertiser,* September 3, 1821). See also Andreas Reichstein, ed., "The Austin-Leaming Correspondence, 1828–1836," *SHQ* 88:250 and 282.

28. "Journal of Stephen F. Austin on His First Trip to Texas, 1821," *SHQ* 7:286–307.

29. Stephen F. Austin, "The Prison Journal," *SHQ* 2:205–206.

30. Austin to Leaming, February 1, 1828, and September 25, 1830, in Thomas F. Leaming Papers, *BTHC,* as well as July 23, 1831, Barker, *Life of Stephen F. Austin,* p. 233.

31. Austin to Leaming, June 14, 1830, *AP* 2:416.

32. Austin to William H. Wharton, April 24, 1829, *AP* 2:211–12.

33. Barker, *Life of Stephen F. Austin,* pp. 254–55 and 448–49.

34. For example, in his letter to William M. O'Hara, June 16, 1819 (*AP* 1:344–45); to Thomas F. Leaming, July 23, 1831 (*AP* 2:677ff.); and to Samuel M. Williams, May 31, 1833 (*AP,* 2:983–84).

35. Margaret Swett Henson also sees things in this light in her biography of Austin's secretary and partner, *Samuel May Williams,* p. 45.

36. See again Barker, *Life of Stephen F. Austin,* p. 21.

37. Gracy, *Moses Austin,* p. 162.

38. See Austin's letter to Emily Perry, July 24, 1828 (*AP* 2:76–77); and from Emily Perry to J. E. B. Austin, November 29, 1828, in which she states that all the records connected with the legal battle were burned in a house fire (*AP* 2:149–50); and for a comprehensive presentation, Barker, *Life of Stephen F. Austin,* pp. 248–49.

39. For the history of this company, see Andrew F. Muir, "Railroad Enterprise in Texas, 1836–1841," *SHQ* 47:339ff.; Eugene O. Porter, "Railroad Enterprises in the Republic of Texas," *SHQ* 59:363–71, and S. S. McKay, "Texas and the Southern Pacific Railroad, 1848–1860," *SHQ* 35:1ff.

40. See *AP* 3:477–78.

41. See Henson, *Samuel May Williams,* p. 77.

42. See the list of his land titles in Taylor, *Spanish Archives,* p. 155.

43. James F. Perry to Thomas F. Leaming, April 21, 1838, Thomas F. Leaming Papers, *BTHC.* That even more than just a little bit was left after paying off the debts and that Perry probably deliberately tried to hold off all too eager relatives is indicated by a letter from Archibald Austin to James Dall of October 6, 1846: "He [a lawyer from Texas] informed us that the Estate [Stephen F. Austin's] was one of the wealthiest Estates in Texas, that it must be worth some six to eight millions of Dollars" (Archibald Austin Papers, *BTHC*). This Archibald Austin might have been the son of Archibald Austin who was the brother of Mary Austin Holley, as in the letter he talked of "aunt Holley," addresses James Dall, who was married to Mary Austin Holley's sister Henrietta, as "uncle," and gives greetings to "uncle Charles," who might be Mary's youngest brother. For the genealogy of the Austins, see Rebecca Smith Lee, *Mary Austin Holley—a biography,* pp. 12–16.

44. See Taylor, *Spanish Archives,* p. 154.

45. Compare Austin's letter to the Ministro de Relaciones interiores y exteriores de los Estados Unidos Mejicanos, October 7, 1828, *AP* 2:122ff.

46. Austin to J. L. Woodbury, July 6, 1829, *AP* 2:226–28; to James W. Breedlove, October 12, 1829, *AP* 2:264ff.; and to Josiah H. Bell, March 17, 1829, *AP* 2:183ff.

47. See Austin to his mother, January 20, 1821, *AP* 1:373–74.

48. Austin to James W. Breedlove, October 12, 1829, *AP* 2:267.

49. See also R. Woods Moore, "The Role of the Baron de Bastrop in the Anglo-American Settlement of the Spanish Southwest," *Louisiana Historical Quarterly* 31:633ff.

50. See also Nacogdoches Archives, vol. 15, pp. 45–46, August 23, 1819, *BTHC.*

51. Moore in "Role of the Baron de Bastrop," *Louisiana Historical Quarterly* 31: 606–81, states: "He [Bastrop] had been instrumental in its [Austin's Colony] conception, initiation, organization and progress" (p. 650). "From the standpoint of achievement, it is sufficient to say that he, more than anybody else, made possible the entrance of Americans into Spanish and Mexican territory" (p. 697).

52. Austin to Caspar Flores, December 6, 1824, *AP,* 1:986.

53. "Information Derived from Col. Heyden Edwards (entered under April 6, 1825)," in McLean, *Papers concerning Robertson's Colony,* 2:292.

54. *WSH* 2:28.

55. *AP* 2:727–28.

56. Austin to James Bryan, April 30, 1820, *AP* 1:358–59.

57. Austin to Emily M. Perry, October 25, 1828, *AP* 2:135–36.

58. He wrote his brother-in-law James Perry on March 28, 1830, "I have raised the name of my family to a respectable standing in this country, and my relations need not be ashamed to own that they are my relations" (*AP* 2:353).

59. Austin to Mary Austin Holley, July 19, 1831, *AP* 2:674ff.

60. See Austin to Thomas F. Leaming, March 15, 1831, Leaming Papers.

61. *AP* 2:207ff.

62. Mary Austin Holley to Orville L. Holley, February 26, 1832 (Mary Austin Letters, 1:217, *BTHC*).

63. Ibid., p. 218. In December, 1831, he had expressed similar thoughts: "We shall go for Independence, and put our trust in our selves, our riffles, and–our God" (Austin to Holley, December 29, 1831, *AP* 2:727–30).

64. Austin to Leaming, San Felipe de Austin, April 20, 1833 (Stephen F. Austin Collection, Special Collections Department, University of Houston Library).

65. Austin to Rafael Llamos, January 14, 1834, *AP* 2:1027ff.

66. Austin to General William H. Ashley, October 10, 1832 (*AP* 2:871ff.).

67. For the political activity of John A. Williams, who had come to Texas with his family as a farmer in 1822, see C. Allen True, "John A. Williams," *SHQ* 47:107–19.

68. See Williams to Austin, December 18, 1832, *AP* 2:903–906.

69. Austin to Leaming, February 16, 1836, Leaming Papers.

70. See Austin's "Explanation to the Public concerning the affairs of Texas, by citizen Stephen F. Austin," a pamphlet that was published in Spanish in 1835. The English translation appears in *SHQ* 8:232–58.

71. Almonte, *Report,* p. 178.

72. For a detailed description of the tension and disturbances, see Connor, *Texas*, pp. 101ff., and bibliographical references on p. 408, and Barker, *Life of Stephen F. Austin*, pp. 400ff.

73. Austin in a proclamation of September 19, 1835, quoted in Barker, *Life of Stephen F. Austin*, pp. 412–13.

CHAP. 6. THE LIFE AND VIEWS OF TEXANS

1. For the history of the newspapers and a detailed characterization of individual papers, see Ben C. Stuart, *The History of Texas Newspapers from the Earliest Period to the Present*; John Melton Wallace, *"Gaceta" to Gazette: A Checklist of Texas Newspapers, 1813–1846*; and Marilyn McAdams Sibley, *Lone Stars and State Gazettes: Texas Newspapers before the Civil War.*

2. See Samuel H. Lowrie, *Culture Conflict in Texas, 1821–1835*, pp. 38ff.

3. Rosa Groce Bertleth, "Jared Ellison Groce," *SHQ* 20:365–66.

4. In her reminiscences Mary Baylor writes further: "Stephen F. Austin was a friend of my father Joseph H. Polley who was one of the men who came with Moses Austin in 1819 but some of the historys say 1820" (Mary A. Baylor Reminiscenses, *BTHC*).

5. See Woodman, *Guide to Texas Emigrants*, p. 27.

6. See Jonnie Lockhart Wallis, ed., *Sixty Years on the Brazos*, p. 10. A good description of a wagon train to Texas was given by Mary Crownover Rabb in her reminiscences, *Travels and Adventures in Texas in the 1820's*, p. 1.

7. Bertleth, "Jared Ellison Groce," p. 359.

8. A contemporary described this in the following manner: "Stephen F. Austin's policy in the management of the relations of the colonies with the Mexican Government was, in the main, prudent and wise. But in every free country there must inevitably arise a party opposed to the 'powers that be' and the Wharton's were recognized as the 'head and front' of such a party in Texas. 'The Austin party' and 'the Wharton party' were designations often heard in the colonial times" (Recollections of J. H. Kuykendall, "The Wharton Brothers," James Hampton Kuykendall Papers, vol. 1, *BTHC*).

9. Mrs. Bertleth repeats an interesting version of this story: "It was a personal letter from William H. Wharton to Sam Houston that brought Houston to Texas. The Whartons had known him in Tennessee, and one night at 'Bernardo' [the name of Jared E. Groce's property] William H. Wharton was telling Colonel Groce about Sam Houston and his success as a fighter. Groce in his impetuous way said, 'That's the kind of men we need in Texas. Sit right down and write to him, urge him to come, and I will send the letter by the next post'" (Bertleth, "Jared Ellison Groce," p. 366).

10. John Austin most likely was not related to Stephen F. Austin. See the biographical sketches in Walter P. Webb, ed., *The Handbook of Texas* (hereafter cited as *HOT*) as well as one for Henry Smith.

11. John Henry Brown, *Life and Times of Henry Smith*, and Henry Stuart Foote, *Texas and the Texans*, 2:160.

12. See the *Texas Almanac* for 1860, p. 43, as well as William F. Gray, *From Virginia to Texas, 1835*, p. III.

13. Barker, *Life of Stephen F. Austin*, p. 402.

14. *Texas Almanac*, 1867, p. 208.

15. For Archer's participation in the conspiracy of Aaron Burr, see Homer Thrall, *A Pictorial History of Texas*, 2nd ed., p. 479.

16. *Texas Almanac*, 1867, p. 208.

17. See also Rosa Belle Wilson, "The Mission of Austin, Archer and Wharton to the United States in 1836" (M.A. thesis, University of Texas, 1937), pp. 38–39.

18. For a biography of William B. Travis and further bibliographical references, see Amelia Williams, "A Critical Study of the Siege of the Alamo and of the Personnel of Its Defenders," *SHQ* 37 (1933): 80ff.

19. Forrest E. Ward, "Pre-Revolutionary Activity in Brazoria County," *SHQ* 64:222.

20. In the beginning stages of the settlement of Texas the transition from farmer to rancher was rather easy. Consequently in what follows, when farmers are mentioned, agriculture as a whole is meant and not a differentiation from rancher. The first census of Austin's colony of March 28, 1826, observes: "All the inhabitants of this colony are farmers and cattle raisers, but there are many artisans among them of different kinds; the number is not stated specifically because now they are following only the occupation of farming." The following numbers were given: 1,800 inhabitants, of whom 750 were single, 335 married, and 37 widowed. Livestock was listed as follows: cattle, 3,500; sheep, 4,500; and horses, 1,000 (Spanish Archives, 54:9–18, General Land Office, as cited in Samuel Asbury Papers, *BTHC*).

21. The statements made here refer only to the period from 1820 to about 1845. For the economic and social conditions, see also William R. Hogan, *The Texas Republic*, 3rd ed., pp. 103ff., and Joseph W. Schmitz, *Thus They Lived*, pp. 8–9, 48–49.

22. On this point, see also the noteworthy study by John William O'Neal, "Texas, 1791–1835: A Study in Manifest Destiny" (M.A. thesis, East Texas State University, 1969), pp. 100ff., in which he investigates a group of 465 settlers. In the division of activists and moderates, he arrived at these interesting percentages:

	Activists %	Moderates %
Years in Texas before the war	7.4	12
Several moves before coming to Texas	54	29
Single	42	18
Married	33	78
Occupation		
Farming and cattle raising	39	72
Keeping a store	61	38
Merchants, bankers, speculators	68	13
Doctors, teachers, lawyers	47	19
Military, politics	25	5

23. October 20, 1834, in Smith's proclamation "Security for Texas," *LP* 1:170ff.

24. Henry Smith, November, 1834, in a supplement to his proclamation, "Security for Texas," *LP* 1:188.

25. Travis to Burnet, April 11, 1835, *PTR* 1:62ff.

26. "The Ayuntamiento of Austin to the Ayuntamiento of Béxar," January 14, 1833, Nacogdoches Archives, December 1832–January 1833, 66:249ff., *BTHC* (copied from the originals in the Texas State Library).

27. Houston to Jackson, February 13, 1833, *WSH* 1:274ff.

28. *Clarion and Tennessee State Gazette,* September 1, 1818, p. 3.

29. Ibid., dated December 11, 1821, appeared January 29, 1822, p. 1.

30. Ira Ingram to Roswell Ingram, May 12, 1830, Ira Ingram Papers, *BTHC.*

31. Ibid., July 23, 1833.

32. Ibid., December 9, 1833.

33. Ibid., May 10, 1834.

34. William B. Travis to David G. Burnet, May 21, 1835, *PTR* 1:121ff.

35. Holman to Moore, April 7, 1835, C. D. and William Donaldson Papers 1806–1860, *BTHC.*

36. See, for example, the letter from James Reily, February 14, 1831, to an unknown addressee in which he complains he had been betrayed in land business (William Pitt Ballinger Papers, *BTHC*). Another man writes to his father on April 20, 1833, that he has no job at the time, wants to move to another place, and that general dissatisfaction prevails there (in the town of Washington) about the judge (Alice Lee Ericson Papers, *BTHC*). In his famous letter to his friend Schwarz in Oldenburg, the first prominent German settler in Texas, Friedrich Ernst, described in 1831 his new homeland in the most colorful terms as a land where milk and honey flowed. After its arrival in Germany, the letter was published in an Oldenburg newspaper and was widely distributed. It is also printed in Detlev Dunt, *Reise nach Texas,* pp. 4–16. For the story of "The First German Settlement in Texas," see Rudolph L. Biesele, *SHQ* 34:334–39. See also the description of Texas by Thomas Decrow in his letter to his brother of June 1831 (Daniel Decrow Papers, *BTHC*) and the letter from Asa Hoxey to Edward Hanrick, May 24, 1834 (Edward Hanrick Papers, *BTHC*).

37. William Hale to his brother Phillip Smith Hale, April 11, 1836 (Phillip Smith Hale Papers, *BTHC*).

38. "Journal of Stephen F. Austin on His First Trip to Texas, 1821," *SHQ* 7:286–307, and representative for the remarks he repeatedly made later, the letters to Thomas F. Leaming, June 14, 1830 (*AP* 2:413ff.) and to the Ministro de Relaciones, July 13, 1830 (*AP* 2:449ff.).

39. "Biography and Lifework of a Prominent Imigrant of 1822," written for the *Post* by W. P. Zuber, Iola, Texas, p. 4 ("His Life in Texas"), Groce Family Papers, *BTHC.*

40. In contrast to the descriptions given by Zuber, who also described the turkey as being unpalatable, Capt. Gibson Kuykendall, who had also come to Texas with his parents in 1821, remembered a somewhat different situation: "We were now without bread. We had about two bushels of corn which we saved to plant the ensuing spring. Deer and turkies were very abundant. The deer was lean, but the turkies were fine and fat and constituted the most valuable part of our subsistence for several months. My father, myself, and two younger brothers were good hunters and our family though large was never destitute of meat. We brought a few cattle with us from Arkansas which supplied us with milk. Bees were plentiful and we

were rarely without honey" ("Recollections of Capt. Gibson Kuykendall," vol. 1, book 1, pp. 42–43, Papers of James Hampton Kuykendall, *BTHC*).

41. See again as an example the letters from Ira Ingram to his uncle Roswell Ingram of December 9, 1833, and January 9, 1835: "The cotton crop is better than it ever has been before. . . . This article is the staple of the country. . . . The corn crop too, is abundant. . . . In fact, the agriculture of the country is in the most flourishing condition" (Ira Ingram Papers, *BTHC*).

42. Hogan, *Texas Republic,* pp. 16ff.

43. See the correspondence of merchant Moses Evans from the Brazos River town of Washington, May 25, 1845, with his supplier on the coast (Schmitz, *Thus They Lived,* pp. 41–42).

44. Ibid., p. 45.

45. Thus the ninety-one-year-old Noah Smithwick in his memoirs, *The Evolution of a State,* p. 15.

46. Schmitz, *Thus They Lived,* pp. 96ff.

47. Smithwick, *Evolution of a State,* p. 14, and John Holmes Jenkins III, ed., *Recollections of Early Texas,* p. 7.

48. See Schmitz, *Thus They Lived,* pp. 86ff.

49. For the various forms of entertainment, especially in the days of the Republic, see ibid., pp. 109ff.

50. For living conditions in Texas, see especially the chapter, "The Necessaries of Life," in Hogan, *Texas Republic,* pp. 25ff.

51. See for example Mier y Terán's report to the Mexican president Guadalupe Victoria, June 30, 1828 (Wallace and Vigness, *Documents of Texas History,* pp. 65–66).

52. See Mary Austin Holley, "Texas," in Mattie Austin Hatcher, *Letters of an Early American Traveller,* p. 156.

53. Since the suppression of the Fredonian Rebellion, it had become much quieter in Nacogdoches. Witness to this is the report of Juan N. Almonte, 1834–35: "Lately, however, very honorable and highly cultured families have begun to establish themselves in Texas, especially in Nacogdoches" (Almonte, "Statistical Report on Texas," p. 211), as well as private correspondence such as, for example, the letter from Isaac Holman to Col. William Moore: "Society is much better here than perhaps you might imagine" (C. D. and William Donaldson Papers).

54. For these figures, see Almonte, "Statistical Report on Texas," pp. 177ff.

55. The most prominent example of such a union was the marriage of James Bowie and Ursula Veramendi, celebrated on April 25, 1831, in the San Fernando church in San Antonio de Béxar. For biographies of Bowie, see J. Frank Dobie, "James Bowie, Big Dealer," *SHQ* 60:337–57, and Virgil E. Baugh, *Rendezvous at the Alamo,* pp. 15–99.

56. The prejudiced opinions ranged from "slovenly" and "unreliable" through "bigoted" to "criminal." See as an example the letters of J. C. Tanner to James B. Austin, January 24, 1827 (*AP* 2:1589–90); Henry Austin to Stephen F. Austin, June 3, 1830 (*AP* 2:407); and from Robert Andrew to Stephen F. Austin, May 15 and 16, 1823 (*AP* 1:640ff.); as well as the characterization by Mary Austin Holley in her 1836 book *Texas,* facs. ed., pp. 127ff. It is exceedingly risky when these prejudices are reproduced today by researchers in a manner that implies they correspond in general to the opinions of the Anglo-Americans of that time. Along with these inadmissible

generalizations, Samuel Harman Lowrie, for example, in his book *Culture Conflict in Texas, 1821–1835*, on pp. 86ff., does not hesitate to adulterate quotations or even to invent them. When Stephen F. Austin describes *one group* in Mexico City one time as ignorant, superstitious, and bigoted, Lowry takes this passage to mean *all* Mexicans (Stephen F. Austin to James E. B. Austin, July 8, 1822 [*AP* 1:530ff.]), just as in citing the letters of Robert Andrew, he suppresses the fact that Andrew, with all his prejudices, still knew how to differentiate enough that he had a number of Mexican friends (Robert Andrew to Stephen F. Austin, May 9, September 5, and October 4, 1823, *AP* 1:637–38, 693–94, and 696–97). Even though he does not use sociological terms, Andrew nevertheless clearly describes in his letters the two prevailing Mexican groups—that is to say, social classes: the uneducated, superstitious poor, and the rich, educated families with whom he kept up friendly relations.

57. See Fane Downs, "The History of Mexicans in Texas, 1820–1845" (Ph.D. diss., Texas Tech University, 1970), pp. 5ff.

58. Again see Mier y Terán's report to the president in Howren, "Causes and Origin of the Decree of April 6, 1830," pp. 378–422, and Almonte, "Statistical Report on Texas," p. 193.

59. Downs, *History of Mexicans in Texas*, p. 272, and also the very good study by Jesús F. De La Teja and John Wheat, "Béxar: Profile of a Tejano Community, 1820–1832," *SHQ* 89:7–34.

60. Documents collected in the Béxar Archives can furnish information here. An example would be a petition in 1787 to the *cabildo* of San Antonio de Béxar in which the citizens emphasized their rights and wanted a guarantee that all the horses and cattle of the province of Texas belonged to the citizens and not to the crown. In it—certainly also for the purpose of justification—they continually speak with proud emphasis of "our province of Texas," which had been looked on with pride as their own and cultivated by the ancestors of those who were petitioning. See John Wheat's translation of this petition, vol. 150 (1787), pp. 3, 7, 15, 16, 20, 21, 31, and 59 (Béxar Archives Translations, *BTHC*).

61. For the biographies of these men with bibliographic references, see *HOT.*

62. For a biography of José Antonio Mexía, see A. Alan Hutchinson, "General José Antonio Mexía and His Texas Interests," *SHQ* 82:117–42.

63. For a biography of Lorenzo de Zavala, see W. S. Cleaves, "Lorenzo de Zavala in Texas," *SHQ* 36:29–40.

64. See F. H. Turner, "The Mejia Expedition," *SHQ* 7:1–28.

65. See also on this theme Eugene Barker, "Native Latin American Contribution to the Colonization and Independence of Texas," *SHQ* 46:313–35, and David Montejano, *Anglos and Mexicans in the Making of Texas, 1836–1986*, pp. 26–35.

66. See the memoirs of the son of Erasmo Seguin, the Juan Nepomuceno Seguin Reminiscences, *BTHC.*

67. Austin to Erasmo Seguin, probably January 1, 1824 (*AP* 1:718–19).

68. William P. Zuber, *My Eighty Years in Texas*, p. 25.

69. See anonymous (most likely Asahel Langworthy) *Visit to Texas*, p. 222; and Charles Douglas to Austin, February 15, 1825 (*AP* 1:1046–47).

70. Ira Ingram to Roswell Ingram, March 29, 1830 (Ira Ingram Papers, *BTHC*). At this point criticism of William Stuart Red's work, *The Texas Colonists and Religion,*

1821–1836, must be established because its primary assertion is: "The war of the Texas Revolution was for religious no less than for civil liberty" (p. 92). Even though a large part of the Protestant colonists rejected the Catholic church as an expression of despotism, they were not fighting for religious freedom, for they possessed it already. See also Howard Miller, "Stephen F. Austin and the Anglo-Texan Response to the Religious Establishment in Mexico, 1821–1836, "*SHQ* 91:310, 316.

71. See Hogan, *Texas Republic,* pp. 21–22.

72. See also Charles S. Sydnor, *The Development of Southern Sectionalism, 1819–1848,* p. 5.

73. See Walter Struve, *Die Republik Texas, Bremen und das Hildesheimische,* pp. 80–81.

74. Austin in a report to the settlers on relations with the Indians (*AP* 1:1211).

75. See the letter from Frost Thorn to Austin, July 22, 1828 (*AP* 2:74–75).

76. Thus William Rabb to Austin, November 24, 1828 (*AP* 2:144–45).

77. Briscoe to J. K. Allen, April 14, 1835, cited in Eugene C. Barker, "Public Opinion in Texas preceeding the Revolution," *ARAHA* 1:222.

78. Declaration of the *ayuntamiento* of Liberty, April 17, 1835 (*Texas Republican,* May 30, 1835), and Briscoe's answer (*Texas Republican,* August 8, 1835, *BTHC*).

79. See the *Texas Republican* of July 18, 1835.

80. Thus Mary Austin Holley in her diary May 15, 1835, ed. J. P. Bryan in *The Texas Quarterly* 18 (1965): 23.

81. See Henson, *Samuel May Williams,* pp. 13ff.

82. For details of the circumstances and the provisions of the law, see ibid., pp. 67ff.

83. For a summary, see Rupert N. Richardson, *Texas, the Lone Star State,* 3rd ed., pp. 80ff., and the bibliographical material on pp. 84–85.

84. See James Harrison to Austin, November 30, 1832 (*AP* 2:895–96), and Thomas F. McKinney to Austin, September 9, 1829 (*AP* 2:254ff.).

85. See Moses Austin Bryan, Austin's nephew, to William W. Hunter, September 15, 1835 (Gerald S. Pierce, "Some Early Letters of Moses Austin Bryan," *SHQ* 70:469ff.); and the same expressed in Bryan's reminiscences in a letter to his son Beauregard of September 25, 1889: "But there was a class of agitators who really precipitated difficulties with Mexico; but for them the rupture might have been postponed. These were ambitious men and speculators, who were looking after changes which would better themselves and hurry up annexation to the U.S. The great mass of the people had their families, homes and property in Texas and wanted peace. They looked to Austin for this and he knew it, and they followed his advice to let Mexican revolutions alone and mind their own business" (Declaration of Independence Autograph Collection, *BTHC*).

86. Compare Zuber, *My Eighty Years,* p. 31. A certain number of the settlers, however, had harsh words for Austin. Lydia Ann McHenry wrote her brother on August 25, 1836: "Austin, imbecile, artful & ambitious, considers himself entitled to every office in the gift of the people. . . . As empresario of this colony he has given to his favorites from 5 to 30 leagues of land & he thinks these illegal doings may be ripped up" (George P. Nielsen, ed., "Lydia Ann McHenry and Revolutionary Texas," *SHQ* 74:404ff.).

CHAP. 7. U.S. ECONOMIC INTEREST IN TEXAS

1. Austin to James W. Breedlove, October 12, 1829 (*AP* 2:264ff.).

2. John P. Austin to Stephen F. Austin, January 1, 1830 (*AP* 2:313–14).

3. John M. McCalla to Austin, October 6, 1829 (*AP* 2:261ff.), and similar letters to Austin from R. C. Nicholas, October 11, 1829 (*AP* 2:263–64), and Henry Austin, December 14, 1829 (*AP* 2:300–301).

4. Jackson to Butler, October 10, 1829 (Anthony Butler Papers, *BTHC*).

5. Butler to Jackson, October 28, 1833 (John S. Bassett, *The Correspondence of Andrew Jackson*, 5:219–20).

6. Jackson to Butler, November 27, 1833 (Anthony Butler Papers).

7. See John S. Bassett, *The Life of Andrew Jackson*, 3rd ed., p. v.

8. See the letters, partly in code, from Jackson to Butler, of February 15, August 17, August 24, and December 9, 1831 (Anthony Butler Papers).

9. The consul in Texas, David Dickson, reported to Secretary of State Henry Clay on January 23, 1827, about the Fredonian Rebellion: "Recent and authentic accounts from there [San Antonio] leaves no longer any doubt of the province of Texas being in a complete state of Revolution" ("Despatches from United States Consuls in Texas, 1825–1844," roll 1, vol. 1, August 15, 1825–September 20, 1844, Record Group 59, National Archives, Washington, D.C.).

10. An accurate biography of Anthony Butler has not yet been written, and so it is difficult to give the particular events of his life with complete accuracy. Born in South Carolina in 1787, he certainly had brothers and sisters, as can be seen from various letters (see John R. Harris to Robert Wilson, June 3, 1828 [Benjamin C. Franklin Papers]); but whether he was the Anthony Butler, son of Maj. Edward Butler, who was raised by Andrew Jackson after his father's death in 1805, is doubtful. As a member of the Freemasons he was grand master of Kentucky in 1812–13 and lived there as the owner of a large plantation. On March 11, 1813, he became lieutenant colonel of the Twenty-eighth Infantry Regiment and on February 21, 1814, colonel of the Second Rifles. In this position he fought under Jackson's command at New Orleans and left the army with many honors on June 15, 1815. In 1818–19 he was a delegate to the state legislature of Kentucky. When he was named as chargé d'affaires for Mexico, he was living in Mississippi. See Bassett, *Correspondence of Andrew Jackson*, 1:207, n. 1; Dunbar Rowland, *A Military History of Mississippi, 1803–1898*, p. 12; Robert V. Remini, *Andrew Jackson and the Course of American Empire, 1767–1821*, p. 160; and Elisabeth LeNoir Jennett, ed., *Biographical Directory of the Texas Conventions and Congresses, 1832–1845*, p. 61. For an assessment of his personality by the historians, see John M. Belohlavek, *Let the Eagle Soar! The Foreign Policy of Andrew Jackson*, p. 228.

11. Butler to Jackson, January 4, 1827, cited in Marquis James, *Andrew Jackson: Portrait of a President*, p. 406.

12. Beales to Butler, June 4, 1833 (Anthony Butler Papers). In the course of time John Charles Beales tried to profit from four different empresario contracts but was unsuccessful. For further details of his life, see *HOT.*

13. James Prentiss was born on March 16, 1782, the second of the six children of Capt. John Prentice and his wife Ann. James changed the family name from Pren-

tice to Prentiss. He was trained to be a merchant and worked from 1803 to 1811 as a partner in the firm of Bond & Prentiss in Boston with a branch in London, where he also worked for a while. Although it was one of the largest import houses in the country, it was slowly reduced by the trade embargo of December, 1807, to March, 1809, and had to declare bankruptcy in 1811. James Prentiss saddled up, moved to Lexington, Kentucky, and went into the clothing business there. Soon he owned the largest herd of merino sheep in the United States and was able to do a lucrative business with the army during the War of 1812. The Peace of Ghent caused prices to fall again and once more Prentiss was out on the street. With his brothers John Mellen, Thomas Green, and Henry Bowdoin, he began to establish his first large land speculation business in Indiana, which then was dissolved in 1820 due to the deaths of John and Thomas. James Prentiss thereupon went to New York, where he was active mostly as a broker. Land business often took him to Washington, D.C. In February, 1857, he became a victim of the mysterious "national hotel poisoning" and died on September 20 at the family home in Rahway, New Jersey. For the genealogy of the extended Prentice/Prentiss family, see Charles J. F. Binney, *The History and Genealogy of the Prentice or Prentiss Family in New England from 1631 to 1883*.

14. Prentiss to Butler, July 27, 1835 (Anthony Butler Papers).

15. Carter, *Masonry in Texas*, p. 214.

16. For the exact boundaries of these empresario contracts, see "Record of Translations of Empresario Contracts," pp. 117, 122, 175, 186 (Spanish Archives, General Land Office, Austin, Texas).

17. Carter, *Masonry in Texas*, pp. 197, 219–20.

18. For a biography of Lorenzo de Zavala, see Cleaves, "Lorenzo de Zavala," p. 29ff.

19. For Burnet's attempt to form a company for this reason, see his letters to Austin, July 18, 1829, (*AP* 2:228–29) and December 4, 1829 (*AP* 2:296ff.).

20. See "Memorial of Anthony Dey, William H. Sumner and George Curtis of New York, Trustees of the Galveston Bay & Texas Land Company of New York to the Board of Commissioners for the Settlement of Claims by American Citizens against the Republic of Mexico, 2nd January 1850," recorded as document 1 of the Galveston Bay & Texas Land Co.'s Case (envelope no. 24, Records of the United States and Mexican Claims Commissions, Record Group 76, National Archives, Suitland, Maryland).

21. See, for example, the letter from Anthony Dey and George Curtis to Austin, December 16, 1830 (*AP* 2:559–60).

22. See also *expressis verbis*, George Curtis to José Antonio Mexía, quoted in Hutchinson, "General José Antonio Mexía," p. 128.

23. See the brochure, *Address to the Reader of the Documents Relating to the Galveston Bay & Texas Land Company, Which are Contained in the Appendix* (New York, 1831), as also "Galveston Bay and Texas Land Company Scrip" (Mirabeau Buonaparte Lamar Papers, *BTHC*). In addition, refer once again to the book that was meant as an advertisement for the company: Woodman, *Guide to Texas Emigrants*.

24. See "Law of Colonization of the State of Coahuila and Texas," art. 8, 9, and 18 (*LOT,* 1:100ff.).

25. Thus Mason to Dey, Sumner, and Curtis, December 7, 1832: "The New York Company may proceed to settle their colonies, nolens volens" (doc. 31, env. 24, Records of the United States and Mexican Claims Commissions).

26. For the detailed statement, see the "Memorial of Anthony Dey" (doc. 1, env. 24, Records of the United States and Mexican Claims Commissions).

27. On January 4, 1851, the engineer Randolph Coyle had figured the area of the designated land in the three empresario contracts of Burnet, Vehlein, and Zavala to be 13,743,163 acres. The company had sold 10,216,635 acres of that (doc. 44, env. 24, Records of the United States and Mexican Claims Commissions).

28. The statements as to the actual sale price fluctuated considerably. Asahel Langworthy of New York wrote Austin on January 5, 1831, that the price for land in Texas fluctuated between 5 and 10 cents (AP 2:574ff.). For other statements see Henderson, "Contracts," SHQ 31:309.

29. As may be seen from the Award Books of the Commission on Claims against Mexico, 2:58, entry 30 (Record Group 76, National Archives, Suitland, Maryland).

30. See anonymous, Visit to Texas, pp. 97ff.

31. A detailed investigation of the Galveston Bay and Texas Land Company and its members is not yet available, and the material that is available is often contradictory. For example, Anthony Dey, one of the attorneys and managers of the company, had 91 of the total of 1,000 shares in the beginning of the venture. On January 12, 1843, he declared bankruptcy in New York. But in 1849 he was again entered as a shareholder with 66 shares. See the list of shareholders in the "Memorial of Anthony Dey" (doc. 1, env. 24, Records of the United States and Mexican Claims Commissions).

32. See "The Texas and New Mexico Act, September 9, 1850," in Henry Steele Commager, ed., Documents of American History, 9th ed., pp. 320–21.

33. For the history and background of this speculation, see Holman Hamilton, "Texas Bonds and Northern Profits: A Study in Compromise, Investment, and Lobby Influence," Mississippi Valley Historical Review 43 (1957): 579–94.

34. See "Texas Debt Claims and Warrants," Record Group 217, Records of the General Accounting Office (GAO), Claim no. 606, Box 12, National Archives, Washington, D.C.

35. See ibid., Claim no. 408, Box 9, and Claim no. 492, Box 11.

36. See "Workbook," p. 11, certificate nos. 619 and 618, Record Group 56, General Records of the Department of the Treasury, National Archives, Washington, D.C.

37. See "Texas Debt Claims and Warrants," Claim no. 688, Box 14, Record Group 217, Records of the GAO, NA, Washington, D.C. That he was a front man is apparent from the documents establishing proof of his claim.

38. Corcoran received $44,854.24, Riggs $115,426.75, and their bank $462,530.83. The successor to this bank, Rigg and Company, then received $63,538.06 more, and Charles St. John Chubb, who was probably acting as agent, received $179,061.05 more, so that the whole sum from which Corcoran, Riggs, and their heirs profited ran to $829,410.93. See "Register of Texas Debt Warrants, 1856–1861," Record Group 39, Records of the Bureau of Accounts, Washington, D.C.

39. See Hamilton, "Texas Bonds and Northern Profits," 592ff.

40. See the power of attorney in doc. 16, env. 24, Records of the United States and Mexican Claims Commissions.

41. For a biography of James T. Mason, see Kate Mason Rowland, "General John Thomson Mason," *SHQ* II:163–98.

42. See Hutchinson, "General José Antonio Mexía," p. 127.

43. See the notice in the *New York Evening Post,* date unknown, but if the average time for mail delivery is figured at from one to two months, it appeared in the summer of 1831 (doc. 28, env. 24, Records of the United States and Mexican Claims Commissions).

44. The date of the letter from Mexía to Prentiss is given as March 24, 1831, in the list of documents, but in the newspaper notice as April 2, 1831 (ibid.).

45. Thus in Hutchinson, "General José Antonio Mexía," p. 131.

46. Ibid., pp. 123ff.

47. See doc. 1, env. 24, Records of the United States and Mexican Claims Commissions.

48. Archibald Austin to Austin, October 10, 1830 (*AP* 2:506ff.).

49. Dr. John Lucius Woodbury, Joseph Vehlein's attorney, received an empresario contract for two hundred families on November 14, 1826. See "Records of Translations of Empresario Contracts," pp. 112–13 (Spanish Archives, General Land Office, Austin, Texas).

50. James F. Perry to Austin, October 27, 1830 (*AP* 2:522ff.).

51. This resulted from the fact that on November 15, 1841, Gilbert Thompson and James Prentiss engaged the lawyer Richard S. Coxe as their legal representative. Coxe also represented Prentiss's other company against Mexico before the Claims Commission. For this and for further details concerning the Union Land Company, see the document "Richard S. Coxe Argument" (doc. 37 of the Papers of the Union Land Company, env. 24, Records of the United States and Mexican Claims Commissions).

52. Ibid.

53. As may be seen from doc. 20 of the Papers of the Union Land Company, env. 24, Records of the United States and Mexican Claims Commissions.

54. See again "Richard S. Coxe Argument" (doc. 37, env. 24, Records of the United States and Mexican Claims Commissions).

55. "Statement of Claims of the Union Land Company" (doc. 11, env. 24, Records of the United States and Mexican Claims Commissions).

56. Award Books of the Commission on Claims against Mexico, 2:56, entry 30, Record Group 76, National Archives, Suitland, Maryland.

57. Ibid., p. 57.

58. See "Contract of G. L. Thompson, Stephen Cleveland, James Prentiss, James Henry Prentiss, and Henry B. Prentiss" (doc. 50 of the Trinity Land Company, env. 24, Records of the United States and Mexican Claims Commissions).

59. See "Remarks Submitted in the Case of the Trinity Land Company" (doc. 4, env. 24, Records of the United States and Mexican Claims Commissions).

60. See "Testimony of the Widow of Henry Prentiss, Elizabeth Prentiss, October 27, 1841 in Vermont" (docs. 14 and 5 of the Trinity Land Company, env. 24, Records of the United States and Mexican Claims Commissions).

61. See Binney, *The History and Genealogy of the Prentice Family,* pp. 127, 156.

62. See "Remarks Submitted" (doc. 4 of the Trinity Land Company, env. 24, Records of the United States and Mexican Claims Commissions).

63. See "Memorial of Anthony Dey" (doc. 1 of the Galveston Bay and Texas Land Company, env. 24, Records of the United States and Mexican Claims Commissions).

64. See Henry B. Prentiss to James Prentiss, April 7, 1833 (Andrew Forest Muir, "The Union Company in Anahuac, 1831–1833," *SHQ* 70:256–68).

65. See George Willich to his family in Germany, September 6, 1834 (George Willich, Jr., Papers, *BTHC*) and anonymous, *Visit to Texas,* 105ff.

66. John Bassett Moore, *History and Digest of the International Arbitrations to Which the United States Has Been a Party,* 4:3450–55.

67. John T. Mason to Anthony Dey, William H. Sumner, and George Curtis, March 23, 1834 (doc. 37 of the Galveston Bay and Texas Land Company, env. 24, Records of the United States and Mexican Claims Commissions).

68. See also Llerena B. Friend, *Sam Houston,* 2nd ed., pp. 42ff. Hogan, *Texas Republic,* assumes this indirectly when he connects Sam Houston with the Galveston Bay and Texas Land Company (p. 82), as does Williams, *The Animating Pursuits of Speculation,* p. 62.

69. Prentiss in his third letter to Butler, July 29, 1835 (Anthony Butler Papers).

70. The J. and L. Joseph Company went bankrupt on March 17, 1837, thus starting the dreadful Panic of 1837. See Robert V. Remini, *Andrew Jackson and the Course of American Democracy, 1833–1845,* p. 427.

71. See "Articles of Association of the New Washington Association" (Samuel Swartwout Papers, *BTHC*). See also Feris A. Bass and B. R. Brunson, eds., *Fragile Empires,* p. xxiv, Samuel Swartwout to James Morgan, November 26, 1837, pp. 53ff.; Morgan to Swartwout, January 12, 1842, pp. 158ff.; and Morgan to Swartwout, May 20, 1842, pp. 175ff.

72. See, for example, the letter from John P. Austin to Stephen F. Austin, November 8, 1835 (*AP* 3:244ff.).

73. For more biographical data concerning George M. Patrick, see Muir, "Union Company in Anahuac," p. 259n14.

74. See Carter, *Masonry in Texas,* pp. 245, 249, and 251.

75. See Bass, *Fragile Empires,* p. xx.

76. Ibid., p. xiv.

77. See Remini, *Andrew Jackson,* p. 148.

78. Ibid., p. 150.

79. Ibid., p. 153, and Bass, *Fragile Empires,* pp. xviiff.

80. Bass, *Fragile Empires,* p. xix.

81. Ibid., p. 172.

82. See the "Articles of Association of the New Washington Association," article 6 (Samuel Swartwout Papers).

83. "Statement of J. Haggerty, Thomas E. Davis, and Alex. H. Dana to the Secretary of the Treasury of the United States," in Texas Debt Claims and Warrants, Claim no. 346, Box 18, Records of the GAO, Record Group 217, National Archives, Washington, D.C.; and the petition of the trustees and manager of the New Wash-

ington Association to Peter W. Gray, judge of the District Court within and for the said County of Harris (Samuel Swartwout Papers).

84. See Texas Debt Claims and Warrants, Claim no. 346, Box 18, Records of the GAO, Record Group 217, NA, Washington, D.C.

85. In Bass, *Fragile Empires*, see Samuel Swartwout to James Morgan, October 2, 1845, pp. 282–83; Morgan to Swartwout, November 6, 1845, pp. 286–87; and Swartwout to Morgan, September 17, 1846, pp. 305–306.

86. Swartwout to Morgan, July 6, 1845 (Bass, *Fragile Empires*, pp. 271–72).

87. Williams, *Animating Pursuits of Sepculation*, p. 177n129.

88. See the letter from John C. Beales to Butler, June 4, 1833 (Anthony Butler Papers), and "Memorial of John Charles Beales" (env. 21, Records of the United States and Mexican Claims Commissions).

89. See Samuel Sawyer to Sam Houston, October 3, 1835 (doc. 88, Andrew Jackson Houston Collection, Texas State Archives), and Houston to Sawyer, February 3, 1837 (*WSH* 2:48–49).

90. See "Memorial of John Charles Beales" (env. 21, Records of the United States and Mexican Claims Commissions), and Charles Edwards, *Rio Grande and Texas Land Company* (n.p., n.d., BTHC).

91. "Memorial of John Charles Beales," (env. 21, Records of the United States and Mexican Claims Commissions).

92. To the Alabama Company belonged, as far as is known, Hooper Coffey (this name is not clearly identifiable) as lawyer, John Austin as agent, Robert M. Williamson as legal adviser, and Asa Hoxey as manager and member of the company. See Asa Hoxey to Robert M. Williamson, March 9, 1833, and John Austin to an unidentified person, February 2, 1833 (Edward Hanrick Papers, BTHC). Nothing is known about Hooper Coffey (if this name is correctly reproduced). John Austin was born on March 17, 1801, in Connecticut, came to Texas with James Long in 1819, was arrested, interned in Mexico, freed at Poinsett's instigation, went to Texas again in 1822, helped Austin – to whom he was most likely not related – and from 1825 on ran a store in Brazoria with Austin's younger brother, James E. B. Austin, until the latter's death in 1829. John Austin was one of the especially active members of the War Party and died of cholera on August 11, 1833. Robert M. Williamson, known as Three Legged Willie because his disabled leg was supported by a wooden leg, came to Texas in 1826 and was an attorney and publisher of various newspapers. Asa Hoxey, born in Georgia on February 22, 1800, was a doctor and came to Texas with his slaves in 1832. Together with Thomas Gray, John W. Hall, and others he founded the Washington Townsite Company for the development of Washington. More concerning the biography of these men as well as further bibliographical references can be found in *HOT.*

93. See John Cameron to Ben R. Milam, December 20, 1827 (Milam-McKinney Collection).

94. See John Exter to Ben R. Milam, March 18, 1828 (ibid.).

95. Listed as founders were Benjamin Reynolds, R. P. Currin, James Davis, William Davis, C. Crusman, John D. Martin, A. V. Brown, Willis W. Cherry, A. R. Covan, and William K. Hill, who also had to straighten out the land business for

the company with the empresarios William Hardin and Josi Dolores, Sterne, and Taylor. See "Articles of Association of the Mississippi Texas Land Company" as well as the "Statement of W. K. Hill (Benjamin C. Franklin Papers). William Hardin, born in Georgia on March 25, 1801, came to Texas in 1827. About Sterne and Taylor mentioned in W. K. Hill's statement, it can only be assumed that this refers to Adolphus Sterne and his brother-in-law Charles Standfield Taylor. For biographies of these men, see *HOT.*

96. Mentioned in Woodman, *Guide to Texas Emigrants,* p. 100.

97. Mentioned in Williams, *Animating Pursuits of Speculation,* p. 206.

98. Ibid., p. 207.

99. Mentioned in Rowland, "General John Thomson Mason," p. 192.

100. See Henderson, "Minor Empresario Contracts," pp. 24ff.

101. Mexía to Prentiss, March 26, June 23, and November 9, 1831 (docs. 28, 32, and 35 of the Galveston Bay and Texas Land Company, env. 24, Records of the United States and Mexican Claims Commissions), as well as Mexía to Austin, March 27, 1833 (*AP* 2:932–33).

102. See Anthony Dey and George Curtis to Austin, December 16, 1830 (*AP,* 2:559–60), as well as January 5, 1831 (*AP* 2:577–78).

103. Austin to Williams, February 19, 1831 (*AP* 2:602), as well as Austin to Thomas F. Leaming, July 23, 1831 (*AP* 2:679).

104. See Austin to Williams, March 21, 1835 (*AP* 3:50ff.).

105. Mason at any rate expresses himself thus in his final report to the Galveston Bay and Texas Land Company (doc. 38 of the Galveston Bay and Texas Land Company, env. 24, Records of the United States and Mexican Claims Commissions).

106. Austin to Mason, April 17, 1833 (Rowland, "General John Thomson Mason," pp. 173–74).

107. As he himself saw it in his final report (doc. 38, env. 24, Records of the United States and Mexican Claims Commissions).

108. Ibid.

109. On January 29, 1834, he wrote to his daughter: "Long since I discovered he was a bad man" (Rowland, "General John Thomson Mason," p. 178).

110. On July 13, 1834, Anthony Butler wrote in his Despatch no. 73 to Secretary of State Louis M. Lane: "After having said this much I must add that Col. Austin does not merit either sympathy or assistance from our government! He is unquestionably one of the bitterest foes to our Government and people that is to be found in Mexico, and has done more to embarras our negotiations upon a certain subject than all the rest of the opposition put together, and I am very sure that he was the principal cause of my being defeated in the last effort made to obtain a [section of Texas] 1022. 236. 1376. 1372. 651. 692" (*Despatches from United States Ministers to Mexico, 1823–1906,* vol. 6 [Sept. 10, 1832–June 9, 1836], Record Group 59, National Archives, Washington, D.C.).

111. See Austin to Williams, November 5, 1833 (*AP* 2:1013ff.); November 26, 1833 (*AP* 2:1016–17); February 14, 1835 (*AP* 3:42–43); and Austin to James F. Perry, March 4, 1835 (*AP* 3:45–46).

112. Henry Meigs to Austin, September 29, 1835, from New York (*AP* 3:140),

likewise in a letter from Alexander Calvit to Mexía, August 29, 1833 (Barker, *Life of Stephen F. Austin,* pp. 390ff.).

113. See the letters under the pseudonym O.P.Q. to Branch T. Archer of January 28 and February 8, 1834, as well as the explanatory article by J. M. Winterbotham, "Stephen F. Austin and Anthony Butler," *MVHR* 11:99–127).

114. He states this in his final report (doc. 38, env. 24, Records of the United States and Mexican Claims Commissions).

115. Austin to James F. Perry, March 10, 1835 (*AP* 3:46ff.).

116. From the letters of Austin to Williams of November 26, 1833 (*AP* 2:1016) and December 31, 1834 (*AP* 3:36–37). See also Yoakum, *History of Texas* 1:325–26.

117. Austin to Williams, April 4, 1835 (*AP* 3:60).

118. On May 6, 1835, he wrote to Williams: "I have never in all my life known so bad, and base a man as Butler—At the time he wrote the OPQ letters he was my enemy" (*AP* 3:73).

119. "Strictly confidential" from William H. Wharton to Austin, June 2, 1836, from Washington (*AP* 3:363ff.).

120. Andrew Jackson's note on a letter to him from Anthony Butler of March 7, 1834 (Bassett, *Correspondence of Andrew Jackson* 5:252–53).

121. See Richard B. Stenberg, "Jackson, Anthony Butler and Texas," *Southwestern Social Science Quarterly* 13:264–86 (hereafter cited as *SSSQ*).

122. Butler to Poinsett, July 8, 1846 (Anthony Butler Papers).

123. Representative are Richard R. Stenberg, "Jackson's Neches Claim, 1829–1836" (*SHQ* 39:255–74); Stenberg, "Andrew Jackson and the Erving Affidavit" (*SHQ* 41:142–53); Stenberg, "The Texas Schemes of Jackson and Houston" (*SSSQ* 15:229–50); Eugene Barker, "President Jackson and the Texas Revolution" (*American Historical Review* [hereafter cited as *AHR*], 12 [1907]: 788–809), as well as the more literary article by Bernard Mayo, "Apostle of Manifest Destiny" (*The American Mercury* 18 [December 1929]: 420–26). In addition, see the biographies by Augustus C. Buell, *History of Andrew Jackson,* pp. 353ff.; James, *Andrew Jackson* 2:406ff.; and Robert V. Remini, *Andrew Jackson and the Course of American Democracy, 1833–1845,* pp. 347–68.

CHAP. 8. ENTER SAM HOUSTON

1. For the events concerning Houston in 1812, as well as for his first military activity, see Marquis James, *The Raven,* pp. 24ff.

2. Houston to General David Parker (*WSH,* 1:8).

3. Sam Houston, *Life of General Sam Houston,* pp. 3–4.

4. See N. M. Ludlow, *Dramatic Life as I Found It,* p. 166, as cited in Friend, *Sam Houston,* p. 8.

5. See the letter of invitation of December 20, 1822 (*WSH* 3:1), as well as McLean, *Papers concerning Robertson's Colony,* 1:369ff. On September 26, 1825, Houston addressed an official letter to "W. Tannehill, esq. Most W. Grand Master of the Grand Lodge of Tennessee, Nashville" (*WSH* 4:2). For membership in the Masons,

see Charles A. Snodgrass, *The History of Freemasonry in Tennessee, 1789–1943*, pp. 23ff.

6. See Friend, *Sam Houston*, p. 8, as well as McLean, *Papers concerning Robertson's Colony*, l:xliii, and p. lxviiin35. On May 5, 1818, a notice from Wilkins Tannehill appeared in the *Clarion and Tennessee State Gazette* in which he announced the publication of *The Masonic Repository*.

7. See *WSH* 4:1–2.

8. See Robert V. Remini, *The Election of Andrew Jackson*, especially pp. 58ff., as well as Friend, *Sam Houston*, pp. 10ff., and James, *Raven*, pp. 53ff.

9. *WSH* 1:130.

10. *WSH* 1:132ff.

11. For Houston's singular relationship with the Indians, see Friend, *Sam Houston*, pp. 24–25.

12. See Jack Gregory and Rennard Strickland, *Sam Houston with the Cherokees, 1829–1833*, p. 126.

13. See Jackson's Executive Book (Jackson Papers, Library of Congress); Jackson to William S. Fulton, January 23, 1838 (Bassett, *Correspondence of Andrew Jackson*, 5:532); and Bassett, *Life of Andrew Jackson*, p. 677.

14. Robert Mayo, *Political Sketches of Eight Years in Washington*, pt. 1, p. 120.

15. Jackson to Fulton, December 10, 1830 (Bassett, *Correspondence of Andrew Jackson*), 4:213.

16. Mayo, *Sketches*, a facsimile of the letter printed between pp. 124 and 125.

17. Ibid., pp. 127ff.

18. John Quincy Adams, *Speech upon the Right of People, Men and Women to Petition (the Texas Speech) Delivered in the House of Representatives between 16th June and 7th July 1838;* he mentions the letter concerned only at the end on Saturday, July 7, 1838, pp. 117ff. On p. 119 the argument appears that the letter was never sent.

19. See the accompanying letter from Fulton of February 15, 1839 (Miscellaneous Letters of the Department of State, Jan. 1–Apr. 30, 1839, M 179, Roll 88, Record Group 59, National Archives, Washington, D.C.).

20. Richard Stenberg, "The Texas Schemes of Jackson and Houston" *SSSQ* 15:239ff.; Henry Bruce, *Life of General Houston, 1793–1863*, pp. 78ff.; Augustus Buell, *History of Andrew Jackson*, p. 351; and Owen P. White, *Texas: An Informal Biography*, pp. 70ff.

21. Jackson to Brigadier General Benjamin C. Howard, August 2, 1838 (Bassett, *Correspondence of Andrew Jackson*), 5:561.

22. Andrew Jackson to Houston, June 21, 1829 (Yoakum, *History of Texas*), 1:307.

23. Wharton to Houston, July 25, 1829 (Yoakum, *History of Texas*), 1:281.

24. Wharton to Houston, October 25, 1829 (Yoakum, *History of Texas*), 1:308.

25. See also *Reports of Committees of the House of Representatives*, 1st Sess., 22 Cong., vol. 5, doc. 502. Houston and Eaton were acquitted of any suspicion of bribery or acceptance of pay for want of evidence.

26. Houston to Van Fossen, April 4, 1830 (*WSH* 1:147ff.).

27. Houston to Van Fossen, August 22, 1830 (*WSH* 1:187–88).

28. See Captain George Vashon to President Jackson, September 12, 1830 (Grant Foreman, *Pioneer Days in the Early Southwest* [Cleveland, 1926], p. 195).

29. See also James, *Raven*, pp. 104ff. For a history of the Chouteaus and their

importance, see William E. Foley and C. David Rice, *The First Chouteaus – River Barons of Early St. Louis.*

30. Thus in his letter to John H. Eaton of June 24, 1829 (*WSH* 1:134ff.).

31. For this business, see Gregory, *Houston,* pp. 127ff., as well as Grant Foreman, "Some New Light on Houston's Life among the Cherokee Indians," *Chronicles of Oklahoma* 9 (1931): 139–52.

32. Houston to Prentiss, March 27, 1832 (*WSH* 1:197–98).

33. In a letter of June 19, 1826, which is difficult to decipher because it was half burned, Samuel Swartwout wrote to Houston that "they"–Swartwout and others–were thinking of establishing a bank and he, Swartwout, hoped that Houston would be governor of Tennessee (Andrew Jackson Houston Collection, doc. 27, Texas State Archives).

34. Prentiss to Houston, April 5, 1832 (*WSH* 1:201).

35. Houston to Prentiss, April 8, 1832 (*WSH* 1:200–201).

36. Houston to Prentiss, March 28, 1834 (*WSH* 1:283–84).

37. See his letter to Prentiss of June 27 and 28, 1832 (*WSH* 1:246–49).

38. "Agreement between Houston and Prentiss," June 1, 1832 (*WSH* 1:229–30).

39. See also James, *Raven,* pp. 163ff., as well as Houston's speech defending himself (*WSH* 1:207–25).

40. Houston to Prentiss, June 9, 1832 (*WSH* 1:234–35).

41. Houston to Prentiss, July 10, 1832 (*WSH* 1:257–58).

42. Houston to Prentiss, September 11 and 15, 1832 (*WSH,* 1:264ff.).

43. Prentiss to Houston, March 8, 1834 (*WSH* 1:280–81), and Houston to Prentiss, March 28, 1834 (*WSH* 1:283–84).

44. Houston to Prentiss, September 15, 1832 (*WSH* 1:266).

45. Houston, *Life of Houston,* p. 5, and compare with Charles Edward Lester, *The Life of Sam Houston,* pp. 64ff.

46. Houston to John H. Houston, December 2, 1832 (*WSH* 6:1ff.).

47. Houston to John H. Houston, July 31, 1833 (*WSH* 5:5–6).

48. See Yoakum, *History of Texas,* 1:308.

49. See Archie P. McDonald, *Hurrah for Texas,* p. ix; James, *Raven,* p. 196; and Carter, *Masonry in Texas,* p. 226.

50. "Application for Headright in Austin's Colony" (*WSH* 1:271).

51. See "Houston's Petition for a Divorce" (*WSH,* 1:277ff.).

52. See Friend, *Sam Houston,* p. 56.

53. This explanation seemed necessary to him for he was trying to defend his right to a piece of land in Burnet's colony against James H. Starr in a lawsuit. Archibald Hotchkiss, who was hired by John T. Mason as agent for the Galveston Bay and Texas Land Company, had only been able to assign land to Houston in the vicinity of Nacogdoches, for Houston had declared he did not want to have any more to do with land in Austin's colony. In November, 1855, after twelve years, the case came to a conclusion in that Starr, according to his own testimony, "capitulated" by buying the piece of land concerned from Houston. Certainly Starr was convinced that Houston had come that far with the help of false testimony. For more about this, see the records of the case in Sam Houston vs. Jas. H. Starr, no.

2188 in the District Court of Nacogdoches County, Texas (Robert Bruce Blake Papers, 27:178–341, *BTHC*).

54. See the memorandum from Williams to Houston of December 26, 1832 (doc. 70, Andrew Jackson Houston Collection, Texas State Archives).

55. Refer again to J. Frank Dobie, "James Bowie, Big Dealer" (*SHQ* 60:344).

56. Houston to Ellsworth, December 1, 1832 (*WSH* 1:267ff.).

57. Houston to Guy M. Bryan, November 15, 1852 (*WSH* 5:364ff.).

58. Ibid., p. 365.

59. Houston to John A. Wharton, April 14, 1835 (*WSH* 1:293–94).

60. Who these friends were who are always being cited cannot be positively ascertained. Moses Austin Bryan wrote about this to his son Beauregard on September 25, 1889: "There is no doubt that the Whartons and Houston worked together at this time, and Houston was greatly helped in the beginning of his political career by the Whartons, for in Texas they were known, and he but little known" (Moses Austin Bryan Papers, *BTHC*).

61. Houston to Jackson, February 13, 1833 (*WSH* 1:274ff.).

62. See the letter mentioned above from Houston to Guy M. Bryan, November 15, 1852 (*WSH*, 5:368).

63. See Augustus C. Allen to Houston, February 28, 1834 (doc. 73, Andrew Jackson Houston Collection, Texas State Archives).

64. See Thomas M. Marshall, "The Whereabouts of Sam Houston in 1834" (*SHQ* 16:328–29).

65. See G. W. Featherstonehaugh, *Excursion through the Slave States from Washington on the Potomac to the Frontier of Mexico*, 2:161, as cited in Friend, *Sam Houston*, pp. 60–61.

66. Houston to John A. Wharton, April 14, 1835 (*WSH* 1:293–94).

67. See Swartwout to Houston, September 12, 1835 (doc. 86, Andrew Jackson Houston Collection, Texas State Archives).

68. See Archibald Hotchkiss to John T. Mason, September 13, 1834 (Rowland, "General John Thompson Mason," pp. 186–87), as well as Austin's letter to Williams of April 15, 1835 (*AP* 3:62–63).

69. See Bass, *Fragile Empires*, p. 42n3, as well as John P. Austin to Stephen F. Austin, January 5, 1831 (*AP* 2:580).

70. Swartwout to James Morgan, April 20, 1837 (Bass, *Fragile Empires*, pp. 40ff.).

71. See Swartwout to Houston, May 18, 1835, and September 12, 1835 (docs. 79 and 86, Andrew Jackson Houston Collection, Texas State Archives). The first name of the lawyer, Mr. Fortune, is not certain, for on September 12, 1835, Swartwout calls him William to Houston and on October 16, 1839, in his letter to Morgan (Bass, *Fragile Empires*, pp. 94–95) refers to him as James. If this is not just an error, perhaps they were brothers.

72. In his letter of May 18, 1835, to Houston, Swartwout still spoke of land on Red River and other enterprises (doc. 79, Andrew Jackson Houston Collection, Texas State Archives). Swartwout certainly had great expectations for his Texas affairs and Houston's help. He expressed this poetically: "When I am King, good Buckingham, claim from me the Earldom of Nacogdoches!–with all the moveables on Thorne's

Land!" (Swartwout to Houston, September 12, 1835, doc. 86, Andrew Jackson Houston Collection, Texas State Archives).

73. Mason to Swartwout, June 4, 1836 (Samuel Swartwout Papers, *BTHC*).
74. Houston to Prentiss, April 20, 1834 (*WSH* 1:289–90).
75. Houston to Prentiss, April 24, 1834 (*WSH* 1:290–91).
76. See reproductions of these portraits in the 1929 edition of James, *Raven*, between pp. 116 and 117.
77. Compare Friend, *Sam Houston*, p. 41, and Yoakum, *History of Texas*, 1:308.
78. See Houston to Jackson, May 18, 1830 (*WSH* 1:149–50).
79. Interesting in this connection also is a letter from Houston to Jackson of September 19, 1829, in which he describes first his passion for politics and then makes vague intimations that fit Texas exactly: "Were I settled in a state; that I might render my aid in some future political struggle between userpation, and the rights of the people" (Bassett, *Correspondence of Andrew Jackson*, 4:75). When one considers that Houston wrote these letters in Fort Gibson, Arkansas, which lay on a main road to Texas, then one can easily imagine that an exchange of information must have prevailed between him and travelers to and from Texas.
80. John F. Kennedy, *Profiles in Courage*, p. 94.

CHAP. 9. MEXICO'S ATTITUDE TOWARD TEXAS

1. See Anne Fears Crawford, ed., *The Eagle*, p. 49.
2. For his report, see the Archivo General de Mexico: Archivo de la Secretario de Fomento Colonización y Terrenos Baldios, Legajo 7, Expediente 47, 1833.
3. See Edith L. Kelly and Mattie A. Hatcher, "Tadeo Ortíz de Ayata and the Colonization of Texas, 1822–1833" (*SHQ* 32:74–86, 152–64, 222–51, and 311–43), as well as Wilbert H. Timmons, "Tadeo Ortíz and Texas" (*SHQ* 71:21–33).
4. *El Fénix de la Libertad*, January 4, 1834; *El Mosquito Mexicano*, August 4 and November 3, 1835; and *El Anteojo*, November 4, 6, 15, and 20 and December 9, 1835.
5. See Brack, *Mexico Views Manifest Destiny*, p. 71.
6. José Maria Tornel Y Mendívil, *Tejas y los Estados-Unidos de América en sus relaciones con la República Mexicana*, here the translation by Carlos Castañeda, *The Mexican Side of the Texas Revolution*, 2nd ed., p. 369.
7. Ibid., p. 342; see also the comments of many Mexican newspapers in December, 1833, as cited in Nettie Lee Benson, "Texas as Viewed from Mexico" (*SHQ* 90:288–89).
8. José Enrique de la Peña, *With Santa Anna in Texas*, ed. and trans. Carmen Perry, pp. 4–5.
9. Ibid., p. 12.
10. See the letters from Mexía to Zavala of January 18 and 24 and March 22, 1833 (Lorenzo de Zavala Collection, *BTHC*).
11. George Fisher to Austin, October 20, 1835 (George Fisher Papers, *BTHC*).
12. For events in California in the 1830s, see David J. Weber, *The Mexican Fron-*

tier, 1821–1846, pp. 242ff. and 254ff., as well as Robert G. Cleland, *From Wilderness to Empire,* 2nd ed., pp. 115ff.

13. See once more the letter from Fisher to Austin, October 20, 1835 (George Fisher Papers, *BTHC*).

14. See Hutchinson, "General José Antonio Mexía," pp. 140–41.

15. "Memoirs of the History of the War with Texas by Vicente Filisola, General of Division and Actual President of the Supreme War and Navy Tribunal of the Republic," trans. Verona Griffith, 1937, vol. 1, pt. 2, pp. 492–93 (Vicente Filisola Papers, *BTHC*).

16. Tornel y Mendívil, *Tejas y los Estados-Unidos,* in Castañeda, *Mexican Side of the Texas Revolution,* p. 380.

CHAP. 10. THE WAR

1. For these circumstances, see also Eugene C. Barker, "Difficulties of a Mexican Revenue Officer in Texas" (*SHQ* 4:190–202).

2. See C. Allen True, "John A. Williams, Champion of Mexico in the Early Days of the Texas Revolution" (*SHQ* 47:107–19).

3. See J. B. Miller to Ugartechea of July 16, 1835, and Wiley Martin for the Brazos District to Ugartechea, Cós, and Santa Anna of July 17, 1835 (*PTR* 1:247 and 249–50).

4. Travis to Bowie, July 30, 1835 (*PTR* 1:289–90).

5. Martín Perfecto de Cós to the Political Chief of the Brazos District, July 7, 1835 (*PTR* 1:212–13).

6. Cós to Political Chief, August 1, 1835 (*PTR,* 1:297–98).

7. See McLean, *Papers concerning Robertson's Colony,* 11:49–57.

8. See Cós to *Gefe Político del Departmento de Nacogdoches,* August 8, 1835 (*PTR,* 1:315–16); Cós to Ugartechea, August 15, 1835 (*PTR,* 1:316–17); Ugartechea to Cós, August 8, 1835 (*PTR* 1:321); and Henson, *Samuel May Williams,* pp. 76–77.

9. See the resolutions of the cities of Columbia, Nacogdoches, and San Felipe (*PTR* 1:342–45 and 370–71).

10. Cós to the Political Chiefs of the districts of Béxar, Brazos, and Nacogdoches, July 12, 1835, which appeared in the *Texas Republican,* August 22, 1835.

11. See the Nacogdoches resolutions, August 15, 1835 (*PTR* 1:344).

12. See Travis to Burnet, Andrew Briscoe, and John M. Moore, all written on August 31, 1835 (*PTR* 1:379–82).

13. Anonymous letter of September 8, 1835, which appeared on October 31, 1835, in the *Niles Register* in Baltimore (*PTR* 1:429ff.).

14. See Benjamin F. Smith to James F. Perry, August 15, 1835 (*AP* 3:98).

15. See F. W. Johnson to Austin, September 5, 1835 (*AP* 3:114–15).

16. See Travis to Austin, September 22, 1835 (*AP* 3:133) and Eli Mercer to Austin, September 23, 1835 (*AP* 3:135).

17. See Miles S. Bennett, "The Battle of Gonzales, the 'Lexington' of the Texas Revolution" (*SHQ* 2:313–16), and Nanna Smithwick Donaldson, "Concerning the Gonzales Cannon" (*SHQ* 5:356).

18. Austin to Burnet, October 5, 1835 (*PTR* 2:42).

19. Barker agrees (Barker, *Life of Stephen F. Austin,* pp. 414–15).

20. For the extremely interesting history of this garrison, which has been restored and is open to the public, see Kathryn Stoner O'Connor, *The Presidio la Bahia del Espíritu Santo de Zuñiga, 1721 to 1846* (Austin, 1966); for the history of this military episode, see Hobart Huson, *Captain Phillip Dimmitt's Commandancy of Goliad, 1835–1836,* pp. 5ff.

21. See the circular "Council to People," October 8, 1835 (*PTR* 2:67).

22. Peter W. Grayson to Austin, October 11, 1835 (*LP* 1:243).

23. Austin to Cós in two letters of October 17, 1835 (*PTR* 2:142–43), and Cós to Austin, October 18, 1835 (*PTR* 2:153–54).

24. See *OCTR* 1:38–39.

25. See once more the letter from Mary Austin Holley to her brother-in-law Orville L. Holley, February 26, 1832, Letters 1:217 (Mary Austin Holley Papers, *BTHC*).

26. Representative is the letter from William R. Carey to William J. Oppelt of January 21, 1836: "I arrived at Washington on the 28th of July [1835]. . . . There I intend to take up my final residence, but the unsettled state of affairs between Texas and the Mexicans aroused our suspicions. They wanted to establish *centralism,* a rather military despotism a government that is repugnant to the principles of free born americans, we remonstrated and sent commissions but we could not positively ascertain on account of their treachery and deceit, they denied it and still they were making preparations for it, but we were on the alert. . . . The Mexican army or rather a part of them came to this place [San Antonio] commanded by Martin Perfecto de Cos, a bold aspiring Young General. . . . The enemy (as I shall call them) sent about 200 of their troops to Gonzales after a cannon. . . . Volunteers were called for to fight for this country" (James H. Collett Papers, *BTHC*). In her reminiscences for October, 1835, when she was ten-and-a-half years old, Dilue Harris described the time: "Our school closed in September. The teacher said there was so much excitement that it affected the small children, and the young men could not be got back in school at all after the election in September. There was a constant talk of war" ("The Reminiscences of Dilue Harris," *SHQ* 4:156).

27. See Eugene C. Barker, "The Texan Revolutionary Army" (*SHQ* 9:227–61). See esp. chap. 7, "The Volunteer Army of the People," pp. 247ff.

28. See Gail Borden to Austin, November 5, 1835 (*AP* 3:238–39; Austin to the president of the consultation, November 5, 1835 (*AP* 3:239ff.); Houston to Fannin, November 13, 1835 (*WSH* 1:305–6); M. A. Bryan to James F. Perry, November 30, 1835 (*AP* 3:268–69); and Austin to F. W. Johnson, December 22, 1835 (*AP* 3:289–90).

29. As seen also by Barker (*Life of Stephen F. Austin,* p. 421) and Friend (*Sam Houston,* p. 63).

30. See Eugene C. Barker, "The Tampico Expedition" (*SHQ* 6:169–86) and "President Jackson and the Texas Revolution" (*AHR* 12:788–809).

31. See Ruby Cumby Smith, "James W. Fannin, Jr., in the Texas Revolution" (*SHQ* 23:79–90, 171–203, and 271–84, esp. pp. 80–81), as well as Clarence Wharton, *Remember Goliad,* pp. 25ff.

32. See Yoakum, *History of Texas,* 2:25.

33. Ibid., pp. 25ff., and M. L. Crimmins, "The Storming of San Antonio de Béxar in 1835" (*West Texas Historical Association Year Book* 22 [1946]: 95–117).

34. Mrs. Harris wrote: "All the men and boys that went to the army from our part of the country had come home and were at work. They seemed to think there would be no more trouble with Mexico" (Harris, *Reminiscences,* p. 159). See also Ernest C. Shearer, *Robert Potter: Remarkable North Carolinian and Texan,* p. 50; Friend, *Sam Houston,* p. 65; and Williams, *A Critical Study of the Siege of the Alamo,* p. 256.

35. For these numbers, see Barker, "Texas Revolutionary Army," pp. 254ff.

36. Compare O'Connor, *Presidio la Bahía,* p. 115.

37. R. C. Stockton to Houston, November 19, 1835, and Henry Raguet to Houston, December 13, 1835 (docs. 122 and 162, Andrew Jackson Houston Collection, Texas State Archives).

38. John Sowers Brooks wrote to his father on December 23, 1835: "It is contemplated to reinforce us and then detach us to attack the city of Metamoras in the State of Tamaulipas. This will be the Commencement of a regular and systematic invasion of Mexico and I trust, I shall live to see it end beneath the walls of the Capitol of Santa Anna's iron rule dominions" (*PTR* 3:293ff.).

39. See Barker, "Texas Revolutionary Army," p. 255.

40. Henry Smith to the Council, January 9, 1836 (*LOT* 1:761ff.); the Council, January 11, 1836 (*LOT* 1:762–63); and Smith to Leonard W. Groce, January 18, 1836 (*OCTR* 1:304ff.). See also W. Roy Smith, "The Quarrel between Governor Smith and the Council of the Provisional Government of Texas" (*SHQ* 5:269–346).

41. See *LOT* 1:650, 660, and 980ff.

42. Ibid., p. 825.

43. Ibid., p. 1063.

44. See the text of the Goliad Declaration of Independence (*LOT* 1:815–20).

45. See the report of the Committee of State and Judiciary, January 3, 1836 (*LOT* 1:735–36), and the report of D. C. Barrett, chairman of the select committee of five, to the Council, December 23, 1835 (*LOT* 1:689).

46. Austin to his cousin Henry Austin, January 7, 1836 (*AP* 3:297–98). On the same date Austin wrote in a still more blatant manner to Houston: "A question of vital importance is yet to be decided by Texas, which is a declaration of independence. When I left Texas I was of opinion that It was premature to stir this question, and that we ought to be very cautious of taking any steps that would make the Texas war purely a national war, which would unite all parties against us, instead of being a party war, which would secure to us the aid of the federal party. . . . I now think the time has come for Texas to assert her natural rights; and were I in the convention I would urge an immediate declaration of independence. . . . The information from Mexico is that all parties are against us, owing to what has already been said and done in Texas in favor of independence; and that we have nothing to expect from that quarter but hostility. . . . If it be true, and I have no reason to doubt it, our present position in favor of the republican principles of the constitution of 1824 can do us no good, and it is doing us harm by deterring those kind of men from joining us that are most useful" (*AP* 3:298–99). His letters to others

are written in this same tone, e.g., to R. R. Royall, Rhoads Fisher, and Mary Austin Holley, all on January 7, 1836 (*AP* 3:299–301).

47. See William H. Wharton, Austin, and Branch T. Archer to Smith, January 16, 1836 (OCTR 1:299–300).

48. For example Fehrenbach, *Lone Star*, pp. 174–75, and Eugene C. Barker, "The Texan Declaration of Causes for Taking up Arms against Mexico" (*SHQ* 15:173–85).

49. See Garry Wills, *Inventing America,* pp. 49ff.

50. The speech was published in the *New Orleans Courier* on December 8, 1835 (*LP* 1:253ff.).

51. See the deed from George Childress to Samuel Swartwout, February 1, 1836, and the "Statement of S. Swartwout against G. Childress," May 18, 1838 (Samuel Swartwout Papers, *BTHC*).

52. See Bass, *Fragile Empires,* p. 12 and n. 2.

53. George C. Childress to Sterling C. Robertson, New York, October 12, 1835 (McLean, *Papers concerning Robertson's Colony,* 11:604–605).

54. See Louis Wiltz Kemp, *The Signers of the Texas Declaration of Independence,* pp. 59ff.

55. See James K. Greer, "The Committee on the Texas Declaration of Independence" (*SHQ* 30–31:239–51, 33–49, and 130–49).

56. Compare the Declaration of Independence of the United States (Commager, *Documents of American History,* 1:100ff.) and the Texas Declaration of Independence (*LOT* 1:1063ff.), and see Garry Wills in regard to the U.S. Declaration of Independence in *Inventing America.*

57. See the entry for this date in Gray, *From Virginia to Texas,* p. 123.

58. Ibid., p. 126.

59. Ibid., pp. 126ff.

60. See *LOT* 1:870–902.

61. The constitutional convention is described in an extremely negative fashion by William Fairfax Gray. In his description of the individual participants he does not spare attributes like "narrowminded," "selfish," and "illiterate." There was a great need for political experience and theory (Gray, *From Virginia to Texas,* pp. 111, 127–28). The accuracy and detail in his report are also vouched for by Andrew Forest Muir (see *HOT* 1:724). In contrast Seymour V. Connor gives the convention high marks (Connor, *Texas,* p. 112). However, when he stresses as praiseworthy the circumstance that the convention did not even require three weeks to complete the constitution, the objection must be raised that the Texans had taken over the entire framework of the American Constitution and some passages word for word, which certainly made their work appreciably easier.

62. Compare Gray, *From Virginia to Texas,* p. 132.

63. See the letter in *LOT* 1:845–46.

64. See Gray, *From Virginia to Texas,* pp. 125–31.

65. James C. Neill to Henry Smith, January 6, 1836, as quoted in Williams, *A Critical Study of the Siege of the Alamo,* pp. 262–63.

66. See Houston to Henry Smith, January 17, 1836 (*WSH* 1:339–40).

67. To form a sound judgment about the true nature of this man is extremely

difficult. "The man was certainly eccentric, perhaps he purposely appeared queer" (Amelia Williams in her short biography in *A Critical Study of the Siege of the Alamo,* p. 109). See also Virgil E. Baugh, *Rendezvous at the Alamo,* pp. 102ff. An interesting article on the various images of Crockett is Frederick S. Voss, "Portraying an American Original: The Likenesses of Davy Crockett," *SHQ* 91:457–82.

68. From the reports it is not clear whether Bowie suffered from pneumonia, tuberculosis, or the result of an accident in which he fell and was seriously injured (Williams, *A Critical Study of the Siege of the Alamo,* p. 17). On that day, February 24, Travis sent out his famous message. For a good account of Travis's life and this special document, see Michael R. Green, "To the People of Texas & All Americans in the World," *SHQ* 91:483–508.

69. See, for example, Walter Lord, *A Time to Stand;* Williams, *A Critical Study of the Siege of the Alamo;* and Lon Tinkle, *13 Days to Glory: The Siege of the Alamo.*

70. Many anecdotes about events in the Alamo have never been unequivocally confirmed or disproved. See Lord, *A Time to Stand,* chap. 15, "Riddles of the Alamo," pp. 198ff., and his "Myths and Realities of the Alamo," in *The Republic of Texas,* ed. Stephen B. Oates, pp. 18–25.

71. See Houston to Fannin, March 11, 1836 (*WSH* 1:362ff.); Lord, *A Time to Stand,* p. 167; and Williams, *A Critical Study of the Siege of the Alamo,* pp. 159–78.

72. Williams, *A Critical Study of the Siege of the Alamo,* p. 279.

73. Travis to Smith, February 13, 1836 (Williams, *A Critical Study of the Siege of the Alamo,* pp. 281–82).

74. Thus Williams in a personal letter of November 7, 1833, to Samuel E. Asbury. She portrays both Fannin and Travis in the most negative terms: "He [Fannin] soon paid the just price for his selfish ambitions." In the same letter she is of the opinion concerning Travis's actions: "It shows a cruel, vindictive nature" (Samuel E. Asbury Papers, *BTHC*).

75. Peña, *With Santa Anna,* pp. 44–45.

76. To give more exact numbers is not possible, for all those who were shot were thrown into a mass grave. Exactly who was with Fannin cannot be determined with accuracy, because of the existing circumstances. For the events transpiring around Fannin and his men, see Harbert Davenport, "The Men of Goliad" (*SHQ* 48:1–41); Smith, "James W. Fannin"; Andrew A. Boyle, "Reminiscences of the Texas Revolution" (*SHQ* 13:285–91); William Corner, "John Crittenden Duval: The Last Survivor of the Goliad Massacre" (*SHQ* 1:47–67); and Castañeda, *Mexican Side of the Texas Revolution,* pp. 18ff.

77. Davenport, "The Men of Goliad," p. 2.

78. See Peña, *With Santa Anna,* pp. 92–93.

79. See Santa Anna's official position, *Manifesto que de sus operaciones en la campana de Tejas y en su cautiverio dirige a sus consiudadanos el General Antonio Lopez de Santa Anna.*

80. See Tornel y Mendívil, *Tejas y los Estados-Unidos.*

81. See Harbert Davenport, "The Men of Goliad," p. 4.

82. See, for example, the *Philadelphia National Gazette,* May 28, 1835, in James E. Winston, "Pennsylvania and the Independence of Texas" (*SHQ* 17:281), and the collection of Texas-related articles from all the newspapers from Cincinnati, Ohio, by

Samuel F. Asbury, especially the *Cincinnati Daily Gazette,* January 12, 1836, with reports from correspondents in New Orleans dated December 27, 1835 (Samuel E. Asbury Papers, *BTHC*). Negative opinions existed also. In the *Virginia Herald* of March 23, 1836, there was the statement: "Volunteers are returning and reporting very discouragingly of the inhabitants of Texas. The inhabitants are poor, and care not a fig under what government they live. The principal object of the majority of the inhabitants that fight is plunder and pillage" (as quoted in James E. Winston, "Virginia and the Independence of Texas," *SHQ* 16:277, n. 1). In the *Cincinnati Daily Gazette* of September 9, 1836, it was even reported that the drawing up of volunteer troops was the same as direct military intervention in Mexico (Samuel E. Asbury Papers, *BTHC*).

83. See Oates, *Republic of Texas,* p. 25.

84. Barker gives these numbers ("Texan Revolutionary Army," pp. 258–59).

85. See Yoakum, *History of Texas,* 2:106ff.

86. For this, see the very graphic description of the flight of her family in Harris, *Reminiscences,* pp. 162ff.

87. See Sam Houston to the chairman of the Military Committee, James Collinsworth, March 15, 1836 (Yoakum, *History of Texas,* 2:475–76).

88. José Enrique de la Peña has only harsh words for his chief (Peña, *With Santa Anna,* pp. 130–31).

89. See Burnet to Houston, April, 1836: "The enemy are laughing you to scorn. You must fight them. You must retreat no farther. The country expects you to fight. The salvation of the country depends on you doing so" (*WSH* 1:412).

90. For the course of events in this battle, see Eugene C. Barker, "The San Jacinto Campaign" (*SHQ* 4:236–345); Connor, *Texas,* pp. 115ff.; and the eyewitness account of Dr. Nicholas Descombo Labadie: "Let us attack the enemy and give them Hell!" (Oates, *Republic of Texas,* pp. 27–34).

91. See the "Official Report of the Battle of San Jacinto," April 25, 1836 (*WSH* 1:416ff.).

92. Houston to Henry Raguet, April 7, 1836 (*WSH* 1:400). By Nachez is meant the Neches River; Jackson assumed it, rather than the Sabine River, was the border.

93. Concerning this theory, see Friend, *Sam Houston,* p. 69, and Eugene C. Barker, "President Jackson and the Texas Revolution" (*AHR* 12:806–807).

94. See Fehrenbach, *Lone Star,* pp. 228–29.

95. Thus William T. Riviere, "Sam Houston's Retreat" (*SHQ* 46:9–14).

96. Houston to Thomas J. Rusk, March 29, 1836 (*WSH* 1:384–85).

97. See Castañeda, *Mexican Side of the Texas Revolution,* pp. 180ff.

98. José Urrea's "Diario de las Operaciones Militares de la Division que al Mando del General Jose Urrea hizo la campana de Tejas," in Castañeda, *Mexican Side of the Texas Revolution,* pp. 264ff.

99. Peña, *With Santa Anna,* pp. 151ff.

100. Houston in a message "To the Troops and People of the East," April 26, 1836 (*WSH* 1:423); for the military aspects of the war, see summary by James W. Pohl and Stephen L. Hardin, "The Military History of the Texas Revolution: An Overview" (*SHQ* 89:269–308).

CHAP. II. THE PHASE OF CONSOLIDATION

1. See Alexander Dienst, "The Navy of the Republic of Texas" (*SHQ* 12:115–203, 249–75; and 13:1–43 and 85–127).

2. Such as John H. Jenkins, "The Texas Navy," in Oates, *Republic of Texas*, pp. 35–41.

3. Not until 1935 were McKinney's descendants awarded the sum that was owed. See Henson, *Samuel May Williams*, pp. 8off. She judges the amount that McKinney and Williams spent for Texas to exceed $99,000.

4. See Swartwout to Morgan, May 16 and 28, 1836 (Bass, *Fragile Empires*, pp. 8ff. and 11ff.).

5. Prentiss to Houston, November 12, 1835 (doc. 116, Andrew Jackson Houston Collection, Texas State Archives).

6. McManus, October 29, 1835, to an unknown person (Jane McManus Storms Cazneau Papers, *BTHC*). Jane McManus, born in New York on April 6, 1807, came to Texas in 1832 at the instigation of Aaron Burr in order to shore up the family finances. For details, see the bibliographical references in *HOT.*

7. Barker thinks that it took nine weeks for news to get to Washington, D.C., from Texas under the most favorable circumstances (Barker, *Life of Stephen F. Austin*, p. 435). This assertion is, however, doubtful as a generality, as can be demonstrated by various letters sent to the North from Texas. For example, a letter written by James Perry from Peach Point in the vicinity of Brazoria, Texas, on April 21, 1838, reached the addressee, Thomas F. Leaming, in Philadelphia on May 30, 1838 (Thomas F. Leaming Papers, *BTHC*). In that letter Perry referred to a letter from Leaming of March 20 that he had received on April 20.

8. See the *Philadelphia National Gazette*, May 17, 19, 23, and 28, 1836 (James E. Winston, *Pennsylvania*, p. 281).

9. Austin to Lamar, June 27, 1836 (*LP* 1:405), and William H. Wharton to Austin, June 2, 1836 (*AP* 3:363ff.).

10. For the opinions of those states and the support Texas got from them, see the various articles by James E. Winston, "Kentucky and the Independence of Texas" (*SHQ* 16:27–62); "Mississippi and the Independence of Texas" (*SHQ* 21:36–60); "New Orleans Newspapers and the Texas Question, 1835–1837" (*SHQ* 36:109–29); "New York and the Independence of Texas" (*SHQ* 18:368–85); as well as Winston, "Pennsylvania," and Winston, "Virginia," and Claude Elliott, "Alabama and the Texas Revolution" (*SHQ* 50:315–28).

11. Printed in the *Courier and Enquirer*, a New York newspaper, as quoted in Winston, "New York," p. 375n20.

12. See the *Clarion and Tennessee State Gazette*, August 24, 1819, p. 3.

13. See Winston, "Kentucky," p. 53.

14. Sterling C. Robertson in an open letter of October 5, 1835, to Mr. Hunt, the publisher of the *Arkansas Gazette*, printed in that paper on October 27, 1835 (*PTR* 2:758 and 5iff.).

15. Barker, "Texan Revolutionary Army," p. 259.

16. *WSH* 1:426–27.

17. See Asa K. Christian, "Mirabeau Buonaparte Lamar," (*SHQ* 23–24 in six parts, here 24:45).

18. See William C. Crane, *Life and Select Literary Remains of Sam Houston,* pp. 112–13; Fehrenbach, *Lone Star,* pp. 241–42; and Friend, *Sam Houston,* p. 71.

19. Friend, *Sam Houston,* pp. 71ff.

20. See Joseph Milton Nance, *After San Jacinto,* pp. 11–12; and Connor, *Texas,* p. 125.

21. See Christian, "Mirabeau B. Lamar," *SHQ* 23:155.

22. See Stanley Siegel, *The Poet President of Texas,* p. 13.

23. Ibid.

24. It cannot be determined from Lamar's statements what company he worked for. On April 10, 1836, he wrote a letter to his brother Jefferson J. Lamar in which he said that he had not yet been able to use the $6,000 that had been entrusted to him for the purchase of land and had therefore deposited it with Lorenzo de Zavala (*LP* 1:350ff.). See also the letter of recommendation from Williams & McKinney to Toby & Brothers in New Orleans in which they attest to Lamar's reliability (*LP* 1:383). Also participating in Lamar's land business was Maj. Robert Eden Handy who, with his business partner, William Lusk, founded the city of Richmond in the vicinity of Houston and, also with Lusk, controlled great amounts of land. See the letter of Robert E. Handy to Lamar, May 28, 1836 (*LP* 1:384) and the biographical sketch of Handy in *WSH* 1:376n3.

25. Poet as he was, he found many flowery phrases for his vindictiveness: "I am certain that there is not a gallant son of chivalry, whose faithful sabre played like a meteor on the plains of San Jacinto, but who will feel that his trusty blade drank the blood of the foe in vain, when he hears that the prime object of vengeance has been permitted to purchase his life and depart the land in liberty and peace" (Lamar to the president of Texas and his cabinet, May 12, 1836, *LP* 1:376).

26. Christian, "Mirabeau B. Lamar" (*SHQ* 23:163).

27. On July 26, 1836, Henry Austin wrote to his sister Mary Austin Holley: "Lamar is a fighting chicken at the head of the army" (Henry Austin Papers, *BTHC*).

28. Lamar to Burnet, July 17, 1836 (*LP* 1:417–18).

29. Entered in Austin's memorandum book under July 20, 1836 (Barker, *Life of Stephen F. Austin,* p. 437); also Austin to the editor of the *Telegraph and Texas Register,* August 4, 1836 (*AP* 3:411–12).

30. See James, *Raven,* p. 266.

31. Houston to Guy M. Bryan, November 15, 1852 (*WSH* 5:364–69).

32. Ibid.

33. See Gray, *From Virginia to Texas,* p. 111.

34. Ibid.

35. Houston to William G. Cooke, end of August (*WSH* 1:446).

36. On September 2, 1836, Austin wrote James F. Perry: "Houston will, I am told, get all the east, and Red river now – Many of the old settlers who are too blind to see or understand their interest will vote for him" (*AP* 3:428). Although Barker sees in this letter only Austin's plan to devote himself to private interests in the coming winter (*Life of Stephen F. Austin,* p. 440), and Ann Hill Froelich in her M.A.

thesis, "The Relationship of Stephen F. Austin and Sam Houston" (Sam Houston State University, 1971, p. 63) considers the letter to be only an example of the fact that Austin was counting on the possibility of defeat. This statement by Austin that the old settlers could only be for Houston because they were "too blind to see" shows that he was neither indifferent to the election nor felt especially friendly toward Houston, and also had not too great an opinion of "his" settlers.

37. The official election results were announced on October 5, 1836, in the new Texas congress (*Journals of the House of Representatives of the Republic of Texas*, 1st Cong. 1st sess., Houston, 1838, p. 31). There were 4,327 votes for president, only 3,922 for vice-president (2,738 for Lamar, 1159 for Rusk, 23 for Zavala, and 2 for H. Smith), and again only 3,922 registered an opinion on the question of annexation. Interestingly enough, the literature on the subject gives different tallies. Friend, *Sam Houston*, p. 76, starts with 6,640, of which 5,119 supposedly voted for Houston, 743 for Smith, 587 for Austin, and 191 for others. These figures for Austin and Smith can also be found in Donald Day and Harry Herbert Ullom, eds., *The Autobiography of Sam Houston*, p. 132; in Crane, *Life and Select Literary Remains*, p. 117, n.*; and Richardson, *Texas, the Lone Star State*, p. 106, but none of the authors give a source for the numbers in question. However, they obviously come from the *Houston Telegraph* of September 23, 1857, and are repeated in Anson Jones, *Republic*, p. 620. The election results for Houston are apparently as different as the eyesight of those who were copying them: Crane: 4,374, Friend: 5,119, Ullom: 5,199, and Richardson: 5,110.

38. Austin to Thomas J. Rusk, August 9, 1836 (*AP* 3:412ff.).

39. *AP* 3:413.

40. Gail Borden, Jr., to Austin, August 15, 1836 (*AP* 3:417).

41. Austin to Gail Borden, Jr. (*AP* 3:418ff.).

42. See Nina Covington, "The Presidential Campaigns of the Republic of Texas of 1836 and 1838" (M.A. thesis, University of Texas, 1929), pp. 28–36.

43. Friend, *Sam Houston*, p. 75.

44. See Henson, *Samuel May Williams*, p. 88. Austin also rejects this reproach in his open letter to Gail Borden, Jr., (*AP* 3:420).

45. Austin to Sen. L. F. Linn, May 4, 1836, a letter that was published in several papers in the United States (*AP*, 3:344ff.). Austin expressed himself in the same way on April 15, 1836, in a letter to "Andrew Jackson, Martin Van Buren, Richard M. Johnson, John Forsyth, Lewis Cass, T. H. Benton, and to any member of the Cabinet or Congress of all parties and all Factions of the United States" (*AP* 3:332–33).

46. See the text of his speech of September 8, 1835, at a public banquet in his honor in Brazoria (*AP* 3:116–19).

47. See the minutes of the Senate meeting of October 28, 1836 in Ernest W. Winkler, *Secret Journals of the Senate, Republic of Texas, 1836–1845*, p. 17; and Barker, *Life of Stephen F. Austin*, p. 442.

48. See Austin to Williams, April 15 and 29, 1835 (*AP* 3:62–63 and 68–69).

49. Austin to Perry, December 25, 1835 (*AP* 3:294–95).

50. See Williams to Austin, August 29, 1836 (*AP* 3:424ff.); concerning the accusations against Austin, see Austin to Rusk, August 9, 1836 (*AP* 3:412ff.).

51. See Austin to Williams, November 3, 1836 (*AP* 3:446–47). For the business connection between McKinney & Williams and Toby & Brothers, see again the let-

ter from the former to the latter of May 25, 1836 (*LP* 1:383), and Henson, *Samuel May Williams,* pp. 89–90.

52. There were 3,277 votes for annexation, 91 against–i.e., 97.3 percent of the electorate voted for annexation by the United States. The constitution of the Republic of Texas was accepted with 3,199 votes. These figures are from the *Journals of the House of Representatives of the Republic of Texas,* p. 31. While 4,327 Texans voted for president, interestingly enough only 3,368 considered it important enough to vote on annexation.

53. See Crane, *Life and Select Literary Remains,* p. 116ff.

CHAP. 12. DOMESTIC POLICIES

1. See the text of the treaty in *WSH* 1:358–60.

2. See Houston to Henry Raguet, April 7, 1836 (*WSH* 1:400) and to Colonel Bowl (i.e., Chief Tewulle), April 13, 1836 (*WSH* 1:409–10).

3. See Siegel, *Poet President of Texas,* pp. 35–36.

4. See "General Lamar's First Message to Congress Communicated December 21st, 1838 (*LP* 2:352 and 354).

5. It is impossible to cover in detail here the events that took place between the Texans and the Comanches from 1840 and 1850. The reports are much too contradictory to allow an accurate picture of the situation. In addition in the Anglo-American literature, the Comanches are generally presented incorrectly as the aggressors and the white men as the defenders. Compare the various treatments in Connor, *Texas,* pp. 142–43 (and bibliographical references on p. 413); Richardson, *Texas, the Lone Star State,* p. 112; Fehrenbach, *Lone Star,* pp. 247–48.

6. Isaac Watts Burton wrote to Lamar on August 25, 1838: "The rebellion of the Mexicans and their attempt to let loose the Indians on this frontier has created a very great excitement among us,–It is now over and we are daily catching the poor devils and I suppose we shall have a fine hanging frolick shortly" (*LP* 2:208–209).

7. See Michael Paul Rogin, *Fathers and Children,* p. 169.

8. As quoted in ibid., p. 206.

9. See James, *Andrew Jackson,* p. 304, and Paul Jacobs et al., *To Serve the Devil,* p. 31.

10. See Christian, "Mirabeau B. Lamar" (*SHQ* 23:155).

11. See J. Warnock to Lamar, December 26, 1840 (*LP* 5:455–56), and William Brookfield to Lamar, January 6, 1840 (*LP* 3:300–301).

12. Lamar's argument is often repeated today by some researchers as fact, without criticism. Stanley Siegel in his biography of Lamar states incorrectly: "Upon the latter tribe's safe return to the United States the former Indian lands of eastern Texas were now ready for despoilment and occupation" (Siegel, *Poet President of Texas,* p. 58). For criticism of Lamar by the citizens, see again William Brookfield to Lamar, January 6, 1840 (*LP* 3:300–301).

13. See Friend, *Sam Houston,* p. 100.

14. See Christian, "Mirabeau B. Lamar" (*SHQ* 23:243).

15. Ibid., p. 244.

16. See Lamar's address to both houses of the Texas congress on November 1, 1840 (*LP* 3:464–70), and his speech at a public banquet also in 1840 (*LP* 3:476–80).

17. That Lamar was greatly hindered in his activities as a politician by his unrealistic dreams and fantasies, along with his great ambition, is even admitted by his extremely well-disposed biographer. See Siegel, *Poet President of Texas,* p. 103.

18. See William C. Binkley, *Expansionist Movement in Texas, 1836–1850,* p. 44.

19. See Lamar's inaugural address, December 10, 1838 (*LP* 2:316–23), as well as his notes about the annexation of Texas, also of December 10, 1838 (*LP* 2:324–27).

20. See D. W. Meinig, *Imperial Texas,* 2nd ed., pp. 39ff.

21. See Dorman H. Winfrey, "Mirabeau B. Lamar and Texas Nationalism" (*SHQ* 59:197).

22. For the history of the Santa Fe Expedition, see Connor, *Texas,* p. 150, and bibliographical references on p. 415; also Siegel, *Poet President of Texas,* pp. 102ff.

23. For these figures, see Christian, *Mirabeau B. Lamar,* p. 246.

24. See Lena London, "The Initial Homestead Exemption in Texas" (*SHQ* 57, 432–53), and *HOT* 1:830–31.

25. For the effort leading up to this law and the text itself, see James D. Carter, *Education and Masonry in Texas to 1846,* pp. 83ff. and 100ff.

26. Concerning the University of Texas system, see the *Texas Almanac* for 1980–81, pp. 396, 617, and 644–45, and for 1986–87, pp. 547–60, 689. For the history of the university, see L. Tuffly Ellis, "The University's Centennial: A Commemoration" (*SHQ* 86:125ff.), and Roger A. Griffin, "To Establish a University of the First Class" (*SHQ* 86:135ff.).

27. Lamar in his first address as president to both houses of congress, December 21, 1838 (LP 2:348).

28. See again Carter, *Education and Masonry;* for Lamar's membership in the Masons, see p. 80.

29. James Morgan to Samuel Swartwout, July 6, 1840, reflects the mood in Texas very well (Bass, *Fragile Empires,* p. 105).

30. For Houston's activities as president, see Friend, *Sam Houston,* chap. 5, "Houston's Republic," pp. 78–114.

31. For details, see Edmund T. Miller, *A Financial History of Texas;* Henson, *Samuel May Williams,* pp. 79ff.; and Hogan, *Texas Republic,* pp. 81ff.

32. As an example, see Swartwout to James Morgan, April 23, 1836 (Bass, *Fragile Empires,* pp. 3ff.).

33. The dissertation by Elgin Williams, "The Animating Pursuits of Speculation," should again be cited here. Although superficial and full of errors, it nevertheless gives a real impression of the extent of speculation in land in Texas at the time of annexation.

CHAP. 13. FOREIGN POLICY AND ANNEXATION BY THE UNITED STATES

1. The complexities of the international relationships of and with Texas have already been illuminated by a number of authors in comprehensive studies, esp. Joseph

William Schmitz, *Texan Statecraft, 1836–1845* (See the bibliography, pp. 239ff.); Marcel Moraud, *The Diplomatic Relations of the Republic of Texas,* Rice Institute Pamphlet, no. 43, pp. 29–54; and Ephraim Douglass Adams, *British Interests and Activities in Texas, 1838–1846.*

2. For Ward's agitation against the United States, see Brack, *Mexico Views Manifest Destiny,* pp. 28ff. and 40ff.

3. See Gustavo Beyhaut, *Süd- und Mittelamerika II: Von der Unabhängigkeit bis zur Krise der Gegenwart,* pp. 25ff.

4. Ibid., p. 72.

5. For these figures and American foreign trade at that time, see Charles Lyon Chandler, *Inter-American Acquaintances,* pp. 22ff. It should not be forgotten that, in spite of all the competition, England was also important for trade with the United States and vice versa. Thirty to 50 percent of the foreign trade of the United States between 1830 and 1840 was carried on with Great Britain, which for its part in those years sent 16 to 25 percent of its exports to the United States. See Harry C. Allen, *Great Britain and the United States: A History of Anglo-American Relations (1783–1952),* pp. 59–60.

6. For the economic power struggle of the Europeans and the Americans in Latin America, see Beyhaut, *Süd- und Mittelamerika II,* pp. 74ff., and David M. Pletcher, *The Diplomacy of Annexation,* pp. 9ff.

7. See Adams, *British Interests in Texas,* pp. 18–19.

8. See the report of the debate in the British newspaper *Courier and Enquirer* (*LP* 5:112–16), and J. L. Worley, "The Diplomatic Relations of England and the Republic of Texas" (*SHQ* 11:1ff.).

9. The problems that Great Britain saw in its relationship to Texas were visible in the correspondence with each other of various public personalities. For example, see Joseph T. Crawford, special agent for the British government, to Sir Richard Pakenham, British minister in Mexico, on May 26, 1837, and James Hook to Lord Palmerston on April 30, 1841; both letters are published in Ephraim Douglass Adams, "Correspondence from the British Archives concerning Texas, 1837–1846" (*SHQ* 15:209–17 and 230–40).

10. Concerning these religious reform movements and their work, see Bailyn, *Great Republic,* pp. 542ff.

11. See the Texas constitution of March 17, 1836 (*LOT* 1:1078–79), and Worley, "Diplomatic Relations of England," p. 4.

12. After this treaty the French received the $600,000 they demanded but not the $200,000 they had meanwhile requested for their expenses in the war. Concerning this conflict, which has gone down in Anglo-American history as the Pastry War, see Meyer, *Course of Mexican History,* pp. 328ff., and Herbert Rook Edwards, "Diplomatic Relations between France and the Republic of Texas, 1836–1845" (*SHQ* 20:210).

13. See the dossier of June 1, 1838, compiled for Molé by Henderson (*DCRT* 3:1208–16).

14. See the memorandum to Molé of September 5, 1838 (Nancy Nichols Barker, *The French Legation in Texas,* 1:47–48).

15. Memorandum to Molé of October 15, 1838 (ibid., pp. 48–49).

16. For this treaty, see again Edwards, "Diplomatic Relations between France and the Republic," pp. 222ff.

17. See *WSH* 3:259; and for Hamilton's role as Texas minister and his relationship with Sam Houston, see Marilyn McAdams Sibley, "James Hamilton, Jr., vs. Sam Houston: Repercussions of the Nullification Controversy" (*SHQ* 89:165–80).

18. Contrary to the version usually repeated in the literature, Belgium never formally recognized the independence of Texas. Compare Connor, *Texas*, p. 147; Friend, *Sam Houston*, pp. 85 and 121; and Richardson, *Texas, the Lone Star State*, p. 125, as well as the contrary view in Pierre Henri Laurent, "Belgium's Relations with Texas and the United States, 1839–1844" (*SHQ* 68:235).

19. In spite of the fact that no treaty was forthcoming, the Republic of Texas kept a consul in Bremen (as also in Antwerp). See Manfred Kossok, "Prussia, Bremen, and the Texas Question" (*Texana* 3:227–69); Schmitz, *Texan Statecraft*, pp. 219ff.; and Jürgen Prüser, *Die Handelsverträge der Hansestädte Lübeck, Bremen, und Hamburg mit überseeischen Staaten im 19. Jahrhundert*, p. 53. Prüser emphasizes that first Lübeck and Hamburg abandoned ratification of the treaty with Texas because of the existing treaty with Mexico after the latter's protest. Bremen nevertheless completed ratification on December 13, 1844. Texas, however, no longer needed to ratify this agreement. See the text of the treaty in *DCRT* 3:1563–69.

20. Dubois de Saligny, cofounder of the Franco-Texian Commercial and Colonization Company, attempted—if also unsuccessfully—to involve France officially in Lamar's Santa Fe adventure. See Nancy N. Barker, "Devious Diplomat: Dubois de Saligny and the Republic of Texas" (*SHQ* 72:330ff.).

21. Saligny's conduct and his advice are still often erroneously seen as the reason the French government refused to give Texas the loan it requested. Thus John Edward Weems, *Dream of Empire*, p. 192. In contrast, Nancy N. Barker records the events correctly (*Diplomat*, pp. 328ff.).

22. See Worley, "Diplomatic Relations of England," pp. 16ff.

23. See Friend, *Sam Houston*, p. 85.

24. See Houston to Joseph Eve, April 27, 1843, as well as the appended Spanish document by Santa Anna of February 18, 1843 (*WSH* 4:181–86).

25. See Harry A. Gailey, Jr., "Sam Houston and the Texas War Fever, March–August, 1842" (*SHQ* 62:37–38).

26. With almost the same words Gen. Alexander Somervell gives the mood in a letter of March 25, 1842, to then Secretary of State Anson Jones: "The hobby on which they ride is, invasion of Mexico, to give peace and happiness to poor suffering Texas, and thereby achieve immortal glory for themselves" (Anson Jones, *Memoranda and Official Correspondence Relating to the Republic of Texas, Its History and Annexation*, p. 173.

27. See Houston to William Henry Daingerfield, April 1, 1842 (*WSH* 3:14ff.), and Gailey, "Sam Houston and the Texas War Fever," pp. 29–44.

28. See Houston's orders to Gen. Edwin Morehouse, March 18, 1842 (*WSH* 2:511).

29. See *WSH* 7:6–7.

30. Compare Houston to Isaac Van Zandt and James Pinckney Henderson, April 16, 1844 (*WSH* 4:298–99), and Houston to Van Zandt and Henderson, May 10, 1844 (*WSH* 4:317ff.).

31. See also Houston's speech in the Senate on August 1, 1854 (*WSH* 6:74–95).

32. See chap. 11, n. 52.

33. Jackson to the U.S. Congress, December 21, 1836, quoted in James, *Raven,* p. 274.

34. See Wharton to Austin, June 2, 1836 (*AP* 3:363ff.) and Wharton to Secretary of State John Forsythe, February 12, 1837 (Francis Richard Lubbock, *Six Decades in Texas,* p. 40); also Remini, *Andrew Jackson and the Course of American Democracy,* pp. 366–67.

35. See Wharton to Austin, May 26, 1836 (*AP* 3:360–61).

36. See James Treat to James Morgan, September 16, 1836 (Samuel Swartwout Papers, *BTHC*), and Swartwout to Morgan, February 6, 1837 (Bass, *Fragile Empires,* pp. 32ff.).

37. See Ashbel Smith, *Reminiscences of the Texas Republic,* p. 80.

38. Sam Houston to John H. Houston, November 20, 1836 (*WSH* 2:27–28).

39. Houston to Robert A. Irion, March 19, 1837 (*WSH* 2:74).

40. Houston to William S. Murphy, May 6, 1844 (*WSH* 4:323).

41. See Houston to Anson Jones, July 8, 1844 (Jones, *Memoranda,* pp. 371ff.); to Andrew Jackson, December 13, 1844 (*WSH* 4:406–407); and to Andrew Jackson Donelson, April 9, 1845 (*WSH,* 4:410ff.).

42. Houston to Isaac Van Zandt and James Pinckney Henderson, the Texas agents in Washington, D.C., on May 17, 1844 (*WSH* 4:325ff.).

43. See once more William H. Wharton to Austin, June 2, 1836 (*AP* 3:364).

44. See Rogin, *Fathers and Children,* pp. 304–305.

45. See Austin to Edmund P. Gaines, July 4, 1836 (*AP* 3:384–85), and Sam Houston in a memo to Gaines in July 1836 (James, *Raven,* p. 261).

46. See Rogin, *Fathers and Children,* p. 305, and Pletcher, *Diplomacy of Annexation,* p. 71. Pletcher thinks that Gaines seriously believed the American settlements were being threatened by Indians, a conjecture that seems doubtful on the basis of the available sources. James, *Raven,* p. 262, indicates that Jackson approved of Gaines's actions, that Jackson only urged the U.S. district attorneys to take care that American neutrality was preserved.

47. David M. Potter, *The Impending Crisis, 1848–1861,* p. 52, and John H. Schroeder, "Annexation or Independence: The Texas Issue in American Politics, 1836–1845" (*SHQ* 89:137–64).

48. See Frederick Merk, *Slavery and the Annexation of Texas,* p. 10.

49. Compare with this the statements of David M. Pletcher, *Diplomacy of Annexation,* pp. 73, 99, and 139.

50. For the eventful history of these parties at the time under discussion, see a summary in Bailyn, *Great Republic,* pp. 473ff.

51. See Frederick Jackson Turner, *The United States, 1830–1850,* pp. 434ff.

52. Concerning this complex political-party scene, see Arthur M. Schlesinger, Jr., *The Age of Jackson,* and Charles S. Sydnor, *The Development of Southern Sectionalism, 1819–1848,* pp. 316ff.

53. For this, see Elisabeth Howard West, "Southern Opposition to the Annexation of Texas" (*SHQ* 18:74ff.).

54. Hamilton to Lamar, November 3, 1838 (*LP* 2:277).

55. For the history of Jackson's Bank War, see Schlesinger, *Age of Jackson,* pp. 76ff., and Turner, *United States,* pp. 402ff.

56. Bailyn, *Great Republic,* p. 484.

57. See the article "Texas and Mexico" in the newspaper *Evening Star,* probably published in New York in August, 1836 (*LP* 1:444–45).

58. These figures are taken from the appendix of Bailyn, *Great Republic,* p. xix.

59. For Van Buren's problems, see James C. Curtis, *The Fox at Bay,* pp. 152ff.

60. See the complete text of the address, *Speech of John Quincy Adams of Massachusetts upon the Right of the People, Men and Women, to Petition; on the Freedom of Speech and Debate in the House of Representatives of the United States; on the Resolutions of Seven State Legislatures, and the Petition of More than One Hundred Thousand Petitioners Relating to the Annexation of Texas to this Union.*

61. See Merk, *History of the Westward Movement,* p. 280.

62. For this see Robert F. Dalzell, Jr., *Daniel Webster and the Trial of American Nationalism 1843–1852,* pp. 42–45.

63. See Pletcher, *Diplomacy of Annexation,* pp. 114–15 and 139ff.; Williams, *Animating Pursuits of Speculation,* pp. 152ff. and 165–66; and Merk, *History of the Westward Movement,* p. 281.

64. Again these figures are taken from Bailyn, *Great Republic,* Appendix, p. xx.

65. Compare the texts of the two treaties of April 12, 1844, and March 1, 1845 (Wallace and Vigness, *Documents of Texas History,* pp. 143–44 and 146–47).

66. See the complete text of the address of Anson Jones (Wallace and Vigness, *Documents of Texas History,* p. 149).

67. See Turner, *United States,* pp. 519 and 526.

68. See Merk, *History of the Westward Movement,* pp. 287–88.

69. See Frederick Merk, *Slavery and the Annexation of Texas,* p. 45.

70. As examples of the discussions within the parties, see the two articles by James E. Winston, "The Annexation of Texas and the Mississippi Democrats" (*SHQ* 25:1–25), and "The Mississippi Whigs and the Annexation of Texas" (*SHQ* 29:161–80).

71. See the official report of Ashbel Smith, the Texas chargé d'affaires in London, to President Anson Jones, June 24, 1844 (*DCRT* 3:1153–56), and R. A. McLemore, "The Influence of French Diplomatic Policy on the Annexation of Texas" (*SHQ* 43:342–47).

72. That this was also very clearly expressed can be discerned from the letter of Ashbel Smith to Anson Jones, July 1, 1844. See Jones, *Memoranda,* pp. 369ff.

73. See the dispatch of the special agent Duff Green to Secretary of State John C. Calhoun on October 9, 1844, mentioned in Pletcher, *Diplomacy of Annexation,* p. 167; and also Ephraim Douglass Adams, "English Interest in the Annexation of California" (*AHR* 19 [1809]: 744–63).

74. Concerning this very extensive area of Pacific trade, as well as the interest of the great powers of the time in California and Oregon, see "The Border Provinces: California and Oregon," chap. 4 in Pletcher, *Diplomacy of Annexation,* pp. 89–110.

75. See the anonymous text, which can be dated as 1838–39 by inner evidence (*LP* 2:384ff.).

76. See A. S. Wright to Lamar, May 4, 1841 (*LP* 3:517).

77. See Dubois de Saligny, the French chargé d'affaires to Texas, to Minister Molé, April 20 and May 1, 1839 (Barker, *French Legation in Texas,* pp. 79ff. and 90ff.).

78. Quoted thus by Dubois de Saligny in his letter to the French Foreign Minister Nicolas Jean de Dieu Soult, Duke of Dalmatia, May 4, 1840 (Barker, *French Legation in Texas,* pp. 138–39).

79. See Friend, *Sam Houston,* p. 151.

80. See Pletcher, *Diplomacy of Annexation,* pp. 134–35, 186–87, and 203–204.

CONCLUSIONS: – A CASE OF MANIFEST DESTINY?

1. Bocanegra to Thompson, August 23, 1843, quoted in Pletcher, *Diplomacy,* p. 126.

2. Juan N. Almonte to José Maria Bocanegra, August 18, 1844 (Eugene C. Barker Papers, transcript vol. 569, p. 89, *BTHC*).

3. Nathaniel Wright Stephenson gives Polk a strange-sounding excuse in *Texas and the Mexican War,* p. 178; "Undoubtedly Polk did not want war; but he was as ignorant of the Mexican character as Adams or Jackson and treated the Mexican ultimatum as of no consequence."

4. See James, *Andrew Jackson,* pp. 333, 379, and 400.

5. See Houston to John H. Houston, November 10, 1828 (*WSH* 2:10–11), and Thomas H. Benton to Houston, August 15, 1829 (*WSH* 1:140); see also Friend, *Sam Houston,* pp. 6, 18–19, 32, and 51, and James, *Andrew Jackson,* pp. 453 and 481ff.

6. On February 22, 1848, Houston made a speech in New York in which he, who still had a very positive relationship with the Indians, put them on a level with the Mexicans and treated them with contempt (*WSH* 5:34–35).

7. Concerning the question of injured Mexican national pride, see Brack, *Mexico Views Manifest Destiny,* pp. 180ff.

8. This follows clearly from Polk's diary entries. See his remarks for May 9, 1846 (Milo M. Quaife, *The Diary of James K. Polk during His Presidency, 1845 to 1849* 1:384–85); Anson Jones expresses himself in the same way in his diary (Jones, *Memoranda,* p. 46).

9. See Isaac J. Cox, "The Southwest Boundary of Texas" (*SHQ* 6:81ff.).

10. See the detailed letter of Andrew Jackson to Moses Dawson, August 28, 1844 (*Letters of Gen. Jackson and Hon. Charles A. Wickliffe on the Re-Annexation of Texas,* Rare Book Collection, Library of Congress).

11. For Lundy's trips to and in Texas, see Merton L. Dillon, "Benjamin Lundy in Texas" (*SHQ* 63:46–62).

12. Thomas Earle, *The Life, Travels and Opinions of Benjamin Lundy, including His Journeys to Texas and Mexico; with a Sketch of Contemporary Events, and a Notice of the Revolution in Haiti,* p. 126, quoted in Dillon, "Benjamin Lundy," p. 57.

13. See Mary Lee Spence, "British Impressions of Texas and the Texans" (*SHQ* 70:163–83).

14. Kennedy, who was in Texas in 1839, certainly viewed the problem of slavery

with the greatest indulgence (William Kennedy, *Texas: The Rise, Progress, and Prospects of the Republic of Texas*, p. xxviii).

15. Straightaway in his introduction Urquhart finds harsh words: "The Great Felony has been consummated. As pirates in disguise steal into a fortress to surprise by cunning, when they cannot overcome by force, so did bands of American outlaws enter the territories of their neighbour" (David Urquhart, *Annexation of Texas: A Case of War between England and the United States* p. 2).

16. See William E. Channing, *A Letter to the Hon. Henry Clay, on the Annexation of Texas to the United States*, 2nd ed.

17. See Eugene C. Barker, "The Influence of Slavery in the Colonization of Texas" (*SHQ* 28:1–33).

18. See Hogan, *Great Republic*, p. 21.

19. The figures are from Kenneth M. Stampp, *The Peculiar Institution*, pp. 31–32. The development, as it is reflected in the percentages, occurred variously in the different Southern states, each according to the economic factors. See Merk, *Movement*, pp. 190–91.

20. As an example, see Ray Allen Billingston, *The Far Western Frontier, 1830–1860*, p. 116.

21. See the compilation by Barnes F. Lathrop, "Migration into East Texas, 1835–1860," *SHQ* 52:198.

22. Ibid., p. 189.

23. Concerning this complex as well as complicated migration, see Merk, *History of the Westward Movement*, chap. 17–32.

24. Concerning the various cultural regions and currents of immigration, see Meinig, *Imperial Texas*, pp. 91ff.; and for the statistics, see again Lathrop, "Migration into East Texas," p. 199.

25. Compare Turner, *United States*, p. 358.

26. Thus also unfortunately Paul D. Lack in his otherwise good study, "Slavery and the Texas Revolution" (*SHQ* 89:181–202).

27. See as examples, Richardson, *Texas, the Lone Star State*, pp. 70–71; Fehrenbach, *Lone Star*, pp. 174ff.; Robert E. Riegel, *Young America, 1830–1840*, p. 74; and Lowrie, *Culture Conflict in Texas*, p. 179.

28. See Oates, *Republic of Texas*, p. 80; Fehrenbach, *Lone Star*, p. 724; and Barbara J. Muse, "The First Phase of the Texas Revolution" (M.A. thesis, University of Houston, 1970), p. 112.

29. See Eugene C. Barker, *Mexico and Texas, 1821–1835*, 2d ed., p. 62. Barker is actually concerned here *expressis verbis* with the problem of religious affiliation, but on the basis of his further statements, he can only have proceeded from a very meager number of sources concerning the other points he also addresses.

30. Compare Noah Smithwick, *The Evolution of a State*, p. 29.

31. See Harris, *Reminiscences*, p. 111.

32. See Barker, *Mexico and Texas*, p. 146.

33. See once more the report of Manuel Mier y Terán to the Mexican President Guadalupe Victoria (Wallace and Vigness, *Documents of Texas History*, pp. 65–66).

34. See Lowrie, *Culture Conflict in Texas*, pp. 157ff., for these various governmental structures.

35. The role of catalyst here is usually awarded to Austin who, returning home from his imprisonment, opened the settlers' eyes concerning Santa Anna's plans. Thus John E. Weems, *Dream of Empire,* pp. 39–40; William C. Binkley, *The Texas Revolution,* 2nd ed., p. 130; and George Pierce Garrison, *Texas: A Contest of Civilizations,* pp. 189ff.

36. See Jones, *Memoranda,* pp. 11ff.

37. See Harris, *Reminiscences,* p. 121.

38. See Pletcher, *Diplomacy of Annexation,* p. 70n17.

39. Eugene C. Barker, "Land Speculation as a Cause of the Texas Revolution" (*SHQ* 10:94–95).

40. See *LOT* 1:103.

41. See Taylor, *Spanish Archives,* pp. 60–61.

42. Concerning this business, see Henson, *Samuel May Williams,* pp. 46ff.

43. See the issue of the *Texas Republican* of May 9, 1835 (*BTHC*).

44. See the *Texas Republican* of June 27, 1835 (*BTHC*).

45. See the circular by Samuel M. Williams to the people of Texas, July 20, 1835 (*LP* 1:216–18).

46. See once more Antonio Tenorio to Martín Perfecto de Cós, April 9, 1835 (*PTR* 1:61), and Carlos O'Campo to Domingo de Ugartechea, May 6, 1835 (*PTR* 1:101).

47. See Robert M. Williamson's address "To the People of Texas," San Felipe de Austin, June 22, 1835 (*PTR* 1:194ff.), and the letter of Benjamin R. Milam to Francis W. Johnson, July 5, 1835 (*PTR* 1:206–7).

48. An addition to Governor Viesca's declaration of April 15, 1835, by "Coahuil-texanus" (*PTR* 1:74–75).

49. See Thomas J. Chambers to James H. C. Miller, July 4, 1835, printed in the *Texas Republican* of July 18, 1835, and James Kerr to Thomas J. Chambers, July 5, 1835 (Microfilm Roll 165, Bexar Archives, *BTHC*).

50. See the public declaration of Martín Perfecto de Cós of May 12, 1835 (*PTR,* 1:104ff.).

51. General Vicente Filisola and the historian Carlos María de Bustamante believed this was murder perpetrated by followers of Santa Anna, but this cannot be proved. See Morton, "Life of Mier y Terán," pt. 8, pp. 541ff.

52. Frequently the behavior of the Texans, in particular Sam Houston, is used as an argument against the thesis that speculators were determining factors in the outbreak of the war. On October 18, 1835, the permanent council accepted the draft of a resolution by Houston that declared all land transactions of the legislature of the state of Coahuila y Texas after 1833 as null and void. This was also later put into the constitution in which John T. Mason was even mentioned by name. But even Barker saw this as probably a purely propagandistic action by the Texans in order not to have their struggle defamed as a war of the speculators. See Barker, "Land Speculation," p. 93. This action naturally drew the fiercest protest from the actual speculators. See Swartwout to Morgan, May 28, 1836 (Bass, *Fragile Empires,* pp. 11ff.).

53. Thus Elesio Paredes, "La Masonería Matamorose en la Historia y en la Leyenda," p. 8 of an unpublished manuscript quoted in Carter, *Masonry in Texas,* p. 255.

54. See also Carter, *Masonry in Texas,* pp. 288ff.

55. Ibid., pp. 306ff.

56. See once more Carter, *Education and Masonry in Texas*.

57. See Carter, *Masonry in Texas*, pp. 350ff.

58. Ibid., pp. 38ff.

59. Ibid., p. 351.

60. See the article concerning a meeting in Nashville, Tennessee, in the *New Orleans Courier*, November 17, 1837 (*LP* 1:253ff.).

61. See Houston's "A Lecture on Trials and Dangers of Frontier Life," given on January 28, 1851, in the Musical Fund Hall in Philadelphia (*WSH* 5:278).

62. See Yoakum, *History of Texas*, 1:329, 364.

63. See Arthur Bauer, "Essai sur les révolutions," *Bibliothèque Sociologique Internationale*, 36:11.

64. For the various assessments and theories having to do with the concept of revolution, see A. S. Cohan, *Theories of Revolution*.

65. See Ted R. Gurr, *Why Men Rebel*, pp. 24ff.

66. Chalmers Johnson, *Revolutionary Change*, p. 143.

67. Johnson himself has to admit that the distinction between rebellion and revolution is very fluid according to his definition. See ibid., chap. 7, pp. 135ff.

68. See Charles Tilly, "Revolutions and Collective Violence," in *Handbook of Political Science*, ed. F. I. Greenstein and N. Polsby, 3:483–501.

69. Hannah Arendt, *On Revolution*, p. 27.

70. Ibid.

71. In this connection it must be stated that a historian like Frederick Merk himself recognizes that the war in Texas was not the result of terrible deeds or tyranny on the part of Mexico – something that did not exist – but rather the result of a mistake on the part of Mexico. However, on the other hand, he accepts the word "revolution" without any criticism. See Merk, *Movement*, p. 274; Barker shows the same inconsistency in *Mexico and Texas*, p. v.

72. Johnson, *Revolutionary Change*, pp. 140–41.

73. See also Andreas Reichstein, "Was There a Revolution at all in Texas in 1835/36?" *American Studies International* 27 (October, 1989).

74. As an example, see Houston's speech in the U.S. Senate, February 19, 1847, concerning the Three Million Bill (*WSH* 4:531).

75. See the declaration by James Kerr, January 4, 1836, distributed as a handbill (*LP* 1:287ff.).

76. Jones, *Memoranda*, pp. 14–15.

77. Thus Garrison, *Contest*, pp. 189ff.; Eugene C. Barker, "The Texas Declaration of Causes for Taking up Arms against Mexico" (*SHQ* 15:173–85); and Fehrenbach, *Lone Star*, pp. 174–75.

78. For the percentages, see the statements and biographies in Louis Wiltz Kemp, *The Signers of the Texas Declaration of Independence*, p. xviff.

79. Lowrie, *Culture Conflict in Texas*, p. 73.

80. Potter, *Impending Crisis*, p. 31.

81. Austin to Thomas F. Leaming, June 14, 1830 (*AP* 2:415).

82. Austin to Thomas White, March 31, 1829 (*AP* 2:197–98) and to Mary Austin Holley, November 14, 1831 (*AP* 2:701).

83. Merk, *History of the Westward Movement*, p. 274. See also the following authors who use the same terminology: Otis Singletary, *The Mexican War*, p. 14; Albert Weinberg, *Manifest Destiny*, 6th ed., p. 250; Dannell George Cottrell, "The Americanization of Texas" (M.A. thesis, University of Utah, 1941), p. 113; and Richardson, *Texas, the Lone Star State*, p. 70.

84. Theodore Roosevelt, *The Winning of the West* (New York and London, 1906), p. 1:43.

85. A contemporary of Travis sketches his character in an interesting and pertinent manner: "He was very ambitious; he hungered and thirsted for fame – not the kind of fame which satisfies the ambition of the duelist and desperado, but the exalted fame which crowns the doer of great deeds in a good cause" (James Hampton Kuykendall, "Sketches of Early Texans," James Hampton Kuykendall Papers, *BTHC*).

86. The lead article by John Louis O'Sullivan is printed in Charles L. Sanford, *Manifest Destiny and the Imperialiam Question*, pp. 26ff.

87. John W. O'Neal, "Texas, 1791–1835," p. 154.

88. Weinberg, *Manifest Destiny*.

89. Ibid., p. 41.

90. Ibid., p. 8.

91. See Brack, *Mexico Views Manifest Destiny*, pp. 172ff.

92. For this reasoning, see Weinberg, *Manifest Destiny*, pp. 72ff.

93. "The removal of all Indians in the 'thirties' – under conditions of hardship described lugubriously in a recent work of Grant Foreman – removed the destiny of this race from the American view" (ibid., p. 89).

94. See ibid., pp. 100ff.

95. Ibid., p. 105.

96. See also the speech of Representative John T. Harding from Illinois, January 15, 1845, who ridiculed the propaganda of the expansionists; part of it is printed in Allan O. Kownslar, *Manifest Destiny and Expansionism in the 1840's*, pp. 69–70.

97. Weinberg, *Manifest Destiny*, pp. 355ff., and Richard W. van Alstyne, *The Rising American Empire*, pp. 165, 176–77.

98. See Walter LaFeber, "A Note on the 'Mercantilistic Imperialism' of Alfred Thayer Mahan" (*MVHR*, 48:683).

99. Weinberg, *Manifest Destiny*, p. 195.

100. This percentage was reached using statements in Bailyn, *Great Republic*, appendix, p. xx.

101. Pletcher, *Diplomacy of Annexation*, p. 99; Robert F. Dalzell, Jr., *Daniel Webster and the Trial of American Nationalism, 1843–1852*, 2nd ed., p. 155; and Daniel Webster's speech in Congress on December 22, 1845 (Kownslar, *Manifest Destiny*, pp. 66–67).

102. See the speeches of representatives Luther Severance of Maine, February 4, 1847; Charles Hobart Carroll of New York, February 22, 1847; Joshua R. Giddings of Ohio, December 15, 1846; Milton Brown of Tennessee, February 12, 1847; and Abraham Lincoln of Illinois, December 21, 1847 (Kownslar, *Manifest Destiny*, pp. 118ff.).

103. On December 30, 1847, R. F. Stockton declared before an assembly in New York: "But we have a duty before God which we cannot – we must not evade. The

priceless boon of civil and religious liberty has been confided to us as trustees." Also, on January 26, 1848, the New York State Democratic Convention published a paper with the following content: "We [the American People] have devolved upon us the great work of restoring to man his long lost rights" (Kownslar, *Manifest Destiny*, pp. 9 and 114ff.).

104. See again O'Neal, "Texas, 1791–1835," pp. 105–106. Frederick Merk attributed a special role to youth: "Youth was responsible, doubtless, for such characteristics of Manifest Destiny as its grandeur and scope and for the moral exaltation with which it was set forth" (Frederick Merk, *Manifest Destiny and Mission in American History*, p. 55).

105. *WSH* 5:34.

106. Williams, *Animating Pursuits of Speculation*, p. 27.

107. Hogan, *Texas Republic*, pp. 86–87.

108. John Delafons in his work *Land-use Controls in the United States*, p. 6, writes: "Speculation in land has been a tradition in America and was in fact a major motivating force in opening the West. It was not the prerogative of the rich but in an undeveloped country land was available to all comers."

109. In 1795 the state of Georgia sold 35 million acres of land in present Alabama and Mississippi to four speculation companies whose members as state representatives had passed the law allowing it. In 1810 the Supreme Court of the United States declared this to be legal. This is taken from Henson, *Samuel May Williams*, p. 62, n. 1; see also Rogin, *Fathers and Children*, p. 81.

110. Rogin, ibid.

111. Michel Chevalier, *Society, Manners, and Politics in the United States*, p. 305.

112. See also Isaac J. Cox, "The Pan-American Policy of Jefferson and Wilkinson" (*MVHR*, 1:212–39).

113. See Rogin, *Fathers and Children*, p. 81; Remini, *Andrew Jackson*, 1:86ff.; and Remini, *The Election of Andrew Jackson*, pp. 51ff.

114. Along this line, see also Carl Russell Fish, *The Path of Empire*, pp. 194–95. The interest in Mexican territory, which consolidated itself into a movement that aimed at annexing all of Mexico, is depicted very well by John Douglas Pitts Fuller, *The Movement for the Acquisition of All Mexico, 1846–1848*, pp. 12ff. Charles Vevier wrote about this in his essay "American Continentalism: An Idea of Expansion, 1845–1910" (*AHR* 65:323): "Relying on its separation from the Old World, the United States redefined the conventional terms of foreign relations by domesticating its foreign policy."

115. See again the letter of October 5, 1835, from Sterling C. Robertson to Hunt, the editor of the *Arkansas Gazette*, which was published on October 27 (*PTR* 2:51ff.), and the letter from Houston to James Pinckney Henderson of February 20, 1844 (*WSH* 4:268ff.).

116. This does not mean that in the course of time all Anglo-American Texans had become hawks. In his narrative description *The Texas Emigrant*, Edward Stiff emphasizes that the Texas "revolution" against Mexico had been illegal, unjust, and provoked by a few hawks (pp. 294ff.).

Bibliography

PRIMARY SOURCES

Public Documents

Archivo de la Secretaria de Fomento, Colonización y Terrenos Baldros, Archivo General de Mexico

Archivo de la Secretaria de Gobierno, Saltillo, Coahuila, vol. 38, 1834

Barker, Eugene C., Transcripts of Official Mexican Papers, BTHC

Bexar Archives, BTHC

Blake, Robert Bruce, Research Collection. 75 vols. Austin, 1958–1959

Despatches from United States Consuls in Galveston, Texas, 1832–1846 (T 151), 2 Rolls, Department of State, Record Group 59, National Archives, Washington, D.C.

Despatches from United States Consuls in Texas, 1825–44 (T 153), Department of State, Record Group 59, National Archives, Washington, D.C.

Despatches from United States Ministers to Mexico, 1823–1906 (M 97), 179 Rolls, Department of State, Record Group 59, National Archives, Washington, D.C.

Miscellaneous Letters of the Department of State, 1789–1906, (M 179), 1,310 Rolls, Department of State, Record Group 59, National Archives, Washington, D.C.

Nacogdoches Archives, State Archives, Austin, Texas, and Transcripts selected from the Nacogdoches Archives, BTHC

Records of United States and Mexican Claims Commissions, Record Group 76, National Archives, National Records Center, Suitland, Maryland

Register of Texas Debt Warrants, 1856–1861, Records of the Bureau of Accounts (Treasury), National Archives, Washington, D.C.

Spanish Archives, General Land Office, Austin, Texas

Texas Debt Claims and Warrants, Records of the General Accounting Office, Record Group 217, National Archives, Washington, D.C.

"Workbook" pertaining to the Texas Debt of 1850, General Records of the Department of the Treasury, Record Group 56, National Archives, Washington, D.C.

Private Papers

Asbury, Samuel E., Papers, BTHC
Austin, Archibald, Papers, BTHC
Austin, Henry, Letters 1806–1846, BTHC
Austin, Stephen F., Collection, University of Houston Libraries
Ballinger, William Pitt, Papers, BTHC
Barrett, Don Carlos, Correspondence 1825–1836, BTHC
Baylor, Mary A., Papers, BTHC
Brooks, John Sowers, Papers, BTHC
Bryan, Moses Austin, Papers, BTHC
Butler, Anthony, Papers, BTHC
Cazneau (Jane McManus Storms) Papers, BTHC
Coles, John P., Papers, BTHC
Collett, J. H., Papers 1810–1876, BTHC
Davenport, Harbert, Collection, BTHC
Dienst, Alexander, Collection, BTHC
Donaldson, C. D. and William, Papers 1806–1860, letters and legal documents, BTHC
Ericson, Alice Lee, Collection, BTHC
Filisola, Vicente, Papers, BTHC
Fisher, George, Papers 1830–1848, BTHC
Franklin, Benjamin C., Papers 1805–1915, BTHC
Groce Family Papers 1824–1871, BTHC
Hale, Phillip Smith, Papers, BTHC
Hanrick, Edward, Papers, BTHC
Harrison, Jonas, Papers, BTHC
Holley, Mary Austin, Letters 1808–1846. 2 vols. BTHC
Houston, Andrew Jackson, Collection, Texas State Archives, Austin
Houston, Samuel, Papers 1815–1928, BTHC
Ingram, Ira, Papers, BTHC
Jackson, Andrew, Papers, Library of Congress, Washington, D.C.
Kuykendall, James Hampton and William, Papers 1822–1897, BTHC
Lamar, Mirabeau Buonaparte, Collection, BTHC
Leaming, Thomas F., Papers, BTHC

McKinney (Thomas Freeman) Papers, BTHC
Milam-McKinney Collection, BTHC
Money, John H., Papers, BTHC
Natchez Trace Collection, BTHC
Perry, Hally Bryan, Papers, BTHC
Perry, James Franklin, Stephen Samuel S., and James Franklin Jr., Papers
    1815–1863, BTHC
Perry, James Franklin and Stephen S., Collection, BTHC
Roberts, Oran Milo, Papers 1815–1853, BTHC
Robinson, Joel Walter, Papers 1835–1891, BTHC
Schoolcraft, Henry Rowe, Papers 1809–1848, BTHC
Seguin, Juan Nepomuceno, Reminiscences, BTHC
Smith, Ashbel, Papers, BTHC
Smith, Henry, Collection I, Letters 1834–1879, BTHC
Swartwout, Samuel, Papers, BTHC
Texas Declaration of Independence Autograph Collection, BTHC
Wharton, Clarence Ray, Collection, BTHC
Wharton, William H., Papers 1837–1877, BTHC
Williams, Sally Trueheart, Papers, Rosenberg Library, Galveston
Williams (Samuel May and Austin May), Papers, BTHC
Willich Jr., George, Papers, BTHC
Yoakum, Henderson, Papers, BTHC
Zavala, Lorenzo de, Papers, BTHC

Newspapers

El Anteojo, Mexico City, 1835
The Bee, New Orleans, 1832, 1833
The Clarion and Tennessee State Gazette, Nashville, 1817–1821
Constitutional Advocate and Texas Public Advertiser, Brazoria, 1832–1833
The Daily Chronicle, Philadelphia, 1839
El Fénix de la Libertad, Mexico City, 1831–1834
El Mosquito Mexicano, Mexico City, 1831–1834
The Nashville Whig, Nashville, 1824–1826
The Nashville Republican & State Gazette, Nashville, 1829–1830
The National Gazette, Philadelphia, 1830–1831
The Saturday Bulletin, Philadelphia, 1830
El Sol, Mexico City, 1821–1830
Telegraph and Texas Register, San Felipe/Columbia/Houston, 1835–1837
The Texas Republican, Brazoria, 183
The Texas Gazette, San Felipe, 1829–1831

Publications of Primary Materials

Adams, Charles Francis, ed. *Memoirs of John Quincy Adams*. 12 vols. Philadelphia, 1877. Reprint, Freeport, N.Y.: Books for Libraries Press, 1969.

Adams, Ephraim Douglass, ed. "Correspondence from the British Archives concerning Texas, 1837–1846." In 24 parts, *SHQ* 15–21 (1912–1918).

Adams, John Quincy, *Speech of John Quincy Adams of Massachusetts, upon the right or the people, men and women, to Petition; on the Freedom of Speech and of debate in the House of Representatives of the United States; on the Resolutions of Seven State Legislatures, and the Petitions of More than one hundred thousand Petitioners relating to the Annexation of Texas to this Union.* Washington, 1838. Reprint, New York: Arno Press, 1969.

Address to the Reader of the Documents relating to the Galveston Bay & Texas Land Company, which are contained in the Appendix. New York: G. F. Hopkins and Son, January 1, 1831.

Almonte, Juan Nepomuceno. "Statistical Report on Texas, 1835" (translated by Carlos E. Castañeda). *SHQ* 28 (1925): 177–222.

American State Papers, 1826–1828, vol. 6, Second Series, Washington, D.C.: Gales and Seaton, 1859.

Anonymous [Langworthy, Asahel?]. *Visit to Texas: Being the Journal of a Traveller through those Parts most interesting to American Settlers.* New York, 1834. Reprint, New York: Readex Microprint, 1966.

Austin, Stephen Fuller, "Description of Texas by Stephen F. Austin, 1828" (translated from the Spanish and edited by Eugene C. Barker). *SHQ* 28 (1924): 98–121.

———. *Establishing Austin's Colony,* ed. David B. Gracy II. Austin and New York: Pemberton Press, 1970.

———. "Explanation to the Public concerning the Affairs of Texas, By Citizen Stephen F. Austin, 18 January 1835" (translated from the Spanish by Ethel Zivley Rather) *SHQ* 8 (1904): 232–58.

———. "Journal of Stephen F. Austin on his First Trip to Texas, 1821" (translated from the Spanish by Ethel Zivley Rather). *SHQ* 7 (1904): 286–307.

———. "Prison Journal." *SHQ* 2 (1899): 183–210.

———. *Some Difficulties of a Texas Empressario.* Washington, D.C., 1899.

Barbey, Théodore. *Le Texas.* Paris, 1841.

Barker, Eugene Campbell, ed. *The Austin Papers.* 3 vols. The two-part vol. 1 = vol. 2 of *ARAHA* for 1919 (Washington, D.C.: GPO: 1924); vol. 2 = *ARAHA* for 1922 (Washington, D.C.: GPO, 1928); vol. 3 (Austin: University of Texas, 1927).

———. "Journal of the Permanent Council (October 11–27, 1835)." *SHQ* 7 (1904): 249–78.

————. "Minutes of the Ayuntamiento of San Felipe de Austin, 1828–1832." In 12 parts, *SHQ* 21–24 (1918–1920).

————. "Texas Revolution Documents." *Publications of the Southern History Association,* vol. 7–9, Washington, D.C., 1903–1905.

Barker, Nancy Nichols, ed. *The French Legation in Texas.* 2 vols. Austin: Texas State Historical Association, 1971, 1973.

Bass, Feris A., Jr., and Brunson, B. R., eds. *Fragile Empires: The Texas Correspondence of Samuel Swartwout and James Morgan.* Austin: Shoal Creek Publishers, 1978.

Bassett, John Spencer, ed. *Correspondence of Andrew Jackson.* 6 vols. Washington, D.C.: Carnegie Institution of Washington, 1926–1933.

Beers, Henry P., ed. "Stephen F. Austin and Anthony Butler Documents." *SHQ* 62 (1958): 233–40.

Benson, Nettie Lee, ed. "A Governor's Report on Texas in 1809." *SHQ* 71 (1968): 603–16.

Binkley, William Campbell, ed. *Official Correspondence of the Texas Revolution, 1835–1836.* 2 vols. New York and London: Appleton-Century, 1936.

Boyle, Andrew A. "Reminiscences of the Texas Revolution." *SHQ* 13 (1910): 285–91.

British and Foreign State Papers. Vol. 5:1817–1818, London, 1837. Vol. 7:1819–1820. London: James Ridgway, 1834, 1837.

Bryan, J. P., ed. "Mary Austin Holley: The Texas Diary, 1835–38." *The Texas Quarterly* 8 (1965): 7–120.

Caro, Ramón Martínez. *Verdadera idea de la primera camnpaña de Tejas, 1836.* Mexico City: Santiago Perez, 1837.

Castañeda, Carlos M., ed. *The Mexican Side of the Texas Revolution.* 2nd ed. Dallas: P. L. Turner, 1970.

Chevalier, Michel. *Society, Manners and Politics in the United States—Being a Series of Letters on North America.* Boston, 1839.

Colección de los Decretos y órdenes generales de la primera Legislatura de las Cortes Ordinarias de 1820 y 1821, Desde 6 de Julio hasta 9 de Novembre de 1820. Madrid: La Imprenta Nacional, 1821.

Commager, Henry Steele, ed. *Documents of American History.* 2 vols. 9th ed. Englewood Cliffs, N.J.: Prentice-Hall, 1973.

Corner, William, ed. "John Crittenden Duval: The Last Survivor of the Goliad Massacre." *SHQ* 1 (1897): 47–67.

Crane, William Carey. *Life and Select Literary Remains of Sam Houston of Texas.* Dallas: William G. Scarff and Co., 1884.

Crawford, Anne Fears, ed. *The Eagle: The Autobiography of Santa Anna.* Austin: Pemberton Press, 1967.

Crockett, David. *The Life of David Crockett.* New York: A. L. Burt, 1902.

Day, Donald, and Harry Herbert Ullom, eds. *The Autobiography of Sam Houston*. Norman: University of Oklahoma Press, 1954.

DeShields, James Thomas, ed. *Tall Men with Long Rifles: The Glamorous Story of the Texas Revolution, As told by Captain Creed Taylor who fought in that Heroic Struggle from Gonzales to San Jacinto.* San Antonio: Naylor, 1935.

Dewees, William Bluford. *Letters from an Early Settler of Texas.* Louisville, 1852. Reprint, Waco: Texian Press, 1968.

Dunt, Detlef. *Reise nach Texas, nebst Nachrichten von diesem Lande; für Deutsche, welche nach Texas zu gehen beabsichtigen.* Bremen: Carl Wilhelm Wiehe, 1834.

Edward, David B. *The History of Texas; Or, The Emigrant's, Farmer's, and Politician's Guide to the Character, Climate, Soil, and Production of that Country.* Cincinnati: J. A. James and Co., 1836.

Ehrenberg, Hermann. *Texas und seine Revolution.* Leipzig: Otto Wigand, 1843.

Escudero, José Agustín. *Memorias del Diputado de Chihuahua,* Mexico City, 1848.

———. *Observaciones sobre Chihuahua.* Mexico City, 1839.

Field, Joseph E. *Three Years in Texas.* Boston, 1836. Reprint, Austin: Steck, 1935.

Filizola, Umberto Daniel, ed. "Correspondence of Santa Anna during the Texas Campaign, 1835–1836, translated, with Introduction and Notes." MA thesis, University of Texas at Austin, 1939.

Filisola, Vicente. *Memorias para la historia de la guerra de Tejas.* 2 vols. Mexico City: Tipografia de R. Rafael, 1848–1849.

Ford, Leicester Paul, ed. *The Works of Thomas Jefferson.* 12 vols. New York and London: G. P. Putnam's Sons, 1905.

Friend, Llerena, ed. "Contemporary Newspaper Accounts of the Annexation of Texas." *SHQ* 49 (1945): 267–81.

Gammel, Hans Peter Nielson, ed. *The Laws of Texas 1822–1897.* 10 vols. Austin: Gammel Book Co., 1898.

Garrison, George P., ed. "A Belated Colonist." *SHQ* 2 (1899): 237–39.

———. *Diplomatic Correspondence of the Republic of Texas.* 3 vols. Vol. 1 = *ARAHA* for 1907. Vol. 2 and 3 = *ARAHA* for 1908, Washington, D.C.: GPO, 1908–1911.

Gray, William Fairfax. *From Virginia to Texas, 1835.* Houston, 1909. Houston: Fletcher Young Publishing Co., 1965.

Green, Rena Maverick, ed. *Samuel Maverick, Texan: 1803–1870.* San Antonio: Alamo Printing, 1952.

Grover, Walter E., ed. "Stephen F. Austin–Charles G. Sayre Correspondence." *SHQ* 63 (1960): 454–56.

Gulick, Charles Adams, et al., eds. *The Papers of Mirabeau Buonaparte Lamar*. 6 vols. Reprint, Austin and New York: Pemberton Press, 1968.

Hamilton, Jeff. *My Master; the Inside Story of Sam Houston and His Times*. Dallas: Manfred van Nort and Co., 1940.

Hammeken, George L. "Recollections of Stephen F. Austin." *SHQ* 20 (1917): 369–80.

Harris, Dilue. "The Reminiscences of Mrs. Dilue Harris." *SHQ* (1901): 85–127, 155–89.

Hatcher, Mattie Austin. *Letters of an Early American Traveller. Mary Austin Holley—Her Life and Her Works, 1784–1846*. Dallas: Southwest Press, 1933.

———. "Letters of Antonio Martinez, the Last Spanish Governor of Texas, 1817–1822." *SHQ* 39 (1935–1936): 66–72, 139–47, 228–38, 327–32.

Holley, Mary Austin. *Texas*. Lexington, 1836. Reprint, Austin: Steck, 1935.

Houston, Samuel. "The Annexation of Texas." *SHQ* 1 (1897): 70–86.

———. *Life of General Sam Houston*. Washington, D.C., 1885. Reprint, Austin: Pemberton Press, 1964.

Huson, Hobart, ed. *Captain Phillip Dimmitt's Commandancy of Goliad, 1835–1836*. Austin: Von Boeckmann-Jones, 1974.

Jackson, Andrew. *Letters of Gen. Jackson and Hon. Charles A. Wickliffe on the Re-Annexation of Texas* (n.p., n.d.), Rare Book Collection, Library of Congress.

Jenkins, John Holmes III, ed. *The Papers of the Texas Revolution 1835–1836*. 10 vols. Austin: Presidial Press, 1973.

———. *Recollections of Early Texas—The Memoirs of John Holland Jenkins*. 4th ed. Austin: University of Texas Press, 1975.

Jones, Anson. *Memoranda and official correspondence relating to the Republic of Texas—its History and Annexation 1836 to 1846*. New York, 1859. Reprint, Chicago: Rio Grande Press, 1966.

Kaiser, Leo M., ed. "Stephen F. Austin's Oration of July 4, 1818." *SHQ* 64 (1960): 71–79.

Kelly, Edith Louise, and Mattie Austin Hatcher, eds. and trans. "Tadeo Ortíz de Ayala and the Colonization of Texas, 1822–1833." *SHQ* 32 (1928–1929): 74–86, 152–64, 222–51, 311–43.

Kemp, Elizabeth, and Katherine Hart, eds. "E. M. Pease's Account of the Texas Revolution." *SHQ* 68 (1964): 79–89.

Kleberg, Rosa. "Some of My Early Experiences in Texas." *SHQ* 1 (1898): 297–302.

Kownslar, Allan O., ed. *Manifest Destiny and Expansionism in the 1840s*. Boston: D. C. Heath and Co., 1967.

Lane, Walter P. *The Adventures and Recollections of General Walter P. Lane, a San Jacinto Veteran, containing Sketches of the Texian, Mexican and Late*

Wars, with Several Indian Fights thrown in. Marshall, Tex.: New Messenger Publishing Co., 1928.

Leclerc, Frédéric. *Le Texas et sa révolution.* Paris: H. Fournier et Cie., 1840.

Linn, John J. *Reminiscences of Fifty Years in Texas.* New York: D. and J. Sadlier Co., 1883.

Lubbock, Francis Richard. *Six decades in Texas; or memoirs of Francis Richard Lubbock, Governor of Texas in wartime 1861–63.* Austin: Ben C. Jones and Co. Printers, 1900.

Mallory, Daniel. *The Life and Speeches of the Hon. Henry Clay.* 2 vols. New York: Robert P. Bixley and Co., 1844.

Malloy, William M., ed. *Treaties, Conventions, International Acts, Protocols and Agreements between the United States of America and Other Powers 1776–1909.* Senate Documents, vol. 48, Washington, D.C.: GPO, 1910.

Mayo, Bernard, ed. *Jefferson Himself.* 4th ed. Charlottesville: University Press of Virginia, 1976.

Mayo, Robert. *Political Sketches of Eights Years in Washington,* Baltimore: Fielding Lucas, Jr., 1839.

McDonald, Archie P., ed. *Hurrah for Texas! The Diary of Adolphus Sterne, 1838–1851.* Waco: Texian Press, 1969.

McLean, Malcolm D., ed. *Papers concerning Robertson's Colony in Texas.* 14 vols. Fort Worth: Texas Christian University Press, and Arlington: University of Texas at Arlington Press, 1974–1988.

Moore, Francis J. *Description of Texas.* New York, 1844.

Moore, John Bassett. *History and Digest of the International Arbitrations to which the United States Has Been a Party.* 6 vols. Washington, D.C.: GPO, 1898. *The Miscellaneous Documents of the House of Representatives in 40 Vols.* (= vol. 39).

Morfi, Juan Agustín. *History of Texas, 1673–1779.* Translated from the Spanish by Carlos E. Castañeda. Albuquerque, N.Mex: The Quivira Society, 1935.

Nielsen, George P., ed. "Ben Milam and United States and Mexican Relations." *SHQ* 73 (1970): 393–95.

———. "Lydia Ann McHenry and Revolutionary Texas." *SHQ* 74 (1971): 393–408.

Peareson, P. E., ed. "Reminiscences of Judge Edwin Waller." *SHQ* 4 (1900): 33–53.

Peña, José Enrique de la. *With Santa Anna in Texas.* Translated from the Spanish by Carmen Perry. College Station: Texas A&M University Press, 1975.

Phillip, Stephen C. *An Address on the Annexation of Texas.* Boston, 1845.

Pierce, Gerald S., ed. "Some Early Letters of Moses Austin Bryan." *SHQ* 70 (1967): 461–71.

Poinsett, Joel Roberts. *Notes on Mexico, made in the autumn of 1822.* Philadelphia: H. C. Carey and I. Lea, 1824.

Quaife, Milo Milton, ed. *The Diary of James K. Polk during his Presidency, 1845 to 1849.* 4 vols. Chicago: A. C. McClung and Co., 1910.

Rabb, Mary Crownover. *Travels and Adventures in Texas in the 1820's.* With an introduction by Ramsey Yelvington. Waco, 1962.

Reichstein, Andreas, ed. "The Austin-Leaming Correspondence, 1828–1836." *SHQ* 88 (1985): 230–82.

Reports of Committees of the House of Representatives at the first session of the Twenty-second Congress, Begun and Held at the City of Washington, Dec. 7, 1831 in 5 Vols. Washington, D.C.: GPO, 1831.

Roosevelt, Theodore. *The Winning of the West.* 6 vols. The Sagamore Series. New York and London: G. P. Putnam's Sons, 1906.

Ruthven, A. S. *Proceedings of the Grand Lodge of Texas.* 2 vols. Galveston: Richardson and Co., 1860.

Sánchez, José María. "A Trip to Texas in 1828" (translated from the Spanish by Carlos E. Castañeda). *SHQ* 29 (1926): 249–88.

Santa Anna, Antonio López de. *Manifesto que de sus operaciones en la campana de Tejas y en su Cautiverio dirige a sus conciudadanos el General Antonio Lopez de Santa Anna.* Veracruz: Imprenta Liberal à cargo de Antonio Maria Valdes, 1837.

Sayles, John, and Henry Sayles, eds. *Early Laws of Texas.* 3 vols. 2nd ed. St. Louis: Gilbert Book Co., 1891.

Schoolcraft, Henry Rowe. *Scenes and Adventures in the Semi-Alpine Region of the Ozark Mountains of Missouri and Arkansas, which were first traversed by de Soto, in 1541.* Philadelphia: Lippincott, Grambo and Co., 1853.

———. *A View of the Lead Mines of Missouri.* New York, 1819. Reprint, New York: Arno Press, 1972.

Sealsfield, Charles. *Das Kajütenbuch, oder Nationale Charakteristiken.* 2 vols. Zurich: Druck and Verlag von Friedrich Schulthess, 1841.

Sedgwick, Theodore. *Thoughts on the Annexation of Texas to the United States.* New York, 1844.

Smith, Ashbel. *Reminiscences of the Texas Republic.* Galveston, 1876. Reprint, Austin: Pemberton Press, 1967.

Smith, Henry, "Reminiscences of Henry Smith." *SHQ* 15 (1910): 24–73.

State Papers and Public Documents of the United States. Vol. 10. 3rd ed. Boston, 1819.

Steen, Ralph W., ed. "A letter from San Antonio de Bexar in 1836." *SHQ* 62 (1959): 513–18.

Stiff, Edward. *The Texan Emigrant: being a Narration of the Adventures of the Author in Texas, and a Description of the Soil, Climate, Productions, Minerals, Towns, Bays, Harbors, Rivers, Institutions and Manners and Customs of the Inhabitants of that Country; together with the Principal Incidents of fifteen Years' Revolution in Mexico; and embracing a condensed Statement of interesting Events in Texas, from the first European Settlement in 1692, down to the Year 1840.* Cincinnati, 1840. Reprint, Waco: Texian Press, 1968.

Taylor, Virginia, ed. *The Letters of Antonio Martinez, Last Spanish Governor of Texas, 1817–1822.* Austin: Texas State Library, 1957.

Terrell, Alexander W. "Recollections of General Sam Houston." *SHQ* 16 (1912): 113–36.

Wallace, Ernest, and David M. Vigness, eds. *Documents of Texas History.* Lubbock: Texas Technological College, 1960.

Wallis, Mrs. Jonnie Lockhart, and Laurance L. Hill, eds. *Sixty Years on the Brazos: The Life and Letters of Dr. John Washington Lockhart 1824–1900.* Los Angeles, 1930. Reprint, Waco: Texian Press, 1967.

Washington, H. A., ed. *The Writings of Thomas Jefferson: Being his Autobiography, Correspondence, Reports, Messages, Addresses, and other writings, official and private.* 9 vols. Washington, D.C.: Taylor and Maury, 1853–1854.

Watkins, Willye Ward, ed. "Memoirs of General Antonio López de Santa Anna: Translation with Introduction and Text," MA thesis, University of Texas at Austin, 1922.

Wharton, William H. ["Curtius"]. *Texas, A Brief Account of the Origin, Progress and Present State of the Colonial Settlements of Texas.* Nashville, 1836. Reprint, Austin: Pemberton Press, n.d.

Williams, Amelia W., and Eugene C. Barker, eds. *The Writings of Sam Houston 1813–1863.* 8 vols. Austin and New York: Pemberton Press, 1970.

Winkler, Ernest William, ed. *Manuscript Letters and Documents of Early Texians 1821–1845.* Austin: Steck, 1937.

———. *Secret Journals of the Senate, Republic of Texas 1836–1845.* Austin: Austin Printing Co., 1911.

Winterbotham, J. M., and Eugene C. Barker, eds. "Stephen F. Austin and Anthony Butler." *MVHR* 11 (1924): 99–127.

Woodman, David, Jr. *Guide to Texas Emigrants.* Boston, 1835. Reprint, Waco: Texian Press, 1974.

Zuber, William Physik. *My Eighty Years in Texas.* Austin: University of Texas Press, 1971.

SECONDARY WORKS

Adair, Anthony Garland, and Ellen Bohlender Coats. *Texas, Its History.* Philadelphia: John C. Winston and Co., 1954.

Adams, Alva. "Texas and Her Liberator–Sam Houston." *The Modern World* (n.d.): 163–67.

Adams, Ephraim Douglass. *British Interests and Activities in Texas 1838–1846.* Gloucester, Mass.: Peter Smith, 1963.

———. "English Interest in the Annexation of California." *AHR* 19 (1909): 744–63.

———. "Manifest Destiny–An Emotion." In Armin Rappaport, ed., *Essays in American Diplomacy,* pp. 75–86. Berkeley and New York: Macmillan, 1967.

Adams, Joseph T. *Lecture on the Subject of Re-annexing Texas.* New Bedford, 1845.

Aguado y Bleye, Pedro, and Cayetano Alcázar. *Manual de história España.* 3 vols. Madrid: Espasa-Calpe, S.A., 1964.

Allen, Harry C. *Great Britain and the United States: A History of Anglo-American Relations, 1783–1952.* New York, 1955.

Allen, John Taylor. *Early Pioneer Days in Texas.* Dallas: Wilkinson Printing Co., 1918.

Alstyne, Richard W. van. *American Diplomats in Action.* Stanford, 1947.

———. *The Rising American Empire.* Oxford: Basil Blackwell, 1960.

Amsler, Robert W. "General Arthur G. Wavell: A Soldier of Fortune in Texas." *SHQ* 69 (1965): 1–21, 186–209.

Arendt, Hannah. *On Revolution.* New York: Viking Press, 1963.

Ashford, Gerald. "Jacksonian Liberalism and Spanish Law in Early Texas." *SHQ* 57 (1953): 1–38.

———. *Spanish Texas: Yesterday and Today.* Austin and New York: Pemberton Press, 1971.

Bacarisse, Charles A. "Baron de Bastrop." *SHQ* 58 (1955): 319–30.

———. "The Union of Coahuila and Texas." *SHQ* 61 (1958): 341–49.

———. "Why Moses Austin Came to Texas." *SSSQ* 40 (1959): 16–27.

Bailyn, Bernard, et al. *The Great Republic.* Boston: Little, Brown, 1977.

Baker, D. W. C. *A Texas Scrap Book.* New York, 1875. Reprint, Austin: Steck, 1935.

Bancroft, Hubert Howe. *History of the North Mexican States and Texas.* 2 vols. San Francisco: The History Co., 1886, 1889.

Banks, Clinton Howe. *The New Texas Reader.* San Antonio, 1960.

Barker, Eugene Campbell. "The Annexation of Texas." *SHQ* 50 (1946): 49–74.

———. "Difficulties of a Mexican Revenue Officer in Texas." *SHQ* 4 (1901): 190–202.

———. "The Finances of the Texas Revolution." *Political Science Quarterly* 19 (1904): 612–35.

———. "The Government of Austin's Colony, 1821–1831." *SHQ* 21 (1918): 223–52.

———. "The Influence of Slavery in the Colonization of Texas." *SHQ* 28 (1924): 1–33.

———. "Land Speculation as a Cause of the Texas Revolution." *SHQ* 10 (1906): 76–95.

———. *The Life of Stephen F. Austin, Founder of Texas, 1793–1836.* Nashville and Dallas, 1925. Reprint, Austin: Texas State Historical Association, 1969.

———. *Mexico and Texas 1821–1835.* Dallas, 1928. Reprint, New York: Russell and Russell, 1965.

———. "Native Latin American Contribution to the Colonization and Independence of Texas." *SHQ* 46 (1943): 317–35.

———. "Notes on the Colonization of Texas." *SHQ* 27 (1923): 108–19.

———. "The Organization of the Texas Revolution." In *Southern History Association Publication* 5 (1901): 451–76.

———. "President Jackson and the Texas Revolution." *AHR* 12 (1907): 788–809.

———. "Private Papers of Anthony Butler." *The Nation* 92 (1911): 600–601.

———. "Public Opinion in Texas Preceding the Revolution." *ARAHA* for 1911, pp. 219–28.

———. *Readings in Texas History.* Dallas: Southwest Press, 1929.

———. "The San Jacinto Campaign." *SHQ* 4 (1901): 236–345.

———. "Stephen F. Austin." *SHQ* 22 (1918): 1–17.

———. "Stephen F. Austin and the Independence of Texas." *SHQ* 13 (1910): 257–84.

———. "The Tampico Expedition." *SHQ* 6 (1902): 169–86.

———. "The Texan Declaration of Causes for Taking up Arms against Mexico." *SHQ* 15 (1912): 173–85.

———. "The Texan Revolutionary Army." *SHQ* 9 (1906): 227–61.

———. "The United States and Mexico, 1835–1837." *MVHR* 1 (1914): 3–30.

Barker, Nancy N. "Devious Diplomat: Dubois de Saligny and the Republic of Texas." *SHQ* 72 (1969): 324–34.

Barnes, Thomas C., Thomas H. Naylor, and Charles W. Polzer. *Northern New Spain: A Research Guide.* Tucson: University of Arizona Press, 1981.

Barton, Henry W. "The Anglo-American Colonists under Mexican Militia Laws." *SHQ* 65 (1961): 61–71.

Bassett, John Spencer. *The Life of Andrew Jackson.* 3rd ed. N.p., Archon Books, 1967.

Bauer, Arthur. "Essai sur les révolutions." *Bibiliothèque Internationale,* vol. 36, 1908.

Baugh, Virgil E. *Rendezvous at the Alamo.* Lincoln and London: University of Nebraska Press, 1985.

Beals, Carleton. *Stephen F. Austin, Father of Texas.* New York: McGraw-Hill, 1953.

Beasley, Norman. *Texas, the Lone Star State.* Garden City, N.Y.: Doubleday, Doran and Co., 1936.

Belaunde, Victor A. "The Frontier in Hispanic-American History." *ARAHA* for 1922, 1:300.

Belohlavek, John M. *Let the Eagle Soar! The Foreign Policy of Andrew Jackson.* Lincoln and London: University of Nebraska Press, 1985.

Bennett, Miles S. "The Battle of Gonzales, the 'Lexington' of the Texas Revolution." *SHQ* 2 (1898): 313–16.

Benson, Nettie Lee. "Texas as Viewed from Mexico, 1820–1834." *SHQ* 90 (1987): 219–91.

Berge, Dennis Eugene. "Mexican Response to United States Expansionism, 1841–1848." Ph.D. dissertation, University of California at Berkeley, 1965.

Bertleth, Rosa Groce. "Jared Ellison Groce." *SHQ* 20 (1917): 358–68.

Beyhaut, Gustavo. *Süd- und Mittelamerika II: Von der Unabhängigkeit bis zur Krise der Gegenwart.* Fischer Weltgeschichte, vol. 23. Frankfurt am Main, 1965.

Biesele, Rudolph L. "The First German Settlement in Texas." *SHQ* 34 (1931): 334–39.

Bill, Alfred Hoyt. *Rehearsal for Conflict: The War with Mexico 1846–48.* New York: Cooper Square Publications, 1969.

Billington, Ray. *The Far Western Frontier 1830–1860.* New York: Harper and Brothers, 1956.

———. *The Frontier Thesis.* Huntington and New York: Robert E. Krieger Publishing Co., 1977.

———. *Westward Expansion.* 4th ed. New York: Macmillan, 1969.

Billington, Ray Allen, and Martin Ridge, eds. *America's Frontier Story.* New York: Holt, Rinehart and Winston, 1969.

Binkley, William Campbell. *The Expansionist Movement in Texas, 1836–1850.* Reprint, Berkeley, 1925. New York: De Capo Press, 1970.

———. *The Texas Revolution.* Baton Rouge: Louisiana State University, 1952.

Binney, Charles J. F. *The history and genealogy of the Prentice, or Prentiss Family in New England, etc. from 1631 to 1883.* 2nd ed. Boston, 1883.

Bogue, Allan, and Margaret Bogue. "'Profits' and the Frontier Land Speculator." *Journal of Economic History* 17, no. 1 (1957): 1–24.

Bolton, Herbert Eugene. "Some Materials for Southwestern History in the Archivo General de Mexico." *SHQ* 6 and 7 (1902, 1904): 103–12, 196–213.

———. *Texas in the Middle Eighteenth Century.* New York: Russell and Russell, 1962.

Bolton, Herbert Eugene, and Eugene C. Barker. *With the Makers of Texas.* New York: American Book Co., 1904.

Bonham, Milledge L., Jr. "James Butler Bonham: A Consistent Rebel." *SHQ* 35 (1931): 124–36.

Bourne, Kenneth. *Britain and the Balance of Power in North America 1815–1908.* Berkeley and Los Angeles: University of California, 1967.

Brack, Gene M. "Mexican Opinion and the Texas Revolution." *SHQ* 72 (1968): 170–82.

———. *Mexico Views Manifest Destiny, 1821–1846*. Albuquerque: University of New Mexico Press, 1975.

Braider, Donald. *Solitary Star: A Biography of Sam Houston*. New York: G. P. Putnam's Sons, 1974.

Braman, D. E. E. *Information about Texas*. Philadelphia, 1858.

Brister, Louis E. "Colonel Eduard Harkort: A German Soldier of Fortune in Mexico and Texas, 1832–1836." *SHQ* 88 (1985): 229–46.

Brown, John Henry. *History of Texas from 1685 to 1892*. 2 vols. N.p., 1892. Reprint, Austin and New York: Pemberton Press, 1970.

———. *Life and Times of Henry Smith, the First American Governor of Texas*. Dallas: A. D. Aldridge, 1887.

Bruce, Henry. *Life of General Houston 1793–1863*. New York: Dodd, Mead and Co., 1891.

Bryan, George Sands. *Sam Houston*. New York: Macmillan, 1921.

Bryant, R. W. G. *Land Speculation*. Institut d'Urbanisme, Université de Montréal, 1975.

Buell, Augustus C. *History of Andrew Jackson: Pioneer, Patriot, Soldier, Politician, President*. 2 vols. New York: Charles Scribner's Sons, 1904.

Bugbee, Lester G. "The Texas Frontier, 1820–1825." *Southern History Publications* 4 (1900): 102–21.

Callahan, Sister M. Generosa. "Henri Castro and James Hamilton." *SHQ* 69 (1965): 174–85.

Cánovas, Agustín Cué. *História social y económica de Mexico, 1521–1854*. 3rd ed. Mexico City, 1967.

Carroll, Bailey H., and Gutsch, Milton R. *Texas History Theses*. Austin, 1955.

Carroll, Benajah H. "Die Annexion von Texas." Ph.D. dissertation, Friedrich-Wilhelms-Universität, 1904.

Carter, James David. *Education and Masonry in Texas to 1846*. Waco: Committee on Masonic Education and Service, 1963.

———. *Education and Masonry in Texas, 1846 to 1861*. Waco: Committee on Masonic Education and Service, 1964.

———. "Freemasonry and Texas History 1800–1835." *SHQ* 56 (1953): 397–406.

———. *Masonry in Texas*. Waco: Committee on Masonic Education for the Grand Lodge of Texas, 1955.

Castañeda, Carlos E. *Our Catholic Heritage in Texas 1519–1936*. 7 vols. Austin: Von Boeckmann-Jones Co., 1931–58.

Caughey, John Walton. *Bernardo de Gálvez in Louisiana 1776–1783*. Berkeley: University of California Press, 1934.

Chabot, Frederick C., ed. *Texas in 1811: The Las Casas and Sambrano Revolution*. Yanaguana Society Publications, vol. 6. San Antonio, 1941.

Chandler, Charles Lyon. *Inter-American Acquaintances.* 2nd ed. Sewanee: University Press of Sewanee, Tennessee, 1917.

Channing, William Ellery. *A letter to the Hon. Henry Clay, on the Annexation of Texas to the United States.* Boston, 1937.

Chase, M. K. *Négociations de la république du Texas en Europe, 1837–1845.* Paris, 1932.

Charlton, George L. "Vince's Bridge, Question Mark of the San Jacinto Campaign." *SHQ* 68 (1964): 342–51.

Christian, Asa Kyrus. "Mirabeau Buonaparte Lamar." *SHQ* 6 parts, 23 (1920): 153–70, 231–70; (1920–1921): 39–80, 87–139, 195–234, 317–24.

Clark, Joseph Lynn, and Julia Kathryn Garrett. *A History of Texas, Land of Promise.* Boston: D. C. Heath and Co., 1949.

Clark, R. C. "The Beginnings of Texas." *SHQ* 5 (1902): 171–205.

Cleaves, W. S. "Lorenzo de Zavala in Texas." *SHQ* 36 (1932): 29–40.

Cleland, Robert Glass. *Wilderness to Empire.* 2nd ed. New York: Alfred A. Knopf, 1947.

———. *This Reckless Breed of Men.* New York: Alfred A. Knopf, 1950.

Cohan, A. S. *Theories of Revolution: An Introduction.* London, 1975.

Cole, E. W. "La Salle in Texas." *SHQ* 49 (1945): 473–500.

Coman, Katharine. *Economic Beginnings of the Far West.* Vol. 2, *American Settlers.* New York: Macmillan, 1921.

Connor, Seymour V. *Texas: A History.* Arlington Heights, N.Y.: AHM Publishing Co., 1971.

Corner, William. "John Crittenden Duval: The Last Survivor of the Goliad Massacre." *SHQ* 1 (1897): 47–67.

Cotner, Thomas E., and Carlos E. Castañeda. *Essays in Mexican History.* Austin: University of Texas Press, 1958.

Cottrell, Dannell George. "The Americanization of Texas." MS thesis, University of Utah, 1941.

Covington, Nina. "The Presidential Campaigns of the Republic of Texas of 1836 and 1838." MA thesis, University of Texas, 1929.

Cox, Bertha Mae. *Our Texas: Explorers, Heroes, Battles, Founders, Makers.* Dallas: Turner Co., 1965.

Cox, Isaac Joslin. "The Louisiana-Texas Frontier." *SHQ* 10 (1906): 1–75; 17 (1913): 1–42, 140–87.

———. "The Pan-American Policy of Jefferson and Wilkinson." *MVHR* 1 (1914): 212–39.

———. "The Southwestern Boundary of Texas." *SHQ* 6 (1902): 81–102.

Creel, George. *Sam Houston: Colossus in Buckskin.* New York: Cosmopolitan Book Co., 1928.

Crimmins, M. L. "The Storming of San Antonio de Béxar in 1835." *West Texas Historical Association Yearbook* 22 (1946): 95–117.

Crisp, James Ernest. "Anglo-Texan Attitudes toward the Mexican, 1821–1845." Ph.D. dissertation, Yale University, 1976.

Culberson, Charles A. "General Sam Houston and Secession." *Scribner's Magazine* 39 (1906): 584–91.

Cumberland, Charles C. *Mexico: The Struggle for Modernity.* New York: Oxford University Press, 1968.

Curlee, Abigail. "The History of a Texas Slave Plantation, 1831–1863." *SHQ* 26 (1922): 79–127.

Curry, Ora Mae. "The Texan Siege of San Antonio, 1835." MA thesis, University of Texas at Austin, 1927.

Curtis, James C. *The Fox at Bay: Martin Van Buren and the Presidency, 1837–1841.* Lexington: University Press of Kentucky, 1970.

Cutrer, Thomas W. *The English Texans.* San Antonio, 1985.

Dalzell, Robert F., Jr. *Daniel Webster and the Trial of American Nationalism, 1843–1852.* 2nd ed. New York: W. W. Norton and Co., 1975.

Daniell, Lewis E. *Texas: The Country and Its Men.* Austin, 1924.

Davenport, Harbert. "The Men of Goliad." *SHQ* 43 (1939): 1–41.

Davis, Mollie Evelyn Moore. *Under Six Flags: The Story of Texas.* Boston: Ginn and Co., 1897.

Dealey, James E. "The Spanish Source of the Mexican Constitution of 1824." *SHQ* 3 (1900): 161–69.

DeConde, Alexander. *This Affair of Louisiana.* New York: Charles Scribner's Sons, 1976.

Delafons, John. *Land-use Controls in the United States.* Cambridge, Mass.: Joint Center for Urban Studies of MIT and Harvard University, 1962.

DeShields, James Thomas. *They Sat in High Places.* San Antonio: Naylor, 1940.

Dickerson, Donna Lee. "The Press and the Presidents of the Republic of Texas." MA thesis, University of Texas at Austin, 1971.

Dienst, Alexander. "The Navy of the Republic of Texas." *SHQ* 12 (1909): 165–203, 249–75; 13 (1909): 1–43, 85–127.

———. "The New Orleans Newspaper Files of the Texas Revolutionary Period." *SHQ* 4 (1900): 140–52.

Dillon, Merton L. "Benjamin Lundy in Texas." *SHQ* 63 (1959): 46–62.

Din, Gilbert C. "The Immigration Policy of Governor Esteban Miró in Spanish Louisiana." *SHQ* 73 (1969): 155–75.

———. "Spain's Immigration Policy in Louisiana and the American Penetration, 1792–1803." *SHQ* 76 (1973): 255–76.

Dixon, Sam Houston. *The Men Who Made Texas Free.* Houston: Texas Historical Publishing Co., 1924.

Dixon, Sam Houston, and Louis Wiltz Kemp. *The Heroes of San Jacinto.* Houston: Anson Jones Press, 1932.

Dobie, J. Frank. "James Bowie, Big Dealer." *SHQ* 60 (1957): 337–57.

Dodd, William E. "The West and the War with Mexico." *Journal of the Illinois State Historical Society* 5 (1912): 159–72.

Doegey, Corayne M. "The Ethos of Sam Houston." MA thesis, Long Beach State College, 1964.

Doggett, A. J. *The Colonization Scheme as Carried out by Moses Austin.* Sherman, Tex., 1912.

Donaldson, Nanna Smithwick. "Concerning the Gonzales Cannon." *SHQ* 5 (1901): 356.

Douglas, Lucia Rutherford. "John Quincy Adams and the Texas Question." MA thesis, University of Texas, 1927.

Downs, Fane. "The History of Mexicans in Texas, 1820–1845." Ph.D. dissertation, Texas Tech University, 1970.

Drinnon, Richard. *Facing West: The Metaphysics of Indian-Hating and Empire-Building.* New York: New American Library, 1980.

Edwards, Herbert Rook. "Diplomatic Relations between France and the Republic of Texas, 1836–1845." *SHQ* 20 (1917): 209–41, 341–57.

Elliott, Claude. "Alabama and the Texas Revolution." *SHQ* 50 (1947): 314–28.

———. *Theses on Texas History.* Austin: Texas State Historical Association, 1955.

Elliott, Sarah Barnwell. *Sam Houston.* Boston: Small, Maynard and Co., 1900.

Ellis, L. Tuffly. "The University's Centennial: A Commemoration." *SHQ* 86 (1982): 125–34.

Estep, Raymond. "Lorenzo de Zavala and the Texas Revolution." *SHQ* 57 (1953): 322–35.

Farber, James. *Those Texans.* San Antonio, 1945.

Farris, N. M. *Crown and Clergy in Colonial Mexico, 1759–1821.* London: Athlone Press, 1968.

Faulk, Odie B. *The Last Years of Spanish Texas, 1778–1821.* London: Mouton and Co., 1964.

Fehrenbach, T. R. *Lone Star: A History of Texas and the Texans.* 5th ed. New York: Macmillan, 1977.

Ficklen, John R. "Was Texas Included in the Louisiana Purchase?" *Southern History Association Publication* 5 (1901): 351–87.

Fish, Carl Russell. *The Path of Empire.* New Haven, Conn.: Oxford University Press, 1919.

Fisher, Lillian Estelle. "Early Masonry in Mexico (1806–1828)." *SHQ* 42 (1939): 198–214.

Flanagan, Sue. *Sam Houston's Texas.* Austin: University of Texas Press, 1964.

Flores, Mena L. *El General Don Antonio López de Santa Anna.* N.p., 1950.

Foley, William E., and C. David Rice. *The First Chouteaus: River Barons of*

Early St. Louis. Urbana and Chicago: University of Illinois Press, 1983.

Foote, Henry Stuart. *Texas and the Texans; or Advance of the Anglo-Americans to the Southwest.* 2 vols. Philadelphia: Thomas, Cowperthwait and Co., 1841.

Foreman, Grant. *Indians and Pioneers: The Story of the American Southwest before 1830.* New Haven, Conn.: Yale University Press, 1930.

————. *Pioneer Days in the Early Southwest.* Cleveland: Arthur H. Clarke, 1926.

————. "Some New Light on Houston's Life among the Cherokee Indians." *Chronicles of Oklahoma* 9 (1931): 139–52.

Frantz, Joe B. *Texas, a Bicentennial History.* New York, 1976.

————. "Texas Giant of Contradictions: Sam Houston." *The American West* 17 (1980): 5–12, 61–65.

Friend, Llerena B. *Sam Houston: The Great Designer.* 2nd ed. Austin: University of Texas Press, 1979.

Froelich, Ann Hill. "The Relationship of Stephen F. Austin and Sam Houston," MA thesis, Sam Houston State University, 1971.

Fuller, John Douglas Pitts. *The Movement for the Acquisition of All Mexico, 1846–1848.* Baltimore: John Hopkins University Press, 1936.

Fulmore, Zachary Taylor. "The Annexation of Texas and the Mexican War." *SHQ* 5 (1901): 28–48.

————. *The History and Geography of Texas – as Told in County Names.* Austin, 1915.

Gailey, Harry A., Jr. "Sam Houston and the Texas War Fever, March–August, 1842." *SHQ* 62 (1958): 29–44.

Gambrell, Herbert. *Anson Jones, the Last President of Texas.* Garden City, N.Y.: Doubleday and Co., 1948.

García, Carlos Bosch. *História de las relaciones entre México y los Estados Unidos, 1829–1848.* Mexico City, 1961.

Gardner, James Alexander. "The Life of Moses Austin, 1761–1821." Ph.D. dissertation, Washington University, 1963.

Gardner, Lloyd C., Walter F. LaFeber, and Thomas J. McCormick. *Creation of the American Empire: U.S. Diplomatic History.* Chicago: Rand McNally, 1973.

Garrett, Julia Kathryn. *Green Flag over Texas.* New York and Dallas: Cordova Press, 1939.

Garrison, George Pierce. "The First Stage of the Movement for the Annexation of Texas." *AHR* 10 (1904): 72–96.

————. *Texas, a Contest of Civilizations.* Boston and New York: Houghton Mifflin, 1903.

————. *Westward Extension, 1841–1850.* 2nd ed. New York and Evanston: Harper and Row, 1968.

Garver, Louis. "Benjamin Rush Milam." *SHQ* 38 (1934): 177–202.

Genovese, Eugene D. *Roll, Jordan, Roll: The World the Slaves Made*. 2nd ed. New York: Random House, 1974.

Gilbert, Charles E. *A Concise History of Early Texas, 1519 to 1861*. Houston, 1965.

Glasscock, Sallie. *Dreams of an Empire*. San Antonio: Naylor, 1951.

Goetzmann, William H. *Exploration and Empire*. 2nd ed. New York: W. W. Norton and Co., 1978.

———. *When the Eagle Screamed*. New York: John Wiley and Sons, 1966.

Gouge, W. M. *The Fiscal History of Texas*. Philadelphia: Lippincott, Grambo and Co., 1852.

Gracy, David B. *Moses Austin: His Life*. San Antonio: Trinity University Press, 1987.

Graebner, Norman A. *Empire on the Pacific*. New York: Ronald Press Co., 1955.

Graebner, Norman A., ed. *Manifest Destiny*. Indianapolis and New York: Bobbs-Merrill, 1968.

Grayson, Peter W. "The Release of Stephen F. Austin from Prison." *SHQ* 14 (1910): 155–63.

Green, Michael R. "To the People of Texas and All Americans in the World." *SHQ* 91 (1988): 483–50.

Greer, James K. "The Committee on the Texas Declaration of Independence." *SHQ* 30 (1927): 239–51; 31 (1927): 33–49, 130–49.

Gregory, Jack, and Rennard Strickland. *Sam Houston with the Cherokees, 1829–1833*. 2nd ed. Austin and London: University of Texas Press, 1976.

Griffin, Roger A. "To Establish a University of the First Class." *SHQ* 86 (1982): 135–60.

Gurr, Ted R. *Why Men Rebel*. Princeton, N. J.: Princeton University Press, 1970.

Haggard, Juan Villasana. "Epidemic Cholera in Texas, 1833–1834." *SHQ* 40 (1937): 216–30.

———. "The Neutral Ground between Louisiana and Texas, 1806–1821." Ph.D. dissertation, University of Texas, 1943.

Hale, Charles Adams. "The Problem of Independence in Mexican Thought, 1821–1853." Ph.D. dissertation, Columbia University, 1957.

Hale, Joseph W. "Masonry in the Early Days of Texas." *SHQ* 49 (1946): 374–83.

Hamilton, Holman. "Texas Bonds and Northern Profits: A Study in Compromise, Investment, and Lobby Influence." *MVHR* 43 (1957): 579–94.

Hancock, Walter Edgar. "The Career of General Antonio Lopez de Santa Anna, 1794–1833." Ph.D. dissertation, University of Texas, 1933.

Harris, Helen Willits. "Almonte's Inspection of Texas in 1834." *SHQ* 41 (1938): 195–211.

Harris, Michael H. *Florida History: A Bibliography.* Metuchen, N.J.: Scarecrow Press, 1972.

Hardt, Annanelle. "The Bi-cultural Heritage of Texas." Ph.D. dissertation, University of Texas at Austin, 1968.

Hatcher, Mattie Austin. "The Louisiana Background of the Colonization of Texas, 1763–1803." *SHQ* 24 (1921): 169–94.

———. *The Opening of Texas to Foreign Settlement, 1801–1821.* Austin: University of Texas, 1927.

Hatley, Roy O. *Texas, Its Storied Past and Thriving Present.* San Antonio, 1976.

Haywood, Harry LeRoy. *Freemasonry and Roman Catholicism.* Chicago: Masonic History Co., 1943.

Held, J. A. *Religion, a Factor in Building Texas.* San Antonio, 1940.

Henderson, H. M. "A Critical Analysis of the San Jacinto Campaign." *SHQ* 59 (1955): 344–62.

Henderson, Mary Virginia. "Minor Empresario Contracts for the Colonization of Texas, 1825–1834." *SHQ* 31 (1928): 295–324, and 32 (1928): 1–28.

Henry, Robert Selph. *The Story of the Mexican War.* 2nd ed. New York: Frederick Ungar Publishing Co., 1961.

Henson, Margaret Swett. *Juan Davis Bradburn: A Reappraisal of the Mexican Commander of Anahuac.* College Station: Texas A&M University Press, 1982.

———. *Samuel May Williams: Early Texas Entrepreneur.* College Station: Texas A&M University Press, 1976.

Hill, Charles Edward. *Leading American Treaties.* 1922. Reprint, New York: AMS Press, 1969.

Hill, Jim Dan. *The Texas Navy in Forgotten Battles and Shirtsleeve Diplomacy.* Chicago: University of Chicago Press, 1937.

Hobby, A. M. *Life and Times of David G. Burnet, First President of the Republic of Texas.* Galveston: Galveston News Office, 1871.

Hofstadter, Richard. *The Progressive Historians: Turner, Beard, Parrington.* 2nd ed. Chicago: University of Chicago Press, 1971.

Hogan, William Ransom. "Henry Austin." *SHQ* 37 (1934): 185–214.

———. *The Texas Republic: A Social and Economic History.* 3rd ed. Austin and London: University of Texas Press, 1980.

Holden, Henrietta A. *Story of the Lone Star State.* San Antonio, 1948.

Houston, Andrew Jackson. *Texas Independence.* Houston: Anson Jones, 1938.

Howe, Paul Sturtevant. *Mayflower Pilgrim Descendants in Cape May County, New Jersey.* Baltimore: Genealogical Publishing Co., 1977.

Howren, Alleine. "Causes and Origin of the Decree of April 6, 1830." *SHQ* 16 (1913): 378–422.

Hume, Martin A. S. *Spain, Its Greatness and Decay, 1479–1788.* Cambridge: University Press, 1925.

Hunley, Josephine Keller. "A Documentary History of Texan Sentiment for Annexation to the United States, 1835–1838." MA thesis, University of Texas, 1937.

Hutchinson, C. Alan. "General José Antonio Mexía and His Texas Interests." *SHQ* 82 (1978): 117–42.

———. "Mexican Federalists in New Orleans and the Texas Revolution." *Louisiana Historical Quarterly* 39 (1956): 1–47.

Hynds, Alexander. "General Sam Houston." *Century Magazine* 28 (1884): 494–506.

Ikin, Arthur. *Texas: Its History, Topography, Agriculture, Commerce, and General Statistics.* London: Sherwood, Gilbert and Piper, 1841.

Ingersoll, C. J. *View of the Texas Question.* Washington, D.C., 1844.

Jackson, Jack. *Los Mesteños: Spanish Ranching in Texas, 1721–1821.* College Station: Texas A&M University Press, 1986.

Jackson, Lillis Tisdale. "Sam Houston in the Texas Revolution." MA thesis, University of Texas, 1932.

Jacobs, Paul, Saul Landau, and Eve Pell. *To Serve the Devil.* New York: Random House, 1971.

James, J. A. "Louisiana as a Factor in American Diplomacy, 1795–1800." *MVHR* 1 (1914): 44–56.

James, Marquis. *Andrew Jackson.* 2 vols. Indianapolis and New York: Bobbs-Merrill, 1937.

———. *The Raven: The Story of Sam Houston.* Indianapolis and New York: Bobbs-Merrill, 1929.

Jenkins, John H. *Printer in Three Republics: A Bibliography of Samuel Bangs, First Printer in Texas, and First Printer West of the Louisiana Purchase.* Austin: Jenkins Publishing Co., 1981.

Jennett, Elisabeth LeNoir. *Biographical Directory of the Texan Conventions and Congresses, 1832, 1845.* Austin, 1941.

John, George O'Brien. *Texas History: An Outline.* New York: Henry Holt and Co., 1935.

Johnson, Chalmers. *Revolutionary Change.* Boston: Little, Brown, 1966.

Johnson, Frank White, Eugene C. Barker, and Ernest W. Winkler. *A History of Texas and the Texans.* 5 vols. Chicago and New York: American Historical Society, 1914.

Johnson, William. *Sam Houston, the Tallest Texan.* New York, 1968.

Jones, Oakah L. *Santa Anna.* New York: Twayne Publishers, 1968.

Jordan, Terry G. "A Century and a Half of Ethnic Change in Texas, 1836–1986." *SHQ* 89 (1986): 385–422.

Kaough, Richard James. "The Annexation of Texas to the United States: A Proposition Analysis." Ph.D. dissertation, Southern Illinois University, 1971.

Kemp, Louis Wiltz. *The Signers of the Texas Declaration of Independence.* Houston: Anson Jones Press, 1944.

Kennedy, John Fitzgerald. *Profiles in Courage.* New York: Harper and Row, 1956.

Kennedy, William. *Texas: The Rise, Progress, and Prospects of the Republic of Texas.* London, 1841. Reprint, Fort Worth: Molyneaux Craftsmen, 1925.

Kidd, J. C. *History of Holland Lodge No. 1.* Houston, 1920.

Kossok, Manfred. "Prussia, Bremen, and the Texas Question." *Texana* 3 (1965): 227–69.

Lack, Paul D. "Slavery and the Texas Revolution." *SHQ* 89 (1985): 181–202.

LaFeber, Walter. *The New Empire.* Ithaca, N.Y.: Cornell University Press, 1963.

Lathrop, Barnes F. "Migration into East Texas 1835–1860." *SHQ* 52 (1948): 1–31, 184–208, 325–48.

Laurent, Pierre Henri. "Belgium's Relations with Texas and the United States, 1839–1844." *SHQ* 68 (1964): 220–36.

Lee, Rebecca Smith. *Mary Austin Holley: A Biography.* Austin: University of Texas Press, 1987.

———. "The Publication of Austin's Louisville Address." *SHQ* 70 (1967): 424–42.

Leming, Sam Kellough. *Leming Family History and Genealogy.* Waldron, 1947.

León, Arnoldo de. *They Called Them Greasers: Anglo Attitudes towards Mexicans in Texas, 1821–1900.* Austin: University of Texas Press, 1983.

Lester, Charles Edwards. *Life and Achievements of Sam Houston, Hero and Statesman.* New York: Hurst and Co., 1883.

———. *The Life of Sam Houston.* New York: J. C. Derby, 1855.

———. *Sam Houston and His Republic.* New York: Burgess, Stringer and Co., 1846.

Lewis, Sarah Elisabeth. "Digest of Congressional Action on the Annexation of Texas, December, 1844, to March, 1845." *SHQ* 50 (1946): 251–69.

Lipson, Dorothy Ann. *Freemasonry in Federalist Connecticut.* Princeton, N.J.: Princeton University Press, 1977.

London, Lena. "The Initial Homestead Exemption in Texas." *SHQ* 57 (1953): 432–53.

Lord, Walter. *A Time to Stand.* Lincoln and London: University of Nebraska Press, 1978.

Lowrie, Samuel Harman. *Culture Conflict in Texas 1821–1835.* New York: AMS Press, 1967.

Lynch, Howard W. "The Attitude of the United States towards Texas, 1803–1845." MA thesis, University of Kentucky, 1933.

Maillard, N. Doran. *The History of the Republic of Texas.* London, 1842.

Manning, William Ray. *Early Diplomatic Relations between the United States and Mexico.* Baltimore: Johns Hopkins University Press, 1916.

――――. "Texas and the Boundary Issue, 1822–1829." *SHQ* 17 (1913): 217–61.

Manuel, H. T. "The Mexican Population of Texas." *SSSQ* 15 (1935): 29–51.

Marshall, Thomas Maitland. "Diplomatic Relations of Texas and the United States, 1839–1843." *SHQ* 15 (1912): 267–93.

――――. *History of the Western Boundary of the Louisiana Purchase.* Berkeley: University of California Press, 1914.

――――. "The Whereabouts of Sam Houston in 1834." *SHQ* 16 (1913): 328–29.

Mateos, Juan A. *História parlamentaria de los congresos mexicanos de 1821 a 1857.* 8 vols. Mexico City, 1877.

May, Ernest R. "American Imperialism: A Reinterpretation." *Perspectives in American History* 1 (1967): 123–286.

Mayes, William Harding. *Struggle of Texas for Independence.* N.p., n.d.

Mayo, Bernard. "Apostle of Manifest Destiny." *American Mercury* 18/72 (1929): 420–26.

Maystrik, Helen. "The Spanish Treaty of 1819 and Its Influence on American History." MA thesis, University of Oklahoma, 1928.

McCall, George. *Stephen F. Austin's Relations with the Mexican Government.* Sherman, Tex.: 1914.

McClendon, James W. *Selected Masonic Writings.* Masonic Home and School Press, 1963.

McCollum, Dudley Foster. "Spanish Texas." Ph.D. dissertation, New York University, 1931.

McConnell, Joseph Carroll. *The West Texas Frontier.* Jacksboro, Tex., 1933.

McCormac, Eugene Irving. *James K. Polk: A Political Biography.* Berkeley: University of California Press, 1922.

McCraw, William. *Professional Politicians.* Washington, D.C.: Imperial Press, 1940.

McDanield, H. F. *The Coming Empire.* Dallas, 1936.

McElhannon, Joseph Carl. "Imperial Mexico and Texas, 1821–1823." *SHQ* 53 (1949): 117–50.

McKay, S. S. "Texas and the Southern Pacific Railroad, 1848–1860." *SHQ* 35 (1931): 1–11.

McKitrick, Reuben. *The Public Land System of Texas, 1823–1910.* Madison: University of Wisconsin Press, 1918.

McLemore, R. A. "The Influence of French Diplomatic Policy on the Annexation of Texas." *SHQ* 43 (1940): 342–47.

McLendon, James H. "John A. Quitman in the Texas Revolution." *SHQ* 52 (1948): 163–83.

Medearis, Mary. *Washington, Arkansas: History on the Southwest Trail.* 2nd ed. Hope, Ark.: Etter Printing Co., 1978.

Meining, Donald W. *Imperial Texas: An Interpretive Essay in Cultural Geography.* 2nd ed. Austin and London: University of Texas Press, 1979.

Merhart, Ulrich von. *Weltfreimaurerei.* Hamburg: Bauhütten Verlag, 1969.

Merk, Frederick. *History of the Westward Movement.* New York: Alfred A. Knopf, 1978.

———. *Manifest Destiny and Mission in American History.* New York: Vintage Books, 1966.

———. *The Monroe Doctrine and American Expansionism, 1843–1849.* 4th ed. New York: Alfred A. Knopf, 1971.

———. *Slavery and the Annexation of Texas.* New York: Alfred A. Knopf, 1972.

Merriman, Roger Bigelow. *The Rise of the Spanish Empire in the Old World and the New.* 4 vols. New York: Cooper Square Publishers, 1962.

Meyer, Michael C., and William L. Sherman. *The Course of Mexican History.* New York: Oxford University Press, 1979.

Middleton, Annie. "Donelson's Mission to Texas in Behalf of Annexation." *SHQ* 24 (1921): 247–91.

———. "The Texas Convention of 1845." *SHQ* 25 (1921): 26–62 (both parts from the author's MA thesis, 1920).

Miller, Edmund T. *A Financial History of Texas.* University of Texas Bulletin No. 37. Austin, 1916.

Miller, Howard. "Stephen F. Austin and the Anglo Texan Response to the Religious Establishment in Mexico, 1821–1836." *SHQ* 91 (1988): 283–316.

Miller, Thomas Lloyd. *Bounty and Donation Land Grants of Texas, 1835–1888.* 2nd ed. Austin: University of Texas Press, 1967.

———. "Fannin's Men: Some Additions to Earlier Rosters." *SHQ* 61 (1957): 522–32.

Montejano, David. *Anglos and Mexicans in the Making of Texas, 1836–1986.* Austin: University of Texas Press, 1987.

Moore, R. Woods. "The Role of the Baron de Bastrop in the Anglo-American Settlement of the Spanish Southwest." *Louisiana Historical Quarterly* 31 (1948): 606–81.

Morand, Marcel. "The Diplomatic Relations of the Republic of Texas." *Rice Institute Pamphlet* 43 (1965): 29–54.

Morison, Samuel Eliot, Henry Steele Commager, and William E. Leuchtenburg. *A Concise History of the American Republic.* New York: Oxford University Press, 1977.

Morphis, J. K. *History of Texas, from Its Discovery and Settlement, with a Description of Its Principal Cities and Counties, and the Agricultural, Mineral, and Material Resources of the State*. New York: United States Publishing Co., 1875.

Morton, Ohland. "Life of General Don Manuel de Mier y Terán." 8 parts, *SHQ* 46 (1942–1943): 22–47, 239–54; 47 (1943–1944): 29–47, 120–42, 256–67; 48 (1944–1945): 51–66, 193–218, 499–546.

Muir, Andrew Forest. "Railroad Enterprise in Texas, 1836–1841." *SHQ* 47 (1944): 339–70.

———. "The Union Company in Anahuac, 1831–1833." *SHQ* 70 (1966): 256–68.

Muse, Barbara Johnson. "The First Phase of the Texas Revolution." MA thesis, University of Houston, 1970.

Nackman, Mark E. "Anglo-American Migrants to the West: Men of Broken Fortunes? The Case of Texas, 1821–46." *Western Historical Quarterly* 5 (1974): 441–55.

———. *A Nation within a Nation: The Rise of Texas Nationalism*. Port Washington, N.Y., and London: Kennikat Press, 1975.

Nance, Joseph Milton. *After San Jacinto: The Texas-Mexican Frontier, 1836–1841*. Austin: University of Texas Press, 1963.

———. *Attack and Counterattack: The Texas-Mexican Frontier, 1842*. Austin: University of Texas Press, 1964.

Nevins, Allan, and Henry Steele Commager. *America: The Story of a Free People*. 4th ed. Oxford: Oxford University Press, 1976.

Newcomb, W. W., Jr. *The Indians of Texas*. Austin: University of Texas Press, 1965.

Newell, Chester C. *History of the Revolution in Texas, particularly of the war of 1835–1836*. New York: Wiley and Putnam, 1838.

Newmann, John B. *Texas and Mexico in 1846*. New York, 1846.

Newton, Lewis W., and Herbert P. Gambrell. *Texas, Yesterday and Today*. Dallas: Turner Co., 1949.

Oates, Stephen B. *The Republic of Texas*. Palo Alto: American West Publishing Co., 1968.

O'Connor, Kathryn Stoner. *The Presidio la Bahía del Espíritu Santo de Zúñiga 1721 to 1846*. Austin: Von Boeckmann-Jones, 1966.

O'Neal, John William. "Texas 1791–1835: A Study in Manifest Destiny." MA thesis, East Texas State University, 1969.

Osler, E. B. *La Salle*. Don Mills, Ont.: Longmans Canada, 1967.

Parish, Peter J. *The American Civil War*. London: Eyre Methuen, 1975.

Parmenter, Mary Fisher, Walter Russell Fisher, and Lawrence Edward Malette. *The Life of George Fisher, 1795–1873*. Jacksonville, Fla.: H. and W. D. Drew, 1959.

Parsons, Edmund Morris. "The Fredonian Rebellion." *Texana* 5 (1967): 11–52.

Parton, James. *Life of Andrew Jackson*. 5 vols. Boston, 1885.

Payne, James Sutton. "Texas Historiography in the Twentieth Century: A Study of Eugene C. Barker, Charles W. Ramsdell, and Walter P. Webb." Ph.D. dissertation, University of Denver, 1972.

Pellow, Robert Emmett. *When Texas Came Romping into the Union*. Waco, 1935.

Pennybacker, Anna J. Hardwicke. *A History of Texas—for schools*. 4th ed. Austin, 1912.

Pessen, Edward. *Jacksonian America: Society, Personality, and Politics*. 5th ed. Homewood, Ill.: Dorsey Press, 1972.

Peters, Robert Kinsley. "Texas: Annexation to Secession." Ph.D. dissertation, University of Texas at Austin, 1977.

Pierce, Gerald S. *Texas under Arms: The Camps, Posts, Forts, and Military Towns of the Republic of Texas, 1836–1846*. Austin: Encino Press, 1969.

Pierson, George Wilson. *Tocqueville and Beaumont in America*. New York, 1938.

Pletcher, David M. *The Diplomacy of Annexation: Texas, Oregon, and the Mexican War*. Columbia: University of Missouri Press, 1973.

Pohl, James W., and Stephen L. Hardin. "The Military History of the Texas Revolution: An Overview." *SHQ* 89 (1986): 269–308.

Pool, William C. *Eugene C. Barker, Historian*. Austin: Texas State Historical Association, 1971.

Porter, Eugene O. "Railroad Enterprises in the Republic of Texas." *SHQ* 59 (1956): 363–71.

Potter, David M. *The Impending Crisis, 1848–1861*. New York: Harper and Row, 1976.

Potter, R. M. "The Colonization of Texas." *Magazine of American History* 8 (1882): 157–67.

———. "The Fall of the Alamo." *Magazine of American History* 2 (1878): 1–21.

———. "The Texas Revolution." *Magazine of American History* 2 (1878).

Pratt, Julius W. *Expansionists of 1812*. New York: Peter Smith, 1949.

———. "The Ideology of American Expansion." In Avery Craven, ed., *Essays in Honor of William E. Dodd*. Chicago: University of Chicago Press, 1935.

Presley, James. "Santa Anna in Texas: A Mexican Viewpoint." *SHQ* 62 (1958): 489–512.

Prüser, Jürgen. *Die Handelsverträge der Hansestädte Lübeck, Bremen und Hamburg mit überseeischen Staaten im 19 Jhdt*. Bremen: Carl Schünemann Verlag, 1962.

Rappaport, Armin, ed. *The War with Mexico: Why Did It Happen?* Rand McNally, 1964.

Rath, Gertrude R. "The Life and Times of Moses Austin in Missouri." MA thesis, University of Texas, 1924.

Rather, Ethel Zivley. "De Witt's Colony." *SHQ* 8 (1904): 95–102.

———. "Recognition of the Republic of Texas by the United States." *SHQ* 13 (1910): 155–256.

Red, William Stuart. *The Texas Colonists and Religion, 1821–1836.* Austin: Von Boeckmann-Jones Co., 1924.

Reeves, Jesse S. *American Diplomacy under Tyler and Polk.* Baltimore: Johns Hopkins University Press, 1967.

Reichstein, Andreas. "Was There a Revolution in Texas in 1835–36?" American Studies International 27 (1989).

Remini, Robert V. *Andrew Jackson and the Course of American Empire, 1767–1821.* New York: Harper and Row, 1977.

———. *Andrew Jackson and the Course of American Freedom, 1822–1832.* New York: Harper and Row, 1981.

———. *Andrew Jackson and the Course of American Democracy, 1833–1845.* New York: Harper and Row, 1984.

———. *The Election of Andrew Jackson.* Philadelphia: J. B. Lippincott, 1963.

Rémond, René. *Les Etats-Unis devant l'opinion française, 1815–1852.* 2 vols. Paris, 1962.

Richardson, Rupert N. "Framing the Constitution of the Republic of Texas." *SHQ* 31 (1928): 191–220.

Richardson, Rupert Norval, Ernest Wallace, and Adrian N. Anderson. *Texas: The Lone Star State.* 3rd ed. Englewood Cliffs, N.J.: Prentice-Hall, 1970.

Riegel, Robert Edgar. *Young America, 1830–1840.* Norman, Okla., 1949. Reprint, Westport, Conn.: Greenwood Press, 1973.

Rippy, Fred J. "Britain's Role in the Early Relations of the United States and Mexico." *Hispanic American Historical Review* 7 (1927): 2–24.

Rives, George Cockhardt. *The United States and Mexico.* 2 vols. New York: Charles Scribner's Sons, 1913.

Riviere, William T. "Sam Houston's Retreat." *SHQ* 46 (1942): 9–14.

Robles, Vito Alessio. *Coahuila y Texas, desde la consumación de la independencia hasta el tratado de paz de Guadalupe Hidalgo.* 2 vols. Mexico City: Imprenta Universitaria Talleres Gráficas de la Nación, 1945–46.

Rogin, Michael Paul. *Fathers and Children: Andrew Jackson and the Subjugation of the American Indian.* New York: Vintage Books, 1976.

Rowe, Edna. "The Disturbances at Anahuac in 1832." *SHQ* 6 (1902): 265–99.

Rowland, Dunbar. *Military History of Mississippi, 1803–1898.* 1908. Reprint, Spartanburg, S.C.: The Reprint Co., 1978.

Rowland, Kate Mason. "General John Thomson Mason." *SHQ* 11 (1908): 163–98.

Ruiz, Ramon Eduardo, ed. *The Mexican War: Was It Manifest Destiny?* New York: Holt, Rinehart, and Winston, 1963.

Rydjord, John. *Foreign Interest in the Independence of New Spain.* Durham, N.C.: Duke University Press, 1935.

Sanford, Charles L., ed. *Manifest Destiny and the Imperialism Question.* New York: John Wiley and Sons, 1976.

Santos, Richard G. *Santa Anna's Campaign against Texas, 1835–1836.* Waco: Texian press, 1968.

Schlesinger, Arthur M. *The Age of Jackson.* New York: Little, Brown, 1946.

Schmitt, Karl Michael. *Mexico and the United States, 1821–1973: Conflict and Coexistence.* New York: John Wiley and Sons, 1974.

Schmitz, Joseph William. *Texan Statecraft, 1836–1845.* San Antonio: Naylor, 1941.

———. *Thus They Lived.* San Antonio: Naylor, 1936.

Schroeder, John H. "Annexation or Independence: The Texas Issue in American Politics 1836–1845." *SHQ* 89 (1985): 137–64.

Sewell, Richard H. *Ballots for Freedom: Antislavery Politics in the United States 1837–1860.* New York: Oxford University Press, 1976.

Shackford, James Atkins. *David Crockett, the Man and the Legend.* Chapel Hill: University of North Carolina Press, 1956.

Sharp, Paul F. "Three Frontiers: Some Comparative Studies of Canadian, American and Australian Settlement." *Pacific Historical Review* 24 (1955): 369–78.

Shaw, Elton Raymond. *The Conquest of the Southwest.* Berwyn, Ill.: Shaw Publishing Co., 1924.

Shearer, Ernest C. *Robert Potter, Remarkable North Carolinian and Texan.* Houston: University of Houston Press, 1951.

Shuffler, Henderson R. "The Signing of Texas' Declaration of Independence: Myth and Record." *SHQ* 65 (1962): 310–32.

Sibley, Marilyn McAdams. "James Hamilton, Jr., vs. Sam Houston: Repercussions of the Nullification Controversy." *SHQ* 89 (1985): 165–80.

———. *Lone Stars and State Gazettes: Texas Newspapers before the Civil War.* College Station: Texas A&M University Press, 1983.

Siegel, Stanley. *The Poet President of Texas.* Austin: Pemberton Press, 1977.

———. *A Political History of the Texas Republic, 1836–1845.* Austin: University of Texas Press, 1956.

Silbey, Soel H. *The Transformation of American Politics, 1840–1860.* Englewood Cliffs, N.J.: Prentice-Hall, 1967.

Silverthorne, Elizabeth. *Ashbel Smith of Texas: Pioneer, Patriot, Statesman, 1805–1886.* College Station: Texas A&M University Press, 1982.

Simmons, Marc S., ed. "Samuel T. Allen and the Texas Revolution." *SHQ* 68 (1965): 481–88.

Simpson, Henry. *The Lives of Eminent Philadelphians, Now Deceased.* Philadelphia: William Brotherhood, 1859.

Singletary, Otis A. *The Mexican War.* Chicago: University of Chicago Press, 1960.

Smith, Justin H. *The Annexation of Texas.* New York: Barnes and Noble, 1941.

———. *The War with Mexico.* 2 vols. New York: Macmillan, 1919.

Smith, Roy E. "The Quarrel between Governor Smith and the Council of the Provisional Government of the Republic." *SHQ* 5 (1902): 269–346.

Smith, Ruby Cumby. "James W. Fannin, Jr., in the Texas Revolution." *SHQ* 23 (1919–20): 79–90, 171–203, 271–84.

Smither, Harriet. "English Abolitionism and the Annexation of Texas." *SHQ* 32 (1929): 193–205.

Smithwick, Noah. *The Evolution of a State; or, Recollections of Old Texas Days* (compiled by his daughter Nanna Smithwick Donaldson). Austin: Steck, 1935.

Smyth, George W. "The Autobiography of George W. Smyth." *SHQ* 36 (1933): 200–14.

Snodgrass, Charles Albert. *The History of Freemasonry in Tennessee, 1789–1943.* Nashville: Ambrose Printing Co., 1944.

Spence, Mary Lee. "British Impressions of Texas and the Texans." *SHQ* 70 (1966): 163–83.

———. "British Interests and Attitudes Regarding the Republic of Texas and Its Annexation by the United States." Ph.D. dissertation, University of Minnesota, 1957.

Steen, Ralph W. "Analysis of the Work of the General Council, Provisional Government of Texas, 1835–1836." *SHQ* 40 (1937): 309–33, and 41 (1938): 225–40, 324–48.

———. *The Texas Story.* Austin: Steck, 1948.

Stenberg, Richard Rollin. "American Imperialism in the Southwest." Ph.D. dissertation, University of Texas, 1932.

———. "Andrew Jackson and the Erving Affidavit." *SHQ* 41 (1937): 142–53.

———. "Jackson, Anthony Butler and Texas." *SSSQ* 13 (1932): 264–86.

———. "Jackson's Neches Claim, 1829–1836." *SHQ* 39 (1936): 255–74.

———. "The Texas Schemes of Jackson and Houston, 1829–1836." *SSSQ* 15 (1935): 229–50.

———. "The Western Boundary of Louisiana, 1762–1803." *SHQ* 35 (1931): 95–108.

Stephenson, Nathaniel Wright. *Texas and the Mexican War.* 1921. Reprint, New York: United States Publishers Association, 1971.

Streeter, Thomas W. *Bibliography of Texas, 1795–1845.* 5 vols. Cambridge, Mass.: Harvard University Press, 1955–1960.

Strickland, Rex W. "Anglo-American Activities in Northeastern Texas, 1803–1845." Ph.D. dissertation, University of Texas, 1937.

Struve, Walter. *Die Republik Texas, Bremen und das Hildesheimische.* Hildesheim: August Lax Verlag, 1983.

Stuart, Ben C. *The History of Texas Newspapers from the Earliest Period to the Present.* Beaumont, 1917.

Sturges, Philip. "Great Britain and the Annexation of Texas." Ph.D. dissertation, University of Utah, 1952.

Sydnor, Charles S. *The Development of Southern Sectionalism 1819–1848.* Baton Rouge: Louisiana State University Press, 1968.

Taylor, Virginia H. *Index to Spanish and Mexican Land Grants.* Austin: General Land Office, 1976.

———. *The Spanish Archives of the General Land Office of Texas.* Austin: Lone Star Press, 1955.

Teja, Jesús F. De La, and John Wheat. "Bexar: Profile of a Tejano Community, 1820–1832." *SHQ* 89 (1985): 7–34.

Terrell, Alexander W. "Stephen F. Austin: A Memorial Address." *SHQ* 14 (1911): 182–97.

Thrall, Homer Spellman. *A History of Texas.* New York: University Publishing Co., 1885.

———. *A Pictorial History of Texas, from the Earliest Visits of European Adventures, to A.D. 1879.* 3rd ed. St. Louis: N. D. Thompson and Co., 1879.

———. "Sam Houston." *Round Table* 4 (1892).

Tilly, Charles. "Revolutions and Collective Violence." In F. I. Greenstein and N. Polsby, eds., *Handbook of Political Violence,* vol. 3, pp. 438–501. Reading, Mass., 1975.

Timmons, Wilbert H. "Robert Owen's Texas Project." *SHQ* 52 (1949): 286–93.

———. "Tadeo Ortíz and Texas." *SHQ* 72 (1968): 21–33.

Tinkle, Lon. *Thirteen Days to Glory: The Siege of the Alamo.* Reprint, College Station: Texas A&M University Press, 1985.

Tjarks, Alicia V. "Comparative Demographic Analysis of Texas, 1777–1793." *SHQ* 77 (1974): 291–338.

Toepperwein, Herman. *Sam Houston.* San Antonio: Hall of Texas History, 1968.

Tolbert, Frank X. *The Day of San Jacinto.* New York: McGraw-Hill, 1959.

———. *An Informal History of Texas—from Cabeza de Vaca to Temple Houston.* New York: Harper and Brothers, 1951.

Tornel y Mendívil, José Maria. *Tejas y los Estados-Unidos de América, en sus relaciones con la república mexicana*. Mexico City: Impreso por Ignacio Cumplido, 1837.

Tracy, Milton Cook, and Bailie Richard Havelock. *The Colonizer: A Saga of Stephen R. Austin*. El Paso: Guynes Printing Co., 1941.

True, C. Allen. "John A. Williams: Champion of Mexico in the Early Days of the Texas Revolution." *SHQ* 47 (1943): 107–19.

Trusty, Norman Lance. "Massachusetts Public Opinion and the Annexation of Texas, 1835–1845." Ph.D. dissertation, Boston University, 1964.

Turner, F. H. "The Mejia Expedition." *SHQ* 7 (1903): 1–28.

Turner, Frederick Jackson. *The United States 1830–1850*. New York: W. W. Norton, 1965.

————. *The Frontier in American History*. The Franklin Center, Pa., 1977.

Tyler, Lyon Gardiner. "The Annexation of Texas." *Magazine of American History* 8 (1882): 377–99.

Uhde, Adolph. *Die Länder am unteren Rio Bravo de Norte*. Heidelberg: J. and B. Mohr, 1861.

Ulibarri, Richard Onofre. "American Interest in the Spanish-Mexican Southwest, 1803–1848." Ph.D. dissertation, University of Utah, 1963.

Urbina, Manuel, III. "The Impact of the Texas Revolution on the Government, Politics, and Society of Mexico, 1836–1846." Ph.D. dissertation, University of Texas at Austin, 1976.

Urquhart, David. *Annexation of The Texas: A Case of War between England and the United States*. London: James Maynard, 1844.

Valadés, José C. *Santa Anna y la guerra de Texas*. 3rd ed. Mexico City: Editorial Patria, 1965.

Vázquez, Josefina Zoraida. "The Texas Question in Mexican Politics, 1836–1845." *SHQ* 89 (1986): 309–45.

Véliz, Claudio. *The Centralist Tradition of Latin America*. Princeton, N.J.: Princeton University Press, 1980.

Vevier, Charles. "American Continentalism: An Idea of Expansion, 1845–1910." *AHR* 65 (1960): 323–35.

Vigness, David M. *The Revolutionary Decades 1810–1830*. Austin: Steck-Vaughn, 1965.

Voss, Frederick S. "Portraying an American Original: The Likenesses of Davy Crockett." *SHQ* 91 (1988): 483–508.

Wade, Houston. *Dictionary with identifying Record of those Master Masons who participated in the Texas Revolution or rendered worthwhile service towards the success of the Republic of Texas*. Houston, 1935.

Walker, Thomas F. "Pre-revolutionary Pamphleteering in Mexico, 1808–1810." Ph.D. dissertation, 1951.

Wallace, John Melton. *Gaceta to Gazette: A Check List of Texas Newspapers 1813–1846*. Austin: University of Texas, 1966.

Ward, Forrest E. "Pre-Revolutionary Activity in Brazoria County." *SHQ* 64 (1960): 212–31.

Ward, John William. *Andrew Jackson: Symbol for an Age.* New York, 1955.

Warren, Robert P. *How Texas Won Her Freedom.* San Jacinto, 1959.

Weaver, Bobby D. *Castro's Colony: Empresario Development in Texas.* College Station: Texas A&M Universtiy Press, 1985.

Webb, Walter Prescott. *The Great Frontier.* 5th ed. Austin: University of Texas Press, 1979.

———. *The Great Plains.* Lincoln and London: University of Nebraska Press, 1981.

Webb, Walter Prescott, ed. *The Handbook of Texas.* 2 vols. Supplementary volume, ed. Eldon Stephen Branda. Austin: Texas State Historical Association, 1952, 1976.

Weber, David J. *The Mexican Frontier, 1821–1846.* Albuquerque: University of New Mexico Press, 1982.

Weems, John Edward. *Dream of Empire: A Human History of the Republic of Texas, 1836–1846.* New York: Simon and Schuster, 1971.

Weinberg, Albert K. *Manifest Destiny.* Chicago: Quadrangle Books, 1963.

Welter, Rush. *The Mind of America, 1820–1860.* New York and London: Columbia University Press, 1975.

West, Elizabeth Howard. "Southern Opposition to the Annexation of Texas." *SHQ* 18 (1914): 74–82.

Wharton, Clarence Ray. *Remember Goliad.* Houston, 1931. Glorieta, N.Mex.: Rio Grande Press, 1968.

———. *Texas under Many Flags.* 5 vols. Chicago and New York: American Historical Society, 1930.

White, Gifford. *1830 Citizens of Texas.* Austin: Eakin Press, 1983.

White, Owen Payne. *Texas: An Informal Biography.* New York: G. P. Putnam's Sons, 1945.

Wight, C. A. *Life and Work of Stephen F. Austin.* Sherman, Tex.: Austin College, 1910.

Williams, Alfred Mason. *Sam Houston and the War of Independence in Texas.* Boston and New York: Houghton Mifflin, 1893.

Williams, Amelia. "A Critical Study of the Siege of the Alamo and of the Personnel of Its Defenders." In five parts, *SHQ* 36 (1933): 251–87; 37 (1933–1934): 1–44, 79–115, 157–84, 237–312.

Williams, Amelia, and Bernhardt Wall. *Following General Sam Houston from 1793–1863.* Austin: Steck, 1935.

Williams, Elgin. *The Animating Pursuits of Speculation: Land Traffic in the Annexation of Texas.* New York: Columbia University Press, 1949.

Williams, Robert H. Jr. "Travis: A Potential Sam Houston." *SHQ* 40 (1936): 154–60.

Williams, William Appleman. *The Contours of American History.* Cleveland: World Publishing Co., 1961.

Wills, Garry. *Inventing America: Jefferson's Declaration of Independence.* New York: Vintage Books, 1979.

Willson, Marcius. *History of Texas.* New York, 1847.

Winfrey, Dorman H. "Mirabeau B. Lamar and Texas Nationalism." *SHQ* 59 (1955): 184–205.

Winkler, Ernest W. "The Cherokee Indian In Texas." *SHQ* 7 (1903): 95–165.

———. "Membership of the 1833 Convention of Texas." *SHQ* 45 (1942): 255–57.

———. "The Twin Sisters' Cannon, 1836–1865." *SHQ* 21 (1917): 61–68.

Winston, James E. "The Annexation of Texas and the Mississippi Democrats." *SHQ* 25 (1921): 1–25.

———. "Kentucky and the Independence of Texas." *SHQ* 16 (1912): 27–62.

———. "Mississippi and the Independence of Texas." *SHQ* 21 (1917): 36–60.

———. "The Mississippi Whigs and the Annexation of Texas." *SHQ* 29 (1926): 161–80.

———. "New Orleans Newspapers and the Texas Question, 1835–1837." *SHQ* 36 (1932): 109–29.

———. "New York and the Independence of Texas." *SHQ* 18 (1915): 368–85.

———. "Pennsylvania and the Independence of Texas." *SHQ* 17 (1914): 262–82.

———. "Texas Annexation Sentiment in Mississippi 1835–44." *SHQ* 23 (1919): 1–19.

———. "Virginia and the Independence of Texas." *SHQ* 16 (1913): 277–83.

Winters, James Washington. "An Account of the Battle of San Jacinto." *SHQ* 6 (1902): 139–44.

Wise, Henry Alexander. *Seven Decades of the Union.* Philadelphia: J. B. Lippincott and Co., 1881.

Wisehart, Marion Karl. *Sam Houston, American Giant.* Washington, D.C., 1962.

Wooten, Dudley Goodall. *A Complete History of Texas.* Dallas: The Texas History Co., 1899.

Wooten, Dudley Goodall, ed. *A Comprehensive History of Texas, 1685 to 1897.* 2 vols. Dallas: William G. Scarff, 1898.

Worley, J. L. "The Diplomatic Relations of England and the Republic of Texas." *SHQ* 9 (1905): 1–40.

Wortham, Louis J. *A History of Texas: From Wilderness to Commonwealth.* 5 vols. Fort Worth: Wortham-Molyneaux, 1924.

Yoakum, Henderson. *History of Texas from Its First Settlement in 1685 to Its Annexation to the United States in 1846.* 2 vols. New York, 1855. Reprint, Austin: Steck, 1935.

Zavala, Lorenzo de. *Ensayo histório de las revoluciones de México, desde 1808 hasta 1830*. 2nd ed. Mexico City: Imprenta à cargo de Manuel N. De la Vega, 1845.

Zuber, William Physik. "Captain Adolphus Sterne." *SHQ* 2 (1899): 211–16.

Zwelling, Shoner S. *Expansion and Imperialism*. Chicago: Loyola University Press, 1970.

Index

References to illustrations are indicated by page numbers in italic type.

Index

Treaty of Friendship, Cession of the Floridas and Boundaries. *See* Adams-Onís Treaty of 1819
Treaty of Velasco, 153–54, 170
Trespalacios, José Félix, 32
Trinity Land Company, 96, 105–107
Trinity River, 70
Troup, George, 154
Tucker, N. Beverly, 176
Turner, Frederick Jackson, 5
Tyler, John, 176

Ugartechea, Domingo de, 77, 91, 133–34
Union Land Company, 105–107
United States: annexes Texas, 89, 132, 153, 165, 170–80, 201; attempts to purchase Texas, 52, 94–96, 112, 118, 123, 125, 127; border disputes of, 11, 17–18, 53, 55, 122, 163; and Canada, 198; claims to Texas of, 24, 49; expansion of, 3–4, 50, 108, 175, 178–79, 197–202; federalism in, 34; financial interest of, in Texas, 109–10; and Fredonian Rebellion, 51; in historiography, 7, 202; image of Texas in, 94; and independent Mexico, 19, 166; and Indians, 161; inquiries from, to Austin, 90; and land titles, 17–18, 49; land speculation in, 23–24, 94, 96–112, 154, 174, 176, 183, 188–89, 198, 200–201; and Louisiana Purchase, 17; Mexicans' view of, 128–29, 186, 189, 191; public debt of, 164; and slavery, 173–77; and trade competition, 50, 167; and war in Texas, 137–40, 144–45, 151–52, 156; at war with Mexico, 178, 181–82; and war of 1812, 21, 113
Universalis Ecclesiae, 206nn7, 8
University of Texas, 164
Upshur, Abel P., 176–77
Urquhart, David, 184
Urrea, José, 144, 146, 154

Van Buren, Martin, 175–76
Van Fossen, John, 116, 118
Van Zandt, Isaac, 177
Vásquez, Rafael, 170–71
Vehlein, Joseph, 51, 97, 100, 103, 111, 228n27
Velasco, Tex., 86–88, 138
Venezuela, 97, 108
Vera Cruz (Mexico), 35, 135, 154, 159, 168
Veramendi, Don Juan Martín de, 88, 122
Veramendi, Ursula, 122, 223n55
vicariato policy, 206n7
viceroy. *See virrey*
Victoria, Guadalupe, 30, 51
Victoria, Tex., 135
Viesca, Agustín, 77, 189–90

Villaveque, Gabriel Laisné de, 48
Virginia, 23–24, 90, 152, 184
Virreinal Audiencia, function of, 15
virrey, 15

Walker, Robert J., 176
Ward, Henry, 166–67
War Party. *See* Wharton Party
Washington, D.C., 51, 113, 116, 119, 120, 129, 159, 171, 178
Washington-on-the-Brazos (Washington, Tex.), 77, 134, 138–39
Washington Townsite Company, 231n92
Waters, John, 115–16
Wavell, Arthur Goodall, 42–44, 109
Webb, James W., 107
Webster, Daniel, 175–76, 199
Weinberg, Albert K., 197–99
Westcott, James D., 117
West Indies, 167
West Virginia. *See* Virginia
Westward Movement, 4–5
Wharton, Jesse, 63
Wharton, John A., 63, 80, 83, 111, 118, 122–23, 131, 134, 136, 188, 199
Wharton, William Harris, *63;* biography of, 63–65, 79–80; in convention of 1832, 63–64; in convention of 1833, 65; as delegate to U.S., 137, 140, 151–52, 171, 173; opposition of, to Mexico, 131, 134, 188, 197; and Sam Houston, 83, 123, 220n9; and Stephen F. Austin, 64, 68, 73, 111, 122–23
Wharton Party, 74, 81–82, 88, 123, 134, 156, 190, 197, 220n8
Whig Party, 152, 174–78
White, William, 38
Whitney, Stephen, 100
Wilberforce, William, 168
Wilkinson, James, 32–33, 35, 108
Williams, Amelia, 143
Williams, Elgin, 200
Williams, John A., 75
Williams, Samuel May, 48–49, 68–69, 77, 91–92, 110, 120, 122, 124, 133, 151, 157–59, 189
Williams & McKinney, 245n24
Williamson, Robert M., 81, 133, 197, 199, 231n92
Woll, Adrian, 171
Woodbury, Dr. John Lucius, 97, 105

Yoakum, Henderson, 6, 193
yorkino, 52, 56, 88
York Lodges, 51–52, 100. *See also* Freemasonry
Yucatán, 89, 99–100, 127, 131, 137, 170, 187

Rise of the Lone Star was composed into type on a Compugraphic digital phototypesetter in ten point Galliard with two points of spacing between the lines. Galliard was also selected for display. The book was designed by Jim Billingsley, typeset by Metricomp, Inc., printed offset and bound by Thomson- Shore, Inc. The paper on which this book is printed carries acid-free characteristics for an effective life of at least three hundred years.

Texas A&M University Press : College Station